WANTED!
A NATION!

Race in the Atlantic World, 1700–1900

WANTED! A NATION!

BLACK AMERICANS AND HAITI, 1804–1893

Claire Bourhis-Mariotti

TRANSLATED BY
C. Jon Delogu

WITH A FOREWORD BY
Ronald Angelo Johnson

The University of Georgia Press
ATHENS

Athens, Georgia 30602
www.ugapress.org

Designed by Kaelin Chappell Broaddus
Set in 10.25/13.5 Adobe Caslon Pro by Kaelin Chappell Broaddus

Most University of Georgia Press titles are available from popular e-book vendors.

Printed digitally

Library of Congress Cataloging-in-Publication Data

Names: Bourhis-Mariotti, Claire, author. | Delogu, Christopher Jon, translator. | Johnson, Ronald Angelo, 1970– writer of foreword.
Title: Wanted! A nation! : Black Americans and Haiti, 1804–1893 / Claire Bourhis-Mariotti ; translated by C. Jon Delogu ; with a foreword by Ronald Angelo Johnson.
Other titles: L'union fait la force. English | Black Americans and Haiti, 1804–1893
Description: Athens : The University of Georgia Press, [2023] | Series: Race in the Atlantic world, 1700–1900 | Original title: L'union fait la force : les Noirs américains et Haïti, 1804–1893. | Includes bibliographical references and index.
Identifiers: LCCN 2023023227 (print) | LCCN 2023023228 (ebook) | ISBN 9780820365893 (hardback) | ISBN 9780820362700 (paperback) | ISBN 9780820362717 (epub) | ISBN 9780820365558 (pdf)
Subjects: LCSH: Free African Americans—Haiti—History—19th century. | African Americans—Haiti—History—19th century. | African Americans—Relations with Haitians—History—19th century. | Immigrants—Haiti—History—19th century. | Haiti—History—19th century. | United States—Relations—Haiti. | Haiti—Relations—United States. | United States—Race relations—History—19th century. | Douglass, Frederick, 1818–1895.
Classification: LCC E185.18 .B6813 2023 (print) | LCC E185.18 (ebook) | DDC 972.94/04—dc23/eng/20230612
LC record available at https://lccn.loc.gov/2023023227
LC ebook record available at https://lccn.loc.gov/2023023228

A Sarah Mills Hodge Fund Publication

This publication is made possible, in part, through a grant from the Hodge Foundation in memory of its founder, Sarah Mills Hodge, who devoted her life to the relief and education of African Americans in Savannah, Georgia.

This book is published with the support of the University of Paris 8 (research center TransCrit).

CONTENTS

FOREWORD

RONALD ANGELO JOHNSON

The success of Laurent Dubois's *Avengers of the New World* in 2004, published during the bicentennial of Haitian independence, expanded the historical literature around the Haitian Revolution. It was exciting to see early Haitian history gain some overdue interest from scholars based in North America. But the focus became overly intense on the slave revolt in the French colony of Saint-Domingue, portrayed as the lost "Pearl of the Antilles." Scholars in the United States by and large ignored Haiti and its people, seeming to prefer writing about enslaved Africans more than the lived experiences of free Haitian citizens.

Soon after its publication, I read the French-language edition of *Wanted! A Nation!* (published as *L'union fait la force* by Les Presses Universitaires de Rennes in 2016) with the intention of highlighting Haitians and free Black people in the United States. The book captured me with its distinctive analysis of the role of Haiti in the evolution of a nineteenth-century transnational Black Atlantic identity. I learned from the bibliography that Claire Bourhis-Mariotti, though based in Paris, had performed research in an archive just miles from my home in central Texas. Professor Bourhis-Mariotti and I had never met. I sent her an email to share my thoughts on the research and to invite her to give a book talk during her next visit to the state. Since her gracious response, we have collaborated, not in Texas, but on two workshops in Paris (one on Frederick Douglass, the other on Black Atlantic migrations) and on a colloquium in Montpellier, France, on Atlantic world slavery. I found in Bourhis-Mariotti not only a brilliant scholar but also a thoughtful, generous colleague. The research in *Wanted! A Nation!* has broadened my historical analyses, evident in an *Atlantic Studies* article on early Haitian and Black American journalism, an edited volume titled *In Search of Liberty* on nineteenth-century African American internationalism, an essay on the diplomacy of Frederick Douglass in the AAIHS's *Black Perspectives*, a *Revue Française d'Études Amér-*

icaines article on Haitian immigration, and in my current book manuscript on revolutionary diplomacy between Haiti and the United States. Few scholars have influenced the development of my thinking around early Haitian-American relations in the Black Atlantic world more than Bourhis-Mariotti.

Wanted! A Nation! presents Haiti studied as a living place, not the lamented Atlantean figure of the bygone Saint-Domingue. In Haiti, Black Americans who had shared similar sufferings at the hands of U.S. oppressors came together with Haitian counterparts to forge a collective identity, to share ideas for expanding education, to establish religious institutions, and to navigate the murky geopolitical waters of Atlantic world diplomacy. The study avoids the trope that life was somehow better in Hispaniola under the French slavocracy, and that Black leaders mismanaged the nation, leading to the misfortunes of present-day Haiti. For the author, Haiti is complex, and so are its people. They interacted, negotiated, and disagreed with famous figures of early U.S. history. Bourhis-Mariotti examines Haiti as a land of free Black people that free Black people from the United States hoped to visit in order to experience freedom alongside other free Black people.

I first encountered *Wanted! A Nation!* during my initial research on the evolution of Blackness in early Haiti and the United States. At the time, few books analyzed the lives and cultural exchanges between Haitians and African Americans. The bulk of the secondary source literature had been published in the French language. Chris Dixon's book *African Americans and Haiti*, published in 2000, was the most accessible English-language volume. Reading Bourhis-Mariotti's analyses provided a scope and depth to transnational Black relations that, to this day, no other book offers. In 2015 Sara Fanning published a wonderful book on Black American emigration to Haiti in the 1820s, and Brandon Byrd later produced a lovely work on Black American engagement with Haiti and Haitians in the late nineteenth and early twentieth centuries. Bourhis-Mariotti's book traverses the nineteenth century, providing readers with distinctive vantage points of Haitian government and life that break new ground in at least two important areas of historical study.

One, *Wanted! A Nation!* advances the understanding of Haiti's role in the evolution of Blackness in the Atlantic world. It argues with vigor that the lives of Haitians and Black Americans were inextricably linked, not only by racist colonialist systems. The two peoples viewed themselves as sharing a Black identity exhibited in their contributions to Atlantic world literature, journalism, art, politics, and religion. This book illuminates extensive, multifaceted relationships across the nineteenth century. As Bourhis-Mariotti puts it, "References to the Black diaspora in the context of the Black Atlantic are rooted in the Atlantic slave trade, but also seek to understand and demonstrate the existence of a specific Black diasporic experience and thought—in other words, studying its nationalist dimension." In the following pages, Haiti is not tangential to early U.S. society and politics but rather central to the way Americans addressed questions of Black freedom and slavery.

The method of studying Haiti through the lens of "Black nationality" from independence to the advent of U.S. occupation brings together the shared history of the first two republics in the western Atlantic world. Historians of the early United States based in North America generally ignore Haiti. They treat the histories of Haitians and Americans as parallel marches, intersecting at a few areas to survey topics like slavery, Black violence, and race. *Wanted! A Nation!* suggests that Black Americans in Haiti carried early American history and culture with them to Haiti. Those who returned to U.S. shores brought Haitian thought and beliefs with them. Newspapers in both countries were covered with stories detailing the exchanges of immigrants and ideas. Despite the refusal of twelve U.S. presidential administrations to recognize Haiti as an independent nation, the Haitian people evoked fear in southerners, instilled pride in Black Americans, and remained a constant factor in the imagination of U.S. policymakers.

Two, Haiti is often overlooked in analyses of early U.S. diplomatic history, which is generally dominated by questions surrounding European balance of power conflicts, American isolationism, and the utility of the Monroe Doctrine. The works of Gerald Horne, Brenda Gayle Plummer, and Julia Gaffield, however, center post-independence Haiti as a determinant of U.S. diplomacy in the Atlantic world. In the recently published *America's Road to Empire: Foreign Policy from Independence to World War One*, Piero Gleijeses argues: "Jefferson loathed Haiti's black rebels and wanted to see the fledgling Haitian state crushed because he feared the example Haiti's successful revolt would set for the enslaved people in the US South." *Wanted! A Nation!* offers one of the most in-depth studies of Haitian-American relations. Its detailed engagement with ongoing, sometimes tense diplomatic negotiations reveals to many U.S. history readers the names and actions of important Haitian leaders like Jean-Pierre Boyer, Fabre Geffrard, Florvil Hyppolite, and Anténor Firmin. By examining bilateral relations across the century, the book posits race, alongside economic and strategic objectives, as an important determinant of American diplomacy.

The book highlights the diplomatic missions of the first five Black American ministers to Haiti. One of America's most famous figures, Frederick Douglass, served within this exclusive cohort of color. He looms large in *Wanted!*

A Nation!, and rightly so. Despite numerous, lengthy, and award-winning biographies of the great abolitionist, orator, and social justice warrior extraordinaire, few of them study sufficiently Douglass's complex diplomatic career. In this area, Bourhis-Mariotti outpaces other scholars. Her expositions of Douglass's diplomacy in Santo Domingo (today the Dominican Republic) and later Haiti are exquisite. She is unafraid to portray the stalwart of Black freedom on unsure footing when trusted white American presidents called upon him to work against the interests of Black people in the Caribbean. The Harrison administration asked Douglass, then serving as minister in Port-au-Prince, to persuade Haitian leaders to sell the strategic Haitian port of Môle Saint-Nicolas to the United States. The book illustrates the instability across Haiti in 1891 caused by the intimidation tactics of a neocolonialist white nation that threatened Haiti's independence with navy warships. Worse, the face of this racist ploy was that of the world's most famous Black man. According to Bourhis-Mariotti, Douglass, "probably bothered by his own role in destabilizing the government of a republic whose stability precisely he had always been quick to praise," tried to reopen more equitable negotiations. Douglass's reputation suffered at home from the incident. Two years later, the Haitian government appointed him first commissioner for the Haitian pavilion at the Chicago World's Fair. There, he delivered a tremendous speech defending Haiti and indicting U.S. diplomacy toward the country. He told the Chicago audience, "Haiti is black, and we have not yet forgiven Haiti for being black or forgiven the Almighty for making her black Haitian culture." Douglass's last act of powerful support for Haiti, perhaps as atonement, remains overlooked by biographers and diplomatic historians, though it vividly illustrates an extensive, racialized relationship between Douglass, Haiti, and the United States.

The ability to read the French language allowed me to engage with and fully appreciate the brilliant scholarship of Claire Bourhis-Mariotti years before an English translation became available. Doctoral programs in U.S. history based in North America do not generally require serious foreign-language studies. Therefore, many scholars of nineteenth-century American history will not possess the capacity to access the book's pioneering research, findings, and conclusions. I am thrilled to see the English translation of *L'union fait la force* published with UGA Press. *Wanted! A Nation!* is a perfect fit for the Race in the Atlantic World, 1700–1900 series, given its strong emphasis on comparative and transnational approaches to racialized inequality in Atlantic culture. This book's greater availability to English-speaking scholars and students will empower it to serve as a foundation for more advanced studies on the role of early Haiti in the development of a shared Black identity across the Atlantic world.

PREFACE TO THE ENGLISH EDITION

The nineteenth century was truly a pivotal century for Black Americans. In the antebellum era, some of them had to endure slavery while others experienced freedom with little or no civil rights. With the end of the Civil War came emancipation, followed by equal civil and voting rights supposedly for all men, a short-lived lull rapidly superseded by the advent of Jim Crow and de facto segregation, the latter being eventually legally upheld by the *Plessy v. Ferguson* decision and its "separate but equal" doctrine in 1896. As a student of American history, and then as a young teaching assistant, I discovered and rediscovered this century of constant struggle through the writings of one of its most famous Black protagonists, Frederick Douglass, whose impassioned and powerful speeches had the power to rouse crowds in the nineteenth century and to captivate my students' attention—an equally outstanding achievement—more than a century and a half later.

When I (re)read the second edition of his last autobiography and his 1893 "lecture on Haiti" in 2009, it became clear to me that Frederick Douglass's extraordinary destiny was intimately linked with that of the small Black republic established on the west side of the Caribbean island of Hispaniola.[1] However, I soon realized that Douglass's special relationship with Haiti—from the beginning of his abolitionist career to the end of his life—remained relatively unknown. The existing historiography in 2009—which was already quite substantial at the time—on the life and career of Frederick Douglass paid little attention to this relationship. Even William S. McFeely, the author of Douglass's most comprehensive biography prior to David W. Blight's 2019 award-winning *Frederick Douglass: Prophet of Freedom,* only devoted a few pages to the relationship between Haiti and Douglass.[2] However, a short but striking passage of his book caught my attention: although Douglass "had fought colonization all his life," McFeely added between brackets that he did so "save for a brief flirtation with James Redpath's plan for settlement in Haiti in the black days after *Dred Scott*."[3] This mysterious phrase prompted me to investigate this so-called plan for settlement and led me to discover that this late 1850s–early 1860s project of emigration to Haiti, in which James Redpath—a white abolitionist and John Brown's biographer—participated as an emigration agent for the Haitian government, was not the first (nor the last) project of emigration to Haiti initiated by and/or for the benefit of free Black Americans. After reading a number of historical sources (such as abolitionist newspapers, the [Black] press of the nineteenth century, Douglass's and other Black activists' personal archives, numerous speeches, pamphlets, and books), I then realized that from its independence in 1804 until the turn of the century, Haiti, as a *Black* republic, had played a major role in the intellectual life, the militant activities, the imagination, and the shaping of the identity of the Black community.[4] Above all, it appeared to me that to free Black Americans, Haiti had not remained an unknown and distant place that they would have only idealized and dreamt of—though this romanticized view of Haiti did play a role in prompting some of them to emigrate there.[5] On the contrary, the Black activists who would become the subjects of my research had very concretely set foot on this land and had physically and truly experienced the place that many of them considered as a "promised land," an example of Black liberation and self-government to follow, a source of political inspiration, or the very place where the "political regeneration" of the "Black race" would happen.

For this reason, I decided to devote my dissertation to examining the peculiar relationship between Haiti and free Black Americans, rethinking the genesis of Black activism, Black diasporic thought, and Black nationalism and internationalism through the lens of Haiti—that nation being viewed as a place for, as well as a means of, expression and development of Black American identity in the nineteenth century. My dissertation naturally focused on the Haitian "experience" in the most prosaic sense of the term, referring to the fact that free Black American individuals physically visited (or settled in) Haiti, and not merely referred to it theoretically or rhetorically in their speeches or writings. It should be made clear that I was far more interested in studying the condition and experience of Black American activists and their community than in studying Black Haitians' experience, for although Haiti had always been a willing partner of Black Americans, it had always struggled to support them, especially financially, and thus failed to organize the development of a common future on its soil. Therefore, I do not claim to have written an exhaustive history of the Haitian American relationship in the nineteenth century but hope to have modestly contributed to shedding new light on this history, through the prism of the relationship between the Black republic and free Black Americans.

Sadly, on the afternoon of January 12, 2010, only a few weeks after I had started working on my dissertation, a magnitude 7.0 earthquake struck Haiti. As we all know, and as of this day, the country and its inhabitants have not fully recovered from this massive and most dramatic disaster. It was logically impossible for me to travel to Haiti during the time of my research, but I was lucky enough to be able to correspond and even meet (in Paris) with academics from the University of Haiti who confirmed I would probably not find anything in the remaining (then available) Haitian archives. This was slightly frustrating, of course, as I would have loved to be able to find and explore Haitian sources that would have helped me better understand the life and experiences of African Americans who emigrated to Haiti in the antebellum era, and better apprehend how they managed or failed to integrate Haitian society. I checked the Haitian newspapers kept in the French National Library in Paris, but there was not much in there on this precise issue. And as the Haitian newspapers available for consultation in Paris were these official newspapers controlled by the Haitian elite and government, they did not really help writing a bottom-up version of this fascinating history.

L'union fait la force has been Haiti's powerful national motto ever since the small Black republic became independent on January 1, 1804. Because it both means "we are stronger together" and "unity makes strength," I chose to use this motto as the title of the book I published in 2016 (in French) with Les Presses universitaires de Rennes, France.[6] This book was a revised version of the PhD dissertation I defended in June 2013 and for which I was awarded, in 2014, the Prix de Thèse de l'Institut des Amériques—an annual doctoral dissertation award given by the Institut des Amériques, a research consortium based in Paris that federates French research on the American continent, in the fields of the humanities and the social sciences.

The idea of publishing an English translation of *L'union fait la force* was first suggested by Ronald Angelo Johnson, the Ralph and Bessie Mae Lynn Chair of History at Baylor University (Texas) and co-editor of *In Search of Liberty: African American Internationalism in the Nineteenth-Century Atlantic World*, who contacted me in 2016 after reading my book.[7] Professor Johnson, a prominent scholar of the Black Atlantic, was probably the first American scholar to read my book in French, and I felt—and still feel—honored by the constructive feedback I received from him. I am grateful that our professional collaboration has never ceased since our fruitful discussion of my book and his own pioneering work, *Diplomacy in Black and White: John Adams, Toussaint Louverture, and Their Atlantic World Alliance,* which he had published with the University of Georgia Press in 2014. This English translation of my own book would not have been possible without Professor Johnson's kind support.

The present book is therefore the translation of a revised and somewhat abridged version of *L'union fait la force*. I have tried my best to adapt what is a monograph initially written for a French readership to a North American or at least anglophone readership, notably by cutting a number of theoretical and contextual discussions that were necessary for French audiences. This being said, as this is a translation of an already published book, I felt I should not try to change the original book and write a new one. That is why this book does not engage with the most recent scholarship published since 2016. It is true that, since I defended my dissertation in 2013 and then published *L'union fait la force* in France in 2016, other scholars have been working and publishing important books on some of the topics my own book covers, thus enriching the historiography. Sara Fanning's 2015 *Caribbean Crossing: African Americans and the Haitian Emigration Movement* particularly focuses on the first emigration movement to Haiti in the 1820s, a subject I discuss in chapter 1 of *L'union fait la force*.[8] Although our conclusions on this first wave of emigration are quite the same—this experience ended more or less in bitter disappointment and failure—my book goes further by examining this episode both as an alternative to the American Colonization Society's African scheme and in relation to subsequent emigration projects to Haiti. Brandon R. Byrd's groundbreaking *The Black Republic: African Americans and the Fate of Haiti*, published in 2019, explores the place of Haiti in Black thought in the second half of the nineteenth century, showing that postbellum Black leaders considered the Black republic as a model of Black self-governance, linking the fate of the small nation to their own advancement in the post-Civil War United States.[9] In *L'union fait la force*, I also argued that Black activists, some of whom had considered Haiti as an ideal and idealized place to which free Black Americans who dreamt of becoming full citizens could emigrate before the Reconstruction amendments were enacted, later promoted the Black republic as an example of Black self-government and a kind of political laboratory for the Black diaspora. Such was the case of individuals like James Theodore Holly, John Mercer Langston, or even Frederick Douglass who, as I demonstrated, sought to draw lessons from the Haitian "model" for their community—lessons that could perhaps be used for the "progress" of Black people in the United States and the advancement of the condition of the diaspora throughout the world. Their observation and experience of Haiti was an opportunity for them to evaluate the ability of their community to rise to influential political positions in the United States. Unlike other works, the present book thus examines the history of Haiti, Haitians, African Americans, and the United States through the complex relationship between the African American community and the Black republic. Because it covers the whole of the nineteenth century, it especially shows how Haiti remained a focus of attention for white as well as Black Americans before, during, and after the Civil War, until the turn of the century.

The story of this special relationship between Black Americans and the Black republic undoubtedly started during the Haitian Revolution (1791–1804), a revolution that contemporary historiography incorporates into the greater movement of the democratic revolutions of the late eighteenth century.[10] As the struggle for racial equality constituted a central element of the Haitian Revolution, some historians such as Sybille Fischer or Laurent Dubois rightly consider Haiti as one of the places where economic modernity arose and where the limits of the European Enlightenment and the French republic's universalism were tested.[11] Other historians such as Ronald A. Johnson or Matthew J. Clavin also argue that the Haitian Revolution, under the leadership of Toussaint Louverture, had long-lasting consequences on American and Atlantic world discussions of race, on American-Haitian diplomacy, and even played a central role in the conflict between the American North and South until the Civil War.[12] In this context, the Haitian Revolution takes on a significant international meaning: as an episode of global history; as the principal crossroads of the Atlantic Slave trade; as the geographic core of Caribbean slavery; and as one of the theaters for the rise of modern capitalism. *L'union fait la force: Les Noirs américains et Haïti, 1804–1893* situates the Haitian republic firmly within recent Atlantic and global historiography by examining the history of Haiti through the complex relationship between the Black American community and the Black Republic in the nineteenth century.

Indeed, this book argues that, before the Civil War, the Black republic was considered by free Black Americans as a place where full citizenship was at hand. Haiti was essentially viewed and concretely experienced as a refuge during moments when free people of color lost hope of obtaining rights in the United States. The thirty years preceding the Civil War saw the emergence of a radical abolitionist movement, particularly among free people of color who, for the most part, adhered to the "stay and fight" ideology. But, as paradoxical as it may seem, while some prominent Black activists then firmly opposed emigration and denounced the American Colonization Society and its African project of mass exile, others advocated relocation to closer places.

Gradually, more and more Black emigrationists started promoting the virtues of emigrating to Haiti, considering the small republic as a "promised land" where their diasporic, separatist, or nationalist ideals converged, as the place where they could build and maintain a "Black nationality," and as the nation where the Black community-in-the-making might fight for the emancipation and the equality of the Black race all over the world. Thousands of free Black Americans thus settled in Haiti before the Civil War, mostly on the occasion of two waves of emigration initiated by the Haitian government in the middle of the 1820s and the early 1860s. During the war, while fighting to save the Union, Lincoln tried to send free Black Americans and contrabands (i.e., slaves who escaped behind Union lines during the Civil War) to various colonies and considered deporting them to a Haitian island (Île-à-Vache), among other places. Sponsored by the U.S. government, the colonization of Île-à-Vache that was launched in early 1863—only a few days after the Emancipation Proclamation was issued—turned out to be a total failure.

After the war, Haiti (recognized by the United States in 1862) gradually became a diplomatic partner, to which the U.S. nominated mostly Black diplomats after 1869. However, Frederick Douglass's mission as the American ambassador to Haiti between 1889 and 1891 reveals the ambiguities of U.S. policy toward the small Black republic at a moment when the United States was trying to impose itself as a dominant power in the Caribbean and as a leading imperialist nation, notably by attempting to establish a military base in Haiti (at the Môle Saint-Nicolas). Douglass's own position and feelings toward Haiti were ambiguous: while (unsuccessfully) negotiating for the lease of the Môle Saint-Nicolas, Douglass was constantly torn between his fraternal love and admiration for his Haitian "brothers" and his paternalistic consideration of Haiti as an "infant" who still needed to "progress."

Haiti and its leaders are also at the heart of this book, even if it does not aim to examine the attitude of the Haitian elites toward their American brethren. Haitian leaders, in particular, supported the American emigration to Haiti, opposed the American geostrategic and diplomatic diktats in the 1870s and 1880s, and offered an international platform to Frederick Douglass at the World's Columbian Exposition in Chicago, thus helping Black Americans who faced discrimination to fight against slavery and the slave trade and to fight for their rights. The closing chapters of the book, which deal with the events that revolved around the Haitian pavilion at the 1893 Chicago Fair, fully illustrate the emancipatory role of the Black republic.[13] By naming Douglass as the first commissioner of its pavilion—a fact still hardly discussed in historiography—Haiti allowed him to use the small building as the "headquarters" of African American activists. Douglass effectively employed the international platform provided by Haiti to denounce the Republicans' abdication to the "values" of the southerners advocating segregation, denying Black Americans the right to vote, and debasing the latter to the position of second-class citizens. The Sage of Anacostia was indeed able to distribute thousands of copies of the famous pamphlet that he had co-authored with Ida B. Wells (*The Reason Why the Colored American Is Not in the World's Columbian Exposition*) to the visitors who had come to visit the Haitian exhibition.[14] Thus, the Black republic gave Black Americans the opportunity to make their voices heard by providing them with the platform their own country had refused them.

By spanning the entire nineteenth century, *Wanted! A Nation! Black Americans and Haiti, 1804–1893* presents a complex panorama of the emergence of Black American identity and argues that Haiti should be considered as an essential prism to understand how Black Americans forged their identity in the nineteenth century. Drawing on a variety of anglophone and francophone sources, *Wanted! A Nation!* goes beyond the usual framework of national American history and contributes to an Atlantic and global history of the struggle for equal rights.

WANTED!
A NATION!

INTRODUCTION

My subject is Haiti, the Black Republic.[1]

—FREDERICK DOUGLASS

The famous nineteenth-century Black American activist Frederick Douglass—one of the principal heroes of this book—was absolutely fascinated by the homeland of Toussaint Louverture.[2] As he saw it, Haiti was the "modern land of Canaan," "a city set on a hill" that "st[ood] forth among the nations of the earth richly deserving respect and admiration."[3] As a Black nation that had won its independence through bloody revolution, Haiti stirred a range of reactions across America throughout the nineteenth century, from obsessive phobia to unbridled admiration, and long remained a topic for debate and controversy among Americans of all races.

The Haitian Revolution undeniably sent ripples across American society, with major consequences for the history of the United States and every segment of the population—Black people, white people, and Native Americans alike—since this was the event that forced Napoleon to sell Louisiana to the young American republic in 1803, laying the foundations for Thomas Jefferson's expansionist program to build an "Empire of Liberty."[4] Clearly, the existence of a free Black nation populated by former slave rebels was bound to influence the development of slavery in the United States after 1800. Although slaveowners were not dissuaded from introducing slavery to new states, they were worried by the success of the Haitian Revolution, leading them to strengthen an already strong proslavery doctrine by, in part, toughening legislation limiting the free Black population's rights.

Focusing more narrowly on the Black community, *Wanted! A Nation!* sets out to demonstrate that the interactions between Haitians and Black Americans, particularly those living in the northern states who were born free or recently emancipated, were plentiful and complex. As soon as the world's first

Black republic achieved independence in 1804, and then increasingly from the 1820s on, it drew the attention of Black American thinkers and leaders eager to further their own struggle for freedom and equal rights. Exchanges between members of the Black diaspora were cultural, artistic, human, religious, diplomatic, political, and commercial, but they were also, inevitably, bound up with issues of identity. Whether Black Americans saw Haiti as an inspirational example of emancipation or a new promised land, whether they left the United States to live there—voluntarily or otherwise—or returned more or less reluctantly to their homeland, Black Americans wrote many pages of their history jointly with Haitians.

One such central actor in this history was Frederick Douglass. Born into slavery in 1817 or 1818, Douglass eventually escaped, purchased his freedom, and became one of the most influential and widely respected Black abolitionist thinkers and orators of the first part of the nineteenth century and a staunch Republican campaigning for equal rights in the second half of the century. In a still-segregated United States, his political career was truly exceptional.[5] Douglass's connection to Haiti dated back to the early years of his career. As early as the 1840s, he was defending what he saw as the first Black republic's right to remain a sovereign, independent nation. Having nearly visited Haiti in 1861—he canceled his planned trip when the Civil War broke out—he finally paid the nation an official visit ten years later as an official representative of the American government, which was then considering potential annexation of the island. He spent two years, from 1889 to 1891, as the U.S. ambassador to Haiti. Haiti, in turn, entrusted him with his last political mission in 1893, appointing him first commissioner for the Haitian pavilion at the Chicago World's Fair, where he gave a lecture on the small Caribbean nation. This last act of support for Haiti, often overlooked and little explored by Douglass scholars, marks the final chapter in a long, complex, ambiguous relationship between Douglass and Haiti. It also reflects his support for a new stage in the defense of Black Americans' rights in the late nineteenth century. Douglass's exceptional career was closely bound up with the Black republic established on the Caribbean island of Hispaniola.[6]

Above and beyond the role of Frederick Douglass, a study of abolitionist newspapers, the personal archives of Douglass and other Black leaders, the nineteenth-century press, and the many speeches, pamphlets, and books written by Black Americans reveals that the Black republic of Haiti was a significant presence in the lives, collective imaginary, and thought of many Black American activists throughout the nineteenth century. Above all, such a study demonstrates that the relationship between Haiti and Black Americans was no mere fantasy or naive, abstract, idealized vision of a far-flung, distant place.

Rather, the Black activists studied in this book traveled to Haiti, breathed its air, and experienced life in a place that many of them considered a promised land—or at the very least an example or model to be proudly praised or copied.

By using Haiti as a lens, *Wanted! A Nation!* focuses on the image of Haiti as a locus for the expression and development of Black American identity. It analyzes the roots of Black American activism, Black diasporic thought, and Black nationalism and internationalism, whose origins are traced back to the 1820s. The book does not seek simply to trace Haiti's influence on the Black American community from afar, a question thoroughly explored in outstanding recent works, but rather the *literal* experience of Haiti by the free Black American abolitionists and activists who traveled there, whether they merely visited, lived there for a while, or settled permanently. In other words, Haiti was for them a real place grounded in concrete personal experience, not simply a theoretical or rhetorical reference.

The relationship between these Black Americans and Haiti throughout the nineteenth century laid the groundwork for a new kind of quest for identity. While slavery had begun to be seriously questioned in the late eighteenth century and the United States was home to ever more free Black men and women, the nineteenth century was a time for the latter to forge a Black American identity. As they wondered what it meant to be Black and free in the United States, Haiti showed them a place where it was possible to be a free, Black citizen. The mere existence of Haiti encouraged and reassured them in their quest for identity, proving that Black men and women could indeed live as free citizens in an independent republic. After 1865, Black Americans, now free citizens of the United States, gradually moved beyond Haiti to espouse a more international approach, eventually opening up the debate on identity to internationalism, Pan-Africanism, and anticolonialism. Haiti was no longer the sole point of reference for oppressed Black people, but to a certain extent, the Haitian experience had enabled the Black Americans who traveled there to develop a diasporic understanding of their community.

The concepts of a Black diaspora and the Black Atlantic are central to the book. They have been widely studied by historians, sociologists, anthropologists, philosophers, literary theorists, and political scientists. Taking a historical approach, we will not seek to take a position on either side of the debates that regularly divide specialists of other disciplines. However, drawing on the concepts of a Black diaspora and Black Atlantic in historical research requires precise definitions of terms that are sometimes used loosely and from different—if not always divergent—perspectives, particularly within French-language scholarship.

Framed in a strictly Anglo-American scientific, political, and cultural context, the Black Atlantic, as defined by Paul Gilroy in 1993, brought a new dimension to American studies and diaspora studies in the early 1990s. Gilroy argued that the history of the Black diaspora was bound up with a topography of movements, shifts, and a network of a number of geographical sites that he identified across Europe, North America, and Africa.[7] His seminal work introduced two major new theoretical approaches: considering the memory of slavery-related violence as the cultural bedrock for the Black diaspora across the Americas, and interpreting expressions of Black culture, particularly music, not as the vestiges of earlier traditions but as what he termed "countercultures of modernity." Gilroy's concept was rooted in the tension between a past recomposed by the experience of slavery and a future shaped by the project to end it.

For several years, scholars working on the multidisciplinary, transnational field of Black studies have been exploring the chronology of the Black Atlantic, extending it to contemporary African diasporas (i.e., those not rooted in the Atlantic slave trade) and to a broader geographical range, looking toward South America and even the Pacific. This tendency to read the African diaspora in more global geographical terms is a fairly recent development, illustrated in Patrick Manning's 2010 study *The African Diaspora: A History through Culture,* which sets out to place the history of the African diaspora in a global context, focusing on the dynamic nature of the interactions between the various Black communities scattered across every continent and taking a *longue durée* approach from the fifteenth century to the present day. Manning extends the Black Atlantic across the Pacific and Indian oceans as far as Asia, applying Gilroy's concept on a global scale.[8]

By demonstrating that Haiti can be read as part of Gilroy's Black Atlantic—though Gilroy himself only mentions it in passing—it becomes clear that *physical* contacts, in the case of Black American emigration to Haiti, along with commercial, and later diplomatic, exchanges, made Haiti a key locus for contact in the heart of the nineteenth-century Black Atlantic.[9] Given that for Gilroy, the study of the Black (and, in terms of this book, specifically the Black American) population can only be understood in terms of Atlantic mobility—in which the Atlantic space is seen as a political and cultural system in its own right, a contact zone between histories and cultures, a place where race, culture, nationality, and ethnicity collide—it is important to locate Haiti in this Atlantic space.[10] The purpose of this book is not to draw up an exhaustive list of every contact between Black Americans and Haiti, but rather to focus on the most significant instances that led to real changes in how the Black American community, and even America as a whole, thought about itself.

Recent decades have built on Gilroy's pioneering research to apply the concept of the Black diaspora across the humanities and social sciences. The term "diaspora," as traditionally applied to the Jewish population, originally pointed at a single community; the Black diaspora, on the other hand, refers to a multitude of peoples from Africa or of African origin, culture, and language. What unites them is, as Gilroy and Manning suggest, the common heritage of slavery and the shared quest for emancipation.[11]

Similarly, using the term "Black" (rather than "African") to refer to the diaspora and the community it studies is important for a couple reasons. First, the geographically rooted term was often rejected by nineteenth-century Black Americans themselves; second, the term "African" maps the diaspora onto the classical model considered solely in terms of the heritage of ancestral Africa, the motherland. The term "Black" is anchored in a more modern, post-African reality. References to the Black diaspora in the context of the Black Atlantic are rooted in the Atlantic slave trade but also seek to understand and demonstrate the existence of a specific Black diasporic experience and thought—in other words, studying its nationalist dimension. In avoiding the terms "African" or "African American" diaspora, this book aims to foreground the *nationalist* dimension of the Black diaspora in the United States. Furthermore, referring to Black people and Black Americans is more in keeping with the rejection of Africa by the majority of Black Americans throughout the nineteenth century, as this book will demonstrate.

Where this study differs from Gilroy's theoretical framework is in its treatment of Black nationalism. Gilroy's work is shaped by his aim of refuting Black nationalist discourse. The starting point for our investigation, however, is that the experience of a multiple, mobile, fluid, intercultural, hybrid diaspora included a nationalist aspect, since Black nationalism was, for its nineteenth-century advocates, a project to build lasting unity. Like Wilson Jeremiah Moses, this book considers Black nationalism as a form of racial nationalism, taking the "race" of the Black people, rather than their skin color, as the foundational link between members of the nation, which it in turn shaped.[12] It follows French anthropologist and geographer Christine Chivallon in reading Black nationalism as "at the same time an instrument of resistance to oppression, a means of restoring dignity that was denied, and the expression of a more political will of self-determination."[13] Since the book's focus is on the diasporic consciousness of the Black American community in the nineteenth century, it uses the concepts of Black nationalism and particularly "Black nationality," anticipating and complementing Pan-Africanism. Many free Black Americans in the first half of the nineteenth century observed the Black republic of Haiti and, aware that they were not considered as citizens on U.S.

soil, considered finding territories where they could form racial communities rooted in a Black nationality. What they called "Black nationality"—not wholly equivalent to what we now call "Black nationalism"—was the idea of bringing all members of the Black community together in a specific place, where they could live freely with all the rights accruing to the citizens of a nation—and why should that place not be Haiti?

Wanted! A Nation! is not a history of ideas but of *men*. Writing a history of the nineteenth-century Black American relationship with Haiti inevitably means writing a history of the Black American elite. In the nineteenth century, only literate Black American activists, abolitionists, and churchmen, and in the first part of the century those who were *free*, were in a position to leave written records of their experiences and the history of their community and its relationship with Haiti. It should be borne in mind that these men were in the minority in the Black community. Yet, like Frederick Douglass, we believe that their role and experience were crucial, as their successes and failures inevitably influenced the community as a whole. As Douglass put it, "Such men increase the faith of all in the possibilities of their race, and make it easier for those who are to come after them."[14]

A study of the Black American community and the Black diaspora is not the study of a homogeneous whole. These issues will be analyzed on a range of levels, both spatially and temporally, from the local (focusing on case studies of certain Black American groups or even individuals in specific regions of the United States or Haitian towns) to the national (the United States and Haiti as a Black republic) and even the global (the Black Atlantic). The shifts between micro- and macroanalysis are important, because taking a wholly collective approach to the nineteenth-century Black American community would inevitably lead to conclusions based on the appearance of homogeneity. This book, rather, seeks to break down this appearance of homogeneity and offer a new reading of the community's journey by studying the place of individuals within the collective experience. Such individual journeys bring a fresh perspective, allowing us to achieve a more nuanced history of the community, with all its diversity of opinions and points of view. The community rarely spoke with one voice on the thorny issues that determined its experience in the nineteenth century. One concrete example is the Black American community's relationship with African colonization and emigration to Haiti, explored in the first three chapters, and one of the leading figures in the community, Frederick Douglass. The latter regularly changed his mind on the issue of emigration to Haiti. Why should the rest of the community not have followed suit? While historiography tends to focus almost exclusively on the Black American community's outspoken opposition to various colonization projects in the first part of the nineteenth century, we will investigate the individual cases of men like Frederick Douglass, Martin Robison Delany, James Theodore Holly, and lesser-known figures to foreground the multiplicity of points of view espoused by the Black American community. According to French scholars Andrée-Anne Kekeh-Dika and Hélène Le Dantec-Lowry, "Black migration to the United States and the Caribbean was long overlooked by scholars. The passivity of peoples with regard to migration has often been pointed out."[15] We will demonstrate that Black emigrationists in fact often actively promoted voluntary migration as a "choice, an act of protest," seeing expatriation as a positive move to a place where they thought they would be able to enjoy the civil and political rights that the United States denied them.[16] Analyzing the experience of James Theodore Holly, for instance, reveals that the Black Americans who campaigned for emigration were not all solely interested in improving the lives of their peers: some also felt themselves to be carrying out a mission to bring religion and/or civilization to Black Haitians and the Black diaspora more broadly speaking. The history of the community's relationship with Haiti will accordingly be studied not in terms of a logical, linear progression but as a disparate range of events that came together to form a single, coherent, yet multifaceted experience of Haiti.

Wanted! A Nation! originally came about in reaction to the feeling that this aspect of the Black community's history had been marginalized in the historiography. The research involved uncovering the traces of Black American experiences of Haiti in the nineteenth century. It quickly became clear that U.S./Haitian relations in the period had, broadly speaking, largely been explored from the point of view of white Americans, particularly in terms of antislavery, abolitionism, colonization, imperialism, and diplomacy. The role of Black Americans in these issues had been overlooked or sidelined; at best, it was assumed that the entire Black American community was of a single mind on the question.

While subjects like slavery and the slave experience, antislavery, abolitionism, emancipation, Abraham Lincoln's relationship with Black Americans and slavery, Reconstruction and its impact on the Black American community, segregation and the struggle for civil rights, Black nationalism and Pan-Africanism, colonization, and the importance of the Christian Church and the press for the Black community have been widely studied in the nineteenth-century context, other issues have been largely overlooked. These include the voluntary emigration of thousands of Black Americans in the first half of the nineteenth century, particularly to Haiti, and the Black American relationship with the Black republic of Haiti throughout the nineteenth century.[17] Why has so little been written on these questions? Part of the answer may lie in the "Atlantic" aspect of this dimension of Black American history, given American history writing's almost exclusively national focus, and on the fact that some of the (primary) sources necessary to answer these questions were not written in English.

The historiography of voluntary emigration is almost nonexistent. Most historians have turned their attention to the Black Americans who rejected emigration and decided to stay in the United States to fight for equal rights and citizenship at home. The few historians who have researched voluntary migration among the Black community have focused almost exclusively on Black Americans moving from the U.S. South (particularly to the northern states) after the Reconstruction era as part of the Great Migration.[18] The more specific issue of Black migration between the United States and the Caribbean has been mainly studied in terms of movement from the Caribbean to the United States in the twentieth century. Little work has engaged with migration from the United States to the Caribbean.[19] One exception is Sara J. Fanning's 2015 book *Caribbean Crossing: African Americans and the Haitian Emigration Movement*,[20] which has a narrow chronological focus on the first wave of migration in the 1820s. The aim of the present book is to fill a historiographical gap in our knowledge of voluntary Black American migration to Haiti in the first part of the nineteenth century.

In terms of the U.S./Haiti relationship, the fear of Haiti—palpable among the white population, especially in the South—has been studied and analyzed. Conversely, however, the Black American interest in and admiration for the Black republic has attracted relatively little attention from scholars. Yet across the nineteenth century, the Black and white elites alike delivered and attended speeches, wrote and read articles, pamphlets, and books praising or criticizing Haiti or even glorifying its heroic leaders such as Toussaint Louverture. This abundant source material sheds light on the real nature of the relationship between nineteenth-century Black Americans and the Black republic. Did they see it as an example to be followed? If so, to what extent? Did they consider traveling there? Why? To what end?

Aside from Sara Fanning's book, only a few works of scholarship, some now a few decades old, have researched the relationship between Black Americans and Haiti. As its title suggests, Floyd J. Miller's 1975 study *The Search for a Black Nationality: Black Emigration and Colonization, 1787–1863* focuses on one aspect of the relationship: Black American emigration to and colonization of Haiti and their role in the emergence of Black nationalism.[21] The few chapters devoted to Haiti grant surprisingly little space to a discussion of Haiti's place in the conceptualization and rise of Black nationalism in the Black American community, though they do offer some leads for analyzing emigration to Haiti in the first half of the nineteenth century. Chris Dixon's *African America and Haiti: Emigration and Black Nationalism in the Nineteenth Century* (2000) aimed to be a more complete study of emigration to Haiti and its relationship with Black nationalism, building on the foundations laid by Miller twenty-five years before.[22] Dixon's subtitle indicates an exploration of the contacts between Black Americans and Haiti across the nineteenth century; however, his chronology, like Miller's, ends with the American Civil War. When the present book was published in France in 2016, no other substantial study of the question was available. In recent years, Brandon Byrd's major work *The Black Republic: African Americans and the Fate of Haiti* (2019) has partially filled the gap in the historiography, analyzing the African American interest in Haiti from the end of the Civil War in 1865 to the American occupation of the Black republic in 1915.[23] Alongside these few books, a handful of articles take a passing interest in the relationship between Black Americans and Haiti in terms of two specific issues: Black American emigration to Haiti and Haiti's "arm's-length" influence on abolitionist movements and the emergence of Black nationalism in the first part of the nineteenth century.

No work to date has explored the concrete contacts between Black Americans and Haiti across the nineteenth century—yet these contacts were richer than is often suspected, from the Reconstruction era to the end of the century. In this postwar period, the leading figure in Haitian/Black American exchanges is undeniably Frederick Douglass, yet this aspect of his political life after emancipation is likewise all too often overlooked. The aim of this work is to fill in this gap in the historiographical knowledge where historians have failed to engage with the "Atlantic" history of Black Americans: it sets out to examine the shifting, nonhomogeneous, rarely harmonious, but always fascinating relationship between Black Americans and the Black republic across the nineteenth century, when Haiti was seen by turns as an example to follow, an ideal to achieve, a model to be defended against white criticism and prejudice, and even an object of critique. For Black activists, it was one of the guiding threads in building not only a Black community per se but also a nationalist and diasporic understanding of the Black American community. Because Haiti was a republic, hence a model of civilized government, and because its citizens were necessarily Black, as stipulated in its many successive constitutions, it represented an attractive prospect for nineteenth-century Black American activists. Furthermore, it was ideally located in the heart of the Americas, unlike the other two Black republics, Liberia and Ethiopia. These were far away in Africa, a continent that, in the white American imaginary (and hence the Black imaginary, which was unavoidably influenced by the codes and values of the white society Black Americans lived in), remained a barbaric, savage place devoid of civilization. In these circumstances, it was hardly surprising that Haiti enjoyed a certain degree of prestige among nineteenth-century Black Americans.

In the first part of the nineteenth century, from Haitian independence to the Civil War, what the Black republic represented above all for free, educated Black Americans was a place where genuine, full citizenship was a reality. Haiti was essentially considered and concretely lived as a refuge at a time when Black Americans thought they would never be granted equal rights on American soil (chapter 1). As the antislavery movement shifted toward radicalization and began to demand immediate abolition, Haiti came to be seen as the ideal (and idealized) site embodying the diasporic, separatist, nationalist ideals of some Black activists, the site where they could root a "Black nationality" to continue their struggle for the emancipation and equality of Black people worldwide, making it a sort of promised land for the Black diaspora (chapter 2). Proponents of voluntary emigration to Haiti firmly opposed the colonizationist program led by the American Colonization Society—a philanthropic society that aimed to send free Black Americans from the northern states "back" to Africa—and considered Haiti as an acceptable alternative that would allow free people of color to enjoy rights that the United States denied them without having to travel halfway around the world. Though two waves of emigration saw thousands of Black emigrants move to Haiti, both waves ended in relative failure. Yet on an individual level the experiment was more or less successful, and the debates surrounding the issue were fertile soil for a theory of Black American identity (chapter 3).

The Civil War turned a new page in the history of Black Americans and Haiti. Abraham Lincoln's recognition of the small Black republic in 1862 and the emancipation of Black Americans the following year opened a new dimension in the relationship. While the period 1862–63 saw Lincoln's project to send Black Americans to colonize the Île-à-Vache in Haiti come to fruition (chapter 4), the fresh hopes raised by emancipation turned the attention of Black American activists away from the island for a while.

Once slavery had been abolished, these activists sought new meaning for their struggle by setting their sights on obtaining full citizenship in the United States and political representation at every level of government. The Reconstruction era from 1865 to 1877 saw a handful of Black Americans achieve success in posts of national, and even international, significance. Unfortunately, the illusion of equality created by these few highly visible and successful Black Americans did not outlast the Reconstruction era. During that same period, Haiti remained dear to the hearts of Black Americans, particularly as from 1869 to the end of the century, every American ambassador to the country was Black (chapter 5). In the meantime, Haiti came to be seen as a site of strategic importance for the United States' imperialist ambitions in the Caribbean. From President Grant's mission to Santo Domingo in 1871 to the Môle Saint-Nicolas affair in 1891—a major event in Frederick Douglass's brief diplomatic career (chapter 6)—Haiti remained central to the interests of both Black and white America in the decades after the Civil War. Two years later, in 1893, Haiti asked Douglass to be its official representative at the Chicago World Fair. Douglass seized the opportunity to return to his pre-emancipation activism (chapter 7). The Haitian pavilion was used as a focal point for Black American discontent: the famous pamphlet *The Reason Why* was published to mark the exhibition,[24] and its co-authors, Ida B. Wells and Douglass himself, handed it out to visitors to the Haitian pavilion.

This final interaction between Haiti and Black American activists marks the end of an era of cooperation—and of this study. The United States, from the great cities of the North to the Deep South, was sinking wholesale into a system of segregation soon to be institutionalized; state-sanctioned racism was creeping into politics at every level, while Black Americans saw their living conditions declining further and faster than at any time since the abolition of slavery, and the Constitution was disregarded every time a Black man was prevented from voting by pseudolegal means. Yet, against all expectations, 1893 was to prove a major turning point for Frederick Douglass and other late nineteenth-century activists. By appointing Frederick Douglass first commissioner for the Haitian pavilion at the 1893 World Fair, the small nation gave Douglass and his peers an unprecedented opportunity to speak on the world stage (chapter 8).

The nineteenth century opened with enslavement for the vast majority of Black Americans and freedom without equality for a tiny minority. And while it ended with freedom without civil rights for all, the vagaries of this century form an overarching dynamic in which Haiti played a major part, underpinning the construction of the Black American community's identity despite that community's almost constant ambivalence toward the Black republic—an attitude that extended to Frederick Douglass himself. The following pages explore the history of the irresistible allure of revolutionary, resistant Haiti, and the power of attraction, in all senses of the term, it held for nineteenth-century Black Americans.

CHAPTER 1

Haiti, the Promised Land?

> I have often asked myself, why Hayti, whose climate is so mild, and whose government is analogous to that of the United States, was not preferred as their place of refuge.[1]
>
> —JEAN-PIERRE BOYER

The first references to the expatriation of Black people date from the colonial era. The historian Walter L. Fleming writes that the idea was as old as racial prejudice and the antislavery movement.[2] But it was during the Revolutionary period, and increasingly during the early years of the young republic, that the idea of colonizing, deporting, displacing, moving, and expatriating free or recently freed Black men and women really developed in the United States.[3] At the same time as a constitution that could federate the largest number of people was being drafted and numerous abolitionist societies were springing up—thus generating heated discussions about the future of the Atlantic slave trade—the *colonization* of Black people outside the American territory was also being seriously considered.

Although the creation of a North American colony in Africa, specifically in Liberia, is well documented and has been the focus of numerous studies, historians have paid much less attention to the emigration of Black Americans to Haiti, and they tend to describe that emigration as something imposed on Black people and therefore accepted under duress.[4] It is likely that the historiography focused principally on the return to Africa because that project was energetically supported or rejected by eminent Black figures such as Martin R. Delany and Frederick Douglass. Except for Abraham Lincoln's backing of the venture to colonize Île-à-Vache, emigration projects from the U.S. to Haiti were undertaken by lesser-known Black activists such as James Theodore Holly and were the object of less controversy and debate in the Black community, sometimes even going totally unnoticed by both Black and white antislavery advocates and abolitionists.

Even if the majority of Black American activists of the first half of the nineteenth century were fiercely opposed to the African colonization project promoted by the American Colonization Society,[5] a sizable number of Black American thinkers and activists spoke out publicly in favor of *voluntary* emigration to freely chosen territories, notably Haiti.

Colonization as an Answer to the Tricky Question of How to Live Together

In the eighteenth century, few people in the English-speaking world doubted that humanity was one. In the Declaration of Independence of 1776, Thomas Jefferson wrote that "all men are created equal." Following that declaration, laws providing for the immediate or gradual emancipation of Black slaves were debated and sometimes passed in northern parts of the country. Starting in the 1780s, however, many observers believed that coexistence between whites and free people of color was inconceivable and that former slaves ought to be isolated, separated, or perhaps deported. This belief would strengthen with the emergence of racist theories in the early nineteenth century. Monogenism gradually yielded to the pseudoscientific belief in a hierarchy of races that conveniently dovetailed with an expansion of slavery in the United States. Indeed, Thomas Jefferson, co-author of both the Declaration of Independence and the U.S. Constitution, already raised the idea of freed Black people "removed beyond the reach of mixture" in his *Notes on the State of Virginia*:

> This unfortunate difference of colour, and perhaps of faculty, is a powerful obstacle to the emancipation of these people. Many of their advocates, while they wish to vindicate the liberty of human nature, are anxious also to preserve its dignity and beauty. Some of these, embarrassed by the question "What further is to be done with them?" join themselves in opposition with those who are actuated by sordid avarice only. Among the Romans emancipation required but one effort. The slave, when made free, might mix with, without staining the blood of his master. But with us a second is necessary, unknown to history. When freed, he is to be removed beyond the reach of mixture.[6]

During the American War of Independence, as former northern British colonies, now becoming states, developed frameworks for the gradual abolition of slavery, no attention was given to the future of freed Black people. The question of cohabitation only came up when poor unemployed Black people, including some falling into prostitution and crime, started filling up cities. People said their ignorance was their own fault instead of taking the necessary measures to help them. Critics saw their poverty as proof of their less than fully human and therefore incompatible status, thus strengthening the idea of their relocation toward other regions and continents. Even though abolitionists considered dark-skinned beings human enough to not be classed as slaves, these same emancipators generally judged freed Blacks to be "inferior" and incapable of assimilating into the general population, becoming true citizens, or governing themselves since they lacked the requisite education.[7] In addition, it was clear that many whites did not wish to live in too close proximity to freed Blacks. Separation in the form of a more or less imposed distancing seemed to be a necessary concomitant of the emancipation of Black slaves. This "solution" to the "Black problem" was hardly a passing fanciful idea. It became the established thinking across the country in both the southern political class and among abolitionists who were mostly in the North but present at the time in the South as well. For everyone there was a burning question that required a quick and efficient answer: What was to be done with all those free people of color?[8] Even if slavery was manifestly barbarous, cruel, and immoral, people were generally not keen on integrating the recently freed populations. It seemed inconceivable to live together, as they saw it, because even though free, Blacks were far from being the equal of whites.

In truth, the idea of a geographical separation between Blacks and whites was not exactly revolutionary at the time. Already at the end of the seventeenth century, a Virginia law required that freed Blacks leave the state.[9] In the North in 1714, a resident of New Jersey had proposed that Blacks "be set free ... [and] sent to their own Country."[10] They were not yet developing a precise program for the emancipation and resettlement of slaves, but clearly a certain mistrust of freed Blacks was already well established in the minds of many. Somewhat later, in the 1770s, the noted Quaker abolitionist Anthony Benezet and even Thomas Paine proposed moving Blacks to the far side of the Allegheny Mountains. None of these expatriation projects was carried out. One reason for these failures was the influence of powerful associations, such as the Pennsylvania Abolition Society, which declared the relocation plans to be morally repugnant and contrary to the humanist principles of the antislavery movement. Others pointed out that there were too few free Blacks to pose a real threat to whites.[11] In addition, Black Americans spoke out massively against such colonization ideas. This did not prevent them from contemplating eventual plans of voluntary emigration,[12] but the vast majority wished to remain on American territory, as abolitionist writings would later attest:

> [T]he coloured people of Philadelphia . . . denounced the [ACS] scheme as injurious and prejudicial to the best interests of their people, and calculated to increase the tension of the chains of slavery, rather than to promote its final extinction.[13]

After receiving limited discussion during the first years of the republic, the idea of resettlement attracted more attention in the northern states at the end of the 1790s and the early 1800s. The principal causes were the imminent termination of the transatlantic slave trade (which was to take effect on January 1, 1808), the proximity of Haiti, and the fear of a revolutionary contagion among the slaves (a concern fueled by the growing number of conspiracies, revolts, rebellions, and other more or less localized and secretive attacks mounted with increasing violence by slaves in the South). Consequently, the colonization talk resurfaced among abolitionists and politicians who were certain they had the solution to all the problems caused by indiscriminate mingling with a free and constantly growing Black population.[14]

A large number of ideas for Black resettlement were hatched at the end of the eighteenth century. For example, in the mid-1780s William Thornton, an eminent Quaker recently arrived from England, and the Reverend Dr. Samuel Hopkins proposed relocating Black people to Puerto Rico or the West Indies, and then to Guinea with the idea of establishing a "Black commonwealth" uniting all the Black population of France, Great Britain, and the United States.[15] Their idea took shape, partially, when friends of Thornton back in London created the colony of Sierra Leone in 1787.[16]

In 1790 the Virginian Ferdinando Fairfax developed his own federal program for the emancipation and displacement of Black people.[17] Fairfax proposed that Congress support the creation in Africa of a colony of emancipated Blacks. Congress would then supervise the defense, financial matters, and political organization of the young colony until it was able to govern itself and become an independent nation-state. In order to assure the success of this colony, Fairfax believed it was necessary to educate the children of the deported and the children of the future émigrés prior to their departure toward the new land that would welcome them. Africa was considered the ideal place to send them on account of its climate and its distance from white populations, which would prevent interracial marriages. Fairfax was convinced that, after a certain time, the United States would see a handsome return on its investment and that the scheme also offered a favorable opportunity to evangelize in barbarous lands.[18]

In 1796 St. George Tucker[19] unveiled his plan for gradual emancipation whereby freed Black people would be denied all civil rights and encouraged to depart in search of such privileges "in some other climate."[20]

The idea of resettlement came into clearer focus in the minds of Virginians after the events of the summer of 1800, in particular the rebellion of the slave Gabriel that was only averted thanks to a tip from two participants.[21] Of course, the argument that resettlement would prevent insurrections was widely invoked as soon as the first news came of the revolution in the French colony of Santo Domingo, but that conviction strengthened in the early 1800s.[22] In 1800, after Gabriel's failed insurrection attempt had traumatized Virginians, Thomas Jefferson, then vice president of the United States, wrote to the governor of Virginia and future president James Monroe about the possibility of systematically "displacing" the rebels and other troublemakers out of the state. "Colonization" in this context now meant protecting the interests of the state, and deportation appeared as a form of punishment for rebellious slaves.[23]

Thus, while certain abolitionists saw resettlement as the logical consequence of emancipation, others, notably gentlemen politicians, saw it as a way to protect economic interests and keep the peace; while others saw it as a way to solve the racial problem of living "next to" free people of color who were considered both inferior and potential catalysts of slave revolts, and who, depending on their state of residence, had few if any legal rights. All that remained was to find a "suitable" location for deportation. On this point opinions were divided, and different proposals enjoyed varying levels of success over the years.

While some proposed the American West, Sierra Leone, Liberia, or Africa more generally, others preferred to privilege Haiti as a possible location for Black resettlement. Its climate, which was said to be similar to Africa's, was a leading argument, including for Thomas Jefferson. In 1801 he stated that the Caribbean zone had the triple advantage of being "inhabited already by a people of their own race & color, [offering] climates congenial with their natural constitution, [and being] insulated from the other descriptions of men"—in other words, far from white people.[24]

But those favoring "the Pearl of the Antilles" were clearly in the minority at the start of the nineteenth century. The proximity of Haiti was a strike against it for most southerners and others opposed to its use for colonization. After Haiti's own war of independence (1791–1804), southern slaveowners were highly suspicious of this new Black republic situated so close to their lands. Between 1793 and 1820, fear of Santo Domingo (renamed Haiti in 1804), in particular the anxiety about a "revolutionary contagion," was palpable among southern planters. A week did not go by without some newspaper commenting on the event.[25] The matter was discussed in every state legislature,[26] while at the same time efforts were made to keep slaves from learning of the event. A sort of "Haiti myth" took hold after 1793 with the arrival in every state of free people of color from the island nation despite numerous laws passed to impede, without success, this undesirable migration. While economic contact with the island decreased after 1806, in accordance with France's request,[27] and the republic experienced its first setbacks, planters feared that mere mention of the island would spark ideas and even hopes of emancipation among their slaves. In the 1790s Thomas Jefferson had already evoked the dramatic consequence of such a domino effect when he remarked that if they did nothing to solve the "Black problem," "we shall soon be the murderers of our own children."[28] This fear was shared by large numbers of his fellow citizens who affirmed the destructive influence of refugees from the "French island" over their own slaves. Consequently, certain states quickly passed laws to block the entrance of refugees and/or their slaves coming from Santo Domingo. Of note are the efforts in South Carolina and Georgia, even though they had no concrete effect. In 1793 Georgia forbade all Black people from the West Indies and Florida (then a Spanish colony) from entering the state. In 1794 South Carolina closed its borders to free people of color coming from the West Indies or anywhere else in the Americas except the United States.[29]

One of the clearest proofs of this haunting fear of Haiti is certainly the series of letters published in the summer of 1794 in a Columbia, South Carolina, newspaper, *The Herald*. These letters, signed by the name "Rusticus" and attributed to Alexander Garden Jr., the son of a famous naturalist, criticized first the misplaced generosity, the excessive humanity of Carolinians who agreed to welcome the refugees from Santo Domingo. He was especially disapproving, however, of southern newspapers that were openly debating the ongoing events on the island. For Rusticus, it was essential to keep quiet about these events and prevent revolutionary and abolitionist ideas from spreading throughout southern society. It was true that many southern newspapers, including the *Courier* in Charleston, the *Virginia Gazette and General Advertiser*, and the *Richmond Enquirer*, reported regularly on the situation in Santo Domingo.[30] But these media outlets were not the only channels for spreading and cultivating the southern fear of contagion. Public speeches, private correspondence, and oral and written travel narratives were also adding to the rumor mill.

At the time, South Carolina was particularly affected by the events in Santo Domingo.[31] It was the only state where Black people constituted a majority of the population, and this probably contributed to the sympathy that Carolinians had toward their white counterparts in Santo Domingo, since a similar revolt might very well have happened in their own state. Planters worried about the negative influence of the revolution, especially since its geographic location made it the leading arrival point for many refugees from Santo Domingo; and with their arrival the rumors of insurrection, more or less substantiated, multiplied such that larger cities and the state were sometimes moved to pass laws in the hope of getting more and better control over these new Black populations.[32] In late 1793, for example, the city of Charleston passed an ordinance "for the better ordering and governing of Negroes and other slaves." Their fears were most certainly justified since the slaves had an excellent communication network, notably thanks to Black people (free or enslaved) who worked on ships, but also because (white) refugees from Santo Domingo were accompanied by their own slaves who had valuable information about the island's violent slave revolt that could certainly be shared with Black Americans.[33] As a result, every slave rebellion in a southern state was analyzed through the lens of Santo Domingo. The insurrection of Gabriel, of Denmark Vesey,[34] and the slave uprising along Louisiana's "German Coast" in 1811 were all discussed in one way or another in relation to Haiti. The American general Thomas Pinckney, for example, declared at the time that Vesey had followed "the example of St. Domingo." In fact, Pinckney predicted that the negative influence of Santo Domingo, which he considered the principal cause of the events in Charleston, would inevitably provoke future problems.[35]

Thus, even though starting around 1800, the idea of "displacing" free people of color was present in everyone's mind—across the political class, abolitionists, and other philanthropic individuals—Haiti was not immediately considered the ideal place of deportation because of the violence on the island that continued until 1804. In the American collective imagination, Haiti was until then associated with unsettling revolts, not with the possibility of peaceful resettlement. This first period of fear was fed and fanned by many newspaper articles or other publications on the subject as well as by verbal communication among Americans (Black or white), especially by enslaved Black people working in ports, sailors, and by refugees (whites or free people of color) from Santo Domingo. It seems to have come to an end in the early 1820s, since it is only then that one begins to hear some, including Thomas Jefferson, calmly invoking Haiti as a favorable destination (and economically advantageous, given the relative proximity of the island) for the free and emancipated Black American population. The leading reasons given were racial and economic. In a second letter dating from 1824, Jefferson calls Haiti an ideal place for the resettlement of Black people thanks to the close proximity of the island, and therefore the substantial savings that such resettlement would imply compared to the high cost of transporting them to Africa. Therefore the "problem" posed by free and emancipated Blacks on American soil was squarely economic and not humanist.[36] Besides the need for apprehensions to subside, another likely factor for the timing of this idea was that the new republic of Haiti was surely preoccupied with its own political, social, and economic affairs. Thus the first truly concrete and documented attempt to relocate a certain number of Black people to Haiti got started in the 1820s.

The First Attempts at Emigration to Haiti in the 1820s

After the more or less fruitful or failed attempts at emigration and resettlement of Black people already mentioned, a young free Black man from New England named Prince Saunders crafted his own plan for emigration to Haiti in 1818.[37] Saunders had received a scholarship to study in England from white philanthropists. While there he met the famous abolitionists Thomas Clarkson and William Wilberforce, who wished to recruit him to persuade Henri Christophe, then king of Haiti (or at least of the northern portion of the island), to agree to accept Black American émigrés to the island.[38] On his first trip to Haiti, Saunders was welcomed by Christophe and then sent to London with the aim of hiring teachers for the new schools of the king. Prince Saunders would later publish in London his *Haytian Papers* (1816) in which he praises Christophe's administration.[39] Christophe's primary concern was the education of his people, as is clear from the Proclamation of January 1, 1817, in which he states:

> Our eyes have been set on public instruction, it being the strongest means to reform and polish the customs and habits of the nation and institute a national character. . . . Moved by principles of justice and liberality, we have wished to favor foreign professors and artists who come set about teaching our youth. And we have declared that all varieties of religion will be tolerated and protected throughout the kingdom.[40]

Christophe asked Saunders to scout out London's best teachers, and he sent $6,000 to Wilberforce to pay advances on salaries and the transportation costs of the future recruits.[41]

Saunders arrived in Philadelphia in the fall of 1818 and did everything in

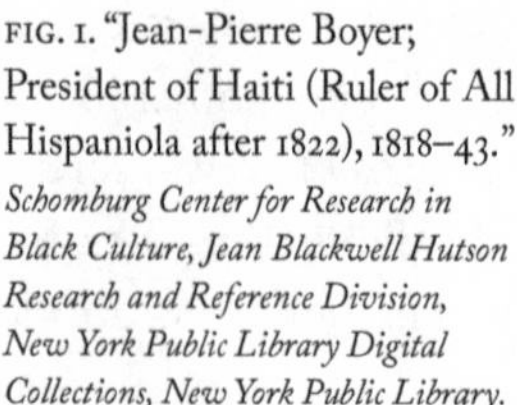

FIG. 1. "Jean-Pierre Boyer; President of Haiti (Ruler of All Hispaniola after 1822), 1818–43." *Schomburg Center for Research in Black Culture, Jean Blackwell Hutson Research and Reference Division, New York Public Library Digital Collections, New York Public Library.*

his power to promote Haiti to white and Black Americans from New York to Boston. His emigration plan to send free people of color to Haiti was now official. Having partnered with Clarkson, Prince Saunders was able to convince Christophe to cooperate as well, and the king seemed willing to provide a ship and make a first donation of $25,000.[42]

In the summer of 1820 Saunders was summoned to Haiti to discuss the logistics of this emigration program. However, just as he arrived on the island, Christophe suffered a paralyzing heart attack. As Saunders waited to be received by the king, a rebellion took place and the king committed suicide on October 8, 1820. These events put an abrupt end to Saunders's project, although he steadfastly maintained that thousands of free and recently emancipated Black men and women were waiting impatiently for a chance to emigrate to Haiti. With the arrival of President Jean-Pierre Boyer as head of state, the plan was finally able to happen.

After annexing the northern territory in 1820 and invading the Spanish portion of the island in 1822, Jean-Pierre Boyer became the successor to Alexandre Pétion, who had been president of southern Haiti. Once recognized as president "by acclamation," he was in need of laborers to carry out his projects for the country.[43] In order to boost the agricultural sector, Boyer turned to the United States and initiated a recruitment campaign that revived the interrupted plans of Christophe and Saunders to encourage Black Americans to emigrate to Haiti.[44] The future émigrés offered a solution to all his problems: unskilled laborers to work in the fields and perhaps beef up his army; and skilled artisans and merchants to revitalize the country's depressed economy. And since he was helping the United States get rid of its undesired free Black population, perhaps Haiti's large neighbor would grant him the diplomatic recognition he desperately needed.[45]

On the other end, in New York, was the Reverend Loring D. Dewey, a white abolitionist and leader within the American Colonization Society (and later a merchant in Haiti). Dewey, having observed that most free people of color in New York did not wish to go to Liberia, decided on his own to write to Boyer about possible terms for a project of emigration to Haiti. He probably counted on the growing notoriety of the American Colonization Society to attract the Haitian president's attention to his overture. Dewey would later admit to not having clearly told President Boyer on whose authority he was writing as "agent."[46] The publication of the complete correspondence between Boyer and Dewey from 1824 is a valuable source of information that clearly states the details of his proposal. In his letters, Dewey makes several explicit requests for details about all aspects of the proposed migration of Black Americans to Haiti, from the amount of aid Boyer was willing to pay to information about how the island operated when it came to schools, religion, marriage laws, and so forth. Boyer's replies were equally clear. To start with, in his letter of April 30, 1824, Boyer expresses surprise that the American authorities could prefer Africa over Haiti as a destination for resettlement.[47] He then answers Dewey's questions one by one, affirming that Haiti is prepared to generously finance the emigration of Black Americans above all for "humanist" reasons, while not denying certain economic and diplomatic motives:

> Animated with the desire to serve the cause of humanity, I have thought that a finer occasion could not have presented itself to offer an agreeable hospitality, a sure asylum, to the unfortunate men, who have the alternative of going to the barbarous shores of Africa, where misery or certain death may await them. . . . Every one can perceive perfectly that it will be an infallible means of augmenting the commerce of the United States, by multiplying relations between two people, the similarity of whose principles of legislation and government ought necessarily to render them friends, although a blind prejudice seems until now to have put obstacles in the way of more direct relations between the one and the other.[48]

In May 1824 Boyer decided to send a Haitian emissary to the United States, Jonathan Granville, with orders to cooperate with American society in general and the American Colonization Society in particular—"the philanthropic society of which [Dewey is] the agent."[49] Granville arrives in New York on June 13, 1824, carrying instructions from his government that Dewey took care to have translated and included in his published correspondence. Among these instructions divided into nineteen articles, Boyer describes the financial aspects of the arrangement, and notably in article 17 specifies the maximum number of Black Americans he wants to see move to Haiti, what precise locations on the island would be reserved for them, and the kinds of crops (coffee, tobacco, chocolate, and so on) they would be expected to grow.[50] In all, Boyer anticipated providing for the arrival of 6,000 people. Given the large number of slaves (or even of free and emancipated Black men and women) present on American soil at the time, this number can seem ridiculously small. In 1820, the Black population was estimated to have been 1,771,656, which represented 18.4 percent of the total population of the United States. It is worth noting that of these roughly 1.75 million Black men and women, only 230,315 or 13 percent were free. Of these, 57 percent (131,280 individuals) lived in slave states in 1820.[51] At the time, however, Boyer's figure did not make the offer any less attractive—in particular to Black Americans, since Boyer was offering to future emigrants, if they behaved themselves as good citizens, the chance to become owners of their own plot of land (roughly thirty-five acres for a group of twelve immigrants and their families), so long as they operated their farms profitably. For the poorest Black Americans, Boyer was even willing to advance a portion of the transportation costs—six dollars per person, to be paid back over the first six months after their arrival on the island.[52]

Many state colonization societies, with almost exclusively white leaders and followers, were enthusiastic about Boyer's proposal since they saw it as carrying out what they viewed as the logical next step after Black emancipation, and it provided the answer to America's perceived racial problems. In fact, though, most of these philanthropic associations ignored, or knew little to nothing at all about, the considerable logistical and psychological challenges of first uprooting, then transporting, and then setting up Black Americans in an unknown environment. Nevertheless, the prospect of distancing themselves from free people of color in order to preemptively avoid the risk of conflict, which they feared would be bloody, along with some undoubtedly good-faith humanist motives to find a suitable solution for their Black brethren, plus a sprinkling of economic calculations, together convinced large numbers of those opposed to slavery to finally choose Haiti rather than Africa as the preferred receiving destination.

One of the most active societies engaged in this search had been the New York Colonization Society. In its first official report from 1823, Haiti is mentioned favorably several times for its economic advantages, principally the cost savings of the transportation to Haiti, compared to shipping Black people to Africa, due to Haiti's geographical proximity.[53] However, because the American Colonization Society was only in favor of Black emigration to Africa, the New York members who favored emigration to Haiti felt obliged to found a parallel organization, the Society for Promoting the Emigration of Free Persons of Colour to Hayti. Little is known about this society other than that it published Dewey's *Correspondence Relative to the Emigration to Hayti, of the Free People of Colour, in the United States*, and that it established partnerships with some northern, Black-led societies, one of which was directed by Samuel Eli Cornish, a free Black man and founder of the Colored Presbyterian Church in New York. After hearing the news of Boyer's offer, some free Black Americans were strongly in favor of emigration to Haiti. In 1824 Richard Allen, founder of the African Episcopal Church (AME) and the Free African Society, and James Forten, a Black abolitionist and businessman, founded the Haytian Emigration Society of Coloured People in Philadelphia with the aim of organizing Black emigration to Haiti.[54] They published a pamphlet intended for free Black people potentially interested in the project. The text is filled with praise for this "promised land," while also giving all the practical details that an aspiring émigré would want to know about the climate, appropriate clothing, how to behave on the island, and religious matters.[55] The optimism of the Philadelphia leaders was shared by those in New York who created their own chapter of the Haytian Emigration Society. The enthusiasm of all of these abolitionist societies, white and Black, differed considerably from the reservations expressed by the American Colonization Society.

Many newspapers echoed this enthusiasm for Haiti, regularly publishing articles filled with praise—either news pieces about the climate, the political and economic organization of the island, and population, or actual letters testifying to the warm welcome extended to Black Americans.

The *Niles Weekly Register* was one of the many periodicals backing the Haitian project.[56] Another was the *Genius of Universal Emancipation* run by the Quaker abolitionist Benjamin Lundy, who started gushing about Haiti in 1824. Using apostrophe to directly address the American government and abolitionist societies, Lundy's infomercials reported on the abundance of food on the island, the supposedly reasonable moving costs, the warm welcome that Black Americans enjoyed, and the possibility for them to successfully flourish and progress.[57] Lundy also published an article about the Haytian Emigration Society that mentions the opening of a new chapter of this organization and insists further on the great opportunity to emigrate being generously offered to Blacks. The *Genius of Universal Emancipation* would also occasionally reprint advertisements used by ship captains attempting to recruit voluntary émigrés.[58]

Convinced that the resettlement of a large number of free people of color outside the United States would bring about the end of slavery throughout the country, Benjamin Lundy thought Haiti was a more suitable destination than Africa based on its proximity and its supposedly more agreeable climate.[59] Lundy made his case at the American Convention for Promoting the Abolition of Slavery and Improving the Condition of the African Race, which held its annual meeting in Philadelphia on October 7, 1823. He was invited by virtue of his standing as president of the Greeneville chapter of the Manumission Society of Tennessee, an association he had founded precisely so that he could join in the Philadelphia convention and deliver his recommendation that the organization send its vice president to Haiti in order to investigate all possibilities for free people of color who wished to move there.[60] In 1824 Lundy let it be known that he would use all his editorial powers to promote Haitian emigration plans and thus positioned himself as a fervent partisan of the project initiated by Boyer and Dewey. Lundy insisted that his support for this project was motivated by a desire to liberate slaves and not a desire to free the (white) country of its Black population. He continued to share his conviction that Black people, once free, had the right to remain on American soil and to become full citizens, but he also acknowledged that the racism they could face would hinder their personal fulfillment.[61] Lundy himself made two voyages to Haiti and continued to praise this destination for free and emancipated Blacks in *A Plan for the Gradual Abolition of Slavery in the United States, without Danger or Loss to the Citizens of the South*, which he published in 1825.[62]

Lundy was not the only white person getting personally involved in the project of resettlement of Black Americans in Haiti during the 1820s. There were many other individual initiatives on the part of planters and antislavery American citizens or residents in the United States. Among them was the plan of a certain Joseph Leonard Smith, Esq., a gentleman of Frederick County, Maryland, whose story is briefly told in the April 1829 issue of the publication of the American Colonization Society, the *African Repository and Colonial Journal*. One learns that Smith "generously" liberated twelve slaves with the aim of resettling them in Haiti—thus giving them not only their freedom but also supplies, including clothing and farm tools, and paying their passage to the island. The article also mentions an unnamed "gentleman" hired by Smith for his local knowledge to assist the newly liberated slaves.[63]

Among the other individual efforts of white people who took up the cause of resettling Blacks in Haiti, there is the example of Frances Wright, a militant Scottish feminist and social reformer and friend of Gilbert du Motier, the Marquis de La Fayette, Thomas Jefferson, and James Madison. Wright threw all her energy into, first, creating a colony of former self-emancipated slaves on American territory, and later worked on a project of emigration to Haiti.[64] Wright first imagined a system that would permit slaves to buy their freedom through labor, and thereby be the agents of their emancipation. She wanted to experiment with a project of gradual emancipation that would involve no financial loss to the planter, an idea she borrowed from the experiment carried out by her friend Lafayette on his property, La Belle Gabrielle, near Cayenne in French Guiana.[65] She was also inspired by the idea of "cooperative community" elaborated in the writings of the Welsh philanthropist and utopian socialist Robert Owen.[66] Frances Wright wrote up her proposal in a publication with the explicit title, *A Plan for the Gradual Abolition of Slavery in the United States without Danger of Loss to Citizens of the South* (1825).[67] She solicited the opinions of Lafayette and Jefferson regarding her colonization project and went so far as to ask Jefferson to actually help make her dream come true. While apparently sympathetic to the idea, Jefferson claimed his age forced him to decline the invitation. It was not exactly clear where she wanted the experiment to take place, although Wright did eventually buy eight slaves and two thousand acres of land north of Memphis, Tennessee. She named her experimental community Nashoba after the Indian name of the river that flowed near the property. She entered into a partnership with George Flower, one of the founders of the English colony Albion situated in Edwards County, Illinois.[68] It is worth noting that at the time Flower had already financed the migration of a certain number of Black people to Haiti.[69]

Wright's project got off to a bad start. The climate was unfavorable and had made her personally ill such that she had to leave her property in the spring of 1827 and take refuge in Europe to convalesce. Also, the wooded landscape had to be entirely clear-cut to allow for planting, an arduous task made worse by swarms of mosquitos. Very soon, public opinion turned sharply against her project. The first to express reservations about the colony was President Madison himself in a letter to Lafayette from November 1826.[70] In Wright's absence, the property manager, James Richardson, took it on himself to publish a description of the community in *The Genius of Universal Emancipation* in which he mentioned his affair with a Black slave. Nothing more was needed for the public to accuse Wright of promoting extramarital interracial sexual relations, and the colony was no sooner nicknamed "Fanny Wright's Free Love Colony." Upon her return in 1828, Wright realized that her colony was a failure and financially ruinous since the slaves, unable to see how eight years of forced labor was going to result in their freedom, would only work under duress.[71] She then decided to accompany her slaves to Haiti herself, and it was there that Frances Wright's experiment in self-emancipation was finally accomplished.[72]

Around the same time, certain Black Americans also sang the praises of the emigration movement to Haiti. Among the most famous, and operating parallel to the actions led by the abolitionists discussed already, there is the commitment of such men as George Boyer Vashon (the first African American graduate of Oberlin College), who spent just under two years in Haiti. Other distinguished members of the Black community had the ambition of moving to Haiti but were forced to change their plans at the last minute. Edward J. Royce was one such case; he would later become the fifth president of Liberia. John B. Russwurm, a Black activist and journalist, chose Haiti as the subject of the speech he gave at the graduation ceremony at Bowdoin College in 1826 ("The Conditions and Prospects of Haiti"),[73] but he never ended up going there. Should one see in these lapses a tacit foreshadowing of the imminent debacle that the emigration to Haiti would become?

The Mixed Results of the First Attempts at Black American Emigration to Haiti

Thanks to these organizational initiatives, of which we have given only a representative inventory, many free and emancipated Black Americans made the voyage to Haiti, although the exact number is unknown. Antislavery leaders of the time estimated that between 1820 and 1840, approximately 7,000 to 10,000 Black Americans had emigrated to Haiti. Of those, it is impossible to say how many survived and permanently settled there, and how many returned to the United States after their stay on the Black Pearl of the Antilles. It appears that after a period of high enthusiasm, many émigrés complained of their situation.[74]

For example, alongside the increasingly positive accounts of Haiti in the *Genius of Universal Emancipation,* letters written by émigrés who were less than enthusiastic would also sometimes get published starting around 1825. These letters spoke often of unkept promises on the part of the Haitian government. In fact, after having subsidized the arrival of 6,000 Black Americans, President Boyer decided in April 1825 to terminate all further financial support. Boyer justified his decision by claiming an American agent had absconded with a portion of the funds allocated for émigré travel subsidies.[75] In fact, the main reason why Boyer lost interest in the fate of Black Americans at that time was more likely the refusal of the United States to recognize Haiti whereas France had recently gone forward with a formal diplomatic acknowledgment of the Black republic. This acknowledgment took place on July 11, 1825, the result of long negotiations that had started as soon as Boyer had taken office.[76] In contrast, American president James Monroe had made no mention of Haiti in his December 2, 1823, Monroe Doctrine speech, thus refusing the coveted recognition that the island had officially requested.[77] Not only was Haiti completely absent from the Monroe Doctrine, but in reply to a formal request for recognition formulated by the Haitian government earlier the same year sent to President Monroe, the American president made the position of the United States regarding Haiti explicit in a special message to Congress dated February 25, 1823. In that message, he expressed the desire to maintain exclusively commercial relations between the two countries. Given that up until that time Haiti had shown no need of the United States to remain independent, there was no consideration given to the recognition of the island nation by the United States.[78] It is probable that this severe rebuke was the true cause for suspending aid to the aspiring Black American émigrés. Another factor was that the official recognition from France was not freely given but, on the contrary, worsened the Black republic's finances since it was accompanied by a royal decree of the French king, Charles X, stating that recognition of the island nation's independence required Haiti to pay an indemnity to French planters corresponding to the losses they suffered during the Haitian Revolution. This indemnity amounted to 150 million gold francs payable over the following five years. This substantial debt would on its own explain Boyer's decision to suspend payments to Black Americans wishing to emigrate to Haiti. And as if that were not enough, in April 1825 the new American president, John Quincy Adams, followed Monroe's example and explicitly objected once again—with his new secretary of state, Henry Clay, as intermediary—to the most recent request for recognition formulated by Haiti on April 18, 1825.[79]

What is clear, in any case, is that after 1825 things only got worse for these voluntary émigrés. It is worth noting that in addition to these financial burdens, other equally troubling obstacles presented themselves. Black Americans had great difficulty overcoming the foreign-language barrier as well as other social and religious differences. Also, they had finally acquired somewhat better living conditions in the United States and were therefore relatively disappointed by what they encountered in Haiti. This disappointment pushed many to return to the American mainland, which, while not exactly favorable to them, was at least familiar territory.

Ultimately, it is difficult to quantify with precision the size of the voluntary wave of emigration to Haiti that occurred in the 1820s. When he traveled to Haiti in 1825, Benjamin Lundy estimated that roughly 8,000 Black Americans were living on the island. James Theodore Holly,[80] a Black bishop and energetic promoter of emigration to Haiti in the 1850s, stated without specifying his source that President Boyer's plan had resulted in the emigration of 6,000 Black Americans.[81] On the other hand, the Haitian historian Leslie Manigat believes the number was as high as 13,000.[82] Without giving a precise figure, another Haitian historian, Georges Corvington, characterizes the emigration as "massive" while adding that some Black Americans "hastily returned to the United States":

> The recruitment campaign that Granville was appointed to lead in 1824 brought hundreds of Blacks to Port-au-Prince, but from the moment of their arrival they encountered severe problems. They had made no plans for adapting to the climate, the language, or the religion of the country. Moreover, the teasing provoked by their bizarre clothing and other accoutrements was very upsetting to them. They refused to settle in the countryside and many hastily returned to the United States.[83]

At the time, Lundy, who was still convinced that Haiti was the ideal solution for free and emancipated Blacks, freely engaged in derisive teasing of his own, calling those who became discouraged and returned to America "effeminate" and lazy.[84] Thus, whatever the true numbers may have been, it is clear that these first emigration attempts were relatively unsuccessful.

The white press was quick to emphasize this failure and occasionally published "reports" or other "correspondence" testifying to the catastrophic living conditions of the Black Americans in Haiti. Most of the time, these newspapers were criticizing resettlement efforts directed at Haiti in order to defend colonization toward Africa instead. For example, the *African Repository and Colonial Journal*, the organ of the American Colonization Society that from the start in 1816 had always come out in favor of colonization to Liberia, published a document in 1829 that consisted of a commentary on a report said to be written by a certain Thomas Kennedy, "a citizen of Wayne County, N.C." (one does not know if he was Black or white, but the use of the term "citizen" suggests that he may have been white), which states that the émigrés were generally "unpleasantly situated, and very much dissatisfied." And regarding their wages, "for two years and a half . . . they had received but from six to ten dollars each, as a compensation for their labor during the above time." Furthermore, says Kennedy,

> They complained to me that the proprietors of the lands for whom they had labored, for two years and a half, had entirely disappointed them . . . and

> said that they had rather be slaves in North Carolina, than to remain there under the treatment they had received since their arrival.

In contrast to the tenor of most articles published up until then in the Black American press and by abolitionists, Thomas Kennedy claimed that the Haitian government was a type of military dictatorship, that Haitians had barbaric manners and were uneducated, and concluded his observations about Haiti by pivoting toward a recommendation that free people of color wishing to leave the United States ought to emigrate to Liberia where they would find a government of laws that would be favorable to them, and enjoy true equal rights, while also—an important bonus—bringing civilization and Christianity to the land of their ancestors.[85]

Shortly afterward, the Black American press also slanted their coverage. Despite the testimonies of failure, abandonment, and returns, numerous articles published in Black American newspapers, journals, and magazines, until late in the 1830s, underscored the freedom and safety guaranteed in Haiti. The *Colored American*, for example, continued to encourage free and emancipated Blacks to emigrate there. Even though the *Colored American* had clearly stated its opposition to the American Colonization Society, voluntary emigration, notably toward Haiti, was not vilified. Many *Colored American* articles were highly critical of the American Colonization Society and of the very notion of "colonization," which the paper labeled a "wicked scheme."[86] Those in favor of colonization were seen as the worst sinners imaginable. They were accused of oppressing, starving, and even assassinating those whom the paper considered to be their victims, namely Africa and African Americans.[87] Along the same lines, one finds in 1838 numerous editorials in the *Colored American* accusing the American Colonization Society and its colonization plans of propagating every evil:

> The colonization scheme is only worthy of designing demagogues who are seeking southern influence and southern votes. Its advocacy is suitable business only for a corrupt clergy, seeking place and money, or for a lazy aristocracy who prefer presidencies, treasuries and agencies to principle. We hope the day is not distant, when every man of piety and principle, will shun that society as he would a bloody banditti or an association of open slave-traders—for it is, morally, no better.[88]

Black American periodicals always clearly distinguished between harmful colonization and voluntary emigration, which was often judged to be a good thing. The editor of the *Colored American* even claimed on occasion that the success of Black Americans outside the United States could only be a positive influence and would, by extension, benefit Black people inside the country. He firmly believed that once it was shown that Black Americans could succeed abroad, the white American population would come around to accepting that Blacks were as intelligent as anyone else, and thereby be forced to grant them more respect.[89]

Between 1837 and 1841, a series of articles appeared on the subject of voluntary emigration to Haiti. They described the political situation, the education system, the culture, and life in general on the island in idyllic terms. These articles, which sometimes resembled travel brochures, praised the island as a place where Black Americans could make progress of every kind since they would be far from the slavery system that still raged through the southern United States. For example, a text from the March 15, 1838, issue of the *Colored American*, while not being overly pushy about Black Americans moving to Haiti, nevertheless does offer an enthusiastic description of the island and its inhabitants:

> The Haytians are a noble, honest, and happy people. . . . Upon the whole, all things considered, Hayti suffers not in the comparison with any other country, neither in her physical, moral nor mental resources.[90]

In these articles from the 1830s, one sees the beginning of a collective consciousness of racial solidarity on the part of Black Americans with their Haitian counterparts. At the time, Haiti was admired because it had managed to free itself from the yoke of slavery, and because its Black population and political class had managed to remain independent. This was taken as proof that Black people were capable of self-government and progress on their own, without the presence of whites. This last point in the argument is essential for a proper understanding of the particular relationship between Black Americans and Haiti.

In sum, the free Black American community may not have completely or massively subscribed to the idea of geographical separation of human beings based on skin color because they did not see spatial segregation as a sustainable solution leading to equality between the "races"; however, at the time they clearly saw the proposals for settling in Haiti as a tempting idea. Alongside their wish to be anchored in North America, which expressed itself over these same first decades of the nineteenth century—since free people of color were perfectly conscious of the role their people had played in the development of the American nation and felt themselves to be American, and not African, as most had been born on American soil—this community increasingly recognized its identity as part of a Black diaspora resulting from slavery. Those in favor of emigrating to Haiti and settling permanently there were affirming their humanity as linked to a diasporic identity and claiming race as a factor of cohesion for an oppressed human group within a context of white racism. Consequently, as will become clear in the following chapters, the relatively unsuccessful emigration projects of the 1820s did not permanently discourage the leaders of the free Black community. Despite the prior setbacks of many of their compatriots, roughly thirty years later other Black Americans would try their hand at settling in Haiti, with varying amounts of success.

CHAPTER 2

Haiti and the "Black Nationality" Project

Go to our brethren, the Haytians, who, according to their word, are bound to protect and comfort us.[1]

—DAVID WALKER

A more radical abolitionist movement took shape over the three decades that preceded the Civil War. It became stridently in favor of immediatism and the doctrine of "stay and fight." Consequently, most Black American abolitionists at the time rejected the project of colonization by free and emancipated Blacks to Africa, which was the defining goal of the American Colonization Society. Yet at the same time some Black American activists openly declared their support for selected projects for emigration by free people of color out of the United States. These "emigrationists," though firmly opposed to the projects of the American Colonization Society, argued in favor of a freely chosen emigration but struggled to agree on a destination. While cities, states, and the federal government were constantly passing restrictive laws against slaves and free Blacks, thus making living conditions for Black Americans ever poorer, some militants, such as William Wells Brown and James Theodore Holly, united at "colored conventions" to discuss emigration, and specifically the idea of emigration to Haiti. From the moment it gained its independence in 1804, the island enjoyed a very favorable reputation among Black Americans, in part because the notion of "race" was prominent and even inscribed in the country's constitution. The revival of interest in Haiti among Black American activists was clearly energized by its legendary reputation.

In point of fact, few Black Americans had ever traveled to Haiti, much less settled there. Given the lack of tangible experience, the choice of Haiti was based on fantasy, a mythic representation of an idealized Haiti that fulfilled the more or less conscious desires of those relaying it who wanted equality and full citizenship. This fantasy circulated among Black elites thanks to the few existing Black American newspapers or those of white abolitionists, which regularly published travel reports, the correspondence of Black activists, or letters sent by an emigrant to their family back in the U.S. This renewed enthusiasm for Haiti was nourished by the collective Black American imagination such that the Black Pearl of the Caribbean was soon considered the "promised land" of a Black diaspora. These feelings were accompanied by the emergence of the notion of "Black nationality" within the Black community, its national conventions, and especially within the emigrationist movement.

The Revival of Abolitionism in the 1830s and the Role of Black American Activists in the Radicalization of the Movement and the Rejection of Colonization

While agreeing that the 1830s saw the emergence of a more radical abolitionist movement, most historians of this period also point out that Black and white abolitionists disagreed on the best means to reach their common goal—especially as the years passed and the philosophy of "moral suasion" preferred by the disciples of William Lloyd Garrison reached its limit.[2] Garrison had advocated a pacifist approach of direct negotiation with slaveowners and refused to involve the slaves directly in the process of their liberation. However some of his followers became impatient and proposed more radical methods of persuasion.[3]

The role of Black people themselves in the radicalization of the abolitionist movement has been little studied, and yet it was not small. The change of direction within the abolitionist movement that took place in the 1830s—shifting from the practice of "moral suasion" toward a radical grievance-based activism of "stay and fight"—occurred thanks to the active participation of Black people who joined the movement. It went from being a combat for gradual emancipation sometimes associated with colonization and compensation for slaveowners to a fight for total and immediate emancipation.[4] Unlike their white northern counterparts, Black people had literally nothing to lose. Most had no possessions, land, reputation, or status. It would be hard to fall any further down the social ladder.[5] They had suffered as slaves, suffered again as free people of color being denied citizenship, and did not fear suffering again in pursuit of freedom for their brethren and to obtain the civil rights that would make them free and equal in rights on American soil. While it is easy to explain the divergent opinions between Black and white activists concerning the best means and timing, it should be said that the whole abolitionist movement was rather fragmented, and the divisions were much more complex than a simple difference of approach based on race. Without claiming to give a definitive explanation for the reasons behind the radicalization, the adoption of immediatism, and the difference of opinion within the movement in the 1830s, it is possible to advance some hypotheses by considering certain contributing factors that would include regionalism, personality conflicts, the economic context, tensions between collective needs and an individualist spirit, and tactical differences.[6]

The national political climate was no doubt a major cause of the deep divisions within all abolition campaigns in every location and of every racial composition. It should be remembered that laws controlling the lives of Black people became tougher in those years, especially after Nat Turner's slave rebellion in 1831.[7] These repressive laws coincided with a doubling of the slave population in the thirty years between 1830 and the start of the Civil War, from 2,009,043 to 3,953,760.[8]

The numerous antislavery pamphlets published between 1830 and 1860 are clear evidence of the majority position among free people of color at the time. Their position, summarized by the words "stay and fight," likely resulted from the degraded living conditions that Black men and women—whether enslaved or free, in northern or southern states, in rural areas or large cities—all had to endure. The goal was to obtain freedom and rights on American soil: in the land where they were born and which they rightfully considered their land. As the years went by and their situation steadily worsened, Black people withdrew from the movement advocating "moral suasion" and gradual emancipation. They turned toward more radical solutions in specific local contexts and separated themselves from most white abolitionists. Some of them, such as Henry Highland Garnet decided to take matters into their own hands:[9] "Brethren, the time has come when you must act for yourselves. . . . Strike for your lives and liberties. Now is the day and the hour. . . . *Rather die freemen than live to be slaves.*"[10]

During these years, free people of color began founding their own associations or "colored conventions." The first national convention of free people of color gathered on September 20–24, 1830, at the Bethel African Methodist Church in Philadelphia. The meeting brought together about twenty delegates from six free states and three slave states. The goal was to study the problems, needs, and interests of free people of color in the United States and to find ways to improve their condition.[11] The moment chosen to unite at such a convention was not random. Gatherings of various societies focused on social ills, whether specific, such as alcoholism, or general, such as the direction of religion or politics, had become a new form of popular collective action. Also, as already noted, the 1830s saw a heightened desire for a more radical abolitionism, and if Black people were going to take a more active role in shaping their community, then the national convention was a logical step in that direction. These conventions were a reflection of their engagement and the forging of their political consciousness. In 1827 Samuel E. Cornish, the editor in chief of the first Black American periodical, *Freedom's Journal*, had already proposed organizing conventions whose goal would be to improve living conditions for free Blacks in the North.

Black Americans who gathered at these political conventions followed classical parliamentary procedures, in other words subdividing into committees to debate a particular aspect of the Black experience. For example, at every such convention there would be a committee on the press, on agriculture, education, commerce, and so on. When these smaller units regrouped in the general assembly, all would participate in an animated general debate on every topic.[12] As their approach suggests, the aim of these conventions was not simply to air complaints about their daily lives, but rather to permit members of the free Black community to define issues, set priorities within their struggle, and also coordinate their efforts nationally, beyond local politics, something that had rarely been done before 1830. The first national conventions were small affairs, but the number of delegates and participants grew each year. There were only fifteen delegates at the second convention in 1831 but nearly seventy in 1847. Moreover, the participants were not always the same from year to year; however, a core group of leaders emerged. The national conventions generally took place in New York and Pennsylvania, but also in Ohio, since many of the delegates and the most influential Black leaders lived in these states. For example. Henry Highland Garnet and Frederick Douglass lived in New York, and John Mercer Langston was from Ohio. These were also, at that time, the states with the highest number of free people of color in the United States.[13]

The minutes of these colored conventions confirm the radicalization of the abolitionist movement and the allegiance of many Black people to the principle of "stay and fight":

> *Resolved*, that, in the language of inspired wisdom, there shall be no peace to the wicked, and that this guilty nation shall have no peace, and that we will do all that we can to agitate! AGITATE!! AGITATE!! Till our rights are restored and our Brethren are redeemed from their cruel chains.[14]

The central idea within the Black abolitionist movement was always the same: stay and fight for rights right here. This is clearly expressed by Robert Purvis in his pamphlet *Appeal of Forty Thousand Citizens*: "We are not intruders here, nor were our ancestors."[15] Another example is the statement of Phillip

A. Bell and Samuel Ennals in their "Address to the Citizens of New York": "This is our home, and this is our country. . . . Here we were born, and here we will die."[16]

Stay and fight was a founding principle of both the first national colored conventions and the first Black American periodicals. It was a natural process when the debates initiated during the convention were extended in the columns of the young Black American press.[17] The first Black American weekly, *Freedom's Journal*, was published between 1827 and 1829 thanks to the efforts of Samuel Eli Cornish, a Black Presbyterian minister in New York, and John Brown Russwurm, a Black abolitionist born in Jamaica and a graduate of Bowdoin College who moved to New York in 1827.[18] The goal of these two men was unequivocal: give Black people a chance to be heard by publishing and circulating their opinions: "We wish to plead our own cause. Too long have others spoken for us."[19]

The central themes that dominated the small world of the early Black American press were fighting for the abolition of slavery, equality, and better living conditions for free people of color. These periodicals also treated other domestic or foreign issues of national or international importance and published opinion pieces by Black leaders and intellectuals on all these topics. Obviously, debates around colonization and emigration were among the most closely followed items in the Black American press between the 1830s and the 1860s.[20]

The Black press played a huge role in Black history at that time because it served to unite and help advance the influence and power of Black elites. Only the Black church and Black music can claim a comparable level of influence within the Black community of the nineteenth century.[21] Indeed, these periodicals were often published by church leaders such as Cornish. The press was a supplemental means to diffuse their ideas beyond the small circle of Blacks who attended their parishes. It was a way to forge a consensus and unite the community around certain key ideas.[22]

It remains difficult, however, to measure the true impact of these periodicals on the Black population. It is also difficult to gauge representativeness of this press; in other words, the extent to which it reflected the views of the Black population as a whole. Black literacy levels were very low in the antebellum era, and Black publications were often sponsored by white abolitionists. This raises the question of the editorial freedom and objectivity of Black editors and, by extension, that of their readers. Frederick Douglass himself, the editor of his own paper, the *North Star*, acknowledged that between 1847 and 1851 he had five times more white subscribers than Black subscribers. At the time, printed matter circulated among many hands; therefore, even if somewhere between 2,700 and 3,000 copies of the *North Star* were sold each week, its readership was far higher than 3,000 people. How much higher is difficult to say, and this is true for Black American readership in general throughout the first half of the nineteenth century.[23] We do know that the Black press often published extracts from the minutes of the colored conventions alongside heated exchanges between radical Black abolitionists and emigrationists. We will return to this active participation in the debates around colonization and emigration later in this chapter.

Their claim to belong to the American soil did not prevent Black abolitionists from seeking aid from outside the country. The decades from 1830 through 1860 were marked by these abolitionists' regular travels to Europe, and especially to Great Britain, to openly denounce slavery, collaborate with other abolitionist societies, raise money for Black churches, associations, and voluntary emigration projects, and to escape the clutches of slave kidnappers.[24] During those years, Black abolitionists went on tour, so to speak, giving talks, publishing slave narratives, and associating with the British with the aim of raising consciousness and the consciences of citizens so as to obtain their moral and financial support. The goal was also to isolate the United States, a rising power on the world's political chessboard, from the influential great powers of Europe by pointing a scolding finger at barbaric American practices and underscoring their incompatibility with the ideals of great civilized nations.[25] At the same time, this attempt to establish a "moral cordon" around the United States enabled Black Americans sojourning in Great Britain to experience for the first time living in an environment more open to allowing them to improve their condition because racial prejudice was not embedded in British society, or at least was not inscribed in law. For example, sending one's children to the best schools, seeking and obtaining important positions within abolitionist associations, and other ambitions not permitted in the United States were now possible. This transatlantic collaboration allowed Black Americans to experience relatively high levels of independence and agency.

However, with few exceptions, Black people crossing the ocean at this time to solicit Great Britain's moral and financial support had no intention of permanently leaving the United States; on the contrary, their goal was to remain in the United States, stay free, and acquire greater freedom and equal rights. Paradoxically, the heightened presence of Black Americans in Canada and Great Britain contributed in some degree to the revival of the emigrationist debate. Martin R. Delany and Alexander Crummell, the most celebrated Black proponents of emigration at the time, even imagined a sort of joint venture that would be mutually profitable: Black Americans would emigrate to Africa, educate and evangelize the Africans; British businessmen would capitalize on the labor of free Blacks who would have received the liberty, equality, and prosperity that was denied to them in the United States. This pro-emigration advocacy between 1830 and 1860 remains an understudied period in the history of Black activism.

The Beginnings of a "Chosen" Emigration Movement

The pro-emigration position was hardly the majority view among Black leaders at the time, but it did exist and had a certain success; all the more when it was linked to a favorably positioned "mythical" land such as Haiti. Emigrationism thus returns at the same time that the abolitionist movement becomes more radical. The emigrationist movement, whose reputation was badly stained by negative associations with the American Colonization Society since its founding in 1816, was nevertheless alive in the minds of some Black activists from the beginning of the nineteenth century. Paul Cuffe, for example, did not wait for the American Colonization Society to launch his own African venture.[26]

In the 1830s there was renewed opposition to the American Colonization Society and its Liberian colonization projects. One Black journalist wrote, "We consider the Colonization scheme the most wily and wicked scheme upon earth."[27] Many articles from that period evoked the existence of an actual government-led nationwide plot whose ultimate goal was the total expulsion of "colored Americans" to Liberia.

> The churches, the schools, the steamboats, the rail roads, the stage coaches, the public houses, and the highways—the priests and the people—all, all are apparatus of torture, *set in motion*, to drive colored Americans to Liberia.[28]

Since free people of color had to face a hardening of the laws that regulated their daily life, and saw the few civil rights they possessed all but taken away entirely, it was clear to them that decisions made in every domain—notably in education, transportation, and their religious life—by (white) church leaders, politicians, and ordinary white citizens across many states (such as in the New Jersey example cited above) as well as by the federal government all had one and the same goal: push Black people to leave the country.

However, this near-unanimous rejection of colonization and the American Colonization Society did not mean that the idea of emigration was thrown out completely. On the contrary, starting in the early 1830s, certain Black thinkers and activists were willing to say that some among them might legitimately wish to emigrate outside America's borders. One striking proof of this paradox is the case of David Walker. Even though the majority of Black activists called for emancipation and equality for all Black people in the United States, in Walker's famous, militant "Call" from 1830, he advised those of his fellows who were considering leaving the United States to go to Haiti. This encouragement to consider Haiti as a place of exile follows a virulent paragraph in which Walker criticizes Black people who have accepted to return to Africa, and affirms that the United States belongs as much to Black as to white people.

> What our brethren could have been thinking ubout [*sic*], who have left their native land and home and gone away to Africa, I am unable to say. This country is as much ours as it is the whites, whether they will admit it now or not, they will see and believe it by and by. . . . If any of us see fit to go away, go to those who have been for many years, and are now our greatest earthly friends and benefactors—the English. If not so, go to our brethren, the Haytians, who, according to their word, are bound to protect and comfort us.[29]

Walker does not specify in what circumstances Haitians supposedly gave their word to protect and comfort Black Americans. Was he alluding to Boyer's letters from the early 1820s? Or perhaps to some later message from the Black republic? It is more likely that this was an eloquent example of the legendary reputation of Haiti as savior, as if in the collective Black American imagination, because of its past, its history, and its military exploits, Haiti was in some way "bound" to welcome oppressed Black men and women from every country.

The ban on whites from owning Haitian land, an interdiction inscribed at the time in Haiti's constitution, may partly explain this reputation that comes through in Walker's statement. Over the nineteenth century, Haiti operated under thirteen different constitutions, not to mention the variations of each of these due to amendments. Starting with the Constitution of 1805, at the moment of Haiti's independence, the matter of race figured prominently:

> Article 12: No white, regardless of national origin, will set foot on this territory with the title of master or owner, nor can they in future acquire any property here.[30]

The Constitution of 1816, which was in force at the time of David Walker's famous speech, repeats this paragraph word for word in its article 38, and specifies further in article 44 the following:

> Article 44: Every African, Indian, and their blood descendants, whether born in colonies or foreign countries, who would come to reside in the Republic are recognized as Haitian, but will only have the rights of citizens after one year of residency.[31]

Given this clear and open path to citizenship, it's hardly surprising that Walker exhorted his fellow Black brethren to move to Haiti.

In the footsteps of David Walker and the national colored convention that took place in Philadelphia in 1830, other Black activists began to speak again about emigration starting in the 1830s but had difficulty deciding what place would be the ideal destination.[32] It is clear that as their enthusiasm for Africa declined due to its association with the negatively perceived American Colonization Society, other territories, especially those located on or near the North American continent, gained favor.[33]

The attraction of Canada, Mexico, and even Trinidad was not new. At the start of the American Revolution, in 1775, the loyalist governor of the British colony of Virginia, Lord Dunmore, offered freedom to the slaves of rebellious planters, if they agreed to fight alongside British troops and help the British crown extend control of its colonies throughout North America. The following year, the British general William Howe added that slaves who fought alongside British troops would receive after the war not only their freedom but also land and supplies in one of his majesty's colonies. Consequently, thousands of slaves fled their plantations to join the British army. At the end of the American Revolution, approximately 3,500 Black loyalists, and hundreds of slaves belonging to loyalist planters, were deported to Canada, specifically to Nova Scotia. After their arrival, these Black loyalists waited years before receiving the land that was promised to them, and when they did it turned out to be poor quality soil. The integration of Black people into Canadian society did not happen without friction. The economic difficulties and discrimination they experienced were enough to convince 1,200 of these Blacks to emigrate to Sierra Leone, another British colony, in the early 1790s. As for the white "Tories" who arrived with their Black slaves, they stayed along with their slaves.[34]

In the 1790s, the legislative assembly in the British colony of Upper Canada initiated a gradual abolition of slavery in that territory thanks to efforts of Lieutenant-Governor John Graves Simcoe and Chief Justice William Osgoode. Even if the first law passed in 1793 freed no actual slaves, it was the first step toward the abolition of slavery throughout Canada. In 1803 Osgoode declared slavery—an institution that had never been well established in Canadian society—to be incompatible with British law. One thousand slaves were freed immediately, and the Canadian abolitionist movement took off. It should be noted that slavery in Canada was of little economic advantage, and the Canadian antislavery reasoning was quite different from American thinking. By freeing slaves and allocating them land, the British were primarily interested in securing the development and safety of their Canadian colonies. The Black people who became free under these auspices were particularly zealous about defending their freedom and were fully willing to join British militias. Thus, the Canadian colonies with the most Black settlers were those that also had a military installation such as the fortified settlement of Amherstburg.[35] In addition, Canadian laws favorable to free Black arrivals and settlement led hundreds of Black Americans to cross the border into Canada in the early nineteenth century.

During the War of 1812 between the United States and Great Britain, the so-called second war of independence, the British vice-admiral Sir Alexander Cochrane offered to Black Americans a proposal similar to the one Lord Dunmore had made forty years earlier: freedom to slaves who left their masters to fight for the British. Same offer, same results. Many slaves rallied to the British side and were able to leave the United States for Novia Scotia or the neighboring province of New Brunswick.[36] But these Black Americans, roughly 1,600 in number, were soon expelled toward Trinidad by the governor of Nova Scotia, Lord Dalhousie, as were hundreds of others who in their case had *chosen* to emigrate to Trinidad rather than to Canada at the conclusion of the War of 1812.[37] These individuals each received sixteen acres of land after their arrival and generally assimilated easily into Trinidadian society. After this first convoy of Black Americans arrived in Trinidad, roughly 1,300 more Black Americans traveled there on their own initiative between 1839 and 1847.[38]

Canada and Trinidad attracted many Black Americans again starting in the 1830s—and even more after the passage of the Fugitive Slave Act in the United States in 1850—because slavery was abolished in those neighboring countries in 1837.[39] Canada, being easier to reach than Trinidad, was one of the logical destinations for fugitive slaves, especially those aided by the abolitionist network known as the Underground Railroad.[40] Moreover, on February 13, 1833, the Canadian government passed a law protecting fugitive slaves from extradition. This law also promulgated high fines and prison sentences for anyone found guilty of kidnapping free people of color.[41] In the 1850s approximately forty settlements with sizable Black populations sprung up across Canada, mostly in Nova Scotia and Upper Canada (renamed Canada West in 1841) in areas geographically close to the American border. It is estimated that roughly 50,000 free people of color and fugitive slaves had emigrated to Canada before the start of the Civil War.[42]

Others chose to flee toward Mexico starting in the 1820s. When Mexico gained its independence from Spain on August 24, 1821, it immediately abolished slavery and granted full citizenship to all inhabitants regardless of skin color. Hundreds of Black people from southern states crossed the border into Texas, which was then under Mexican control. However, after Texas became an independent slavery-permitting republic in 1836, and all the more after it was annexed by the United States in 1845, free people of color and fugitive slaves who had taken refuge in Texas were again threatened with being turned back into slaves. Consequently, those who could do so fled to Mexico, which remained one of the final destinations of fugitive slaves also aided by the Underground Railroad.

At the same time, certain Black Americans, even though favorably disposed toward Canada, also spoke of Haiti as a last resort: "It is true that . . . Hayti, and perhaps some other countries, will still afford us a place of refuge."[43] Among the periodicals singing the praises of Haiti was the *Colored American* (mentioned in chapter 1). It regularly published flattering descriptions of life on the island—always the ideal weather but also its democratic institutions, including the protection of religious freedom so cherished by Americans.

Sometimes it was a short piece simply describing the prosperity of the little republic, sometimes a travel narrative, or a letter of a Black American settled in Haiti sent to their family back in America. In certain cases, the goal of these authors was clearly to encourage others to emigrate by underscoring the opportunities they would have for decent work and attractive salaries.[44] Laws favorable to Black people and the absence of racial prejudice in Caribbean societies was particularly emphasized:

> Colonization to Africa holds out to view no prospect for benefitting Americans. Voluntary emigration to other countries presents to individuals a better field for improving their condition; but it is only certain classes who can accept the advantages. . . . The islands of Hayti, and Trinidad are open to us; there no distinctive persecuting laws present insurmountable barriers to our advancement; nor does the monster prejudice arise like our evil genius to thwart us in our career of usefulness and virtue.[45]

Obviously, the fact that slavery had already been abolished in the Caribbean islands was seen as a distinct advantage. Even if there was no recommendation for massive emigration, it was clear that people were not being discouraged from trying to improve their life security by emigrating to politically more acceptable and accepting countries such as the British West Indies or Haiti, the Black republic:

> The subject of West India emancipation is exerting considerable interest in this part of the country. Port au Plot [*sic*] in the island of Hayti, and the island of Trinidad are the places to which several of our friends look as their future homes. We would not recommend general emigration, as our opinions have always been quite clear on that point, but we would not discourage individuals from trying to improve their condition anywhere.[46]

The goal of these articles was probably to allow readers to form their own opinion about the island by furnishing trustworthy information passed on by travelers—Black or white men mostly—who had concrete experience of life in Haiti.[47]

It should also be noted that at the time Haiti enjoyed a rather special status among Black Americans. It was and would always be the first Black nation-state, and it was the only place in the Americas where black skin guaranteed citizenship instead of the reverse. The influence of the Haitian Revolution on Black Americans has been amply discussed and is undeniable. All Black American activists, and certainly all the most influential ones (David Walker, Frederick Douglass, William Watkins, Alexander Crummell, Henry Highland Garnet, Martin Robison Delany . . .) took the Haitian Revolution as proof that Blacks were not inferior. And while many did not approve of the violence that occurred, they applauded the revolutionary spirit and made Toussaint Louverture into a hero of the Black race.[48] The speech by David Walker discussed earlier, in which he allows himself a brief digression to evoke Haiti, was preceded by many others delivered by influential activists, among them Prince Saunders and John Brown Russwurm.

While these two men were each interested in the prospect of emigrating to Haiti, praising such an undertaking was not their only objective. One of the striking characteristics of their evocations of Haiti is their idealist and idealized description of the island and its inhabitants. Haiti was described as wonderfully beautiful, blessed with an ideal climate, and extraordinarily abundant in natural resources. For Saunders, Haiti was indeed "naturally beautiful and (as to soil and yields) [an] astonishingly luxuriant island."[49] Haitians were generally described as courageous people who had chosen for themselves a form of republican government. This was considered the ultimate proof of Black, not just Haitian, noninferiority.

> The Haytiens have adopted the republican form of government: and so firmly is it established, that in no country are the rights and privileges of citizens and foreigners more respected, and crimes less frequent. They are a brave and generous people.[50]

This praise of Haiti was followed by much more; for example, the speech of James McCune Smith at New York's Stuyvesant Institute in 1841 and William Wells Brown's encomium, *St. Domingo: Its Revolutions and Its Patriots*, published in 1855.[51] The common thread in all these documents and others from the same period is that they used the Haitian Revolution and Haiti's republican institutions as proof of the noninferiority of Black people while enshrining Toussaint Louverture in the pantheon of heroes of the Black race.[52]

In the 1830s and '40s, the question of formal recognition of Haiti was often raised by Black activists seeking legitimacy. The refusal of the United States to recognize Haiti was incomprehensible to Black Americans, who took it as a sign of contempt on the part of a powerful white nation toward its Black neighbor. Many articles were published on this topic, notably in the late 1830s when the question of the annexation of Texas was a pressing concern. These often emotionally charged pieces openly reproached the American government for its "*exceedingly little and unwise*" conduct toward a republic that, as they saw it, had proved it deserved as much respect as any other people that had embraced democracy.[53]

Never lacking arguments, these partisans for the recognition of Haiti also underlined American economic interests in Haiti, insisting on the commercial ties that already existed between the two nations and how they would only strengthen. They even elevated Haiti above Texas, which was then at the center of American political discussions: "As a matter of dollars and cents, . . . we have stronger reason for acknowledging Haytian than Texan independence." In addition, for Black Americans, recognizing Haiti was fundamentally a moral obligation. The editor of the *Colored American* reminded readers that a seventh of the troops (two hundred men) who fought alongside General Andrew Jackson on December 23, 1814, in the Battle of New Orleans, which ended with Britain's defeat on January 8, 1815, were Haitian volunteers. "Is not gratitude due to the people of Hayti, for the timely and indispensable succour rendered by them in 1814?"[54] James McCune Smith also deplored America's lack of gratitude toward a nation that had undeniably played an important role in the preservation of American liberty:

> The independence of this Republic [Haiti] has been acknowledged by France and Great Britain. Our Great Republic, which was signally aided by

Haytien soldiers at the Battle of New Orleans, pitifully withholds a like acknowledgement of the independence of Hayti.[55]

It is clear that the idea of emigration and the idea of Haiti never disappeared from the debates within the Black American community between 1830 and 1850. The nearly diasporic thinking about a "promised land" that would welcome Black Americans was gaining acceptance. And very naturally this idea of distancing or separation—temporarily or permanently—from the white population, and why not by means of emigration to Haiti, was very soon linked to the idea of uniting the Black community around the concept of Black nationality.

The Apogee of the Emigrationist Movement and the Emergence of the Idea of "Black Nationality"

Most historians are in agreement that Black nationalism was born out of a visceral reaction to the Compromise of 1850, in particular the provision in it called the Fugitive Slave Act. They agree that it is difficult to speak of Black nationalism before the 1850s, and all evoke the same turning point, the Compromise of 1850, as being the catalyst of this movement.[56] However, not all make the connection between Black nationalism and the emigrationist movement. It should be noted that few historians have studied the question of the emigrationist movement to Haiti. An analysis of the first wave of emigration to Haiti in the 1820s has led to the claim made here that it was closely linked to the emergence of the idea of Black nationalism—even if the term "nationalism" was not then explicitly used—or at least to the idea of a Black nationality. To sum up what has been said above, the emigration movement's goal was to permit free Black Americans to pursue their lives on an island where, one must not forget, skin color was inscribed in the Constitution, and where, consequently, citizenship and all the rights that follow from it (notably the right to own property) were accorded exclusively to Black people.

We will show for the remainder of this chapter that the new projects of emigration to Haiti that multiplied from the 1830s through the 1850s were inseparable from the development of the concept of Black nationality in a way not dissimilar from their parallel development in the 1820s. Furthermore, we will insist on the involvement of Black people in this emigration project—an involvement that can also be explained by the correlation between emigration and Black nationality.

Black nationalism is traditionally defined as a development of race consciousness associated with positive pride, the consciousness of belonging to a community founded on ideas of race and color, and experienced through the search for common experiences and the Black community's economic self-reliance, with as an ultimate goal the creation of a "black nation-state."[57] This definition logically implies a certain form of economic separatism, but also physical distance.

We prefer to use instead the term "Black nationality" to designate the new diasporic consciousness of the Black American community in the decades leading up to the Civil War. Starting in the 1830s, Black Americans spoke up and wrote about their feeling of belonging to a unitary racial community. They themselves used the expression "Black nationality" and sometimes "Negro nationality." This concept was especially used by Black emigrationists, and often with Haiti as the emigration destination. The principal difference between it and the Black *nationalism* that would emerge later was that within the expression "Black nationality" was a positive connotation of the experience of Haitian citizenship. In other words, Blacks who argued in favor of establishing Black nationality did so with the example of Haiti in mind. They considered that the diasporic Black nationality which they wished to see come about could be "created" in Haiti, where Black people already enjoyed all the rights associated with citizenship. Thus, Black nationality was that which would unite all Black people around the world—the Black diaspora—preferably in Haiti, the country that promised to offer both refuge and a nationality.

> Mr. W[atkins] then alluded to the inducements offered by the Government of Hayti to the colored people of the United States and the Canadas, to emigrate to that island. *A home and a nationality are offered*, where they can demonstrate their capacity for self-government.[58]

Establishing this nationality, in particular in Haiti, would allow Blacks to then be heard throughout the world, to have standing on the geopolitical chessboard, and thereby leverage to fight effectively for the abolition of slavery and the slave trade, and improved conditions for the Black diaspora.

> [T]here is no powerful and enlightened negro nationality anywhere existing to espouse the cause and avenge the wrongs of their race. Let such a nationality be at once developed and brought upon the stage of action, equal in every respect to the demands of the nineteenth century, and the African slave-trade must not only instantaneously cease, but negro slavery itself must also be speedily abolished throughout the world. Such a nation would have the power and prestige of making itself heard, felt and respected on this question in the councils of the world.[59]

This idea of "Black nationality" developed and quickly spread, notably thanks to Black periodicals and the colored conventions discussed above. It is clear that the wish to create Black nationality advanced in tandem with a growing consciousness of belonging to a diaspora and the desire to work collectively toward the progress of the Black race around the world.

> The nineteenth century . . . desires to establish a Nationality for the purpose of lifting the [Black] race to the level of civilization, and enabling it to contribute its share to the progress of the age. *The nineteenth century wants a Black Nationality, because it is an instrumentality that cannot be dispensed with in the rehabilitation of the black race*, and it looks to us to furnish the energy, the enterprise, the men to aid in its development.[60]

The first shared experience within the Black American community was slavery, but free Black people would soon have other forms of community experience, notably gathering in large cities after the War of Independence and assembling at the colored conventions and within other organizations fighting against slavery and for civil rights. Chosen, voluntary emigration was another of these forms of Black community experience.

It is impossible to neatly distinguish two groups among Black activists—those in favor of emigration versus those firmly opposed—not least because many changed their minds on the matter. Since on one hand they may have been vociferously opposed to the very idea of leaving the United States, while on the other hand more moderate and even attracted by the possibility of emigrating under certain conditions, many Black activists were frankly torn by this question and spoke and wrote about it in ways that many today would find contradictory. Likewise, among those whom one might identify as emigrationist at a certain point in time, there is little consensus about where to actually go: Africa, Canada, the West Indies. All these destinations were evoked, debated, and tested.

A key moment in the resurgence of emigrationist ideas within the discourse of Black activists was the 1847 National Convention of Colored People and Their Friends held in Troy, New York. As the minutes of the convention prove, delegates were clearly aware that the Black struggle transcended borders. They took interest in what was happening in Trinidad and Jamaica, for example. This renewed interest appears as another step toward separatism and the idea of Black nationality. The idea that all Black people, both inside and outside the United States, had a "common cause" was taking shape.[61] Even Henry Highland Garnet, who up until then had mostly defended the idea that Blacks ought to be free and equal on American soil, came around to stating that emigration might be a feasible alternative for those who considered improving their situation within the United States to be impossible. In a letter to Frederick Douglass published in the *North Star* in January 1849, he confessed that his feelings about colonization had changed: "I would rather see a man free in Liberia, than a slave in the United States."[62] This altered position caused a rift between Garnet and Douglass, but some months later the adoption of the Compromise of 1850 and the loathsome Fugitive Slave Act sent shockwaves through the Black community, forced now to think more concretely about fleeing, notably to Canada.

The most well-known partisans in favor of Canada in the 1850s were Henry Bibb, Mary Ann Shadd, and James Theodore Holly.[63] Like many Black Americans, they were particularly discouraged by the adoption of the Fugitive Slave Act, which wiped out all hope for improving their life security in the United States. Therefore in 1851 they emigrated to Upper Canada. It can be noted that before his tilt toward defending emigration to Canada, Holly had been attracted by the idea of emigration to Africa. For a time, Holly was even in correspondence with the American Colonization Society and expressed a wish to emigrate to Liberia, but only if he could teach and practice medicine there. He had asked the American Colonization Society to fund his medical studies, but this request was denied in 1850. He then turned to supporting emigration to Canada starting in 1851 with a series of articles published in the Black periodical *Voice of the Fugitive.* He was careful to clearly distinguish between the emigration he favored and the colonization he rejected. Holly also thought it would be possible to establish a Black association in Canada whose goal would be to aid all Black people throughout North America. A North American Convention of colored people was organized in Toronto in September 1851 that Bibb, Shadd, and Holly all attended. Understandably, the delegates present at the convention exhorted all Black Americans to emigrate to Canada. They advanced the idea of creating a North American "agricultural league," an organization whose mission would be to purchase Canadian land for resale to emigrants.[64]

The emigrationist debates between 1850 and 1852 are mostly centered on Canada. But in June 1853, during the General Convention for the Improvement of the Colored Inhabitants of Canada that took place in Amherstburg in Upper Canada, other destinations were discussed, notably Haiti. It would seem that Bibb and Holly, who had undergone in Canada the same racial prejudice and discrimination as in the United States, were seeking other more favorable conditions for their emigrationist projects. Bibb and Holly turned this convention into a critical moment for the emigrationist movement in the United States. Believing now that the revolution imagined by some was in fact unattainable, members of the convention proposed that Black Americans turn toward emigration. The authors of the report published in the wake of the convention wrote favorably about the possibility of emigrating to Haiti. In a paragraph from the minutes of the convention entitled "Hayti," the members praised the Black republic and the benefits for Black Americans of emigrating to Haiti and making a fresh start on this sheltering island. Beyond simply mentioning Haiti as a possibility, the convention members expressed a striking sentiment of fraternity toward Haitians. They considered that Black Americans had the "duty" to celebrate and contribute to the prosperity of the Black Republic. It was said that emigration to Haiti would help reinforce the power of the Haitian government to counter external threats—meaning possible attacks from white republics such as France or Spain. Thus, emigration was considered both possible and highly beneficial to the entire Black community, and more generally for a Black diaspora without borders, because the focus was not only on Haitians and Black Americans. The Blacks in Cuba were evoked, and indeed all Blacks throughout the Americas were encouraged to unite to form "a Continental League of the Africo-American race."[65]

But it was the following month, in July 1853, at the Colored National Convention held in Rochester, New York, that the notion of Black nationality truly emerged out of the ideas under discussion. The advocates of stay and fight on one side and the emigrationists on the other agreed on one point: a belief that the destiny of all Blacks was conjoined, and that therefore united collaboration was necessary for the progress of the community.

In 1853 the most energetic advocate for emigration was without question Martin Robison Delany. After 1851 Delany emerged as the leader of the nationalist-emigrationist philosophy. He had inherited this line of thinking from his mentor, Reverend Lewis Woodson, a free Black from Pittsburgh. Woodson did not have the temperament to become a great national leader, but between 1837 and 1841 he laid the groundwork for the nationalist-emigrationist doctrine later disseminated by Delany. For Reverend Woodson, the author of many articles published under the pseudonym Augustine in the *Colored American*, Black Americans were a distinct caste within the American republic. He claimed that for there to be "uplift," Black people needed to have a specific feeling emerge within their community that he named "national feeling."[66] Delany expressed sympathy for this nationalist-emigrationist philosophy in his book entitled *The Condition, Elevation, Emigration, and Destiny of the Colored People of the United States, Politically Considered* (1852). While he refused the idea of leaving the American continent entirely (i.e., the "New World"), he did not think emigrating to Canada was a good idea since Canada might easily be annexed by the United States one day. He spoke more favorably of Central America and the British West Indies as possible emigration destinations, suggesting that Black Americans might create their own nation in those places. In addition, he insisted that Black people ought not count on the help of whites, even white abolitionists, whom he considered hypocrites. In other words, he recommended separatism and the establishment of Black nationality outside the sphere of influence of the United States.[67]

Coincidentally, Delany's book was published the same year as Harriet Beecher Stowe's bestseller *Uncle Tom's Cabin*.[68] The rapid and wide dissemination of Stowe's best-selling novel certainly contributed to the renewal of debates on colonization on the edges of the conventions of colored people, and it gave new energy to the emigrationist movement in the early 1850s.[69]

Uncle Tom's Cabin succinctly evokes colonization through the voice of the character George Harris, a fugitive slave who, after spending nine years outside the United States (in Canada, then France), makes the decision to commit to the idea of "African nationality" and emigrate to Liberia. He explains his choice to one of his friends in a letter:

> The desire and yearning of my soul is for an African nationality. I want a people that shall have a tangible, separate existence of its own; and where am I to look for it? Not in Hayti; for in Hayti they had nothing to start with. A stream cannot rise above its fountain. The race that formed the character of the Haytiens was a worn-out, effeminate one; and, of course, the subject race will be centuries in rising to anything.
>
> Where, then, shall I look? On the shores of Africa I see a republic,—a republic formed of picked men, who, by energy and self-educating force, have, in many cases, individually, raised themselves above a condition of slavery. Having gone through a preparatory stage of feebleness, this republic has, at last, become an acknowledged nation on the face of the earth,—acknowledged by both France and England. There it is my wish to go, and find myself a people.[70]

In this passage, George Harris clearly states his contempt for Haiti and Haitians. This is not surprising since, as noted above, those favoring colonization, and the American Colonization Society in particular, had no fondness for Haiti. Later in the same letter, Harris affirms that "Africans" have different physical and mental characteristics than whites; but in the service of Liberia, their characteristics would permit it to join the ranks of civilized nations. Stowe's critics understandably reproached her for making her character be a spokesperson for the pro-African colonization position.

In truth, the novel received diverse interpretations among Black American readers. While some, such as Frederick Douglass, responded enthusiastically, seeing the novel as a means to mobilize white opposition to slavery, others were highly critical, in no small part because of Stowe's pro-colonization digression via Harris's letter. For Martin Delany, Stowe was a patronizing and racist colonizationist. For Douglass, Delany's criticisms of Stowe were contradictory and incompatible with his (Delany's) own pro-emigration stance. In Delany's view, Douglass, by approving of the novel, was aligning himself with the racism and paternalism of white America, whose favor he was manifestly trying to cultivate.[71] The antagonism surrounding Douglass's and Delany's opposing views of *Uncle Tom's Cabin* is the clearest sign that the debates in the 1850s about "stay and fight" versus emigrationism were intense and complex, with interests and arguments sometimes oddly overlapping despite apparent divergence. Douglass and Delany probably locked horns over *Uncle Tom's Cabin* in part because both sought to be the preeminent leader of the Black community, and partly because they disagreed on emigration and about the separatism that emigrationism and a search for Black nationality entailed. Clearly, debates about emigration, colonization, and Black nationality, which were already active in the Black American community since the 1830s, intensified after the publication of *Uncle Tom's Cabin.*

Delany, though strongly opposed to colonization, was also clearly in favor of voluntary emigration because for him it was closely linked to the nationalist ideology he supported. At the same time, however, some of his critics were beginning to doubt their own anti-emigrationist position, and some even switched sides on this question in the space of only a few months. This was the case for James Whitfield, for example.[72] At first he was a fervent supporter of the "stay and fight" position at the July 1853 convention,[73] but some months later he declared his complete support for emigration in a statement published in *Frederick Douglass' Paper* on the occasion of epistolary debates on this subject with William J. Watkins.[74] In a letter addressed to Watkins dated December 30, 1853, Whitfield first asks, "What then are the causes of the degradation of the black race in this country, and what are the measures adequate to remove them?" He then places the question within a wider comparison of the persecution of "American Negroes" and "the case of the French Huguenots [and] the British Puritans." And he concludes:

> [W]hen the oppressed class are but a small minority, scattered through the country, and the whole organization of government is in the hands of their enemies, with all its power wielded to crush them, as in the case of the

> French Huguenots, the British Puritans, and the American Negroes, Emigration is the only resource.[75]

One may wonder why Whitfield compares a community defined by color or "race" with a religious community. Was this an indication that Whitfield was then thinking of himself and his fellow Blacks as belonging to a diaspora and to a group that transcended borders? Of course Whitfield's primary concern was surely to highlight the oppression that Black people faced by comparing them to other minorities who in earlier times had been forced to flee their countries to escape persecution, but there may also be in this letter the early germination of Black diaspora thinking.

Shortly after these debates, a "National Emigration Convention" took place in Cleveland, Ohio, in 1854.[76] One hundred and two delegates attended this convention from eleven U.S. states that spanned every region of the country as well as Canada. While it is difficult to measure levels of support, these numbers and the geographic diversity are proof of the importance of the emigration question among free people of color during this period of tighter enforcement of slavery and worsening conditions for Black people generally in the United States.

During this convention, Delany presented "A Report on the Political Destiny of the Colored Race, on the American Continent," adapted from a work he had published two years earlier, *The Condition, Elevation, and Destiny of the Colored People of the United States*. In this report, Delany takes up the problem of the white population's refusal to grant full citizenship to Blacks, even calling it a disease before stating categorically, "We propose for this disease a remedy. That remedy is Emigration."[77] Delany then attempts to specify a destination for this emigration. After ruling out contiguous territories on the North American continent, which he thinks may fall one day into the hands of white Americans, as well as areas already densely settled by white people, he states his preference for the West Indies and Central and South America. Armed with facts and figures, Delany attempts to prove that the surface area of these lands is sufficient to receive the entire Black population of the United States. Delany also mentions Haiti, a country he deeply admired.[78]

> [T]he Island [*sic*] of Haiti, in the West Indies, peopled by as brave and noble descendants of Africa, as they who laid the foundation of Thebias, or constructed the everlasting pyramids and catecombs [*sic*] of Egypt.—A people who have freed themselves by the might of their own will, the force of their own power, the unfailing strength of their own right arms, and their unflinching determination to be free.[79]

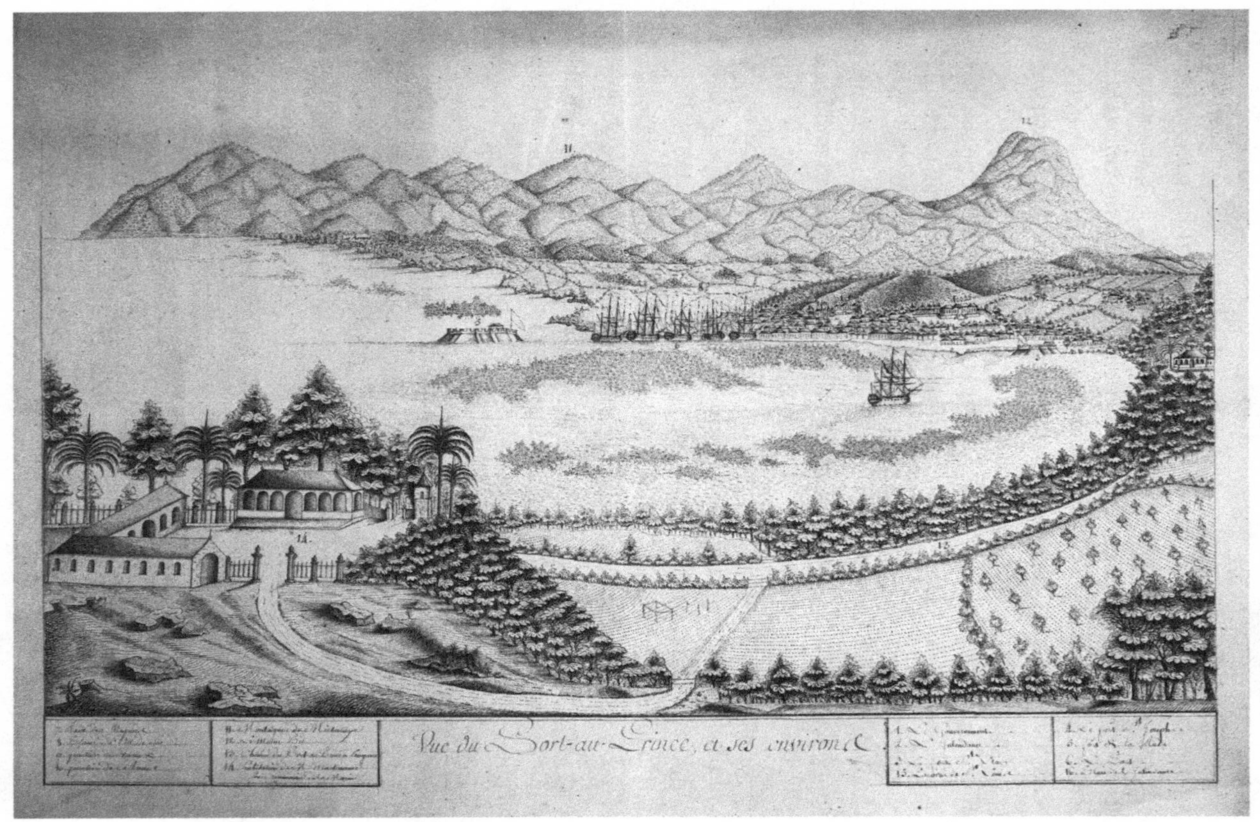

FIG. 2. Map of Port-au-Prince, 1800. *Reproduction courtesy of the Norman B. Leventhal Map & Education Center at the Boston Public Library.*

The convention of 1854 passed many resolutions in favor of emigration, but it is worth noting that the delegates were still unable to reach unanimous agreement about the emigration destination. As a result, the convention created a National Board of Commissioners with Delany as president, the goal being to facilitate the emigrationist movement by studying and evaluating various emigration projects that were serious candidates. This fact-finding committee in turn conferred on James Theodore Holly, a young Episcopalian, the task of studying the feasibility of Black Americans emigrating to Haiti.

The emigrationist movement expanded even more the following year at the Colored National Convention of 1855. It became clear that Black people were tempted by all sorts of emigration schemes so long as they had nothing to do with the American Colonization Society. Not even the most ardent defenders of the "stay and fight" position could resist the debates around emigration and Black nationality that were the principal focus of the delegates assembled at the convention. Especially influential was a letter from J. W. C. Pennington[80] addressed to the convention in which he calls for the organization of an even bigger convention that would assemble Black people from every country—"gentlemen of talent from the British, French, Spanish and Danish Dominions, and also from Mexico and Central America"—and for which Haiti would be the ideal location.[81]

It is in this context, then, with sympathies in favor of emigrationism clearly linked to the establishment of Black nationality, that James Theodore Holly emerged as the principal emigrationist leader promoting Haiti as the ideal destination by virtue of it being already a "Black" republic, ready to welcome Black Americans and to become the "promised land" of a Black diaspora.

CHAPTER 3

The Second Wave of Emigration to Haiti

Colored American emigrants will find among the Haytians
the most favorable field in which to obtain their manly growth
to the full stature of free and independent men.[1]

—JAMES THEODORE HOLLY

James Theodore Holly is certainly not recognized around the world today as a major African American leader of the nineteenth century.[2] However, he was acquainted with the greatest figures of his time—Martin R. Delany, Frederick Douglass, Henry Highland Garnet—and collaborated with other Black activists who made their mark in the years leading up to the Civil War. Holly is still famous in Haiti today, not as a charismatic leader of the Black American cause, but as the founder of the Episcopal Church in Haiti.

Holly was born in 1829 in Washington, D.C., the son of free parents. He was baptized and raised as a dutiful Roman Catholic in Washington until age fifteen. In 1852 Holly converted and became a member of the Episcopal Church in Detroit, Michigan. On June 17, 1855, he was ordained deacon in Detroit's Saint Paul's Church. Holly then moved to Connecticut and was ordained to the priesthood at Saint Luke's Church, New Haven, where he was rector, on January 2, 1856. His rapid rise within the Episcopal Church ran parallel to his energetic devotion for Haiti. Holly was clearly an early sympathizer with the Haitian cause and shared his interest in Haiti in various letters to Episcopal authorities: "he . . . vowed before he was ten years old to become a Minister of God to labor among the Haïtien people as their Apostle and evangelist."[3]

Holly participated in the lively debates between Black emigrationists and their critics that took place throughout the 1850s and was already by then a fervent activist convinced that the first Black republic was the place where Black Americans would permanently settle and elevate themselves.[4] He also thought that Black American emigration would be beneficial to Haiti and the Haitians. On numerous occasions, Holly emphasized this "civilizing" aspect of emigration, arguing that Black Americans were more advanced than Haitians thanks to the privilege of their contact with whites, and hence would be able to extend "American civilization" to Haiti. In conjunction with this quasi-imperialist outward discourse, Holly claimed that by serving the Haitian cause, Black American émigrés would also be serving the cause of Black people who remained in America by participating at a distance in the collective struggle to eliminate discrimination inside the United States.[5] In the following chapters it will become clear that by defending the Haitian cause and contributing to its "progress," Black Americans aimed to prove that Black people in every country were human beings and equal to whites, and not inferior beings incapable of governing themselves. In this way, Haiti was used as a "laboratory," a large-scale experiment that was to serve the cause of the Black diaspora around the world.

James Theodore Holly's Haitian Dream

James Theodore Holly committed himself to the cause of emigration to Haiti at the time when the missionary movement was in full swing in the United States. Churches were establishing missions in the western United States as well as in foreign countries, notably in Africa with the Anglican (or Episcopal) Church having the largest presence there.[6] It is known that churches often sent Black missionaries to Africa. For these individuals, accepting to head up a mission in Africa was a form of social promotion superior to remaining in the secondary roles they occupied in churches within the United States.[7] Of course, these Black missionaries were accepting to travel to Africa with the goal of "civilizing" it. They arrived as representatives of American culture. It was therefore also an opportunity for them to gain the respect of whites and improve their own condition in the United States. They would have many of the same stereotypes about Africans as whites, and were convinced that converting Africans to Christianity was necessary to avoid the degradation of the continent.[8]

Holly was not so different from the Black Americans who decided to evangelize Africa. His preference for Haiti was probably based on its proximity and the favorable reputation of Haiti, and by his own conflicts with the American Colonization Society. For Holly, Black Americans ought to feel invested in the mission to safeguard the independence of Haiti. By emigrating there and increasing the ranks of its workers and citizens, Black Americans were help-

FIG. 3. Right Rev. James T. Holly, D.D., first bishop of the National Haitien Church, ca. 1875.
New York: Currier & Ives. Photograph. Library of Congress, Washington, D.C.

ing ensure that Haiti would remain independent and not fall into the hands of whites—whether the Spanish, who at the time were taking control of the Dominican Republic, or the Americans, who could very well have expansionist ambitions. It is very likely that this unambiguous position worked in his favor at the Emigration Convention of 1854, thus resulting in his nomination as commissioner in charge of evaluating the feasibility of emigration to Haiti.

Having already the ambition of becoming a missionary in Haiti, Holly next attempted to convince the Episcopal Church to finance his first voyage to the island. On July 1, 1855, only weeks after being ordained a deacon, Holly traveled to New York with the aim of being named a missionary to Haiti by Episcopal authorities. His request came before the Foreign Committee of the Episcopal Church, which, though refusing to sponsor an official mission in Haiti at that time, did permit Holly to travel there to collect information about an eventual "opening" for establishing an Episcopal Church in the Black republic.[9] He left New York on July 11, 1855, and arrived in Port-au-Prince on August 1, 1855.[10]

Upon arrival, Holly quickly met with religious leaders (mostly Methodists and Baptists) already present on the island with the goal of evaluating the possibility of an opening for the Episcopal Church.[11] He was soon introduced to a Haitian judge, Émile de Ballette, to whom he could present his project.[12]

Ballette, who had studied in London and converted to the Anglican Church there, was entirely receptive to the idea of establishing an Episcopal Church in Haiti. Ballette underscored that the laws and constitution of Haiti protected all religions, without exception, but confided to Holly that the secret to a successful mission was "a free school." "[A] free school is necessary; attached to the church, it will recommend it to public notice"; plus, some medical knowledge and paying all the bills would also be helpful, he added.

> [I]f a little knowledge in medical relief, that is to say family and home remedies, can be now and then given to the poor, it will have a great effect. . . . [T]he necessary materials for the school must not be forgotten; it would cost too much here, everything must be in French of course, and the more complete the better.[13]

After a few weeks, Holly had no more money and was forced to return to the United States before he could pursue any further specific negotiations with Haitian authorities. However the outlook was favorable—not so much about emigration of Black Americans to Haiti but for Holly's own plans to establish a permanent Episcopal Church on the island. When he arrived back in New York in September 1855, Holly tried again to convince the Episcopal authorities of the suitableness of a religious mission in Haiti, but with no success. Holly had prepared a series of lectures about "the condition and wants of St. Domingo" that he wished to deliver in various places across America.[14] In November 1855 he toured the parish churches in New York state, relating the substance of his stay and praising Haiti to all who would listen. By the end of November, he had to face facts: even if some free people of color who came to hear his lectures were interested, the Episcopal Church was still refusing to underwrite a full-fledged mission in Haiti.[15] He would therefore have to seek out other sources of financial assistance. Some months later Black Americans who gathered for the Emigration Convention in August 1856 in Cleveland, Ohio, were still unable to agree on an emigration destination, and to his great disappointment Holly was not able to get the necessary funds for his Haitian project from that source either.

With the need to raise money still on his mind, Holly spent the summer of 1856 preaching for Haiti and in 1857 published a collection of his lectures from the past two years. This publication, which explicitly promoted Haiti as a prime destination for Black American emigration, was made possible thanks to the support of an association sponsoring Black American literature that was itself created under the auspices of the Emigration Convention of 1854, the Afric-American Printing Company.[16] The ostensible purpose of Holly's book, entitled *Vindication of the Capacity of the Negro Race*, was to use the Haitian Revolution and the subsequent history of the island as proof that Black people could govern themselves and thereby contribute to building Black American dignity and pride in their "race"; however, the primary motive was to advertise Holly's emigrationist project. This is clear from his conclusion that comes after a lengthy presentation of the admirable stability of the Haitian governments that have succeeded one another since the founding of the independent Black republic:

> Her rich resources invite the capacity of 10,000,000 human beings to adequately use them. It becomes then an important question for the negro race in America to well consider the weighty responsibility that the present exigency devolves upon them, to contribute to the continued advancement of this negro nationality of the New World until its glory and renown shall overspread and cover the whole earth.[17]

Claiming the island could easily provide for ten million inhabitants,[18] Holly pressed Black Americans to contribute to Haiti's development and thereby contribute to the advancement of Black nationality on the island and by extension in Africa and throughout the world. With this clearly nationalist and diasporic position, Holly was exhorting his Black brethren to unite around the grandeur of Haiti and join in a civilizing mission that somewhat resembled the discourse around "Manifest Destiny" launched by John L. O'Sullivan in 1845; in other words, a duty to enlighten Black people around the world by transmitting the knowledge, know-how, civilization, and Christianity they had acquired from their (beneficial in these respects) contact with whites. By allowing the institution of slavery to develop, God had an ulterior plan for Black people. This plan was to first send the latter to America where they would create the Haitian nation, and from that fount would come the "regeneration." For Holly, the source of renewal was Haiti, and it was the role of Black Americans to support it.

> God, therefore in permitting the accursed slave traffic to transplant so many millions of the race, to the New World, and educing [eliciting] therefrom such a negro nationality as Hayti, indicates thereby, that we have a work now to do here in the Western World, which in his own good time shall shed its orient beams upon the Fatherland of the race. . . . And in seeking to perform this duty, it may well be a question with us, whether it is not our duty, to go and identify our destiny with our heroic brethren in that independent isle of the Caribbean Sea, carrying with us such of the arts, sci-

> ences and genius of modern civilization, as we may gain from this hardy and enterprising Anglo-American race, in order to add to Haytian advancement; rather than to indolently remain here, asking for political rights, which, if granted a social proscription stronger than conventional legislation will ever render nugatory and of no avail for the manly elevation and general well-being of the race.[19]

Holly was clearly borrowing from the discourse of American exceptionalism. If (white, Anglo-Saxon) Americans were indeed the chosen people, endowed by their creator with a civilizing mission in the Western Hemisphere, Black Americans were no less endowed with their civilizing mission toward their colored brethren, and had been transported from Africa to America to be in contact with civilization in order to then spread it far and wide, including in the Eastern Hemisphere (i.e., Africa). Haiti offered a political model, and it was the duty of Black Americans to help that nation survive. Rather than seeking additional rights in the United States, Black Americans ought to bring to Haiti their material and technical aid to make Haiti rich and respected. Holly played down the importance of the struggle for civil rights within the United States, considering that obtaining those rights would bring nothing to Black people in other countries, whereas the mission Holly conceived would have a universal impact. For Holly, what counted most was not improving the living conditions of just Black Americans but "saving" the entire race—the Black diaspora.

In this regard, Holly's project was quite distinct from the emigration projects of the 1820s but also from the Black emigrationist intentions of the 1850s, whereby the main goal of resettlement was to save Black Americans from the cruel fate they were allotted in the United States.

Since he knew that money was indispensable for his plan to succeed and accepted his failure to obtain funds for his Haiti mission from the Episcopal Church, Holly decided to turn to Frank P. Blair Jr., a Republican congressman from Missouri who was known to be favorable to Black resettlement in Central America.[20] Blair saw this colonization project as a chance to take control of Central America while also getting rid of America's free Black population. While on one hand insisting on the impossibility of assimilating the Black population within the American territory, Blair simultaneously considered these same Black people as the perfect, because educated, representatives of the United States abroad. "The American-born and American-instructed African" would be the guarantor of civilization in places "where the people of their own color prevail." In Blair's vision, "emigrants in thousands would soon find their way to freedom" and occupy positions of responsibility, "holding office both in church and state." Above all, Blair saw the extraordinary commercial potential if the United States could send their free and emancipated Blacks as colonizers "to the vacant regions of Central and South America."[21] On January 24, 1859, Blair presented his argument to businessmen who belonged to the Mercantile Library Association of Boston, Massachusetts, and soon published his speech along with letters of support he had received from certain Black activists and emigrationists. These letters were meant to prove that Black Americans themselves were favorable to this idea of colonization toward Central America or Haiti.[22] However, another contributing factor that may explain the renewed interest in colonization and emigration precisely at the end of the 1850s needs to be remembered. Blair's speech occurred not long after the Supreme Court's decision in the *Dred Scott* case (March 6, 1857). At the time, this decision was experienced like a thunderbolt among Black activists who concluded, if they had not already, that the U.S. Constitution would never defend them and that it was probably useless to hope to become full-fledged citizens of the United States.[23]

It is in this context that Holly took up his pen to write to Blair. He sent several letters, including one dated January 30, 1858, that Blair chose to publish in its entirety. In this letter, Holly returns to the details of his Haiti emigration project and his lack of funding, which, in Holly's view, explains why for the moment few Black Americans have expressed interest in moving there. Holly lists all the measures he had already taken as of January 30, 1858, to favorably prepare this emigration project, claiming that the Haitian government was completely ready to receive Black American emigrants, though without specifying on what conditions. Curiously, in the rest of this letter, Holly seems to have abandoned the Haitian project and turns to supporting Blair's Central American idea instead. Holly even gives several pieces of advice to Blair to better succeed with his project and would seem to be almost volunteering to help him with it. He explicitly recommends that the project go forward under the auspices of an association supported by influential members of the U.S. Congress, one that Black emigrationists would be welcomed to join. Furthermore, he recommends that the association name an "able commissioner" who, "accompanied by some intelligent colored man," would enter into negotiations with "the Central American Government."[24] Blair did not reproduce his own letters in this volume, but it is clear that Holly received no financial backing from Blair and his allies toward the Haiti emigration project.

Without Blair's financial assistance, but no less committed to his project, Holly then participated in a third Emigration Convention in 1858 in Chatham, Upper Canada. Once again, no consensus is reached. The delegates refuse to support a particular destination and merely give their blessing to all those who have plans to leave the United States. They do change their name, however, to the "Association for the Promotion of the Interest of the Colored People of Canada and the United States," thereby signaling their support for all initiatives whose goal is the improvement of Black lives, not just emigration. Holly and the other emigrationists thus lost an important source of support for their projects. Delany managed to win approval for the creation of an "African Commission" to explore Niger, but with no financial assistance since the leaders of the convention were not inclined to encourage Black emigration to Africa. Some weeks earlier, Henry Highland Garnet had created the African Civilization Society in New York, whose goal was to evangelize and civilize Africa.[25] This organization was harshly criticized by some Black American activists who suspected it to be in league with the American Colonization Society given the similarity of names, although Garnet always denied any such alliance.[26]

Although he had always refused to partner with whites and had doubts about the source of funding for the African Civilization Society, Delany ended up joining it in March 1859 and obtained funding for his African voyage in May of the same year—an arrangement that can be seen as a tactical concession on his part.[27] Meanwhile, Holly was still seeking financing for his Haiti project, but he was less interested in the new organization that emerged from the 1858 convention and therefore continued to speak out in favor of Haiti but on a more individual basis.[28]

In 1859 Holly published several articles in the *Anglo-African Magazine* in which he analyzed the reasons behind the failure of the emigration wave of 1824 with the aim of storing up lessons that could be used for his Haiti project. For Holly, the institution of slavery as experienced by Black Americans was partly to blame for this failure. He cited a "paralyzing effect of slavery" that was long-lasting and debilitating as it sapped the confidence of Black Americans who were then less psychologically prepared to be their own bosses. Thus they arrived in Haiti in the 1820s with the idea of finding "servile employment" of the kind they had been used to in the United States. Furthermore, Holly argued, some went to Haiti with an overly colonialist attitude, believing they could take the lead "in order to teach the Haytians how to rule" their own country. Holly seemed to be suggesting that with an attitude like that, emigration to Haiti was bound to fail because a feeling of North American superiority present in the Black American community ran counter to an understandable spirit of proud independence among the native Haitians.[29] That being said, and even though he regretted the attitude of the first Black Americans who emigrated in 1824, Holly was still willing to claim Black American superiority over Black Haitians, indeed over all other Black people around the world, which is paradoxical to say the least.[30] In Holly's view, Haiti was in need of specific qualities possessed by Black Americans; however, this did not prevent him from considering Haiti as the political model for the Black diaspora. The idea of Black Americans guiding the Haitian people toward civilization, and that their union could then provoke a chain reaction that would in turn help all Black people around the world free themselves from their state of barbarism, was at the center of Holly's reasoning and can be found in all the articles he wrote in favor of emigration to Haiti. He often compared Black Americans and Black Africans, and used pejorative language to characterize the inferiority of the latter. Here, for example, is the conclusion to the third article in his series "Thoughts on Hayti":

> It would be useless for me to enter into an examination of the claims of Africa as a field from whence Hayti might be supplied with emigrants. The barbarism of the inhabitants of that savage continent could not do otherwise than retard, instead of promoting, the national development of that people.[31]

This denigration of Africans can certainly be interpreted as a way to indirectly reject all projects of emigration and resettlement toward Africa. Africa was being discredited by Holly with the implication that what ought to be avoided was any future arrival of Black *Africans* to Haiti.

Starting from the premise that the Black man could not be equal to the white man within the United States, Holly explains how successful emigration to Haiti would have a positive effect on American slaves and improve the destiny of all Blacks around the world:

> [A] successful emigration of colored people from this country to Hayti will exert a reflex influence on the condition of the slaves in this country, and on the destiny of the negro race throughout the world, that shall secure in the speediest manner, their ultimate disenthrallment and complete political regeneration.[32]

The "political regeneration" necessary for the progress of the Black race in the United States and in the world but also for the "national regeneration" of Haiti, which Holly evokes in several of his articles, could only be achieved, he believed, through the emigration of educated Black Americans to Haiti through a program that would be voluntarily chosen, not massive or imposed.

Holly's core conviction is clear: "Emigration alone is the only means by which a suffering people can seek their political regeneration."[33]

James Redpath and the Haitian Proposal

After the Compromise of 1850 with its Fugitive Slave Act, and even more so after the *Dred Scott* decision of 1857, emigration, exile, and the search for a better life outside the United States was more important than ever for hardened emigrationists. Therefore, it is not surprising to find in Black periodicals between 1858 and 1862, alongside Holly's specifically pro-Haiti articles, many others as well as pamphlets and open letters all taking a favorable view of emigration. It is not unusual to find numerous references to Haiti in these other materials as well as truly passionate debates about this destination. Even if, as stated previously, the immediate American context and political direction were tilting more people toward a favorable outlook on emigration, another factor fueling interest in Haiti was emerging in the form of a new direct offer from the Haitian government.

Général Guillaume Fabre Nicolas Geffrard became president of Haiti in January 1859, and soon after taking power he initiated on his own, and without anyone's help on the American side, a campaign to bring Black Americans to Haiti. Starting in March 1859, *Frederick Douglass' Paper* published articles about Haiti and the new Geffrard presidency, and referred to the offer the new Haitian president was making to Black Americans wishing to emigrate. One March 1859 issue of the paper makes a favorable allusion to Geffrard's proposal: "We are glad to see that the new President of Hayti proposes to solicit immigration into Hayti by the free colored people of these United States."[34] One month later, the same newspaper printed an "invitation" from the Haitian government.[35] The following week, Frederick Douglass published an article, which had first appeared in the *Chicago Press and Tribune*, reporting and praising the decision of certain Black Americans to form a committee with the goal of organizing the departure of those who wished to leave the United States and take advantage of the Geffrard invitation, while at the same time regretting that this emigration would deprive the city of "good citizens" and "honest men."[36]

In early May 1859 *Frederick Douglass' Paper* published a letter signed by a certain James Redpath in which the latter advised Black Americans to be cautious. The letter states that at the moment Redpath is writing, April 23, 1859, Geffrard's "scheme" is still very unclear and that he has thus far made no official commitment about the terms and conditions for receiving potential emigrants. Though Redpath states, "I like this Geffrard," he remains suspicious given the silence he's encountered in answer to specific questions he put to the Haitian president about details of the offer. Therefore, he says to Black people eager to emigrate, "You had better turn your faces to the snow-drifts of Canada" rather than to Haiti.[37] Meanwhile, the abovementioned Black committee organized a meeting, one learns from the same article in the *Chicago Tribune* that was reprinted in the same issue of *Frederick Douglass' Paper* that printed Redpath's letter, and it voted to officially approve the Geffrard offer and thereby encourage voluntary emigration by free people of color. It even proclaimed that emigration to Haiti was a "duty" that a Black free man owed himself, and to "the four millions of his friends in bonds."[38] Subsequently, some weeks later Frederick Douglas reprinted an article from the *New Orleans Delta* dated June 21, 1859, in which one learns that "large parties of free persons of color have lately, at intervals, emigrated to Port-au-Prince, in Hayti, for the purpose of settling there." A first group of 150 people is said to have left Louisiana in May 1859 aboard the ship *West Indian,* and a second group of 195 people is said to have left New Orleans on June 20, 1859. Also noteworthy are certain details about the conditions offered to these émigrés leaving Louisiana. It is stated that the Haitian government would be giving them each a plot of land and had paid for their passage to the island.[39]

It is believed that in the summer of 1860 Geffrard decided to engage the services of an American to accelerate the recruitment process directed at Black Americans.[40] The person turns out to be the very same James Redpath, a white abolitionist and loyal friend of the famous abolitionist John Brown who was executed the same year.[41] Redpath is given the title general agent of emigration to Hayti for the United States and the Canadas and is to work on behalf of the Haitian government in its emigration offices in Boston. Redpath writes in his *Guide to Hayti* (1861) that he had been to the island on two occasions in the winter and summer of 1859, and made a third trip in the summer of 1860.[42] The manuscripts of Redpath's correspondence with Victorin Plésance, then secretary of state for foreign relations in the Haiti government, reveal that the campaign to recruit candidates for emigration really got going in the fall of 1860.[43]

Obviously, Redpath's mission was to attract potential candidates for emigration from among America's free Black population. Geffrard, who believed he had found the ideal solution for the labor shortage that was a major problem for his country, was knowingly encouraging Black American emigration to Haiti on terms less favorable than those offered by Boyer in the 1820s. Those terms are spelled out in Redpath's *Guide to Hayti.* For example, one reads, "It is chiefly to the development of Agriculture in Hayti that the Government wishes to make this enterprise subservient." Besides, the Haitian president agrees to encourage the emigration of Black Americans by paying up to fifteen dollars toward the passage "for each able-bodied man or woman," and eight dollars per child for those under age twelve and the same amount for people over age sixty. He also agrees to free room and board for a period of eight days while the new arrivals find living arrangements of their own. It is furthermore stated that the émigrés will enjoy the same state protections as native Haitians, the same ease for enrolling their children in school, practicing their religion freely, and could become Haitian citizens after one year of residency on the island. Finally, the émigrés would be exempt from military service, which was normally a nine-year duty for Haitians. On the other hand, unlike Boyer, Geffrard initially had no plans to offer a plot of land to émigrés. Instead, they were free to rent plots and cultivate them with a payment of 50 percent of production to the owner; or they could buy plots from private owners or from the state at supposedly advantageous prices. Furthermore, if they were dissatisfied, émigrés were free to leave whenever they liked, unless they had received a travel subsidy from the government, in which case they would be free to leave after a nonnegotiable three years of service cultivating Haitian lands.[44]

The initial conditions that stated émigrés were free to settle wherever they liked on the island were subsequently modified by a presidential order dated August 14, 1860, which stipulated that émigrés would be restricted to settling in Cap-Haïtien, the Gonaïves, Saint-Marc, Port-au-Prince, or in Les Cayes.[45] Finally, it is worth noting that the Law on the Emigration into the Country, of Persons of African and Indian Race promulgated on September 1, 1860, improved emigration conditions compared to those of 1859 by stating "five carreaux of land will be granted, free of all charge, to every family of laborers or cultivators of African or Indian race who shall arrive in the Republic," though the grant would be reduced to two carreaux if the émigré farmer was unmarried.[46]

Beyond his wish "to improve the methods of agriculture and come to the aid of Black Americans who were victims of race prejudice,"[47] Geffrard had the same motive as his predecessor from thirty years earlier: to obtain the recognition of his country by the American government. In the early 1860s this need for official recognition was closely linked to the local foreign affairs of the little Black republic surrounding the tense relations between Haiti and the country that controlled the other two-thirds of the island of Hispaniola—namely, the Dominican Republic.

When he arrived in power, Geffrard faced a dilemma: should he continue the war against the Dominicans or make peace? Since the creation of the Republic of Haiti, the question of its relationship to the Dominican Republic was raised many times by a succession of leaders without ever receiving a definitive answer. With the help of two powerful mediators, France and England, Geffrard chose to enter into a five-year cease-fire with the Dominicans in 1859. This agreement did not last long, however, because on April 6, 1861, the Spanish general counselor in Port-au-Prince officially informed the Haitian government that by virtue of an accord between General Pedro Santana, president of the Dominican Republic, and the Spanish court in Madrid, all Dominican territory was now annexed by the Spanish crown. On March 18, 1861, President Santana had turned his country over to Spain while remaining in power with the title of governor-general. Immediately, Haitian authorities, who ever since 1804 had feared that a great power might one day conquer the eastern portion of the island and invade Haiti, publicly protested. Geffrard even published a call to arms in *Le Moniteur.* Haiti also organized some insurrectional expeditions into the Dominican Republic and welcomed anti-Santana forces into the country. Because Haiti was sheltering Santana's adversaries, the Spanish admiral Rubalcava sailed swiftly into Port-au-Prince on July 6, 1861, and ordered that the Geffrard government fire twenty-one cannon shots as a pledge of allegiance to the Spanish flag and the payment of two hundred thousand Spanish dollars within forty-eight hours. Thanks to the intervention of Henry Byron, the English governor-general and head of diplomatic and consular services, Rubalcava softened his conditions somewhat, with Geffrard forced to pay only twenty-five thousand Spanish dollars and to perform the salute to the flag. Afterward, Geffrard proclaimed official neutrality but continued to secretly support the insurgency.[48]

For its part, the United States protested against Spain's clear violation of the so-called Monroe Doctrine; however, since the American government was then preoccupied by a civil war within its own territory, it had neither the means nor probably the desire to enforce the doctrine at that inauspicious moment. Obviously, President Santana's decision to have the Dominican Republic revert to the status of a Spanish colony on March 18, 1861, caused great alarm in Haiti, which feared the Spanish presence in its midst and thus immediately sought protection from the United States, beginning with a new request for official recognition addressed to President Abraham Lincoln on May 22, 1861.[49]

Interestingly, the first exchange between Redpath and Plésance from seven months earlier on November 3, 1860, already raises the matter of Haiti's desire for official recognition. Clearly, one of Redpath's missions as the agent in charge of organizing American emigration to the island was to obtain the American government's recognition of Haiti. Indeed, in this report Redpath states that he had obtained assurances of cooperation on this topic from Republican senator Charles Sumner.[50]

On October 24, 1860, Redpath began a propaganda campaign in favor of emigration to Haiti, and he was to keep Plésance regularly informed of his efforts. As he says himself in his first report, the main strategy was the publication of his *Guide to Hayti* and its dissemination to prospective émigrés. Redpath also counted on a sympathetic American press, both white and Black, that would publish pro-emigration articles. Finally, he cultivated the support of Black American activists who were openly in favor of emigration.[51]

Redpath succeeded in recruiting Black activists with budding reputations in 1860 and 1861, giving them the title "agent of emigration" with the role of helping spread the word within the Black community about Geffrard's generous offer. Among these agents were James Theodore Holly, H. Ford Douglas, William Wells Brown, and Henry Highland Garnet. Once recruited, each of them received a letter with instructions in which their mission as agent was defined. For example, they were to travel to different American states trying to recruit "citizens of African descent, of the class, chiefly, of farmers and laborers." They were to inform these individuals about "the offers of the Haytien Government, and the advantages of Hayti as a home for the colored races of America." They were also to distribute wherever they went English translations of Haiti's laws, send to Redpath the addresses of families expressing the intention of emigrating, and submit reports about their activities twice a week.[52]

The Haitian emigrationist propaganda operated through the production of verbiage by these noteworthy agents (or by their emigrationist and abolitionist friends) and the reproduction of their discourse in popular white and Black newspapers.[53] Redpath worked closely with the Black periodical *Weekly Anglo-African,* which in 1860 was one of only two such publications, the other being the newspaper of Frederick Douglass; but he also made sure he had the support of prestigious white publications such as the *New York Tribune*, which in 1860 enjoyed the record-setting circulation of two hundred thousand sales per day.[54] Redpath considered the *New York Tribune* as "the organ of the Republican Party," which in 1860 he believed "promises to be the next dominant power here." He was therefore proud to have "succeeded in securing the immense influence of the *Tribune*" to advance the twin goals of promoting emigration to Haiti and obtaining official American recognition of the Black Republic. In his first report, Redpath states that he ordered thousands of copies of the *Tribune* and *Anglo-African* (forty thousand and ten thousand copies, respectively) that contained the English translation of Haiti's laws as well as Redpath's pro-emigration infomercial so that they could be distributed by him and his agents at emigration rallies they planned to organize throughout the country.[55] Redpath also sought out the support of the other Black periodical of the day published by Frederick Douglass in 1860 under the name *Douglass' Monthly*. Given the official opposition of Douglass to emigration at the time (as noted in the previous chapter, Douglass was vigorously opposed to emigration of his fellow citizens in the 1850s), one can imagine that Redpath's efforts in this direction were unsuccessful. Redpath remained careful but optimistic, knowing that Douglass was not favorably disposed for the moment at least:

> I am negociating [*sic*] for the support of the other of the two papers published by colored men in the United States, and although its editor has always hitherto opposed Emigration, I am likely to obtain his aid.[56]

And Redpath was right to think so, since Douglass would soon be regularly publishing pro-Haiti, pro-emigration pieces in his periodical. The most striking example of his overall approval of the emigration project occurs in the pages of the January 1861 issue of *Douglass' Monthly*. After first repeating his own reservations and general optimism about America, Douglass is willing to concede that emigration may be extremely advantageous for a large number of Black American families:

> While we have never favored any plan of emigration, and have never been willing to concede that this is a doomed country, and that we are a doomed race in it, we can raise no objection to the present movement towards Hayti. For years we have looked to such emigration as a possible necessity to our people; and though we do not think that necessity has yet fully come, we can no longer throw our little influence against a measure which may prove highly advantageous to many families, and of much service to the Haytian Republic. . . .
>
> Let every emigrant go to Hayti with the purpose to give the country his best energies, and we will be bound that the country will take care of him and fulfill his highest expectations.[57]

It is difficult to say how much this changed attitude was new and surprising. Although up until then Douglass had never openly expressed support for emigration to Haiti, he had also never disguised his curiosity and even admiration for the Black republic. As early as April 1848, Douglass praised Haiti and regretted that Americans generally and Black people in particular knew little or nothing about this republic that he described as "most interesting."[58]

To affirm this observation, Douglass decided to start regularly publishing in the *North Star* the correspondence of a certain Harold that details his pilgrimage to Haiti.[59] Further proof of his admiration for Haiti is published in July 1861 when Douglass uses the occasion of another piece devoted to emigration to Haiti to declare that he "rejoices in her prosperity" and considers one should "look to her example with pride and hope."[60] Further testimony of his implicit sympathy for the emigration project, or at least a certain attraction to Haiti, can be seen in his project to travel there himself with his daughter in the spring of 1861 at the invitation of the Haitian consul in Philadelphia; however, the outbreak of the Civil War forced him to defer that journey.[61]

Month after month, James Redpath and the Bureau of Emigration he directed managed to get pro-Haiti articles, speeches, and personal narratives published in numerous American periodicals—white and Black, in the North and the South. One example is a letter addressed to President Geffrard by George W. Wilson, an "Ohio Agent," and sent from Port-de-Paix on July 10, 1862. The letter was printed in New Orleans on the front page of the *Union* newspaper on October 1, 1862. This ostensibly private letter not intended for mass diffusion throughout the country was in fact an ingenious propaganda tool, because the agent writing to Geffrard about a colony of 250 "intelligent, industrious, practical-minded farmers possessing a capital of 30,000 dollars" is an endless text of praise for Haiti and the generosity of its government. Wilson brags about the success of his settlement and concludes that he hopes to return to Haiti with "many other" Black volunteers.[62]

Redpath sought to quickly extend his sphere of influence and did not limit himself to recruiting Black agents and diffusing his propaganda in the periodicals mentioned above. He also cultivated a network of white abolitionists by staying in regular contact, with encouragements to relay the terms of Geffrard's offer in their speeches and writings, and to rally behind the cause of official recognition of the island republic.[63] Redpath also creates his own periodical, the *Pine and Palm*, specifically dedicated to emigration to Haiti, even though this would not be officially its only mission, but it did build further visibility for the project. In the opening sentence of the first editorial of the *Pine and Palm*, the abolitionist clearly states the goals of his new propaganda tool: "This journal will be devoted to the interests of freedom, and of the colored races in America." In the interest of freedom and the races of color in America, he understood his mission as defending the cause of emigration to Haiti, first to encourage the country's development and elevate it into a great American power, and second because he considered Haiti to be the ideal place to efficiently and enduringly establish "Black nationality."

> THE PINE AND PALM will advocate—The building up of Hayti, by an enlightened and organized emigration, into the rank of a great American Power. . . . We must create a great Negro Nation. Where? Hayti alone affords us a foundation near enough to influence Slavery and its brood of prejudices here, broad enough to establish a nationality of the necessary importance and durability there.[64]

One sees here that Redpath's goals perfectly align with those of Holly, namely building up Haiti through emigration, which will lead to political regeneration and the emergence of a powerful and respected republic.

The *Pine and Palm* is clearly a propaganda tool designed to advance emigration to Haiti. Alongside direct advertisements praising the emigration plan proposed by the Haitian government were the transcriptions of grandiloquent speeches by Black Americans speaking in favor of emigration to the island. Among the different arguments advanced by these emigrationists, one was no doubt particularly captivating to free people of color in the early 1860s; namely, Haiti's offer of ownership of a plot of land. It is well known how important property was to every American—it being a fundamental right protected by the Constitution. It was also an integral part of the aspiration of Black Americans to become full citizens and leave behind the second-class status they were customarily forced to accept. Legally owning land was a necessary condition of full citizenship, and it was very difficult to obtain within the United States, including in northern states, because most Black people were too poor. Therefore, Haiti's offer of land in a place relatively close to the United States and within a republican political space populated by other Black people was attractive. This argument was made many times by William Wells Brown, a former slave who was for a time the agent of the Haytian Bureau of Emigration. He was considered a gifted orator, a talent he exercised on the occasion of a speech he made at the Twelfth Baptist Church in Boston on August 8, 1861, about Black Americans and their relation to the Civil War. Near the end of his speech, he exhorts the latter to seriously consider the option of emigration to Haiti that was being offered to them:

> Now where shall we go to? This must be decided each one for himself. . . . Twenty years ago I visited Hayti andJamaica, and have ever since felt that those regions justly belonged to the sons and daughters of Africa. But I feel more interested in Hayti than the other islands.[65]

In another speech also reprinted in the *Pine and Palm,* the idea of an inheritance through the transfer of property, a key component of property owning, is Brown's central concern; but one also finds the idea of the universality of the Black cause that was important to Redpath and Holly:

> Now if we may go to California, Oregon, and other places to better our condition and to give an inheritance to our children, why should we not go to Hayti? It is conceded by all whites that with regard to situation and commercial advantages, Hayti is the most valuable of all the West India Islands. . . .
>
> The West India Islands are eventually to fall into the hands of the sons and daughters of Africa, and the sooner we take possession of them and develop their resources, the better it will be for ourselves, our children, and for humanity.[66]

Brown logically considered emigration as a chance to more quickly gain access to property ownership, and therefore to citizenship, and from there to secure a future for one's descendants. Even though he also considered the possibility of emigration toward the western territories of the United States, emigration to Haiti was for him, as it was for other Black emigrationists and Redpath, a means to build a Black community and found Black nationality in a place where skin color was not an obstacle to the "pursuit of happiness" spoken of in the American Declaration of Independence.

On the Failure of the Second Wave of Emigration to Haiti and the Relative Success of Holly's Haitian Mission

It is difficult if not impossible to know with certainty the exact number of Black Americans who left the United States to settle in Haiti, especially since all émigrés were not necessarily accounted for by the Bureau of Haitian Emigration. Some departed on their own without notifying the bureau, which had its own difficulties keeping accurate records of lists of candidates and actual departures. Others had no sponsorship from the Haitian government; this would include all those free people of color who made the journey before Fabre Geffrard's official invitation or even his arrival in power, in other words under the government of Faustin Soulouque. Other factors that make the counting complicated include deaths during the journey (the number of Black people boarding a ship could be higher than the number disembarking in Haiti) and last-minute cancellations (some who volunteered might simply change their mind and not show up at the dock).[67] One can also ask if the proper count for this second wave of emigration during the early 1860s should include those who left the United States between 1859 and 1860, in other words during the Geffrard period after the announcement of the invitation but before the involvement of James Redpath and the creation in Boston of the Haytian Bureau of Emigration.[68]

Secondary sources remain circumspect or vague about the numbers. For example, the historian William Seraille writes, "the fate of the approximate 2,500 emigrants [responding to Geffrard's invitation] remains basically unknown." He cites no source for that number, speculating simply, "perhaps many died in Haiti while others, unable to pay for their return passage, quietly assimilated into the society." Seraille also gives no information about the emigrants' states or cities of origin, writing only that they came from the East Coast of the United States.[69] Historian Willis D. Boyd claims that based on a review of notices published in the *Pine and Palm,* he was able to establish that the first sixty-two emigrants left New York on January 3, 1861, and that by December 31 of the same year 1,172 Black Americans had arrived in Haiti.[70]

Concerning the émigrés who departed before the creation of the Boston bureau, there are some clues in newspapers from 1859 that run somewhat counter to Seraille's claim about the provenance of the emigrants. The *Baltimore Sun* of April 28, 1858, for example, reports that "a large number of colored people in Chicago" are preparing to leave the country for Haiti.[71] The *New York Daily Tribune*, reprinting a notice that had appeared in the *New Orleans Bulletin* of May 4, 1859, notes some weeks later that a ship, the *West Indian*, reportedly left New Orleans for Port-au-Prince on May 1, 1859, with 150 free people of color onboard. It also states that the *West Indian* is the very first ship to transport free Black Americans from New Orleans to Haiti.[72] The following month, the *Sun* reports that a ship will be leaving New Orleans on July 7, 1859, for Haiti with 700 emigrants and that "Louisiana has already lost over 1,000 of these people" leaving for Haiti.[73] Meanwhile the *Daily Confederation* of Montgomery, Alabama, claims that a ship transporting 200 free Black Americans to Port-au-Prince already left New Orleans on June 20, 1859.[74] Around the same time (June–July 1859), the *New York Daily Tribune* and *Frederick Douglass' Paper* published the same article that first appeared in the *New Orleans Delta* on June 21, 1859, in which it is said the first ship to leave Louisiana, and specifically New Orleans, to transport 150 free Blacks to Haiti was the *West Indian* on May 1, 1859; and that a second ship, the *A. C. Brewer*, cast off on June 20, 1859, with "about 195 persons" on board.[75] These sources lead one to believe that it was mostly free people of color from New Orleans and the surrounding area, in other words from the South and not the eastern United States, who were leaving for Haiti; though it should be noted that these reports concern only the first half of 1859 and that the Boston bureau was not yet organized.[76]

As for the first ship to leave the United States for Haiti under the auspices of the Haytian Bureau of Emigration, the information in periodicals from the year 1860 seems to contradict Boyd's claims. The *Commercial Advertiser* in New York reprints information from the *New Orleans Picayune* stating that regular departures of free people of color leaving for Haiti will be set up by the Haitian government starting November 1, 1860 (in other words, roughly at the same time Redpath's bureau was created).[77] The *Liberator*, whose offices were in the same building as the *Pine and Palm*, states that "the first vessel sent by the Haytian Bureau of Emigration will sail from Boston on the 22nd of December next."[78] These two sources would seem to prove that the ship leaving New York in January 1861 was not the first voyage organized by the Boston bureau, and this is further confirmed by information in the *Weekly Anglo-African*, which states that a ship left Philadelphia on January 1, 1861, transporting a large number of Black people to Haiti.[79] Even without a complete list of every article mentioning ships (often generically with no name) or Black men and women traveling to Haiti (often without exact numbers or details about origin), it is clear that not all were leaving from New York and Boston, and that New Orleans was a busy port of emigration to Haiti. Indeed, the latest announcement we have been able to find about a group of Black Americans traveling to Haiti appeared in a French-language newspaper in New Orleans dated January 28, 1864. It states that "a ship will leave for the port indicated [Port-au-Prince] on March 20 if between now and then enough passengers show up."[80] There is no information about whether this scheduled departure actually took place.

The handwritten document of the Boston bureau mentioned earlier in this chapter also gives some clues about the number of emigrants wishing to voluntarily leave the United States for Haiti, but it provides no proof about the numbers of Black people who really left. Redpath did not keep lists of emigrants by name; at least none figure in this document. For example, in the report sent on January 21, 1861, Redpath states that one of his agents, George Lawrence, "informed him that within two weeks he expected to have fifty or more emigrants from Charleston, South Carolina" ready to embark for Haiti. A week later on January 27, he writes that "A second colony is already prepared to sail" and that "This colony will be composed of exiles from South Carolina." Redpath was never very precise about the numbers and admits that it always depended on the Black people themselves, who were free to back out of their commitment. "If the emigrants all keep their promises, the next vessel will convey over a hundred to Hayti," he writes in his report for February 2, 1861.[81] James Theodore Holly was similarly imprecise in his correspondence with the

Episcopal authorities when discussing Black American emigration to Haiti in May 1862. "Thousands of American emigrants are now here" on the island, he states, and he anticipates "thousands more."[82]

Finally, knowing what actually became of these emigrants is not easy because of challenges in evaluating the "qualitative" experience of the new arrivals in Haiti. Newspapers publishing letters sent home by emigrants or by abolitionists visiting the island testify that life there was no picnic. Like their predecessors in the 1820s, most of these Black emigrants were unprepared to face circumstances considerably different from what they had previously known. Some complained about the climate, but almost all mentioned their trouble with the language barrier, as well as a sort of culture shock around religion, customs and habits, and education that took them by surprise. In addition, many were not former slaves but born free, and many were also city dwellers unaccustomed to tilling soil as they were expected to do. As before, it seems that the majority of those who survived the journey and the living conditions on the island ended up turning back within a few months or years following their arrival. Some newspapers allude to these return voyages to the United States in articles that are far less encouraging about the situation of Black Americans in Haiti. For example, the April 5, 1862, issue of *Weekly Anglo-African* prints a letter of a Black American returning from Haiti who is clearly disillusioned and dissatisfied about the welcome they received and their stay. The letter is sharply critical of the Haitian government and the local inhabitants. This witness, referred to as "another returned emigrant from Hayti," claims the Haitian government did not keep its promises, that the agents on the island were incompetent, and that the plots of land allocated were of very poor quality and situated far from water sources. The author goes on to say that emigrants were dying of hunger and that the native Haitians themselves were generally uncivilized, had barbaric customs, and were unfriendly to emigrants:

> Freedom of speech does not exist in Hayti. . . . The Haytian government is a military despotism in the strictest sense of the term. . . . The natives, male and female, generally go half clad, bordering on nudity.[83]

This former emigrant concludes by saying one must not trust the many letters published in the *Pine and Palm* that paint a rosy picture of emigration, even alleging that they are forgeries written in the offices of the Boston Bureau of Emigration itself. In 1863 only James Theodore Holly would still be sending positive news about Haitian emigration,[84] a fact that is rather hard to believe when one recalls that Reverend Holly lost several members of his family, including his mother, wife, and two of their children, during the first year after their arrival.[85]

Even before unhappy emigrants started making the return journey back from the island, several agents of the Haytian Bureau of Emigration had already distanced themselves from the project. Henry Highland Garnet resigned in March 1861, as did H. Ford Douglass, who then enlisted in the Union army in 1862. The same year William Wells Brown, probably influenced by the hope ignited by the Civil War in the Black community, turned toward fighting alongside partisans of "stay and fight." James Redpath himself resigned fairly quickly from his position at the Haytian Bureau of Emigration in Boston. Perhaps frustrated by the failure of his enterprise, he abandoned the project in 1862 and became a war correspondent on the Union side during the Civil War.[86]

Things turned out better for James Theodore Holly, who managed to solidly implant the Episcopal Church in Haiti after many years of suffering. In the spring of 1861 Holly left Connecticut for Haiti along with 110 other emigrants.[87] Upon arriving, he and the other Black American settlers were allocated farmland near Port-au-Prince by the Haitian government, but this farming colony would soon prove to be a failure. In the first year after getting settled, approximately a third of the emigrants died of various diseases, and many others returned to the United States. Since Holly left America without the financial backing of the Episcopal Church, his first months in Haiti were enormously challenging for him and his companions: "twelve months of intense suffering, labor, and affliction; (in which time he [Holly] has buried the larger half of his family—mother, wife, and two children)."[88] On rare occasions Holly received sums of money from the Episcopal Church, though it still refused to grant him official missionary status. Happily, these occasional payments became more regular after Holly's first year on the island.[89] By early 1863 Holly and his parishioners had left the farming community and settled in the center of Port-au-Prince. In May 1863 there was an inauguration ceremony for the Holy Trinity Church, the first parish of the Episcopal Church in Haiti.[90]

Through ups and downs Holly held firmly to his convictions and became a Haitian citizen in 1864: "I am now a Haïtien citizen, entitled to all the rights and immunities guaranteed to the same by the constitution and laws of my adopted country. I expect to live and die here."[91] By 1866 Holly had established three additional missionary parishes in Cape Haitian, Les Cayes, and Cabaret-Quatre. Though Holly initially preached essentially to the Black Americans who had emigrated with him, he soon devoted himself mostly to the native Haitians since his emigration project was in truth part of a larger project to evangelize and educate the Haitian people. His followers who eventually became ordained leaders were all Haitian. The first Haitian priests and deacons were ordained in 1866 by the bishop of Maine, who was sent to Haiti especially for this purpose. In 1874 the General Convention of the Episcopal Church created an independent church named the Haitian Apostolic Orthodox Church and conferred on Reverend Holly the title of bishop of Haiti. As an independent church, it received only a small annual grant that was barely enough to feed the clergy. Nevertheless, Holly stayed on the island until his death on March 13, 1911. According to the archives of the Episcopal Church, at the time of Holly's death the Orthodox Apostolic Church of Haiti was composed of fifteen parishes, seven missions, six primary schools, and a clinic. There were fifteen priests and two thousand members.[92] Thus, even if Holly's plans for Black American emigration to Haiti mostly failed, his Haitian evangelization project was a success.

Over the century that followed Haitian independence, the country was looked on with mistrust by whites as a symbol of violent revolution and an emancipation that came with enormous bloodshed. However, for Black Americans, Haiti was a place where full citizenship was accessible. Thus, even if the bloody revolutionary images of Haiti were also present in the minds of some, the Black republic, while not ideal in every way, represented an idealized place as the locus of a harmonic convergence of the values of the diaspora, separatism, and nationalism that animated certain Black American activists. Perhaps for these activists the idea was to follow Haiti's example, but over the first half of the nineteenth century Haiti was especially looked to as a potential refuge at a time when Black Americans were despairing of ever being able to obtain basic rights within the American territory. Haiti had inscribed color within its very constitution and was therefore the only place in the world (besides Liberia after 1847) where Black people could claim to be full citizens of a Black republic; and to a certain extent this gave Haiti the status of "promised land" for the Black diaspora. Emigration to Haiti offered an acceptable alternative that permitted Black Americans to enjoy the rights that were denied to them in the United States—rights that they were mostly disinclined to acquire by emigrating to the African continent, which they considered barbarous.

Black American interest in Haiti during the nineteenth century was not incompatible with their struggle for emancipation and, eventually, equal citizenship inside the United States. In certain respects, Haiti functioned just as Canada had for fugitives along the Underground Railroad, as the North Star that guided abolitionists and other Black American activists toward an ideal of liberty and equality. It stood as an example that could be followed and incarnated the hope of improving one's condition and becoming free citizens with equal rights. In short, despite its unstable political reality, Haiti was an ideal, a model that the Black community turned to many times during the nineteenth century.

Following the example of James Theodore Holly, and notwithstanding the failed experiments of many of their earlier Black brethren, other Black Americans would attempt to settle in Haiti in the second half of the nineteenth century after 1862. Despite all, Haiti would remain an irresistible temptation and source of inspiration for Black Americans. It is worth noting that after finally gaining official U.S. recognition in 1862, only *Black* Americans such as John Mercer Langston and the celebrated Frederick Douglass were sent to Haiti with the title of minister resident and consul general between 1869 and 1900. Although Abraham Lincoln would be the one to nudge the American government into recognizing Haiti, he was not the first American president to name a Black ambassador to Haiti. As the Civil War was raging, the man who would soon emancipate four million Black slaves had other projects in mind for these people, including a colonization project that would involve Haiti.

CHAPTER 4

Abraham Lincoln's Project for Haiti

> It is better for us both, therefore, to be separated.[1]
>
> —ABRAHAM LINCOLN

Abraham Lincoln was a superstitious person. Two of his biographers, Noah Brooks and Carl Sandburg, retell in similar terms how Lincoln supposedly saw his doppelgänger appear in a mirror on the very evening of the day he was elected president of the United States, November 6, 1860.[2] His wife, Mary Todd Lincoln, interpreted this at the time as auguring both Lincoln's future reelection and his premature death: "She thought . . . that the paleness of one of the faces was an omen that [he] should not see life through the last term." Lincoln had seen "*two* separate and distinct images" of himself in a swinging glass.[3] The incident may also be interpreted as symbolizing the allegedly divided or double personality of Lincoln, a man said to be tormented by the conflict between his antislavery convictions and his racial prejudices. The clearest proof of the uneasy reconciliation of these two aspects of his personality can be found by examining his strong inclination in favor of colonization.

Two schools of thought concerning Abraham Lincoln and colonization have coexisted since the earliest days of the first Lincoln biographies.[4] The first believes he was honest, sincere, and direct in his support of colonization.[5] They claim Lincoln was a true colonizationist who supported a project of separation of the races—described by some as "ethnic cleansing"—via an African colonization program.[6] According to this view, colonization was the genuine political preference of the president and not merely a propaganda tool used to mollify Democrats, reassure northern Republican moderates, and calm the white population in the border states—Delaware, Kentucky, Maryland, and Missouri—that practiced slavery but did not secede from the Union and struggled to maintain a precarious neutrality.[7]

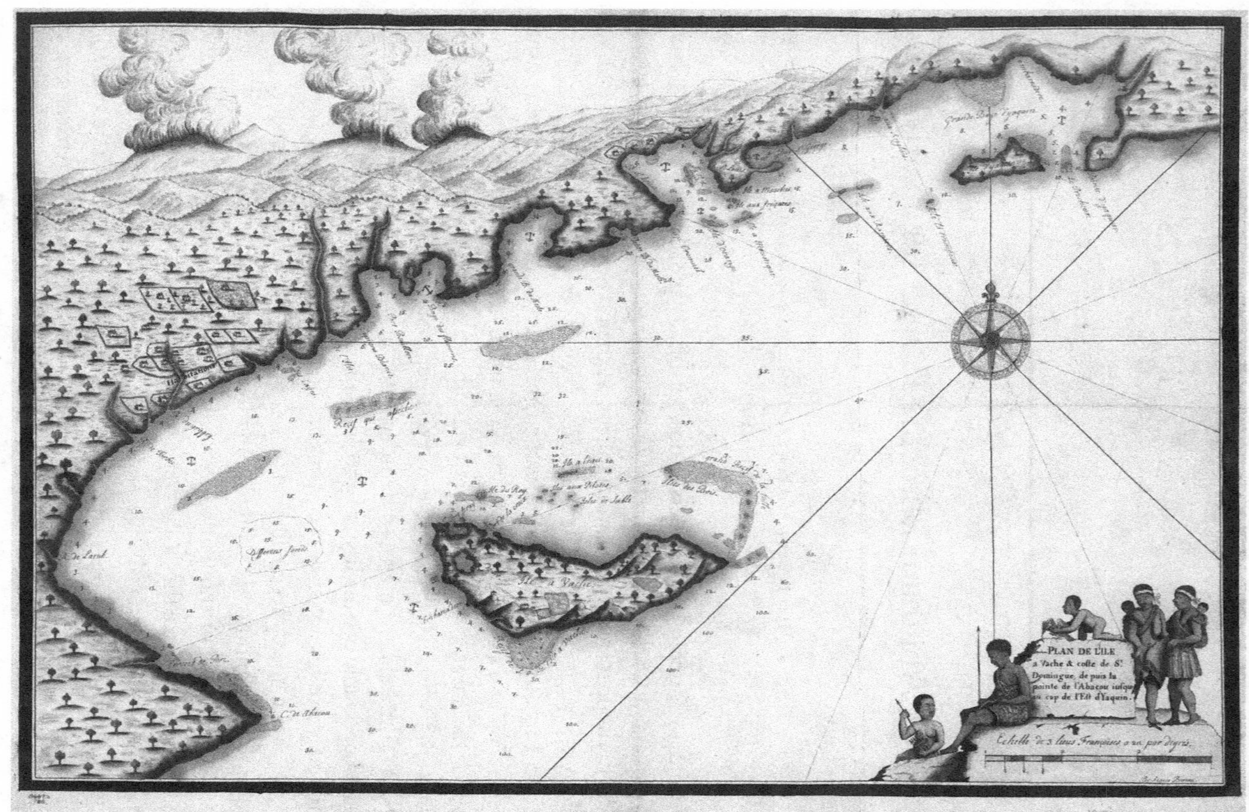

FIG. 4. Jacques Bureau, "Map of Ile à Vache," *Plan de l'Ile a Vache & coste de St. Domingue de puis la pointe de l'Abacou iusquau cap de l'est d'Yaquin,"* [?, 1700]. *Geography and Map Division, Library of Congress, Washington, D.C.*

As one would expect, historians in the other camp take the exact opposite position and claim that prior to 1863 Lincoln was using colonization as a propaganda tool. They believe it was part of a public relations strategy, and therefore they see his procolonization stance as merely a pose and not proof of racism. They say it was Lincoln's way of responding to concerns among Democrats about the race-mixing that would eventually follow emancipation, and to the growing fear in the North about a wave of emancipated slaves flooding northern cities.[8] In this view, colonization would be a smokescreen that allowed Lincoln to advance his emancipation project while deflecting the barbs of public opinion and his political adversaries with a colonization scheme that he knew full well to be unworkable.[9]

To this day, there has been no resolution of these opposing views. It is likely that Abraham Lincoln did not have just one plan for saving the Union but several. Colonization was one option among many, and it is easy to imagine that while Lincoln may have been perfectly lucid about the impossibility of deporting and resettling elsewhere the entire Black American population, he may have yet genuinely wished to reduce the number of Black people in America as a way to lower racial tensions by having fewer free people of color inhabiting the cities and states of the Union.

Lincoln may have had antislavery convictions and believed "that all mankind should be free";[10] but he had also inherited the practices and beliefs of the people native to the Old Northwest where he had been raised and where he would spend much of his life.[11] Most in this region were partisans of "free labor." This ideology, the centerpiece of Lincoln's Republican Party, considered all labor in a free society to be honorable. Slavery, by dint of its mere coexistence alongside free labor, devalued the latter and the free laborers who were de facto placed in competition with slaves. For Lincoln, free and honest men who worked hard could improve their lot in life and rise up the social ladder. He himself had done physical labor, first with his father, then as a regular employee, and therefore came to believe that any man could improve his condition through work, and that Black people, being men, also had the right to have their chance at improving their condition by freely working, harvesting, and storing up the fruits of their labor.[12]

That said, and regardless of what the true motives of the Great Emancipator may have been, like many politicians, antislavery partisans, and abolitionists before him, Lincoln turned to colonization to get around the tricky problem of how to live together. Thus he sought to promote a procolonization policy right up to the enactment of the Emancipation Proclamation and arguably until his assassination in 1865.

The Recognition of Haiti: A Means toward Colonization?

Historian Benjamin Quarles claims that "In Lincoln's thinking, compensated emancipation was doomed unless it could be tied in with deportation." With colonization, "Slavery and the race problem would thus vanish simultaneously."[13] Lincoln only had to find the ideal place where he could deport Black people "emancipated" by his future proclamation. Although for a time he had been a member of the Illinois branch of the American Colonization Society and had also received the former president of Liberia at the White House in August 1862, Lincoln believed that Africa was much too far away to imagine resettling a large number of Black people there—the transportation costs alone being enormous. He was also aware that most Black Americans who wished to emigrate wanted to stay on the American side of the Atlantic Ocean.[14]

One of the options geographically ready to hand at the start of Lincoln's first term was Haiti. At the time Lincoln took office, emigration to Haiti was fully underway, and it is impossible that Lincoln did not get wind of it since the text of President Geffrard's offer and the propagandistic articles of his official agent, James Redpath, were then being published in various periodicals and in every state. In 1861, therefore, Haiti was a tempting option that offered several advantages: free people of color had already been going there voluntarily for many years without the American government needing to participate in cost-sharing; the Haitian government was manifestly desperate to attract this labor force; and geographically speaking, one could not imagine a better solution than this close but not too close location. Thus, in addition to the purely commercial and diplomatic reasons, it is the possibility of relocating free Black Americans to Haiti that leads Lincoln to ask Congress to formerly recognize Haiti as a nation-state.

At the time Abraham Lincoln raises the possibility of recognizing Haiti (and Liberia, the other Black republic) before the U.S. Congress on December 3, 1861, it had already been a long-standing request of Black Americans as Lincoln must also have known. And Black Americans were not the only ones pleading the case for recognition. Many white businessmen and politicians were also airing their grievances and underlining the regrettable negative influence that the nonrecognition of the Black republic had on their affairs and for the country.

However, regarding emigration to Haiti in the 1820s at least, the Haitian historian Jacques Nicolas Léger, who would later serve his country in the U.S. as envoy extraordinary and minister plenipotentiary, points out that

> There was nothing to be hoped for [from the U.S.]; slave holders were all-powerful. As such, they could hardly go along with seeing former slaves build themselves into a sovereign nation, and would certainly not pardon the audacity of Haitians turning their island territory into an asylum of freedom for those whose skin color had until then forced them to put up with a degrading yoke [in the United States].[15]

In other words, the nonrecognition of Haiti by the United States could be explained by the skin color of the island's inhabitants and the political sway of slaveholders over American foreign policy.[16] The enormous amount of trade between Haiti and the United States at the time ought to have been reason enough to justify recognition. Granted, on the American side it was mostly northern states that had trade relations with Haiti. Southerners, especially after the insurrections led by the slave Gabriel and then by Denmark Vesey, were less interested in the Haitian market.[17] In any case, the federal government completely ignored the question of recognition for over fifty years.

When Lincoln finally made a formal request to Congress for the recognition of Haiti and Liberia, the great European powers of the day—France, Great Britain, Spain, but also smaller countries such as Denmark, Holland, Belgium, Portugal, Sweden, and Austria—all already had a diplomat stationed in Haiti. Liberia had been recognized by Great Britain a few months after it declared its independence (1848), and French recognition came in 1852.[18] Thus it may be that Lincoln's first reason for deciding to seek official recognition for Haiti was a hope that doing so would improve American's reputation abroad and lead the great European powers to side with the North.[19]

Meanwhile, James Redpath was doggedly continuing with his efforts to gain official recognition for Haiti, notably by using his network of acquaintances. In his communication with the Haitian government, he mentions Senator Charles Sumner, the editor in chief of the *New York Tribune*, a newspaper closely aligned with the Republican Party, but also Montgomery Blair, an abolitionist and Radical Republican, who held the position of postmaster general under Lincoln from 1861 to 1864.

There is no trace of any private correspondence between James Redpath and Abraham Lincoln. However, when Lincoln took office, it is likely that he knew of the movement of Black voluntary emigration to Haiti and knew Redpath was one of the driving forces behind the movement because of the many articles he had published on the subject in several periodicals, including some prominent ones in the North, and also because Lincoln and Redpath had some common acquaintances. It is worth noting that Redpath began publishing the *Pine and Palm* to promote emigration to Haiti and American recognition of the country just weeks after Lincoln's inauguration. Certain documents within the archives of the Haytian Bureau of Emigration also confirm that Lincoln was aware of the efforts of Redpath and Geffrard, which suggests that he called for official recognition of Haiti in December 1861 because Black emigration to the island was already well underway.

Before Lincoln took office, Redpath had already arranged an interview between the future president and one of his white agents, Richard J. Hinton, who had been involved in the creation of the Republican Party. This is one sign among others of Redpath's lobbying efforts in favor of recognition for Haiti.[20] Shortly after this first indirect contact with Lincoln, Redpath had a letter about his emigration plan delivered to Lincoln by way of Judge W. M. F. Arny of Kansas. Redpath hoped to convince Lincoln "how a hearty endorsement of this scheme of Emigration will help the Republican party" and that it was already as popular as the California gold rush: "It takes like the California fever." He then expresses his preference for indirect support: "I don't ask Mr. Lincoln publicly to endorse or say anything about this scheme, but his private influence might be of service to it." Redpath announces that "Mr. Hinton has already spoken in my name to the President elect—with regard to the Question of a recognition of Haytian Independence" and claims "leading Republicans [George Andrews Greely, Montgomery Blair, Charles A. Dana] approve this future Question, one which Mr. Lincoln will have to meet." Aware that receiving a Black ambassador or a Black diplomatic agent could harm the Lincoln administration, Redpath promises that the Haitian government shall send no emissary while Lincoln is in office, if only the president could assure him that he would work toward a rapid recognition of Haiti.[21]

Redpath also directed his lobbying at Senator Charles Sumner of Massachusetts, who was already supportive of his cause. In one of many letters to Sumner dated March 17, 1861, Redpath asks the senator to intercede on his behalf with Lincoln's cabinet on the matter of diplomatic relations with Haiti:

> The recognition of Haytian Independence would greatly facilitate my work. It would give a greater impetus to emigration than anything that the Cabinet could do. Mr. Blair is strongly in favor of any [unreadable] and intimated that wherever he could he would use his influence for Recognition.[22]

At the same time Redpath was continuing his propaganda campaign in the *Pine and Palm*, he kept close tabs on the actions of certain political groups that favored recognition and regularly sent detailed updates to the Haitian government. In one of his reports from March 1861, Redpath announces that the Ohio state senate recently passed a resolution calling for the U.S. Congress to recognize Haiti, adding that the resolution was the result of his handiwork.

> Last Week the Senate of Ohio passed a Resolution urging the Congress of the United States to recognize the independence of Hayti. This was the result of movements inaugurated by this Bureau.[23]

Redpath's best allies in the fight to obtain recognition for Haiti were the American merchants adversely affected by the taxes imposed by Haiti on goods originating in countries that did not officially recognize the Black republic. These merchants used business associates they sent to Haiti to express sympathy with the Haitian cause.[24] Seth Webb, for example, an American businessman in Port-au-Prince, sent a letter dated September 4, 1861, to Lincoln's secretary of state, William H. Seward, in which he forcefully explains that not recognizing Haiti is a disaster for American commerce and is destroying the influence of the American government and its business interests in Haiti.[25] There is no doubt that pressure from merchants and businessmen like Webb was as important as pressure from politicians in moving Lincoln toward his decision in favor of recognition and to call for it in his annual message to Congress on December 3, 1861.

Lincoln raises the question of official recognition of the two Black republics, Haiti and Liberia, in fairly straightforward terms: "If any good reason exists why we should persevere longer in withholding our recognition of the independence and sovereignty of Hayti and Liberia, I am unable to discern it."[26] In less than thirty words, Lincoln puts an end to fifty-eight years of American dithering about recognizing Haiti and grants Liberia the recognition it so clearly needed.[27] But Lincoln was not only defending American business interests, since later in the same address he also evoked contrabands (i.e., fugitive slaves) and colonization—clear proof that emancipation, recognition of the Black republics, and colonization were intrinsically linked in the mind of the Great Emancipator.

As for the practical details of the recognition itself, the day after Lincoln's address, Charles Sumner took up the complex task of defending Haitian and Liberian (and American) interests by immediately calling for a vote to authorize the government to send diplomatic representatives to Haiti and Liberia. On December 4, 1861, on Sumner's request, the question of establishing diplomatic relations with the governments of Haiti and Liberia was forwarded to the Congressional Committee on Foreign Affairs, and on February 4, 1862,

Sumner read aloud on the Senate floor "A Bill to Authorize the Appointment of Diplomatic Representatives to the Republics of Hayti and Liberia." After a second reading on April 22, 1862, it was decided that it would be further debated in the Senate the next day.[28]

After opening with a brief idyllic description of the two Black republics and their respective histories, Sumner uses his Senate speech on April 23, 1862, to point out that this recognition was first requested by Boston and New York merchants of every political persuasion many years ago, as well as by distinguished politicians such as John Quincy Adams, in the interest of improved commerce. Sumner reinforces his argument with statistical evidence stating that Haiti ranks twenty-seventh among America's trading partners, well above Sweden, Norway, and Austria, as well as the French West Indies and British colonies.[29] Sumner next turns to the threat of a possible invasion of Haiti by its Spanish neighbor or its former occupier, France, to say that Haiti desperately needs America's recognition to protect itself from malevolent European powers while also recalling that these and other powers had already granted recognition. Sumner gives little attention to the matter of America's recognition of Liberia since it is a fundamentally different case with its American and pacific (not French and revolutionary) origin story under the auspices of the American Colonization Society. In Sumner's concluding remarks in favor of true ambassadors and not mere consuls to give the proper weight to America's future diplomatic presence in Haiti, he subtly and succinctly introduces the notion that "Emigrants to these republics will be multiplied by such a recognition."[30] Colonization by free people of color was more present than ever in public discussions at the start of 1862 and was indissociable from the question of recognition for Haiti and Liberia within Lincoln's emancipation project. After some lively exchanges about the inevitable obligation for the U.S. to welcome on its soil dark-skinned ambassadors from these newly recognized republics, the bill passed in the Senate with thirty-two votes in favor and seven opposed.[31]

On June 2, 1852, House member Daniel Gooch, another Massachusetts Republican, calls for a vote on the Senate bill:

> Justice, sound policy, political wisdom, commercial interest, the example of other governments, and the wishes of the people of our own, all demand that we recognize the independence of Hayti and Liberia, and that, in our intercourse with them, we place them on the same footing as other independent nations.[32]

However, Gooch's generous spirit was not widely shared in the House of Representatives. Democrat Samuel S. Cox of Ohio proposed an amendment calling for the appointment of a consul general to the two republics for the sole purpose of negotiating trade deals. Claiming the bill to recognize Haiti was "literally a Black Republican measure," Cox confessed his disgust at the idea of "receiving a black man on an equal footing with the white men of this country" and added that his view was backed by "Every objection which instinct, race, prejudice, and institutions make." According to Cox, white Americans would mock such ridiculous ambassadors, and contrabands would welcome them as "ebony demi-god[s]."[33] Cox, along with other House Democrats such as Charles J. Biddle of Pennsylvania, claimed that the Senate bill was a disguised maneuver to prepare the way for emancipation, to which Congressman Blair of Missouri replied with a call for resettling the future emancipated Black people outside the country, which then gave rise to a heated discussion about colonization to Haiti and Liberia.[34]

Cox's amendment was finally rejected, and the Senate bill was approved in the House by a vote of eighty-six to thirty-seven. This legislation, "An Act to Authorize the President of the United States to Appoint Diplomatic Representatives to the Republics of Hayti and Liberia, Respectively," was signed into law by Abraham Lincoln on June 5, 1862.[35] The law authorized the president to nominate ambassadors who, after consent of the Senate, would take up their diplomatic posts in Haiti and Liberia under the title commissioner and U.S. consul general. The next day, Lincoln submitted his nomination of Benjamin F. Whidden of New Hampshire to be commissioner to Haiti, and confirmation from the Senate occurred on July 12, 1862, this being then the date we may consider as the official starting point of America's recognition of Haiti.[36]

The recognition of Haiti and Liberia was not the only business undertaken in Lincoln's Annual Message of December 3, 1861. Lincoln also broached the matter of fugitive slaves, the so-called contrabands, which he proposed to relocate while adding that it would be wise to include Black Americans who were already free in this colonization project. Through this message Lincoln clearly revealed the line of thinking in the area of race relations that he would pursue over the next two years.

Abraham Lincoln's Colonization Project in Central America

The Lincoln administration included three notable colonizationists, besides Lincoln himself, and each held a key post within the government: Edward Bates was Lincoln's attorney general; Montgomery Blair served as postmaster-general; and Caleb B. Smith was secretary of the interior until health problems forced him to resign in late December 1862. Lincoln and his allies quickly joined forces to make colonization "one element of a strategy for promoting gradual abolition in the border states."[37]

Together they promoted their "hobby" in a variety of subtle and secretive ways.[38] In March 1861, just one month into the war, Lincoln had already instructed Elisha Crosby, his newly appointed ambassador to Guatemala, to acquire land for the establishment of a Black colony to be managed "more or less under the protection of the U.S. Government."[39] But Guatemala was not the only possible location imagined by Lincoln's cabinet. As already mentioned, Lincoln was not generally interested in Africa, which among other factors he considered too far away; and therefore he focused his attention on Central and South America. For example, there was the small region of Chiriquí, a disputed territory between Colombia and Costa Rica.

Several years before colonization became an official pursuit of the Lincoln administration, Ambrose W. Thompson, a Philadelphia shipbuilder who had also founded a coal mining company, the Chiriquí Improvement Company (CIC), had already reached out in 1858 to Lincoln's predecessor, President James Buchanan, to encourage colonization in Chiriquí—but without much success. Thompson did not give up, however, and contacted Lincoln at the start of his presidency through Gideon Welles, then secretary of the navy, sometime between May and August of 1861. In early August, a brother-in-law of Lincoln's wife, Ninian W. Edwards, submitted a report on Thompson's proposal. The report makes subtle allusion to the possibility of resettling Black Americans in Chiriquí. About this same time, Lincoln appears to have decided to withdraw the dossier from Welles and turn the idea over to Caleb B. Smith, whom he knew was favorably disposed to colonization. It is also believed he advised Thompson to make contact with the colonizationist Francis Preston Blair Sr. (Montgomery Blair's father) in order to draft a new project before the end of the year that would combine coal mining and colonization.[40]

The project was probably abandoned in early 1862. During his annual message of December 3, 1861, Lincoln made plain his colonization ideas, though without specifying a destination. In that message he asks Congress to conceive of establishing colonies, preferably in Central America, for the resettlement of emancipated slaves, contrabands, and also Black Americans who had already been free for some time. It is worth noting that in midsummer 1861, Congress had passed a law authorizing Union soldiers to seize slaves from their Confederate owners on the grounds that the slaves were "property used for insurrectionary purposes."[41]

By recommending the resettlement of Black slaves recently confiscated from their masters, Lincoln was attempting to relieve the Union of a considerable financial burden, since these confiscated pieces of property were now dependent persons, in effect temporary wards of the state. And by proposing to extend the colonization option to all free Black Americans without distinction, Lincoln was probably hoping to kill two birds with one stone: solving both a budgetary problem and the vexed problem of how the different "races" would live together, which was a divisive issue among northerners. Without naming any particular location, Lincoln advanced his view that colonization could take place "at some place, or places, in a climate congenial to them." And he made this recommendation to Congress in the same speech, let us remember, in which he called for official recognition of Haiti.[42] Although most historians believe Lincoln was thinking of Chiriquí during his annual message of December 3, 1861, we believe he probably also had his eyes turned toward Haiti, in no small part because Redpath had already been pulling at his ear about the favorable possibilities for both colonization and business on that island.

Moreover, while the Senate Foreign Relations Committee was still occupied with recognition of Haiti, in the House of Representatives on April 7, 1862, a nine-person committee was charged with a complementary mission:

> to inquire and report to this House . . . whether any plan can be proposed and recommended for the gradual emancipation of all the African slaves, and the extinction of slavery in the States of Delaware, Maryland, Virginia, Kentucky, Tennessee, and Missouri . . . ; and . . . whether colonization of such emancipated slaves on this continent or elsewhere is a necessary concomitant of their freedom.[43]

Momentum in favor of colonization grew quickly, and Lincoln soon had the financial backing from Congress to go forward with his project. A first step was a law passed on April 16, 1862, abolishing slavery in the District of Columbia, which also allocated $100,000 to finance colonization. The law stipulated that the president would be able to freely spend this money on the project so long as payments per emigrant did not exceed $100.[44] Some months later, on July 16, 1862, a second law in Lincoln's favor budgeted an additional $500,000, "to be used at the discretion of the President" for relocating newly freed Black men and women from the District of Columbia or "to colonize those to be made free by the probable passage of a confiscation bill."[45] A third law, known as the Second Confiscation Act, was passed on July 16, 1862:

> [T]he President of the United States is hereby authorized to make provision for the transportation, colonization, and settlement, in some tropical

> country beyond the limits of the United States, of such persons of the African race, made free by the provisions of this act, as may be willing to emigrate, having first obtained the consent of the government of said country to their protection and settlement within the same, with all the rights and privileges of freemen.[46]

On April 1862, some days after colonization became federal policy, Ambrose Thompson (the son of Ambrose W. Thompson) wrote at length to Abraham Lincoln with the aim of reviving his father's project. After claiming that Liberia and Haiti were "strongly objectionable" destinations, Thompson launched into a long plea for Chiriquí, including an itemization of expected costs.[47] Starting in early May 1862, Caleb B. Smith supposedly tried to convince Lincoln to make a contractual arrangement with Ambrose W. Thompson for the colonization of free and emancipated Black people to Chiriquí while specifying that it was impossible to offer any guarantees about it ever becoming a future sovereign colony.[48]

Meanwhile, U.S. relations with Costa Rica, one of the two nations claiming sovereignty over the province of Chiriquí, were not altogether sunny. In June 1862, after hearing rumors about a pending colonization expedition to Chiriquí, the Costa Rican ambassador in Washington spoke with the American secretary of state, William H. Seward, to say that the United States ought not to attempt building independent colonies there, and he reminded Seward of the already tense territorial dispute between Colombia and Costa Rica. In addition, since 1860, Colombia had been experiencing civil war and had even sent two separate delegations to the United States, which made it all the more difficult for the Americans to understand who controlled what and who had the real negotiating power to sign an agreement concerning the colonization of Chiriquí.[49] However these rather farcical circumstances did not slow Lincoln's determination to carry on. Even though no proper contract was able to be signed with any diplomatic representative of either Costa Rica or Colombia, Lincoln continued to believe in the project and understandably sought to persuade Black Americans to sign up.

In the summer of 1862 Lincoln gave further momentum to the Chiriquí emigration project by naming Reverend James Mitchell as his commissioner of emigration. Mitchell's first task was to convene a meeting of leading Black Americans in Washington so that Lincoln could convince them of the merits of his emigration project, with the idea that they would then enthusiastically relay the plan throughout the Black community.[50] Lincoln had met Mitchell in 1853,[51] and since that time the two colonizationists had corresponded regularly, as one can tell from the large number of letters preserved in the Abraham Lincoln papers.[52]

Although the way in which this delegation of Black leaders was constituted did not please everyone,[53] the upshot was that five leading members of the free Black community in Washington, D.C.—John T. Costin, Cornelius Clark, John F. Cook Jr., Benjamin McCoy, and their leader, Edward Thomas—arrived at the White House on August 14, 1862. However, this meeting only occurred after an earlier assembly at the Union Bethel AME Church, where two resolutions were adopted expressing the group's reticence about emigration and their refusal to make a firm and definitive decision about a question that in truth ought to be put to the four million people concerned.[54] It should be added that on the same day they received the president's invitation, Lincoln was welcoming to the White House the former president of Liberia, Joseph J. Roberts, and a representative of the American Colonization Society—a meeting that the Black people gathered at the Union Bethel Church believed did not augur well for them.

The five men quickly understood that they were not being invited to a respectful dialogue with the president but instead had been recruited to be a passive audience listening to emigrationist propaganda, with the idea that they were to be the vehicle to make Lincoln's colonizationist position known and promote it both in the Black community of Washington, D.C., and more generally to the entire population, Black and white, of the whole country. It should be noted that this interview took place with a stenographer present, and Lincoln's statement was soon published in newspapers across the country.[55]

The purpose of the statement is easily summarized. A first goal was to inform the Black Americans that a sum of money had been granted to the president by Congress that would facilitate the emigration of free and emancipated Black people who wished to leave the United States. The related goal was to get them to think seriously about taking advantage of this financial assistance from the government. Lincoln used arguments tinged with racism to convince his audience. They should leave, he said, because their very presence was a source of mutual suffering for Blacks and whites. Lincoln affirms that their presence and the institution of slavery caused the Civil War—"But for your race among us there could not be war, although many men engaged on either side do not care for you one way or the other"—and so, "It is better for us both, therefore, to be separated."[56]

Furthermore, Lincoln calls Black people who would refuse to the leave the country "selfish," and recommends instead that they act in the general interest of their community, by which he meant also the slave population. Lincoln argues that the first phase of this colonization effort should not be undertaken by slaves or recently freed Black people, on the grounds that they were less intelligent and capable than Black Americans who were free from birth or had been so for a long time. He also tries to convince his listeners that on American territory they would never gain equality and that as members of the Black elite (as free people of color of long standing), they should set a good example to the rest of their community, especially those still operating under the yoke of slavery, and leave. He asks the free people of color of Washington, D.C., whom he compliments as being "capable of thinking as white men," to accept to leave the country of their birth for the good of their "race."[57] All that remained was the matter of choosing the place for their resettlement.

Realizing with some surprise that Black Americans wished to remain geographically close to whites to whom they seemed "attached," Lincoln rejected Liberia as a destination.[58] Instead, he tells them, "The place I am thinking about having for a colony is in Central America." Without revealing its name or exact location, he says, "The country is a very excellent one for any people, and with great natural resources and advantages, and especially because of the similarity of climate with your native land—thus being suited to your physical condition."[59] These favorable natural conditions, which "afford an opportunity to the inhabitants for immediate employment," make it an ideal destination. Lincoln ends by conceding that the "the political affairs in Central America are not in quite as satisfactory condition as I wish," but he promises to do everything in his power to guarantee that they will be treated well, at least as well as the local elites: "Besides, I would endeavor to have you made equals, and have the best assurance that you should be the equals of the best." In concrete terms, Lincoln wished this Black delegation to commit to finding at least fifty Black volunteers for starters—among whom "twenty-five able-bodied men, with a mixture of women and children" willing to accept deportation and resettlement "for the good of mankind." After Lincoln had finished his presentation, Edward M. Thomas stated that he would consult among his peers and provide an answer as soon as possible, to which Lincoln replied, "Take your full time—no hurry at all," and their meeting came to a close.[60]

The answer was not long in coming. Thomas, the leader of the delegation, sent Lincoln a letter only two days after their interview. In the letter, Thomas expresses his support for Lincoln's plan, and his use of the pronoun "we" suggests that he is speaking with the general accord and in the name of the Black community. Thomas says that he wishes to discuss the "movement of emigration" Lincoln favors with the "leading colored men in Philadelphia, New York and Boston." Furthermore, he adds, although his community had been "entirely hostile to the movement" before their meeting of August 14, 1862, he now says, "we believe that our friends and co-laborers for our race in these cities will . . . join heartily in sustaining such a movement." Thomas also announces that he will be sending two Black emissaries to each of these cities to enlighten the Black population about the advantages of emigration (suggesting in passing that these emissaries have their expenses paid out of the newly created colonization fund) and he promises to keep Lincoln informed about the "success" of this mission.[61]

Although Thomas gave no indication that there was anything less than a total consensus about colonization in Washington's Black community, there is evidence that he was actually operating on his own and had consulted with no one before writing to the president.[62] In truth, the subject of colonization was more than ever a source of conflict and division, and Thomas was only one among those of his peers, such as Henry McNeal Turner (an influential Black pastor in Washington, D.C.) or Henry Highland Garnet, who supported the various colonization projects that had emerged off and on over the previous decade.[63]

After his meeting with the delegation of Black leaders, Lincoln asked Caleb B. Smith to recruit a supervisor for the future Chiriquí colony. The Republican senator from Kansas Samuel Pomeroy was contacted, and he accepted to play a role in the colonization project. The choice of Pomeroy is rather mysterious given that in April 1862 this radical abolitionist had voted against granting Lincoln a colonization fund and had publicly mocked the emigration plan in June of the same year.[64]

At any rate, the letters that autumn from Pomeroy to Smith and Lincoln clearly indicate that the Chiriquí project had some support within the Black community. Despite the internal divisions we have mentioned, as well as the strong opposition of certain radical abolitionists,[65] thousands of Black people volunteered to emigrate to Chiriquí. According to Senator Pomeroy, as many as 4,000 Black Americans had come forward by mid-September 1862, which was the moment when Lincoln approved the CIC contract prepared by Caleb Smith that explicitly named Pomeroy as supervisor.[66] This number climbed to 13,700 by the end of October. In a letter to Lincoln dated April 16, 1862, in which Pomeroy deeply regrets the abandonment of the project, he alludes to 14,000 volunteers, a figure, if true, that would have represented a higher number of Black people than the total emigration to Liberia since the founding of the American Colonization Society in 1816. Pomeroy's numbers may be questioned, but there is little doubt that a large number of Black men and women had volunteered—perhaps encouraged by the publication on September 22,

1862, of the preliminary Emancipation Proclamation that clearly disclosed colonization as intrinsically linked to freeing the slaves.[67]

Quite suddenly, on September 24, 1862, Lincoln decided to halt the project before a single ship had sailed for Chiriquí. There were many reasons, including suspicion of corruption. Pomeroy and Thompson were suspected of embezzlement and accused of using colonization funds in ways that were not transparent.[68] Another reason was that the dispute between Costa Rica and Colombia showed no sign of resolution. In addition, it was determined that the coal in Chiriquí was of poor quality.[69] A final reason for shutting down the Chiriquí project definitively was that Colombia supposedly did not want to welcome Black people to the region because they would endanger the fragile racial balance in the country. At the time, Chiriquí was "the whitest part of the country," and Black Americans might have suffered even more from racial prejudice there than in the United States.[70]

At the very least, the Chiriquí failure served to push Lincoln to change strategies for carrying out his colonization vision. It is said that the impediments encountered in that first experiment encouraged Lincoln to abandon partnerships with private companies and to turn instead to direct negotiations with nations accepting to receive Black Americans. One sign of this change was that supervision of the whole matter passed from the Department of the Interior to the State Department tasked with managing foreign affairs.[71] However this shift was not immediate, as can be seen in the Île-à-Vache experiment.

The Colonization of Île-à-Vache: Abraham Lincoln's Haitian Experiment[72]

Though disappointed by the failure of his Central American project, Lincoln was unwilling to renounce all colonization. For instance, he requested that Secretary of State William H. Seward draft and send a letter to European powers (notably Great Britain, France, the Netherlands, and Denmark) and to the new republics in Central America. The letter announced that President Lincoln was ready to enter into negotiations with any nation willing to welcome Black Americans in their territory or in their tropical colonies. The letter had little success.[73]

Furthermore, while Congress, his secretary of the interior, his commissioner for emigration, and many Black Americans (especially after the August 14, 1862, meeting) were all focused on the Chiriquí project, Lincoln was laying the groundwork for a parallel colonization project in Haiti. The historiography considers the Haitian project of secondary importance, claiming that it only really came into existence following the aborted Chiriquí project. And yet there is evidence that Lincoln had already been thinking of Haiti somewhat earlier and then continued to consider the possibility of colonization there in parallel with the Chiriquí project.[74] In this view, Haiti was not a last-ditch effort by Lincoln but rather a project of long-standing interest on a par with Chiriquí. The advancement of the former after the abandonment of the latter can be understood as related to the timeline of U.S. recognition of Haiti. Indeed, before diplomatic relations between the two countries existed, it was difficult to seriously present such an option to the American people. In calling for American recognition of Haiti, Lincoln clearly had colonization in mind, as we have already established by noting its evocation in the famous December 3, 1861, annual message to Congress, and in Lincoln's indirect contact with James Redpath prior to December 1861. Lincoln was fully aware of all that Haiti represented in the minds of the Black American community, and he knew that several thousand Black men and women had already left for Haiti between 1859 and the day of his December report to Congress.

Lincoln's Haiti experiment began nine months later in the fall of 1862 when Bernard Kock, an American businessman, signed a ten-year contract with Haiti giving him permission to pursue agricultural projects on Île-à-Vache. Kock met with Caleb B. Smith at the start of September 1862—in other words, a few weeks before the collapse of the Chiriquí project—to discuss the idea of resettling Black Americans in Haiti. Kock was very persuasive as he shared the details of his contract with the Haitian government—claiming that nothing could be done on the island without his permission, that no Haitians lived there year-round, and that after ten years the whole island would belong completely to him. Furthermore, Kock promised to furnish all the infrastructure, materials, and services necessary for the well-being of Black arrivals on the island—including doctors, churches, and schools. He asked only that the American government accept to pay for the transportation of the future settlers and a lump sum for the purchase of the first provisions and other essentials to get the colony started properly. Smith is said to have been pleased with this idea, which seemed easier to accomplish than the Chiriquí project.[75]

Following this first promising meeting, Kock sent and soon published an open letter to Lincoln restating all the points he had gone over with Smith. In this pamphlet-like document, signed by Kock and bearing an unidentifiable seal, the businessman asks Lincoln for assistance "in providing immediate employment and permanent homes for five thousand or more of these destitute people"—referring to "contrabands who have found their way within the lines of our [Union] armies." He mentions the geography and climate of his "plan of colonization" on what he refers to as "my island," and tells Lincoln that, originally, he had planned to recruit German and Swiss laborers, but his sympathy for the contrabands and his desire to serve his president's "desire to colonize them" have given him this other idea:

> My original intention was to employ Germans and Swiss to cultivate cotton; but, after seeing the contrabands, and learning their destitute condition, their anxiety to be employed, and Your Excellency's desire to colonize them, I yielded to the solicitation of their friends, and have determined, with your assistance, to take at least five thousand.

In this letter, signed "Bernard Kock, Governor of A'Vache Island," the businessman promises to reimburse the American government for all the expenses the latter would pay over the first two years, with the exception of transportation costs and the cost of feeding the colonists during the initial period of acclimatization.[76] Three days later, Kock sent a second personal letter to Lincoln requesting a private interview with the president to discuss "the subject of *colonizing* the Island of A'Vache (Hayti), with Contrabands."[77] The same day (a coincidence or planned?), Jacob R. S. Van Vleet, co-editor of the *National Republican,* also wrote a long letter to the president in which he supports Kock's project, reviewing all the same points though with some key differences, such as the duration of Kock's contract (twenty years and not ten, as Kock had said) or that Kock was only asking for financial assistance for the first thousand colonists and would pay all expenses of the other four thousand himself.[78] Kock next sent a letter to James Mitchell similar to the one he had sent to Lincoln. Meanwhile, President Geffrard of Haiti ordered Colonel Ernest Roumain to Washington, where he supposedly convinced Mitchell of the plan's interest. To avoid a repeat of the Chiriquí debacle, Lincoln asked Pomeroy to do a background check on Kock, which resulted in a very favorable report about the businessman.[79] Kock was also highly recommended to Lincoln by William E. Robinson, a New York editor and politician. Therefore, in December 1862, it is unlikely that Lincoln had any reason to doubt Kock's honesty.[80]

In his annual message on December 1, 1862, Lincoln reaffirmed his support for colonization, giving it now both an economic and social justification: "[to] reduce the supply of black labor by colonizing the black laborer out of the country, and by precisely so much you increase the demand for and wages of white labor."[81] He is also no longer speaking in favor of Central America as a destination but instead recommending Haiti and Liberia. He expresses regret that Black Americans are not more enthusiastic about these destinations, but he says he is optimistic about their future support for these colonization plans.[82]

At the end of the month, on December 31, 1862, the eve of the publication of the Emancipation Proclamation, Lincoln signed a contract with Bernard Kock. Even though colonization does not appear in the final Emancipation Proclamation of January 1, 1863,[83] it is difficult to not see the connection between it and the signing of the contract with Kock, especially in light of Lincoln's procolonization statements in the annual message of December 1, 1862. It is clear that in Lincoln's mind colonization and emancipation were closely linked. One could call the former the doppelgänger of the latter, its "evil twin," the morally dubious double alongside the benevolence and altruism of emancipation. And those two were indissociable from the third step of granting formal recognition to the Black republics in what would then be a sort of Lincoln triptych or equilateral triangle.

Shortly after signing the contract with Kock, Lincoln received news about Kock's dishonesty. The source was probably William Seward,[84] but the news also came from John Palmer Usher, who had taken over from Caleb B. Smith, and from Benjamin Whidden, the American diplomat stationed in Port-au-Prince. Whidden urged Lincoln to renounce the contract by getting Seward to not allow the government's seal to be placed on it. It turns out Kock was not the sole architect of the Haitian project. He had two associates, both New York businessmen, Charles K. Tuckerman and Paul S. Forbes, who had already invested $70,000, and they were unwilling to simply walk away from the project.[85] After learning that the contract between Kock and the American government had been suspended, they traveled to Washington to negotiate directly. Tuckerman and Forbes stated that Kock deeded exploitation rights on Île-à-Vache to them, and the pair now proposed an initial transport of five hundred Blacks financed by the American government in the form of either fifty dollars per emigrant or, alternatively, the payment of all transportation costs and all means of subsistence necessary for their first six months on the island.[86] To save money and time, the two men pressed the Lincoln administration to allow them to transport the first emigrants before the signing of an accord with the Haitian government that was intended to guarantee decent living conditions for the new Black settlers—an accord that, in fact, would never be signed.[87] Thus, on April 14, 1863, the *Ocean Ranger* left Fort Monroe, Virginia, with roughly five hundred African American emigrants aboard and headed to Île-à-Vache. The emigrants, probably contrabands, were accompanied by Bernard Kock, who had been named governor of the future colony by

Tuckerman and Forbes—a detail that the two men scrupulously withheld in their talks with Lincoln's advisers.[88]

Very soon, the Haitian dream of the few voluntary Black American emigrants to Île-à-Vache became a nightmare. Kock seized all their belongings and exchanged their American dollars for bank notes he had fabricated himself. He also mistreated them to the point of provoking their open revolt. At least these are the allegations that appear in a June 25, 1863, letter written by James De Long, the American consul present in Les Cayes. According to De Long, the emigrants, about 450 in number, were living in rustic conditions, sleeping on the ground, and had been physically and psychologically abused by Kock. He adds that Kock had swindled the Blacks, forcing them to exchange their goods for "Kock dollars," and was selling at exorbitant prices provisions that he had received at no cost from the American government.[89] In sum, De Long's letter describes a tyrannical and corrupt state of affairs on the island.[90]

Fearing the increasing anger of the Black colonists he had exploited, Kock took refuge in Les Cayes on July 3, 1863. At that point Tuckerman and Forbes realized Kock was only interested in personal gain, and they named a replacement, A. A. Ripka, who would in turn abandon the project a few months later in early January 1864. At the end of 1863, with numerous disturbing reports about the colony reaching Washington, the American government decided to dispatch a special envoy to the island to evaluate the situation. The man appointed, D. C. Donnohue, a supporter of colonization from Indiana and acquaintance of Secretary of the Interior John Usher Palmer, arrived on December 15, 1863. He would state in his report, "What they had suffered since coming to Haiti was by far worse than the slavery they experienced before they were free." Many had died of sickness. The survivors were suffering from malnutrition and wore the same clothes they had had on when they left the United States eight months earlier. On top of that, the soil of the island was infertile, and all their efforts to grow food on it had failed.[91]

By all accounts, the experience had been a total fiasco, and the Black colonists wished to return to the United States. Donnohue counted 292 survivors on the island, and 73 more who had fled Kock's autocracy were on the neighboring island. Though his first thought was to transport these survivors to Jamaica, Donnohue learned in February 1864 that Washington had decided to bring the Île-à-Vache colonists back to American soil. On February 29, 1864, the *Marcia Day* arrived at the island and on March 20, 1864, the survivors disembarked in Alexandria, Virginia.[92]

This marked the end of the Lincoln administration's project to resettle Black Americans in Haiti. This attempt was the last official colonization ef-

FIG. 5. Banknote of five Haitian dollars, created by entrepreneur Bernard Kock after he got a rent contract for the Haitian island Île-à-Vache to grow cotton, using freed slaves from the United States. January 1, 1863. *Wikimedia Commons.*

fort of the American government, and historian Eric Foner claims it was Lincoln's very last colonizing effort, period.[93] The Île-à-Vache disaster was viewed by Congress as unfortunate proof of the failure of the colonization position. Already on March 15, 1864, before the emigrants had returned, Senator Morton S. Wilkinson of Minnesota presented a bill in the Senate calling for the cancellation of the funds allocated for colonization. The bill passed on July 2, 1864, and received Lincoln's immediate signature.[94] It turned out that of the $600,000 that had been approved for Lincoln to finance his colonization efforts, less than $40,000 had actually been spent up to that point of which roughly $25,000 was paid as salary to Pomeroy and the remaining portion as salary to Mitchell.[95]

Most historians believe that Lincoln definitively abandoned all ideas of colonizing Blacks after the publication of the Emancipation Proclamation on January 1, 1863, and that the Île-à-Vache attempt was Lincoln's and his administration's last colonization project. As proof, they point to John Hay's remark in his diary for July 1, 1864: "I am glad the President has sloughed off the idea of colonization."[96] However, recent research suggests that Hay probably misinterpreted Lincoln's public silence on the matter of colonization. The historiography generally accepts Lincoln's public silence on the matter after January 1, 1863, as proof that he had completely dropped the whole idea, which is taken further by some to mean that his opinion about Black people drastically changed and that he now embraced egalitarian thinking. Yet there is evidence that other colonization projects were launched during his presidency after 1863. In other words, Lincoln may have continued dreaming of colonization right up to the moment of his assassination. Of note is Lincoln's reception of British immigration officials and also his decision to maintain James

Mitchell as commissioner of emigration, even after Congress had voted to rescind the colonization funding, precisely so that Mitchell could negotiate a colonization accord with Lord Richard Bickerton Pemell Lyons, the British ambassador in Washington, which grew out of Lincoln's general call for colonization partners that Seward had circulated on September 30, 1862. In early 1863 Mitchell also received official permission to hire J. Willis Menard, a pro-emigration Black American, as his secretary at the Bureau of Emigration.[97] In truth, the main obstacle to the plans of Lincoln and Mitchell at the time was the American secretary of war, Edwin M. Stanton, who was firmly opposed to resettling contrabands abroad when they could just as well be enlisted to fight in the Union army.[98]

Nevertheless, the Lincoln administration pursued negotiations with Great Britain and other countries too. It seems that Seward's circular did not fall on deaf ears and produced several proposals from foreign powers, notably by Ecuador, where several colonization efforts were attempted between 1861 and 1864.[99] In addition, several attempts were made to create colonies of emancipated slaves within the United States or the North American continent starting in 1863, in particular between 1865 and 1871 when President Grant considered annexing part or all of the island of Hispaniola in order to create a place of refuge for southern Black people fleeing the terror of the Ku Klux Klan. The proponents of *domestic* colonization saw it as a way to guarantee the separation of the races while permitting the territorial expansion of the nation and conservation of newly acquired civil rights for Black Americans.[100]

As for Haiti, one thing is certain: the year 1862 marked a turning point in the relations between Black Americans and the little Caribbean republic. Up until the time of recognition, they had regarded Haiti as an ideal republic, the place where they could project their dreams of liberty, equality, and citizenship, and therefore hold it up as the perfect emigration destination. However after January 1, 1863, when emancipation and the hopes it nourished definitively changed their circumstances, they began to look at the Black republic differently.

After having participated actively in the Civil War by enlisting in the Union army, Black Americans, especially newly freed southern Black people, were emotionally more inclined to integrate within the American nation and seize all opportunities offered to them to become full-fledged citizens. These included exercising the right to vote, to run for office in state assemblies or even at the federal level, to settle in the South thanks to the new system of sharecropping that had been devised, or to emigrate to the West to acquire land. Black Americans received aid from their abolitionist supporters and from the federal government, notably under the auspices of the newly created Bureau of Refugees, Freedmen and Abandoned Lands, commonly called the Freedmen's Bureau, and the Freedman's Bank, which Frederick Douglass would unhappily preside over for a time. All these changes led Black Americans to think they could place their trust and hopes in the American nation where they had been born.

Thus, at the end of the Civil War and during the entire period of Reconstruction that followed, Haiti was no longer a country of hope or symbol for Black nationality but rather a respected neighbor. This different relationship between Haiti and Black Americans corresponded to a changed attitude toward Haiti by Americans in general. The first idea was no longer that of a country liberated by force of arms but one that occupied a specific geopolitical position. Since equality and citizenship on American soil now seemed more achievable, Black activists and new Black American *citizens* initiated a new relationship with Haiti, one based less on utopian feelings and more on pragmatism. An important step in this direction was the new chapter of diplomatic relations between the United States and Haiti initiated with the appointment of the first African American ambassador to Haiti, Ebenezer Don Carlos Bassett.

CHAPTER 5

Haiti's Growing Strategic Importance for U.S. Imperialist Ambitions

It is a great thing for Hon. John Mercer Langston to represent this republic at Port au Prince, . . . but it would be indeed a step in advance, to have some colored men sent to represent us in white nationalities.[1]

—FREDERICK DOUGLASS

The Civil War, the recruitment of Black men within the Union army, and then the emancipation of all Black Americans that was made the law of the land with the passage of the Thirteenth Amendment to the Constitution—these events together brought the emigrationist movement to a temporary halt, at least when it came to emigration projects outside U.S. borders. That movement had grown out of the frustration felt by a portion of the Black community about not being able to obtain equality and full citizenship in the country where they had been born; and with that came the contemplation and for some the experimentation of fulfilling those desires in another country. But that frustration gave way to renewed hope once the Civil War ended.

The year 1865 would mark the beginning of a new chapter in the history of the United States, especially for its Black citizens: the postslavery era. The congressional approval and ratification by the requisite number of states of three amendments to the Constitution, known as the Reconstruction Amendments, between 1865 and 1870 sparked hope within the African American community that they could take full advantage of the civil rights now granted and in theory protected by the U.S. Constitution. The support received from the federal government and the Republican Party, while timid in certain respects, gave Black people reason to believe that they could now place their trust and hope in their birth nation. Notably, the right to vote allowed them to have a political stake in their country because it was now legal to elect Black representatives in state legislatures and to Congress.[2]

Unfortunately, however, the hope kindled by the favorable outcome (for Black Americans) of the Civil War did not last long, especially in the southern states of the former Confederacy. In truth, despite (or because of) the formal end of slavery, racial segregation also began to be implemented starting in 1865 with the passage of the first segregationist laws under President Andrew Johnson. State legislatures in the South, probably fearing that Black people were plotting their revenge, began to impose rules of physical and social distance between the two races. Another goal of the southern states was to maintain control over Black labor, now free and no longer slave labor, but as essential as ever to the plantation economy of the South.[3] The result was that most southern states passed laws collectively known as Black Codes. These paternalist measures would regulate Black social life in public and address pressing economic concerns.[4] Although the Republican majorities in many states, aided by the Freedmen's Bureau, organized public services and constructed schools, hospitals, asylums, and so forth, segregation was the rule, whether institutionalized or not. Churches, schools, and the military continued to be segregated just like before the Civil War—nothing new under the southern sun. That being said, one should keep in mind that Black people themselves, desiring autonomy—in other words independence both as individuals and as a community—would consolidate and extend further the Black institutions created by free people of color or by slaves before the Civil War. These included newspapers, neighborhoods, churches, schools, and social and cultural institutions (secret societies and social clubs), and mutual aid societies.[5] Even in the North, Black people often lived in particular neighborhoods and villages on account of widespread racial prejudice. It can be said that in all areas of social and economic life, Black Americans remained, sometimes voluntarily, separate from whites.[6] Thus, as soon as the Civil War was over, de facto segregation was established in the North and South, and de jure segregation existed principally in southern states. Even though the first state-level segregationist laws passed in 1865 were quickly overturned by the federal government, racial separation insinuated itself into all aspects of African American lives.[7] In the early 1870s, the situation of Black Americans was very different from one state to another, and between one city and another. Sometimes there was more or less informal separation of Blacks and whites, and yet some interracial contact remained possible. The strict separation within cities was most visible in churches, public transportation, and schools.[8]

Nonetheless, the three Reconstruction Amendments and the various bills that were voted on and signed into law between 1865 and 1870, notably to guarantee Black people the right to vote in southern states, made a significant contribution to improving living conditions for them. This improvement was particularly visible in the political sphere since roughly two thousand Black men were elected to local, state, or federal offices during Reconstruction.[9]

Ebenezer D. C. Bassett, the First African American Diplomat

Despite all these domestic changes, Haiti did not drop out of view for long among Black Americans. Once official recognition had been achieved, the Black republic saw its status change from that of a simple trading partner to one with a political and diplomatic relationship to the United States. Part of this more prestigious status was the appointment of an American diplomat who would reside in Haiti. The first three Americans to serve as commissioner and consul general of the United States in Haiti, and then as United States minister resident (starting in 1866), were three white politicians: Benjamin F. Whidden (1862–65), Henry Everard Peck (1865–67), and Gideon Hiram Hollister (1867–69).

By naming the African American Ebenezer Don Carlos Bassett to the post of minister resident and consul general of the United States in Haiti in 1869,[10] Republican president Ulysses S. Grant instituted a tradition that would last for roughly fifty years: sending Black diplomats to the Black republic. It was thus through the diplomatic corps that Black Americans would renew their relationship with Haiti during America's Reconstruction period. At the time Bassett's nomination was naturally the subject of much commentary, in the American press especially, since he was the first Black American ever appointed to a diplomatic position on the international stage.

As soon as the first rumors of Bassett's nomination began circulating, both Black and white American periodicals covered the story, each with its own interpretation and often with racial prejudice sprinkled in. The nomination of a Black man to non-elective office, especially in the wake of a tense presidential election, was hotly debated in a country still reeling from the consequences of slavery and the Civil War and by no means totally reunited. Thus even rather out-of-the-way newspapers such as the *Leavenworth (Kansas) Bulletin* took an interest in the nomination of Ebenezer Bassett as ambassador and reported that "he is endorsed by a national committee of colored men" as well as by prominent white and Black figures such as "Fred[erick] Douglass, [George T.] Downing, Langdon and many others white and black."[11] Some news outlets considered it rather logical that a Black man be named to this important position since it concerned a Black nation:

> A number of prominent gentlemen in and out of Congress, believing that the mission to Hayti can be best filled by a colored man, are urging as a candidate for that position Ebenezer D. Bassett, principal of the Colored High School in Philadelphia.[12]

The argument that a Black man was better suited to take up a diplomatic position in Haiti than a white person was not taken for granted by everyone, however, neither in the press nor, it would seem, among the American people, and certainly not in Congress. The *Manufacturers' and Farmers' Journal* of Rhode Island commented on the Senate confirmation process for civil servants newly nominated by the president: "The democratic Senators opposed Bassett as minister to Hayti simply on the ground that he is black. They were not willing that a republican President should send a colored minister to a colored court."[13] Shortly after Bassett's nomination was confirmed by a majority of the senators, other newspapers, including some in northern states, circulated rumors that Bassett had turned down the honor on the grounds that he did not want to serve in a country inhabited solely by Black people. Recalling that some years earlier African Americans had refused to resettle in Liberia for the same reasons, the *New York Herald* claimed that Bassett preferred "to stay among white people" and that Black people "recoil from the idea of living in a community where there is nothing but niggers," concluding "for Bassett [there is] too much of the nigger in Hayti."[14] Angling off the *New York Herald* piece, the *Weekly Telegraph* in Macon, Georgia, went further and denounced "the philosophic absurdity of mixing negroes in politics." According to the author of this piece, Black men like Bassett never seek to gain respect for their race or "to elevate it" but instead have as their sole ambition a personal ascent above the level of Blacks to enter the company of whites.

> Clay, Bassett and Fred Douglass . . . have no pride of race and no real ambition to exalt their own—no faith in its capacity and no genuine hope for its future. . . . [T]he negro appointee values office only as he thinks it confers a buckra distinction and makes him a great man among whites.[15]

In sum, Black people who succeeded in politics were depicted as egocentric individualists whose real goal was not to defend the Black community but to flee from it.

When Bassett was not being criticized for the color of his skin, he was criticized for lacking the legitimacy to exercise the function of minister resident and consul general in Haiti. Although some newspapers, Black and white, praised his personal and professional rise as irreproachable,[16] others expressed their surprise at this nomination, claiming Frederick Douglass would have been more qualified for this mission. The latter view appears in a piece published by the *New York Daily Tribune:*

> It is understood that Mr. Frederick Douglass declined the latter position [minister resident in Hayti]—the only reason which could warrant the appointment of any other person of his race to it.[17]

Indeed, it seems that Douglass and other prominent Black men had refused the position because all entertained the hope of being nominated for a more prestigious position within Grant's administration.[18] While not saying he was holding out for something better, Douglass does claim in his autobiography that he preferred to yield the position to Bassett and support him rather than take the job himself, which he could "easily have secured."

> I could easily have secured the appointment as Minister to Hayti, but preferred to urge the claims of my friend, Ebenezer Bassett, a gentleman and a scholar, and a man well fitted by his good sense and amiable qualities to fill the position with credit to himself and his country.[19]

The *National Republican* newspaper, on the other hand, claims that Douglass was never offered the post, stating that he would have accepted it immediately had it been offered. The piece goes on to say that Douglass deserved a post within Grant's administration and that he had been the victim of a plot to exclude him from the political arena.[20] The ability to know the full truth of the matter probably died with Douglass himself, and it would therefore be unprofitable to speculate excessively about the conditions of Bassett's appointment. It is at least plausible, however, that Douglass at first declined the offer because he felt confident that he would be offered something better, then regretted his decision when he realized that Grant was not going to include him in his cabinet.

These disputes, which were very common in both northern newspapers and those published in ex-Confederate states, only exacerbated racial tensions in the precariously reunited American nation. At the same time, Black newspapers as well as white-controlled Republican news outlets generally applauded Bassett's nomination, and overall they congratulated Black men for taking an active role in the political life of their country. *The Elevator* and other Black periodicals castigated their white counterparts for their casual display of race prejudice while reaffirming their own support for the Grant administration. As the Fifteenth Amendment granting Black citizens the right to vote was making its way through the ratification process, the pro-Black press argued that the nomination of people like Bassett was a boon to the Black community and to the successful reconstruction of the nation.

> [W]e hold that the policy which [Grant] adopted of appointing negroes to public positions, fulfils the intent and determination of the reconstruction measures, and prepares the basis of the efficiency of the 15th amendment.[21]

In the end Ebenezer Bassett became the first minister resident and consul general of the United States in Haiti, and the first African American in U.S. history to occupy an official diplomatic position, on April 16, 1869.[22] It is of symbolic importance that a Black man was invited to take up this post in the Black republic, and it represented an opportunity for the Black community to reconnect with Haiti, no longer around emigration but now on a diplomatic footing.

Historian Daniel Brantley has lamented that the role of African Americans in the history of American diplomacy has so far not been covered by the historiography on this topic. Their role has been generally misrepresented and often totally ignored.[23] The story of Ebenezer Bassett is no exception. There are few publications about his diplomatic career. The very first, published in 2005, is a short biography of Bassett that usefully summarizes his career in a few pages, but it is too superficial for anyone to fully measure the important role he played in Haiti and the implications of his appointment for African Americans.[24] The second, more complete study, *Hero of Hispaniola: America's First Black Diplomat, Ebenezer D. Bassett*, by Christopher Teal, was published in 2008.[25] The author provides more details about Bassett's achievements in Haiti, but the book's primary interest for us is its analysis of the circumstances and stakes surrounding his nomination as ambassador. Teal claims that Bassett asked President Grant for the appointment in private correspondence, wherein he stated that he had been encouraged by both whites and Blacks to seek the post. In his letter, Bassett tried to argue in favor of his candidacy in two distinct ways. On one hand, he pointed out his "unchallenged character of probity and patriotism";[26] in other words, the favorable character traits exemplified by his engagement in the Civil War to recruit Black soldiers on the Union side. On the other, he underlined the guaranteed positive consequences that his nomination would have for Grant, insinuating that his appointment would encourage Black Americans, who were now voting citizens, to massively support him and his party in future elections. It is unlikely that such an argument would have left Grant unmoved. It was certain that the general-turned-politician would seek reelection, and that he had the power then and there to name Black people to prestigious posts and thereby win the gratitude of the entire Black community, which could be converted into support for Grant in future elections. It is thus easy to conclude that Bassett's nomination was purely an electoral calculation. It should be noted that Grant and most Republicans probably underestimated at the time the lengths to which southerners would go to in order to keep Black men from voting. Although southern efforts to block the Black vote were not yet on the front burner in 1869, the White House had already anticipated the outcry from all political parties at the news of Black nominations to posts, such as ambassador, which would have national and international visibility. This is no doubt why Grant requested that the Senate ratify the Bassett nomination as quickly as possible. Bassett's nomination was approved by the Senate only four days after Grant had officially announced it; he thus became ambassador to Haiti, taking the place of the manifestly corrupt white Republican appointee, Gideon H. Hollister.[27]

Bassett presented his credentials to the Haitian government in early September 1869. By that time, diplomatic relations between the United States and Haiti were already well organized. In addition to Bassett's appointment as minister resident and consul general,[28] the American government dispatched six consular agents.[29] During his time as minister resident, Bassett, like his predecessors, was essentially managing claims by American citizens over trade-related issues, defending the diplomatic immunity of American consular agents and merchants, and responding to material events such as storms, fires, and the numerous tropical diseases that affected American citizens residing on the island. Bassett also had to deal with Haiti's angry reaction in 1871 when President Grant attempted to annex the Spanish Santo Domingo portion of the island—an incident we shall return to later in this chapter. Bassett's greatest challenge, however, was coping with the increasing number of Haitian political refugees who sought shelter within his embassy compound, particularly after Great Britain announced in 1874 that its embassy would no longer provide asylum to these individuals.[30] The case of General Boisrond-Canal would prove to be the most delicate among them.

The general was one of a small group of Haitian insurgents who had successfully removed the former president, Sylvain Salnave, from power in December 1869.[31] Jean-Nicolas Nissage Saget replaced Salnave and was in turn replaced by General Michel Domingue in 1874. Domingue had some success in foreign policy matters—notably the establishment of a peace accord and mutual recognition of borders with the Spanish portion of the island, Santo Domingo—but Haiti's domestic finances were in a disastrous state and made worse by crippling levels of corruption and fraud. Domingue's main political adversary, Pierre Théoma Boisrond-Canal, openly criticized the government's economic policies and specifically a loan it had taken out with France. Wishing to eradicate corruption and silence his political opponents, Domingue had all those whom he considered to be threats to his personal power executed. It is in this context that Boisrond-Canal took refuge in the American embassy and asked to be granted political asylum by Bassett. An intense confrontation followed, leading to a siege of Bassett's residence by more than a thousand soldiers acting on Domingue's orders. At the end of this standoff that lasted over five months, Bassett was successful in getting the death sentence against Boisrond-Canal changed to forced exile for life to the island of Jamaica.[32] (His forced exile only lasted a few weeks, and he then became president of Haiti from July 1876 to July 1879.)

Bassett remained in his post as minister resident and consul general of the United States in Haiti for just under the eight years of Grant's two terms as president. This was longer than the tenure of his three white predecessors combined. As is the custom, Bassett submitted his resignation in 1877 as Grant was leaving office. But the end of his service as minister resident was only a temporary interruption of his relations with Haiti. After returning to the United States, Bassett would serve in New York as Haiti's consul general to the United States from 1877 to 1888, after which he returned to Haiti in 1889 and lived there until 1898.[33]

Although the rare biographies of Bassett provide information about the living conditions in Haiti and the various tasks related to his service on the island, it is impossible to learn from them whether his mission had a wider symbolic dimension for Bassett. It is difficult to know what Bassett thought about Haiti and if the service to his country in the Black republic had a particular emotional significance for him. Given that he left no autobiography or even an essay or article about his Haitian experience, taking stock of it is a delicate matter. The Frederick Douglass archives contain some private correspondence between the two men, but with two exceptions (one from 1869, the other from 1888), all fifty-five letters sent by Bassett to Douglass start in 1889, the year Douglass was named the U.S. minister resident and consul general in Haiti. In these letters, Bassett is above all trying to convince Douglass to accept the post of minister resident. Bassett offers his assistance and will in fact follow Douglass to Haiti and serve as his secretary. The only letter from Bassett to Douglass from the earlier period that concerns us here is dated July 3, 1869; in other words, a few days after his arrival on the island. The letter speaks of Bassett's difficult crossing to the island, his eventual arrival, and his first meetings with Haitians but also with Reverend James Theodore Holly. It also mentions the climate, apparently very unpleasant during the dry season of Haiti's summer, and the island's natural beauty. Bassett writes that he is happy to be on the island but provides few details, saying only, "Society here is in a very *unAmerican* state." To this rather enigmatic pronouncement he adds, "Everything is in extremes. There is no middle class." He tells Douglass the society is divided in two: on one side a wealthy, educated, superior class, on the other a mass of poor, illiterate laborers.[34]

In contrast to Bassett, who shared so little about the personal, interpersonal, or transpersonal significance of his Haitian experience, much more is known about what his successor, John Mercer Langston, thought and said about Haiti. Besides his official diplomatic correspondence, Langston wrote an autobiography in which he describes at length his mission in Haiti, including its emotional and symbolic dimension both for him personally and for the Black community more generally.[35]

"It took people like John Mercer Langston to pave the way for Barack Obama": Black Diplomats in Haiti from Langston to Thompson[36]

Less than one year after the election of the Republican Rutherford B. Hayes in 1876, the new president nominated John Mercer Langston, another prominent African American activist, to the post of minister resident and consul general of the United States in Haiti, and as special envoy to the Santo Domingo government, on September 27, 1877.[37] Like Bassett, Langston was a longtime acquaintance of Frederick Douglass. These three men, despite their quite different backgrounds (Douglass was born into slavery and rose as an autodidact; Bassett and Langston were born free and had access to a formal education), came to know one another through their abolitionism, respected one another, and all held for a time this same post as minister resident and consul general in Haiti.[38]

Soon after his arrival in Haiti, Langston quickly joined other foreign diplomats present on the island to protest against Haiti's taxes that targeted foreign merchants. As a model civil servant, he corresponded regularly with those who held the position of U.S. secretary of state over his period of service in Haiti, reporting in great detail on the economic and political evolution of the country. These reports included information about the succession of local insurrections and the bloody repressions associated with each one: assassinations, executions, burnings, and other scenes of looting and disorder that shook the Black republic during his time there. He also informed Washington of the daily grievances filed at the embassy by Americans residing in Haiti who had endured damages caused by these revolts.[39] The events that marked Langston's years as ambassador are well documented but are not the primary focus here, which is instead the less well-known overall conception that Langston and, by extension, the whole Black community had about his Haitian experience. He devoted two whole chapters of his autobiography to his diplomatic service in Haiti. The first, entitled "Appointed Minister to Haiti," offers a rich array of Langston's personal comments about how he conceived of his mission and its symbolic implications for the Black community, Black nationalism, and the internationalism of the Black diaspora.[40]

As with Bassett, John Langston attributed the Haiti assignment to his patriotism and unfailing devotion to the Republican Party. After recalling his unconditional support of the party since its creation in 1856, Langston states that Hayes named him to the post in Haiti as a token of appreciation for the work he had done to secure the Black vote for Hayes in the presidential election of 1876.[41] However he adds that he was rather looking forward to being named to a higher post within the Hayes administration, one with national significance on American soil.[42]

In the autobiography, Langston goes on at length about what Haiti always meant to him. It also reveals the extent to which the Haitian experience represented for him a unique opportunity to be part of "an actual negro nationality." Langston was no doubt curious and enthusiastic about observing firsthand the Haitian people:

> He had learned how for more than seventy years, in spite of frequent revolutions, destructive often of thousands of lives and incalculable amounts of property, this people had maintained their nationality and independence.

The goal was clear: to see a dream come true.

> [H]e would find in this negro country, with its Black Republic, a condition of life which . . . would justify the dream of his youth with respect to an actual negro nationality.[43]

Reading Langston's words here, one understands that Haiti, once the ideal and idealized emigration destination for Black Americans who dreamed of becoming full-fledged citizens, was now viewed more by those Black Americans, who had by that time officially obtained citizenship, as a laboratory experiment at a national scale for the diaspora community. It was an experiment that would now have to be observed up close, and in Langston's case this meant living there temporarily in order to learn the lessons that could be useful for the whole community, lessons that could perhaps help improve the conditions of Black Americans in the United States. Indeed, Langston reports that he was pleasantly surprised by the success of Black Haitians, and more specifically intrigued by the observation that in Haiti Black people were important citizens with access to the highest public positions, notably in government:

> He had never seen up to that time men of their complexion holding such positions and performing such duties. His curiosity therefore was profoundly excited, so that he inquired of the captain who they were and what they came aboard of the ship for? To these questions he replied in full explanation, adding at the same time, "You are now, Mr. Minister, in a negro country, and as I intend to invite you to go ashore with me, I will show you sights which shall be new, and perhaps a little surprising."[44]

What Langston observed were the effects of the "colorism" practiced in Haiti from the beginning when it was enshrined in the Constitution of 1805. Thus his first contact with Haitians was truly, as he says himself, a "revelation":

> This introduction to Haiti and the Haytians was in every sense a new revelation to Mr. Langston. He had hitherto only seen the negro in his best estate at home, in nominal freedom and dependence. Now he beholds him the owner of a great country, the founder and builder of a great government, with a national sovereignty and power respected and honored by all the great Christian civilized powers of the earth.[45]

Langston was conveying the importance for Black Americans of concrete physical contact with the island. Despite everything that Langston, an educated man, had read or heard about Haiti, it was only through his actual contact with the island that he understood that its success inevitably impacted the entire Black community around the world. By experiencing Haiti and seeing for himself the achievement of this Black nationality, Langston was also having a transnational experience. By accepting the post of minister resident to Haiti, Langston had become the tie that linked Black Americans and Haitians. He thus became a witness of the diasporic experience in the transatlantic context, a binding agent of two national communities (Black Americans and Black Haitians) within the Black Atlantic, fusing them into one and the same diasporic racial community: the Black diaspora. An optimist, Langston concludes by affirming that the vision he had was entirely positive and pleasant:

> Once there, the vision and reality of absolute, positive negro nationality presented itself to him, in boldest, most striking features, and yet without such

> disagreeable and unpleasant circumstances as to cause the least anxiety or regret that he was at last in the capital of the country, near whose government he should reside.[46]

The shared sense of belonging of Black Americans and Black Haitians within the same racial community appeared all the more plain to him on the occasion of his visit to the palace of President Boisrond-Canal. There Langston was especially and agreeably surprised to discover that Haitians admired the same heroes as Black Americans—and that they were American heroes. One was the abolitionist John Brown, a second was Senator Charles Sumner. Portraits of these two white heroes of the Black cause were hanging on the wall in the presidential palace. It may be that the portrait of Brown had something to do with the nomination of his biographer, James Redpath, as agent of the Haitian Bureau of Emigration in the early 1860s, and that Sumner's portrait was intended to honor the man who had guided the U.S. recognition of Haiti through the U.S. Senate in 1862. Langston claimed "[t]he Haytian people loved John Brown because he stuck [*sic*], against every odds [*sic*], for the freedom of the slaves of the United States" and "would immortalize the name of Charles Sumner because . . . he opposed the annexation of Santo Domingo to the United States"—an annexation that would have threatened the independence of Haiti.[47] Langston's interpretation receives confirmation from Haitian historian Jacques-Nicolas Léger:

> When the United States Senate refused to approve the annexation treaty, some Haitians started a public collection of funds to offer a gold medal to Mr. Sumner. . . . In accordance with a law passed on July 27, 1871, his portrait was placed in Haiti's Chamber of Deputies, and when he died, the Haitian flag flying over all public buildings remained at half-mast for three days of mourning.[48]

It is clear that the minister resident was generally charmed by the island's beauty and the success—or at least the apparent success—of its inhabitants. Thus Langston's Haitian experience, which was supposed to be only a diplomatic mission, was also for him a life-size experience of Black nationality and occasion for reflecting on the capacities of his "race" to gain access to posts and duties of national scope.

As mentioned above, Langston devoted a second chapter of his autobiography to his Haitian mission. This chapter, entitled "Diplomatic and Consular Services," describes his specific duties as minister resident and consul general of the United States in Haiti. Langston relates many of the situations he had to face, both in Haiti and in the Dominican Republic, where he was chargé d'affaires and consul general from 1877 to 1885. Generally speaking, this chapter offers little information about the significance of the Haitian experience for Langston personally or for his community. However, in the last few pages he does affirm the overall success of his mission, a success that he sees as his personal achievement but also an accomplishment for the entire Black American community. Langston believed that his personal success as minister resident would necessarily have positive effects for his community. It is clear that were a Black man to be seen failing at this job, the American government would be less inclined to dispatch other Black diplomats to Haiti. Clearly proud of his success, Langston documented it in detail by completely transcribing the report that was prepared from the testimony of Reverend James Theodore Holly concerning Langston's eight years of service and published in an enigmatic book entitled *Our Representatives Abroad* in 1879. We have been unable to acquire a copy of this work, however the online archives of American libraries contain a book with a similar title from 1876 published by a white man, Augustus C. Rogers: *United States Diplomatic and Consular Service: Our Representatives Abroad: Biographical Sketches of Embassadors* [sic], *Ministers, Consuls-General, and Consuls of the United States in Foreign Countries; Including Also a Few Representative Americans Residing Abroad in Unofficial Capacities* (2nd ed.). This work includes a short biographical entry on Langston's predecessor, Ebenezer Bassett.[49] We can deduce that such sketchbooks were probably published fairly regularly with each change of administration. In any case, it is clear that the profile of Langston was published in a work whose readership was not exclusively Black, and probably mostly white given that it was prepared under the auspices of an American government agency, and also because at the time illiteracy among Blacks was seven times higher than in the general population. In 1880, 70 percent of Black people were illiterate compared to 9.4 percent of whites, immigrants included, giving an overall illiteracy rate throughout America then of 17 percent.[50] It is thus legitimate to claim that the success of men who belonged to the Black elite at the time such as John Mercer Langston could only be beneficial to the entire community of their "race."

Langston submitted his resignation, as was the custom, when a new president was elected in the fall of 1884, and would thus terminate his service as minister resident in Haiti. Not long after his return to the United States in December 1885, Langston accepted the offer to become president of the Virginia Normal and Collegiate Institute. Now called Virginia State University, it was the first school of higher education for Black people founded and publicly financed by the state of Virginia starting in 1882.[51]

The administration of Republican president Chester A. Arthur made the curious choice of naming a mixed-race person, George Washington Williams, to be Langston's successor as minister resident in Haiti on March 2, 1885, two days before Democratic President-elect Grover Cleveland's inauguration. The choice of Williams was ill-timed and controversial to say the least. He had been implicated in a financial scandal in Europe involving loans contracted with both Europeans and American officials stationed in Europe whom he never paid back. In the end Williams, who had enthusiastically accepted the job, was not allowed to take up the post in Port-au-Prince before the next president, Grover Cleveland, named another Black man, John E. W. Thompson, in his place.[52]

Thompson was from New York and a graduate of the Yale School of Medicine, but also a francophile and an expert on international law. Even though the Democratic Party did not favor naming Black people to high positions, it seems that the president of Yale, Dr. Noah Porter, and the mayor of New York City, Agram S. Hewitt, were able to convince President Cleveland to nominate Thompson to the post in Haiti.[53] Like his predecessors, Thompson's main job was to deal with complaints lodged by American citizens and merchants about Haitian taxes or about the wrongful seizure of their merchandise. His term of service in this role was especially marked by the civil war that divided the country for nearly a year between September 1888 and August 1889.

When Thompson arrived in Haiti on June 30, 1885, the president was Louis Étienne Félicité Lysius Salomon, known as Lysius Salomon Jeune. He was elected for a seven-year term on October 23, 1879. At the end of his first term, Salomon was reelected on June 30, 1886, and inaugurated one year later on May 15, 1887.

However, shortly thereafter the Haitian people expressed their concern that Salomon was perhaps aiming to remain president for life, and General Séïde Thélémaque became the spokesperson for their discontent. On August 4, 1888, a rebellion broke out in Port-au-Prince that led the ailing Salomon to renounce his mandate on the morning of August 10, 1888, and to leave the very same afternoon for France where he would die some weeks later. After Salomon's departure, two presidential candidates emerged: Thélémaque and François Denys Légitime, a former senator and secretary of agriculture. During a conflict between their supporters on September 22, 1888, Thélémaque was killed. At that moment a new candidate, General Hyppolite, emerged with support from Haitians in the north, northwest, and the Artibonite region. Hyppolite considered Légitime, who had support in western and southern provinces, to be responsible for Thélémaque's death. Assemblies in the departments of the west and south named Légitime as chief executive on October 14, 1888.[54] Noting the absence of support from assemblies in other departments, and although Hyppolite had named his own cabinet in Cape Haiti on December 1, 1888, the others named Légitime president on December 16, 1888.

Légitime was immediately recognized by the European powers but not by the United States, which was supporting General Hyppolite more or less directly. It should be noted that on October 22, 1888, the American steamship *Haitian Republic* had been captured by the small warship *Le Dessalines* when the Haitian government under Légitime suspected it of transporting arms and other supplies to Hyppolite's supporters. In order to avoid having this diplomatic incident expand into open war with the United States, Légitime authorized the ship to be released on December 21, 1888, after Thompson communicated the discontent of the American government (who suspected France and Spain, Légitime's allies, to be behind the seizure), but the damage had been done. Légitime's government also had difficulties with Santo Domingo, the neighboring republic suspected of furnishing arms and ammunition to Hyppolite. Finally, after nearly a year of fighting between partisans of Légitime and Hyppolite, Légitime fled to France on August 22, 1889, leaving the way open to Hyppolite, who was proclaimed president of Haiti by the Constitutional Assembly on September 9, 1889, and took the oath of office the following week on September 17.[55]

In poor health, Minister Resident Thompson had submitted his resignation to the American president in March 1889, but his replacement did not report for duty until eight months later.[56] The Republican president, Benjamin Harrison, who had taken office on March 4, 1889, decided not to name a new minister resident to Haiti until June 1889, and the new appointee arrived some months later in the fall of 1889. By that time the outcome of the conflict between Légitime and Hyppolite had been decided, and the new minister resident presented his letter of credence to the newly named President Hyppolite on November 14, 1889. The new minister resident was none other than Frederick Douglass, probably the most famous American, Black or white, ever sent to Haiti in an official capacity. Douglass, as we have said, had great respect for the Black republic. In truth, this appointment was not exactly Douglass's first diplomatic mission, nor was his arrival the first time he had set foot on the Caribbean island of Hispaniola. Nearly twenty years earlier Douglass had been assigned to a diplomatic mission in the Caribbean that had disastrous consequences for the imperial ambitions of then-President Ulysses S. Grant.

Frederick Douglass and the Failed Annexation of Santo Domingo

In order to better understand what was at stake in the mission Douglass was given in 1871, one must first go back a few years to try to understand the new American interests regarding the island of Hispaniola.

After the Civil War, the United States focused most of its attention on the country's internal affairs during what is known as the Reconstruction. In keeping with this, at the end of 1867 the House of Representatives passed a resolution aiming to block all future acquisition of territory, largely because territorial expansion was commonly associated with slavery. The United States no longer sought to acquire new lands, since expansion was to be no longer territorial but economic. New foreign markets were needed to sell U.S. agricultural and industrial products.[57] Paradoxically, the Civil War–era hostility toward the North on the part of Great Britain, France, and Spain encouraged the United States to seek out locations for naval bases in the Caribbean so that it could respond quickly in case European nations attacked America from their Caribbean colonies.[58] Thus, after the Civil War, American newspapers generally positioned themselves in favor of the annexation of the Dominican Republic, which they continued to refer to as Santo Domingo, or even of Haiti. They claimed that this annexation—perhaps of the entire Caribbean—was part of the "manifest destiny" of the United States.[59] However, not everyone was in favor of annexation. Those opposed underscored especially the racial problem that was already complicated enough in the United States without having to add to it the challenge of integrating a people of assorted racial backgrounds such as the Dominicans.[60] However those reservations were set aside as Haiti and the entire island of Hispaniola fell within the expansionist vision of the United States in the Caribbean. The island that had once been a symbol of Black freedom would now become part of a strategic objective.

The Grant administration and its secretary of state, Hamilton Fish, took a particular interest in Môle Saint-Nicolas, a small area in the northwest of Haiti that was ideally situated a mere ninety-four miles from the coast of Cuba. Fish had barely taken up his duties when he sent Lieutenant Commander Thomas Selfridge to conduct a discreet reconnaissance mission along the coasts of the Dominican Republic and Haiti with the aim of establishing a naval base there.[61] Selfridge returned to the United States in mid-July 1869 and described the very precarious situation of Haiti's president, Sylvain Salnave, who would be easy to overthrow. In short, he advised Grant to take advantage of the situation to acquire Môle Saint-Nicolas. Salnave, who was indeed in great difficulty in his country, planned "to remain in power by defeating his adversaries thanks to an intervention by the United States from whom he expected money, arms, and ammunition in exchange for Môle Saint-Nicolas that he would sell or lease." Thus, in September 1869, with his situation worsening, Salnave paid a visit to the American minister resident Ebenezer Bassett to obtain from the United States a loan of two or three million dollars "to be paid with the revenue from duties or by ceding Môle Saint-Nicolas." Bassett, however, warned Secretary of State Fish against the offer to take Môle Saint-Nicolas, "because he knew the universal feeling of Haitians against any surrender of their territory."[62] The American government hesitated to respond favorably to Salnave's offer. Meanwhile, in December 1869 Haiti's legislative assembly voted in favor of offering the United States the free use of one of its ports, in fact the very same Môle Saint-Nicolas, as a storage depot for coal and naval base in exchange for American protection and a loan of twelve million dollars. But the Grant administration still held back from concluding the deal with Salnave, and the execution of the Haitian president by his enemies on January 15, 1870, put an end to negotiations between the two countries on this matter.[63] On March 19, 1870, Nissage Saget was elected president of Haiti.[64]

For its part, the Dominican Republic renewed its efforts to form closer ties with the United States. Ever since gaining its independence from Haiti in 1844, the country had sought American protection to ensure against a possible future Haitian invasion.[65] Thus, shortly after Salnave's execution, the Dominican president at the time, General Buenaventura Báez Méndez, communicated to President Grant that Dominicans were in favor of being annexed by the United States.[66] Although in January 1870 Grant did order two ships to be stationed off the Dominican coast to discourage Haiti from invading the Dominican Republic, the United States rejected annexing Santo Domingo in a close Senate vote in June 1870. Haitian historian Jacques-Nicolas Léger underscores that this opposition to the annexation of the Dominican Republic by the U.S. Senate was energetically led by Senator Charles Sumner, who was convinced that a first such annexation would lead to the annexation of Haiti. Grant had to resign himself to subsequent refusals when he attempted to convince the House of Representatives to annex the island via a joint resolution in early 1871, and turned then to sending an American delegation to the island.[67]

After having supported the presidential campaign of Ulysses S. Grant in 1868, Frederick Douglass cherished the hope of obtaining an important government appointment. Even though, as we have seen, the post of minister resident to Haiti eluded him, his political career in the Caribbean nevertheless took shape in 1871 when he was chosen to be a member of the commission that would travel to the Dominican Republic to discuss a possible annexation. Douglass viewed this appointment as a victory not just for him but for the entire Black community, because he considered his nomination as proof of the government's respectful recognition of Black citizens. However, it is worth noting that Douglass, the preeminent Black activist who up until then had always supported the independence of Caribbean countries and notably Haiti, was accepting to travel to Hispaniola to take part in a project whose ultimate goal was the extinction of at least one and perhaps both Black republics on the island. It may be that the difficulty he had reconciling this contradiction explains why this high-stakes mission is passed over in only a few lines in Douglass's third autobiography. He merely names the three other members (all white) of the commission and briefly comments on the awkward behavior of the Black servants onboard the ship that was taking them to the Dominican Republic. Douglass summarizes the experience as "highly interesting and instructive" without providing any further details.[68]

After having already attempted to annex Santo Domingo in 1854, 1866, and 1868, the United States under President Grant decided to try again in 1870. This effort was undertaken in part to reaffirm in the eyes of the world the famous Monroe Doctrine, which was compromised by European activities on several Caribbean islands, and also to boost foreign trade. It seems as though Grant thought that if the United States did not acquire Santo Domingo, then this small country would turn toward Europe for political and financial support. Unlike Senator Sumner, Grant believed that the Dominican people wished to become part of the United States and benefit from the advantages of America's democratic institutions. Consequently, following the Senate's rejection of the annexation proposal in June 1870, Grant did not back down from his Caribbean ambitions and instead formed the commission that included Douglass. Its mission would be to travel to the Dominican Republic to gather information about the political and economic circumstances on the island, study closely the Dominican positions regarding the allocation of territory to Americans who wished to start a business there, and to determine if the Dominican people truly wished to be annexed by the United States.[69]

Douglass's appointment to this commission provoked polemical reactions. He was to be the commission's secretary, and many Black Americans attacked the Grant administration for assigning the great Frederick Douglass a subordinate role that they considered beneath his dignity.[70] However, Douglass seems to have seen it differently and accepted the appointment alongside the three commissioners: Benjamin Wade, Samuel Gridley Howe, and Andrew D. White. The few historical accounts that mention Douglass's willingness to go along with the annexation of the Dominican Republic provide few details about the mission's work, stating merely that the annexation Grant so desired did not happen. One must therefore turn to periodicals of the day to learn more about how this expedition played out.

An article in the *New York Herald* states that the commission was created by resolution through a vote (103 in favor, 63 opposed) in the U.S. House of Representatives on January 10, 1871. The resolution authorized the president to name a three-member commission and a secretary. Their role would be to travel to the island of Hispaniola to take stock of its politics, society, climate, and economy, among other aspects, "in order that Congress, before proceeding to its annexation, may be better posted than it was in the purchase of Alaska," which had been finalized in 1870.[71] After summarizing the arguments of those in favor of annexing Santo Domingo as well as those—particularly Democrats—who were firmly opposed, the *New York Herald* concludes that the annexation will probably take place "within the next three months" and then adds: "before the expiration of twelve months the republic of Hayti will follow suit, thus giving us the whole island of Hayti or Santo Domingo." In sum, for this newspaper, the naming of the commission was tantamount to approval of the annexation.

On the composition of the commission, an article in the same newspaper and another in the *New York Daily Tribune*, both dated February 21, 1871, note that the three members will be accompanied by a secretary who will himself have two assistants, and each commissioner will have a personal secretary. Also traveling will be a botanist, geologist, and other scientists each with his secretary, as well as half a dozen journalists, thus bringing to thirty-two the expedition's total number of participants who set off on the frigate *Tennessee* on January 17, 1871.[72] Strangely, Douglass's name and title as secretary appears fifth on the full list of passengers onboard the *Tennessee* that was published by the *New York Daily Tribune*. His was mostly a symbolic role without great importance, which may explain why Black Americans, but also Senator Sumner, complained about "the ill treatment of Fred Douglass by that commission." In their view Douglass was clearly treated as inferior to the other commissioners, and President Grant was disrespecting Douglass by appointing him as a simple secretary.[73]

FIG. 6. Unknown maker (American), "Frederick Douglass with the Commissioners to Santo Domingo, Brooklyn Navy Yard, January 1871," January 1871, albumen silver print. *J. Paul Getty Museum, Los Angeles.*

Articles published at the time about the mission itself are a rich source of information about the commission's activities, the Dominican Republic (its climate, beauty, and resources), and especially about the local population, described as "for annexation and the stable government they expect from it."[74] Newspaper articles published in February and March 1871 insist particularly on the tense relations between Santo Domingo and the neighboring republic of Haiti, evoking a possible imminent invasion of the former by the latter.[75] There are also many details about various trips within the Dominican Republic by the commissioners and their attendants. They visited Samaná as well as the cities of Santo Domingo and Puerto Plata, and had discussions with the Dominican president, Báez. It is reported that Douglass gave a speech in Samaná on January 28, 1871, to two hundred Black people who were the descendants of the free people of color who had emigrated to the Dominican Republic in 1825 when the territory was still controlled by Haiti.[76]

The commission was also charged with traveling to Haiti, among other things to meet with Minister Resident Bassett and eventually with the Haitian government. President Báez seems to have feared a Haitian invasion arriving from the eastern part of the island, but the newspapers claim that the annexation of Haiti by the United States would also happen soon and are more apprehensive about the difficult future assimilation of the Black Haitian population. The *New York Herald* used harsh words to claim that they were unassimilable because "the Haytien niggers . . . have set themselves up as superior to white men" and because "the Haytien blacks have legislated against white equality and to keep off white men."[77] The *New York Daily Tribune* published an article about the commission's short visit to Haiti that seems to echo the views of its famous secretary:

> Even Frederick Douglass, the most generous of critics and the most devoted friend of his own race and a believer in its latent ability for self-government, confesses to a feeling of sorrow and disappointment at the spectacle presented. . . . They all acknowledge that the Negro Republic of Hayti is a failure. . . . The feeling of the people here . . . is strongly against the United States.[78]

After a brief meeting with Haiti's president, Jean-Nicolas Nissage Saget, the commissioners returned to the United States, with a short refueling stop in Jamaica, and arrived in Washington on March 27, 1871.

During the few weeks of his mission (January to March 1871), Douglass was both fascinated by the country's beauty and troubled by the poverty of its people. He would return convinced that annexation could only benefit the Dominicans who would thereby become American citizens. It was on this point that Sumner and Douglass were in disagreement, though it did not harm their friendship according to Douglass. For Sumner the annexation of the Dominican Republic meant the extinction of a Black or "mulatto" republic, to use the term commonly repeated in the newspapers of the day; while for Douglass, on the other hand, annexation was about delivering aid to a defenseless people whose nationhood was being eroded by constant internal fighting, and thus for Douglass it meant peace, prosperity, and stability for the Dominicans. Douglass, who up until then had always pleaded in favor of independence for Black republics,[79] justified his new position by specifying that although during the time of slavery in the United States he was opposed to American expansion at the expense of Black people, after Black emancipation and the end of the Civil War, he judged the country to be sufficiently evolved to not expand at the expense of Black populations but genuinely in their interest. The United States was now a democracy with egalitarian principles and other values that he supported seeing fully spread around the world.[80]

It seems, however, that in addition to Senator Sumner, William Lloyd Garrison and many educated Black people—Henry Highland Garnet first among them—also disagreed with Douglass about the hypothetical annexation of the Dominican Republic.[81] On March 30, 1871, in other words almost immediately after the commission's return, there was a gathering of Black Americans at the Cooper Institute of New York (better known as the Cooper Union for the Advancement of Science and Art) to commemorate the ratification of the Fifteenth Amendment. One speaker at the event, Reverend Wyland Garnett, clearly stated his opposition to annexation and criticized the commission and especially Douglass, whom he accused of being allowed to be a part of the commission in exchange for promising in advance to draft and sign a report in favor of annexation.[82]

It was particularly awkward for Douglass that his name was being used by every local and national newspaper as a justifying endorsement of Santo Domingo's annexation. At other times it was being done to lend credibility to fantastical ideas published in some white newspapers that were revealing about persistent southern resistance to accepting equality between Blacks and whites and moving toward a postslavery future of peaceful coexistence of the races. For example, the *Richmond Whig* echoed the Baltimore newspaper the *American* in suggesting in its issue for April 7, 1871, that annexing Santo Domingo would offer a place to resettle all Black Americans, that Frederick Douglass would be installed as governor, and that this was "the only mode of restoring peace and order in the South."[83] In addition, since he had added his signature at the end of the commission's report, which was of course in favor of annexation, Douglass saw his name being used every which way in many white newspapers seeking to justify their pro- or anti-annexation position, and generally marked by strong anti-Black prejudice or even anti–Fifteenth Amendment propaganda to undermine Black voting rights. In one example from the *Georgia Weekly Telegraph*, an article entitled "Negro Barbarism and Suffrage" ascribes to Douglass feelings that it is hard to believe he ever held about Dominicans, claiming "Frederick Douglas [*sic*] returned . . . with tears of sorrow in his eyes at the evidence of the backward progress of his race in civilization, if not their near return to barbarism." The ascription then serves as cover for diffusing the newspaper's racist propaganda and its militant opposition to granting equal rights to African Americans.[84]

The various attacks that Douglass endured from certain members of the Black community and the exploitation of his name by malicious white newspapers forced Douglass to fight back. After returning from his mission, Douglass regularly had articles published in the *New National Era* that all supported annexing the Dominican Republic;[85] but he also felt obliged to justify his position and rebut the accusations of adversaries in rival publications. One example from April 1871 is a letter of his sent to the editor of the *New York Daily*

Tribune in which he tries to refute the accusations made against him by Henry Highland Garnet.

> The Rev. H. H. Garnet is wrong in attributing to me the crazy statement "that the people of Hayti are an inferior race to those of Santo Domingo." . . . If I am for annexing Santo Domingo, and am not for annexing Hayti, it is because the one is in favor of being annexed while the other is not.[86]

If Garnet accused Douglass, perhaps unjustly, of considering Dominicans as superior to Haitians, it may be because Douglass had in fact affirmed in the same article that a certain anarchy was prevalent in Haiti whereas the political situation in the Dominican Republic seemed more tranquil. What is certain is that Garnet and other Black activists as well as Senator Sumner were all extremely touchy about Douglass's support for an annexation project that threatened the independence of a Black population but also, in a possible domino effect, the independence of the homeland of Toussaint Louverture, whom he so admired.

In his articles promoting the advantages of annexing Santo Domingo, Douglass insisted above all on economic considerations. He praised the fabulous resources of the island—wood, fruit, and other goods. But he also noted its strategic importance in accord with the imperialist discourse of the day. Third, he touted the humanitarian and humanist dimension of the annexation. Douglass seemed convinced that by annexing Santo Domingo and thereby gaining a permanent physical presence in the Caribbean, the United States could fight efficiently for the abolition of slavery in the region, particularly in Cuba.[87] It is clear from his articles that Douglass was not taking into account the "race" of the potential annexers and that of the annexed. He was acting not as a Black man but as a Republican, which may explain the provenance of Garnet's animosity toward him.

Douglass did not hide his support for the Republican Party and his sympathy with the ideology of Manifest Destiny. For him it was the worldwide role of the United States in the postslavery era to spread freedom among oppressed peoples along with the superior Western civilization's democratic and republican ideals. At the time Douglass was convinced that one ought not leave Santo Domingo to simply evolve on its own because he considered the country too weak to survive. Annexation, he believed, would bring civil peace and progress to the island and its inhabitants, whom he believed had been impoverished by years of slavery and civil wars.[88] It is likely that Douglass genuinely believed that American citizenship would offer this oppressed people the stability and prosperity they desired, just as it had brought liberty and equal civil rights to Black Americans.

His attitude toward the Dominican Republic and support for the expansionist preferences of the Republican Party show Douglass in a new light. The former abolitionist and champion of the Black cause was now an unapologetic imperialist. Perhaps Douglass was somewhat blinded by a desire to see the Republican Party—the political force that had gained Black American emancipation, equal civil rights, and the right to vote—continue to dominate throughout the American political landscape. And perhaps at the start of the 1870s this made him see the struggle for progress in the Black community as of lesser importance. Douglass probably did not fully appreciate at the time how fragile the recently acquired rights were and how more than ever they needed to be ardently defended. Perhaps he did not see that Reconstruction was coming to an end, and that the Republican Party was gradually reducing its commitment to the African American community, especially in southern states, and instead focusing its energies on the concerns of the white majority—perhaps in part out of electoralist motives—and pursuing imperialist ambitions. As we shall see in the next chapter, it was only after a new and longer association with Haiti and at the conclusion of a bitter diplomatic experience on the island that Douglass would realize how far the goal of equal rights was from being fully achieved and the extent to which racial prejudice was strongly rooted in the institutions of his country.

CHAPTER 6

Frederick Douglass's Diplomatic Career in Haiti

> One ever feels his twoness,—an American, a Negro; two souls, two thoughts, two unreconciled strivings; two warring ideals in one dark body, whose dogged strength alone keeps it from being torn asunder.[1]
>
> —WILLIAM EDWARD BURGHARDT DU BOIS

At the advanced age of seventy-two, Frederick Douglass was appointed minister resident and consul general to Haiti by the Republican president Benjamin Harrison.[2] Public opinion was immediately divided by his nomination. Some responded favorably to the news, believing that Douglass was the best ambassador the United States could send to the Black republic. Others were more reserved about it; some were angry. Certain newspapers, including Black-led presses, and some of his own friends considered the post to be not sufficiently prestigious for someone of his standing. Douglass himself had wanted his former post as recorder of deeds.[3] Some news outlets considered him too old for the job, others said Haiti would be offended by the nomination of a *Black* minister resident, and some believed that not knowing any French would be an insurmountable handicap for Douglass.

A Contested Nomination in a Special Context: An Imperialist America Confronts a Haiti Destroyed by Civil War

As Douglass states in his last autobiography, none of his nominations to prestigious posts, in other words to jobs that had not traditionally been assigned to Black people, happened without comments in the press or without the open hostility of conservative voices.[4] Before Douglass had even accepted the job of minister resident and consul general to Haiti, American papers, white and Black, were already discussing the nomination. One could expect that white newspapers would be more unfavorable of Douglass's nomination than Black ones, but in fact voices for and against came from all quarters. Not surprisingly, the *New York Daily*, a paper closely aligned with the Republican Party, declared it was pleased with Douglass's nomination and that, despite his advanced age, he was more suited for that honorable position than any younger man.[5] The *Washington Bee*, a Black newspaper, celebrated Douglass's nomination, adding about Haiti, "that unfortunate country, which is in a state of chronic revolution," would benefit from the positive influence of the Sage of Anacostia.[6] In a similar vein, the *Omaha Daily Bee*, another white Republican paper, claimed Douglass would be very influential in Haiti and therefore in a better position to defend American interests on the island, and also that he could serve Haitian interests well by protecting residents "against foreign machinations in Hayti."[7]

The *Pittsburgh Despatch*, however, yet another white Republican paper, was less enthusiastic about the nomination. It raised doubts about Douglass's ability to do the job. In an article from June 29, 1889, the paper claimed that the Black American community itself was divided over the nomination, affirming that Douglass was out of touch inside Washington's Black elite, that his marriage to a white woman had discredited him in some parts of the Black community, and that certain Black people were angry at him for having placed members of his family in important positions whenever he had the chance.[8] The same paper published a second negative article the next day, which stated that Stephen Preston, the Haitian diplomat stationed in Washington, D.C., admired Douglass the orator but feared that Douglass as minister resident would be ineffective because he did not speak French.[9] This argument was often repeated in papers opposed to the Douglass nomination, even if it was somewhat specious given that neither Bassett nor Langston spoke French when they first arrived in Haiti as minister resident.[10] Douglass was fully aware of the attacks mounted against him in various newspapers. He mentions this in his last autobiography, attributing them to the race prejudice of the time and to his refusal to enter into dealings with certain New York merchants.[11]

Friends and acquaintances of Douglass also shared their encouragements, regrets, or objections in private correspondence. His friend Robert James Harlan—a mixed-race former slave born in 1816 who had purchased his freedom in the 1850s—congratulated Douglass on his nomination while adding his "regret you did not receive a place commensurate with your ability and position."[12] A certain Isaiah Mitchell asserted that Haiti "is too small and the people too barbarous for a man of your size." He goes on to claim the post is a trap set by Americans who want to punish Douglass and his white wife for daring to marry.[13]

> There are many people in this country who would like to see you out of it and many who would like to have Mrs. Douglass punished for her treachery to the Anglo-Saxon race and both of you buried among the "niggers" of the island.

But Douglass cast aside these criticisms and accepted the position enthusiastically. To some extent he believed that conferring the post of minister resident to a Black man and former slave was a form of official recognition of his "race" by the U.S. government, a gesture of reconciliation of sorts, but also a strong message addressed to Haiti's Black population. Because even though he was not the first Black minister resident to Haiti, who better than Frederick Douglass could represent the United States before a people whose independence he had always defended and admired?

Douglass was a proud man—proud of the way he had thrown off the yoke of slavery, proud of the way he had led his life, defended the abolitionist cause, and had become an influential figure—and people generally granted that he deserved to be. His was an irresistible ascension: born a slave on American soil, he would finish his public life as minister resident to Haiti representing the American government in a foreign country. However, the arc of his life seems to have caused him some misgivings—torn between a desire to serve his country and the pain of being rejected by it because he was Black. Douglass was indeed proud to have this mission conferred on him, but he remained upset by his own conflicted feelings. While he fought to be recognized by his own country—and this post was certainly a form of recognition—he also positioned himself as a Black man belonging to the Black race, and even to a Black diaspora; therefore he was not going to serve his country in any way that would be detrimental to other Black populations. Nothing illustrates this personal conflict better than the complicated relations Douglass would have with the Black republic of Haiti. During the two years he spent in Haiti, a time when America was revealing to the world its new imperial ambitions, Douglass would reveal this somewhat hidden and little-known side of his character. His complex personality comes through when reading his diplomatic writings, such as the letter from June 25, 1889, in effect his first piece of diplomatic correspondence, in which he officially accepts with pride and enthusiasm the post being offered:

> I am deeply sensible of the honor the President has conferred upon me by assigning me this very important mission, and I am especially touched by

> the confidence expressed in the possible influence I may exert upon the people among whom he would send me.
>
> I therefore feel it my duty to accept the mission thus tendered me by His Excellency, the President of the United States.[14]

It is possible, though, that his pride temporarily blinded Douglass, and that he lacked discernment during the two years of his mission in Haiti. The incredibly warm welcome he received on his arrival further elevated the high opinion he had of himself and somewhat diverted his attention from certain fundamental political realities. The Môle Saint-Nicolas affair, which was so central to Douglass's mandate in Haiti, revealed the paradoxes of a man and a nation. Emotions, ego, and affect would become the key elements in this affaire d'état, which had undeniable strategic implications for the resolutely imperialist United States at the end of the nineteenth century.

Douglass's nomination happened at the start of 1889 when a civil war was still raging in Haiti between the supporters of François Denys Légitime, who had temporarily taken power and whose government was rapidly recognized by the United States and the European powers, and those of Louis Mondestin Florvil Hyppolite. The Americans were nervous about the friendlier relations between Légitime and the French government and as a result "did not hesitate to show the preference they had for the cause defended by General Hyppolite."[15] In truth, shortly after Légitime was recognized by Great Britain and France in early 1889, Hyppolite attempted to purchase ships, weapons, and ammunition. Although the American government had decided to remain neutral, Hyppolite found a receptive audience in a certain William Pancoast Clyde, a New York shipbuilder. Wishing to make money off the conflict, Clyde dispatched Frederick Elie as his agent to negotiate with Hyppolite. At the same time (in mid-January 1889), Hyppolite had begun to request American aid through Stanislas Goutier, the American consul posted to Cap-Haïtien. It is rather complicated to establish with certainty the tenor of these various negotiations, but it appears that Hyppolite definitely proposed to both Elie and Goutier the leasing of Môle Saint-Nicolas in exchange for their aid. Specifically, it seems Hyppolite conditioned the lease on the American government's recognition of his claim to power, and that he pushed Clyde and apparently his friend Admiral Bancroft Gherardi, a close associate of Secretary of State James G. Blaine, to furnish him with arms and ammunition.[16]

Thus the year 1889 opened in Haiti with a bloody civil war that in the end was favorable to Hyppolite. "At first, the war in the north was favorable to Légitime. . . . But at the start of May, the lack of energy of the government in

Port-au-Prince, the absence of a shared ideology among its members, and the simultaneous military buildup in the north swung things in the other direction."[17] It is therefore rather surprising that President Harrison's administration would recognize the ailing government of Légitime at the end of June 1889 and nearly simultaneously name Frederick Douglass as minister resident. The circumstances surrounding these two official actions remain mysterious. It seems that Harrison was acting to counter his secretary of state, James G. Blaine, who he knew was close to both Admiral Gherardi and Clyde, who were at the time unofficially providing aid to Hyppolite.[18] In the end, Hyppolite emerged victorious from this civil war. On August 22, 1889, Légitime left the country onboard the French ship *Kerguelen,* and the next day Hyppolite and his army entered Port-au-Prince. On September 9 the national assembly proclaimed General Florvil Mondestin Hyppolite president of Haiti for a seven-year term, and he took the oath of office on September 17.[19]

When he accepted the post in Haiti, Douglass must have been aware of the imperialist ambitions of President Harrison and Secretary Blaine, who had never disguised their aspirations regarding Haiti. In the spring of 1889 they officially announced a plan to send emissaries to Haiti who would meet with the two warring generals and attempt to use diplomacy to untangle this conflict and its international ramifications.[20] It should be noted that with the Nicaragua canal project then under study, Harrison's government could not remain neutral regarding the conflict in Haiti, and he probably preferred to see Hyppolite become president rather than Légitime, who was supported by the French.[21] Like his predecessor, Grover Cleveland, President Harrison feared that Môle Saint-Nicolas might fall into the hands of the Europeans.[22] The expansionist obsession was central to the Harrison-Blaine administration at the same time that Douglass was minister resident in Haiti. The search for new foreign markets was closely linked for Blaine and Harrison to establishing naval stations in the Caribbean at strategic locations that would guarantee a secure trade route toward future canals through the isthmus of Latin America.[23]

Frederick Douglass, who had always supported Republicans, more or less sided with American expansionism, or at least with the expansion of his country's cultural influence and civilization. As we have seen, before emancipation, Douglass was quick to oppose any expansion of the United States that would jeopardize Black people; however, he adopted a different position following the Civil War. He then argued that his country, which had successfully abolished slavery, was now sufficiently enlightened to not develop at the expense of Black populations but would, on the contrary, act in their interest. Douglass was basically sympathetic to the idea of Manifest Destiny and therefore held a pro-expansionist position implying increased American influence in Haiti, but in a way that he saw as advantageous to both peoples. One sees this position clearly expressed in many of his diplomatic communications.[24] For him, the expansion of American civilization, including by annexation, perhaps, would be a way to bring peace and stability to Black peoples in the Caribbean.

Though his appointment became official at the end of June 1889, Douglass did not go to Haiti immediately. Political events on the island delayed his arrival but allowed him to initiate correspondence with Ebenezer Don Carlos Bassett, the first Black American minister resident to Haiti. Bassett would not be taking up that post again and encouraged Douglass to accept it. Through Bassett, Douglass also began corresponding with Stephen Preston, Haiti's minister resident to the United States. An examination of their many exchanges, which included Bassett mailing to Douglass translations of his own correspondence with Preston, reveals that Preston and Bassett were trying to convince Douglass to do everything in his power after his arrival on the island to preserve Haiti's independence and prevent the United States from acquiring Môle Saint-Nicolas. Bassett concludes one letter with a wished-for affirmation: "The Môle Saint-Nicolas will not be occupied either by France or the United States—vive Haïti."[25]

Bassett, Preston, and Douglass seem to have agreed on the necessity of not allowing the post of minister resident to be held by a white man. Contrary to reports in some New York newspapers, Preston was delighted with Douglass's appointment to the Haiti post, especially because the choice had been made by the president himself, and not by Blaine for whom he had less sympathy: "It was the President who chose and named Mr. Douglass. The President is against American intervention in Hayti. He would accept mediation. He does not regard lightly the colored vote as Mr. Blaine does."[26] Moreover, Preston knew that the Sage of Anacostia was strongly disliked by New York merchants, the same ones who had helped Hyppolite defeat Légitime. Their criticisms of Douglass were clearly business-related and therefore made Douglass an excellent nominee, because uncorruptible, for the minister resident post in Haiti: "All the merchants of New York, *without a single exception*, are furious that a *negro* is going to represent their interests in Hayti. They do not conceal it. . . . They know that Mr. Douglass is not to be bought, and that *he* will *not* be their instrument."[27]

Bassett's energetic efforts to convince Douglass to take the job were clearly not disinterested. In the end, receptive perhaps to some of the criticism he was hearing, Douglass agreed to go to Haiti accompanied by Bassett, who spoke fluent French; and Basset was happy to go along as a simple secretary.[28]

Frederick Douglass as Diplomat and His Lack of Discernment in His Analysis of the Local Situation and His Own Mission

Leaving behind the swirl of debate around his nomination, Douglass finally arrived in Haiti, the Black republic he had been eager to finally witness up close. Eager to prove to the American government that it had made the right choice in quickly recognizing Hyppolite,[29] Douglass sent off a first reassuring diplomatic dispatch to Blaine entitled "Mr. Douglass' View of the Political Situation":

> I have reached the conclusion that Haïti has now entered upon a condition of settled peace and prosperity under the guidance of a wise and stable administration. . . . It is admitted that order and tranquility have never been so universal and complete in Port au Prince, at the close of any revolution, as under the provisional government of General Hyppolite.[30]

Some days later, his fifth dispatch was similarly sunny:

> [There are in Haïti] many demonstrations of popular confidence in the new President of the Republic. . . . There is now no visible serious opposition to the newly organized government under General Louis Mondestin Florvil Hyppolite. Every one with whom I talk expresses the conviction that Haïti has had enough of war and is willing now to acquiesce in a condition of peace.[31]

Douglass would continue to regularly underline in exaggerated tones the stability of the Hyppolite regime and the overall peaceful situation, thus systematically minimizing the various crises that Haiti experienced between October 1889 and the summer of 1891. What was motivating this optimism and the proliferation of compliments toward the Black republic? To anyone reading these dispatches while keeping in mind Douglass's personal history up until then, it is clear that he was trying to prove to Americans that this government of Black people for Black people was a success; and he did this by exaggerating the island's prosperity and stability. Beyond the Haitian people themselves, it was the entire Black race that had a stake in the successes and failures of the first Black republic. Affirming Haiti's success was implicitly recognizing that all Black people around the world were capable of self-governance and advancement without the help of whites, and thereby a refutation of the paternalist ideas that had served as justifications for Black enslavement and Black segregation in the United States and elsewhere.

FIG. 7. "General Hyppolite; President of Haiti; 1889–96." *Schomburg Center for Research in Black Culture, Jean Blackwell Hutson Research and Reference Division, New York Public Library.*

One of the first specific tasks that Douglass had to carry out was collecting sums of money of varying amounts that Haiti owed to certain Americans.[32] Meanwhile, he seems not to have grasped right away the reason for his presence in Haiti nor the true reason for the American support of Hyppolite, which were really one and the same: the desire to acquire a strategic position in Caribbean waters—the famous Môle Saint-Nicolas.[33]

Soon after arriving, Douglass was made dizzy by some of the attention he received. On November 14, 1889, he met with President Hyppolite on the occasion of his predecessor's formal withdrawal and the start of his term as minister resident. But what was to be a simple succession ceremony became a moment of glory for Douglass, who eagerly recounted every detail of the event in his diplomatic dispatches: the minister resident was received with great honor; the street leading to the presidential palace was lined with soldiers saluting as he passed by; as he entered the building the American national anthem was played. Rendered lightheaded, perhaps, by a welcome that befitted a head of state, Douglass seized the occasion of his formal acceptance speech before members of the Haitian government to loosen his reserve and expound on his personal experience and feelings. It was no longer the diplomat speaking but instead Frederick Douglass the man, the former slave, the abolitionist, the defender of the Black race:

> Mine has been a long and eventful life, identified with the maintenance of principles illustrated in the example of Haïti.
>
> My country has conferred upon me many marks of its favor, but in view of the heroic devotion to liberty and independence exemplified by your brave countrymen in the darkest hour of their history, I can say, in all sincerity, that I have received at the hands of my government no honor that I prize more highly than the honor of my appointment as Minister Resident and Consul General to the Republic of Haïti.[34]

It was not simply a matter of Douglass expressing America's friendly feelings toward Haiti, but of explaining how much his selection for this post was in his eyes a personal victory, and stating the degree to which he, as an individual, felt close to Haiti and to its struggle for independence. This is hardly surprising coming from someone who had always defined Black liberation as a struggle. It was plain from the many details he shared in his autobiographies about this struggle with his former master, Edward Covey, and from his support in favor of recruiting Black troops to fight for the Union in the Civil War.

The admiration that Douglass had for Haiti was clearly reciprocal, if one accepts the declaration made by President Hyppolite following Douglass's speech:

> As you know, Mister Minister Resident, your reputation is known in both worlds. You are the incarnation of the idea that Haiti pursues: the intellectual and moral development of men of the African race through personal effort and intellectual cultivation. I could easily return the favor of your statement: the United States has already given several marks of its consideration and esteem to the Republic of Haiti, but it will never be able to give a higher testimony of its interest than that of sending you here as Minister Resident and Consul General.[35]

Beyond simply flattering the ego of his guest, Hyppolite seemed to genuinely admire Douglass. By transcribing these words in the dispatch that he later sent to Blaine, Douglass was probably hoping to prove to the American government that he could be counted on as the man with the extraordinary destiny who transcended national borders and whose influence was undeniable. He also took the opportunity to refute rumors circulating in American newspa-

FIG. 8. "Frederick Douglass at His Desk in Haiti," Photograph, Paper, 20.3cm x 25.4cm. *Frederick Douglass National Historic Site, Washington, D.C.*, FRDO *3899*.

pers that the Haitian people would have preferred it if the United States had sent a white emissary.[36]

In any case, without knowing it, Douglass's act of thinly disguised bragging worked to the advantage of the American government. Harrison had not sent the Sage of Anacostia to Haiti by chance. The Republicans clearly aimed to make use of his charisma, thinking perhaps that his notoriety and popularity with the Haitian people would permit them to easily and successfully carry out the negotiations necessary to obtain Môle Saint-Nicolas. After all, the prize was clearly Môle Saint-Nicolas, and the Haitians were fully conscious of that.

On November 21, 1889, an American warship, the U.S.S. *Yantic*, was cruising near the Haitian coast and dropped anchor off the shore of Môle Saint-Nicolas.[37] Anténor Firmin, Haiti's foreign minister, naturally asked Douglass for an explanation of the unusual presence of the American ship. But Douglass, who had not been informed of this American military maneuver, had difficulty responding. Not only had the American leadership kept Douglass in the dark about how it coveted Môle, but the minister resident would learn about it through rumors in the press.[38] Douglass relayed his exchanges with

Haitian officials about the ship in his diplomatic dispatches and was forced to recognize that an anti-American sentiment was spreading through the Haitian population.[39] Understanding that Haitians were very sensitive about anything to do with their territory, Douglass used all his rhetorical skill to diplomatically convey to the Harrison administration that this show of force was unwelcome. The Haitians were not naïve, and their nervousness was palpable.

This incident was the first in a long series that showed how Douglass was being used as a pawn by the United States. The unstated purpose of his presence on the island was to smooth over relations with the Haitians. But what is obvious to us in hindsight when reading his diplomatic correspondence was seemingly much less so for Douglass at the time. Douglass did his best to convince the Haitians, and perhaps himself, that the American naval presence in Haiti was there to reinforce Hyppolite's power. Douglass seems to have been overconfident, perhaps because somewhat blinded by protocol and the extreme courtesy the Haitians showed toward him. He did not really see, or did not wish to see, the local political stakes and the intentions of his own government.

Thus the incident is quickly forgotten, at least by Douglass, and life goes on more or less normally. Each visit to the presidential palace is recounted in a dispatch, and each contains a dose of Douglass's self-flattery intertwined with a summary of his exchanges with the Haitian president. These dispatches also reveal how much Haiti's success was important to Douglass. That success, and especially the capacity of Hyppolite's government to maintain peace and order, was proof for the minister resident of the capability of Black autonomy in general. One can easily imagine that Douglass sent off his dispatches with the goal of proving to his government that if Haiti's Black citizens were capable of successfully governing themselves, then Black people in the United States were fully capable of doing the same. If one recalls the political context within the United States in 1889—one year before New Orleans passed its first openly segregationist law regulating public transportation, seven years before the infamous *Plessy v. Ferguson* decision—in other words, a rather somber period that sees the rise of the first Jim Crow laws principally in southern states and the simultaneous collapse of the promises of the Reconstruction period, one cannot help but hear Douglass the defender of civil rights and equality speaking in these dispatches.

Nevertheless, Douglass continually sought to reconcile his Black identity and status as a colored "brother" to Haitians with his patriotism and proud attachment to his American citizenship. For example, in one dispatch dated December 14, 1889, Douglass transcribes a speech he gave in the presence of

Hyppolite to justify the recent American presence in Môle. To explain that Americans had no intention of harming Haiti, Douglass makes the weighty argument that the United States is no longer the country of slavery that it was thirty years earlier but instead a country where all "races" find their place. The argument was supposed to be reassuring, a way to convince Hyppolite that the United States did not consider itself superior to Haiti.[40] He of course also included in his dispatch Hyppolite's response, which continues with the customary high praise of Douglass, attributing to him an important role in the history of his country, recognizing him as a leading architect of Black emancipation:

> It is glorious for you to have worked personally toward the outcome that you affirm today, an outcome no one thought possible a quarter century ago. You have been one of the great laborers for the progress of liberal ideas in your great and noble country. When you are received here with such honor and all present themselves with such veneration before you, know for certain, Mister Minister Resident, that we count you as one who contributed mightily so that the great starry Republic would no longer limit human rights to one particular branch of the family of man, but salute with satisfaction the progress toward liberty of all—regardless of race, color, and background.[41]

The months that followed these exchanges passed without any major incident to trouble the peace and tranquility on the island that Douglass so cherished. In his dispatches Douglass would regularly give updates on the situation in Haiti, usually very favorable updates that were even exaggeratedly optimistic. One example is a communication dated January 17, 1890, in which Douglass offers his opinion on the elections that had taken place the previous week on January 10 and whose outcome was still undetermined. Despite the "considerable disorder and violence in some quarters" and the as yet unannounced results, Douglass nevertheless concludes his observations by affirming that the election went rather well and demonstrates the country's high level of political stability: "In the main, I think that the election has been fair and that the result reached is in favor of the stability of the Government and of the peace of the country."[42]

But now and then American warships cruise by off Haiti's shores, and each time they provoke Haitian distrust. Douglass makes scrupulous accounts of all these incidents in his dispatches, noting that they gave rise to all sorts of conjecture: "the presence of one of our national vessels in these waters is apt to attract general attention and to awaken curiosity and speculation."[43] Knowing that the Haitians were quick to rise up over anything, Douglass did everything he could to dissuade the American government from doing maneuvers in Haitian waters, especially since it was happening without advance notification. He warned the Americans about the particularly sensitive and nervous Haitian character, describing them as almost paranoid and obsessed with the idea that a large nation might attack them and seize their territory—and understandably so. Indeed, the demonstration of force in Caribbean waters was in fact part of the display of President Harrison's new imperialist politics. Harrison inaugurated America's imperialism notably by conferring on Benjamin F. Tracy, his secretary of the navy, a program of renovation and expansion of America's naval fleet. Thus, under Tracy's leadership, wooden vessels were replaced by powerful steel ships at a rapid pace. It was under Tracy that the battleships *Maine*, *New York*, and *Oregon* as well as the flagship *Olympia* would all go into service (in 1890, 1891, 1893, and 1892, respectively).[44] It is therefore safe to say that the American incursions off the coast of Haiti were hardly random cruises.

This series of maneuvers off the coast of Haiti does not seem to have alerted Douglass; or, if he did have suspicions, they were kept out of his diplomatic correspondence. Is it possible Douglass was perfectly naïve about what was happening? He was an intelligent man, and though advancing in years it is hard to imagine he would allow himself to be fooled in this way. And yet subsequent events suggest this may have been the case. It should be said that Hyppolite did nothing to help open his eyes, continuing instead with his endless compliments toward Douglass and public declarations of his friendship with the United States.[45] Even though Douglass warned the United States that those opposed to Hyppolite's regime were using this vaunted Haitian-American friendship to destabilize it, he remained very positive about the country's political situation and continued to reassure his government about its relations with Haiti.[46] At the same time, Douglass used his report to U.S. officials about Haiti's peace and prosperity to justify an extended leave of absence. After reporting how martial law, which had been in place in Port-au-Prince since May 24, 1888, was now lifted, Douglass turned to a request of sixty days off island on the grounds that Haiti's summer climate would be damaging to his health.[47]

In the last days before Douglass returned to the United States in the summer of 1890, Hyppolite's government was formally recognized by three European powers: France, Great Britain, and Italy.[48] At the end of the two-month summer leave that he obtained, Douglass was instructed by the State Department, with no explanation, that he was not to return to Haiti. Eventually,

Douglass left from New York on December 7 and resumed the duties of his appointment in Haiti on December 13, 1890.[49] Thus Douglass had been sidelined for roughly five months from the place where he had been named minister resident. Why? If he had his suspicions, he again kept them out of his diplomatic correspondence. Historians say only that Douglass was held up in the United States at the request of the shipbuilder Clyde.[50]

Whatever the cause, during these five months of leave (two voluntary plus three forced), Douglass must have kept himself informed about American political life and in particular about the imperialist public declarations of the U.S. government. For example, Douglass was surely not unaware of James G. Blaine's speech in Waterville, Maine, on August 29, 1890, which clearly spelled out America's imperialist intentions. However, that speech and the unjustified extension of his leave of absence do not seem to have upset Douglass, who simply returned to his post as soon as he received instructions to do so. And yet another political event might have piqued Douglass's curiosity about his government's true intentions: namely, the passage of the protectionist Tariff Law of August 1890, which stands as further proof of the imperialist strategy being adopted then by the American government in the Caribbean region. Haiti's refusal to submit to American threats when it declined to sign the reciprocal treaty specified in the text of the Tariff Law ought to have been understood by Harrison and Blaine as a clear sign that Haiti was determined not to yield to outside pressure.[51]

Most historians who have studied the Môle affair claim that before allowing Douglass to return to Haiti in December, Blaine supposedly asked him informally, perhaps only orally, to try and negotiate with the Haitian government to obtain the sale or lease of land to allow for a coal refueling station at Môle Saint-Nicolas.[52] There is no trace of that exchange in Douglass's diplomatic papers. In fact, the first known evocation of the subject occurs in a confidential private letter from Douglass to Blaine in which the general topic is a new year's ceremony in Haiti in early 1891. During this ceremony, Firmin informed Douglass that the American press was claiming that Hyppolite had promised Môle to the United States. Douglass was apparently very embarrassed and attempted to deny that the American government had its eyes on Haitian territory, but he did concede that it would like to establish a coaling station in the Môle area. Firmin did not respond to this quasirequest, and Douglass realized immediately that he was heading into a veritable land mine. In a letter dated January 6, 1891, Douglass reminds Blaine how touchy the Haitians become as soon as they suspect anyone might be wishing to seize any of their territory. However, he goes on to say that he considers the acquisition of such a coaling station at Môle would be advantageous for Haiti and promises to do all he can to obtain such a base.[53] Douglass, the committed expansionist, the devoted American citizen, and perhaps Douglass the vainglorious, convinced of his high influence over the Haitian government, was clearly overtaking Douglass the sage, the representative of the Black diaspora, who was completely aware of and perhaps also admired the Haitians' instinctive attachment to their property.

Meanwhile, a new diplomatic incident involving American ships was unfolding. The American company G. A. Brett Son and Co. had complained to Secretary Blaine about its ships being arbitrarily detained in Haitian ports at great cost to the ships' owners. In a diplomatic dispatch dated January 9, 1890, Blaine informs Douglass that the captains of these ships are complaining that they "receive no help from their representative in Haiti"—meaning from Douglass.[54] In reply, Douglass states that the matter is largely out of his hands and that he had done all he could—namely, attempt to untangle the situation with Firmin, Haiti's foreign minister and minister of commerce. Firmin had reminded him of Haitian law in this area: ships could be detained by authorities until taxes on their cargo had been paid, and in this case the party in charge had not paid the taxes in question. What might have remained an insignificant matter took on greater importance in the following months and became the trigger for the Môle Saint-Nicolas crisis. Throughout, Douglass revealed his limitations as a man of influence and negotiator, whereas the Haitians showed their determination and a capacity to resist American pressure. The tiny little nation of Haiti, so weak and isolated, had already and would again stand up to the American steamroller without giving in. It is in this context that the Môle Saint-Nicolas affair began in earnest.

The Môle Saint-Nicolas Affair: A Stinging Defeat with Disastrous Consequences for the Political Career of Frederick Douglass

The affair itself is easily summarized. On January 1, 1891, Blaine sent instructions about his wish to acquire Môle Saint-Nicolas to Douglass and to Admiral Bancroft Gherardi (the same person who had supported Hyppolite against Légitime). Douglass was asked "to co-operate to the best of your ability in bringing about the end to which the Admiral will give all his energies." Furthermore, he is told that "President Harrison considered our acquisition of the Môle to be in full conformity with Haiti's interest as well as those of the United States."[55] However, Douglass does not immediately receive these instructions. It is likely that he received them at the end of January, and they came in a surprising fashion, delivered by Admiral Gherardi, which suggests that Blaine was deliberately keeping Douglass away from his plans.

Douglass quickly understood that he was no longer in charge and that Blaine had chosen Gherardi to lead the negotiations. Gherardi was a rather awkward man and had little diplomatic skill. As his means of persuasion, he would switch randomly from an argument based on Manifest Destiny to threats to direct intimidation, but at each turn he encountered Haiti's surprising self-assurance. In the end he was forced to accept reality: Haiti had no intention of selling or leasing Môle Saint-Nicolas and felt under no obligation to do so simply because the United States wanted it to.[56] What is particularly interesting in this affair is not the negotiations themselves—in short, Haiti dragged the matter out for several months before finally refusing categorically to bend to the wishes of the United States—but rather the way in which Douglass experienced the negotiations, and the way he reacted to Gherardi's statements and those of the Haitians. It is also interesting to observe in what way Douglass's double personality emerges as the weeks pass and the Americans approach their final defeat.

At first it is Douglass, the uninhibited expansionist, who speaks. During a first interview between Douglass and Gherardi on one side and Firmin and Hyppolite on the other, Douglass attempts to persuade the Haitians to give up Môle. He argues that their stubborn refusal to yield a part of their territory, while formerly understandable and praiseworthy, could only be a source of danger in 1891.[57] But as the negotiations continued, Gherardi became more insistent and threatening while Douglass almost totally withdrew from the conversation, allowing his compatriot to draft on his own an official letter requesting the yielding of Môle and allowing him to pursue the oral discussions with the Haitians on his own as well. This self-erasure is palpable in the minister resident's dispatches, which become shorter, more infrequent, and less precise over time. It is likely that Gherardi's arguments were no longer agreeable to Douglass, who realized that the admiral was ready to use force and seize Môle no matter what the Haitians thought. Gherardi, who indeed seemed ready to do anything to acquire the Môle territory, took the bold step of sending a misleading letter to Blaine in which he attributed to Douglass the view that it would be best to bypass negotiations and seize Môle by force, and that doing so would supposedly be in the interest of the Haitian government, which would then not have to justify to the people this yielding of territory.[58] In his dispatches, Douglass obviously never raised the possibility for the United States to acquire Môle by force. In his many interviews with Hyppolite or Firmin or both, Douglass had always insisted repeatedly that the United States was a friendly nation and would never use force against the Black republic. There is no reason to think he would suddenly alter his beliefs about that.

Finally, on April 22, 1891, after more than two months of unfruitful negotiations, Firmin sent an official message to the two American emissaries stating his government's refusal to give up Môle Saint-Nicolas. In a laconic telegram dated April 23, 1891, Douglass tells his government, "Hayti has declined lease of Môle."[59] The telegram was followed by a more detailed dispatch, drafted the same day, entitled, "Mr. Firmin's Refusal to Lease the Môle." In it Douglass joins a copy of Firmin's note of April 22, 1891, as well as the official written response, signed by Douglass and Gherardi, that he sent to Firmin on April 24, 1891. The note was unequivocal: Firmin refused to lease Môle Saint-Nicolas to the United States for the purpose of establishing a coaling station for American navy ships. Surprisingly, Firmin claimed that his refusal was due to a clause that the United States would have tried to impose in the lease arrangement for Môle Saint-Nicolas. The clause forbid Haiti from giving control over Môle Saint-Nicolas or any other portion of its territory to any other nation, which would have amounted to a type of colonial domination by the United States over Haiti. Therefore, Firmin declared that "the acceptance of your request with such a clause included would be in the eyes of the Haitian government an insult to the Republic's national sovereignty and a flagrant violation of Article 1 of our Constitution, since by renouncing the right to freely dispose of our territory, the acceptance would have amounted to consenting to a tacit alienation from it."[60]

This clause was thus the first reason explaining "the impossibility in which the Haitian government found itself regarding the lease to the American government of Môle Saint-Nicolas on the latter's conditions." Firmin added a second reason for this refusal, namely:

> The arrival in this port of two American squadrons, comprising the most powerful warships of the U.S. Navy, made a disastrous impression to the whole country which finds it alarming or worrisome. Supposing even that the national Constitution were not an obstacle to the acceptance of the request presented by your excellencies in the name of the president of the United States, the Haitian government could hardly, in the present circumstances, enter into negotiations to lease Môle Saint-Nicolas without appearing to yield to foreign pressure and in so doing compromise our existence as an independent people; all the more since several American newspapers, with an unknowable goal in mind, are spreading untrue propa-

> ganda that tends to lead one to believe that there were signed agreements between the President of Haiti and the United States of America for ceding of this same bay of Môle Saint-Nicolas that his Excellency the U.S. President Harrison wishes to have as a naval station for use by the American navy.[61]

This frank and definitive response closes with a more diplomatic tone whereby Firmin attempts to flatter the United States, recalling as he does his "fervent sympathy and sincere attachment for the most glorious and most generous republic in the New World and perhaps the entire modern world."[62]

Douglass may have got it exactly right: the presence of seven American ships off the coast of the island may have inclined the Haitians to decide against ceding Môle Saint-Nicolas while simultaneously giving them a solid pretext to justify their decision. It may also be that Hannibal Price, Haiti's ambassador in Washington, D.C., at the time, also played a significant role in Firmin's decision-making by sending him a telegram from the United States dated April 18, 1891, in which he assures Firmin that the United States would not use force but was trying to simply intimidate Haiti by sending their squadrons: "The fleet is there for the purpose of intimidating. Do not yield. Nothing will happen."[63]

The United States had suffered a rather humiliating setback. The great American nation had lost face to a tiny republic, and moreover one governed by Black people. The Republicans in charge of segregationist America had a lot at stake in this affair, first of all their credibility both at the federal level and internationally. The United States attempted a last intimidation maneuver that took the form of circling the island with U.S. navy ships. However, this only made people more agitated since the effort to take control of Môle was perceived by Haitian people as proof of neocolonialism on the part of the American government. Haitians could not help but think that this was white and racist America trying to seize Môle from the Black republic. The Haitian government was even obliged to refute rumors about a hypothetical government handover of Môle to the Americans in a public declaration in the *Moniteur* for April 25, 1891.[64] The Haitian government was clearly destabilized by the agitation and alarmism caused by the presence of the ships and the rumors about a handover of Môle:

> Neither Môle Saint-Nicolas nor any other territory will be leased. Our relations with the republic of the United States will continue on the same foundation of sympathy and cordiality from which they have never departed,

> because our Great Friend will be able to understand our refusal thanks to its spirit of generosity and fairness so well known throughout the world.[65]

Frederick Douglass was aware of the implications of these accusations of neocolonialism tinged with racism, and he tried to calm the situation. He was probably very upset himself since he knew his country was entering into a dark period of its history with Black Americans now free and equal on paper but not in actual fact, as Jim Crow laws aiming to keep Black men from voting were spreading through every southern state. Looking to reduce tensions, and probably bothered by his own role in destabilizing the government of a republic whose stability precisely he had always been quick to praise, Douglass tried one last time to reopen negotiations with Firmin for the leasing of Môle. But Firmin repeated his refusal and let it be known that his "no" was definitive.[66]

This was the last interview between Douglass and Firmin, who resigned some days later and was replaced by Saint-Hilaire Hugon Lechaud, formerly Haiti's minister of public works.[67] Public opinion found the acceptance of this resignation surprising, seeing it as sign of the government's weakness and of further problems to come. It is true that complications were only just beginning. In early May, Douglass witnessed acts of violence and repression on the island. The city of Port-au-Prince and the surrounding area were placed under martial law, and the government, fearing an insurrection, made numerous arrests.[68] President Hyppolite tried to restore calm and silence the persistent rumors about Môle Saint-Nicolas in a speech published in the *Moniteur* on May 6, 1891. He repeated that he had not signed over Môle nor any portion of territory and that such a thing would never happen.[69] He even promised to publish the correspondence between the United States and Haiti about Môle, and openly accused Légitime's supporters of having planted the rumors.

Douglass then asked permission to leave the island for sixty days, claiming he had urgent affairs that required his attention back in America.[70] As riots were multiplying, Douglass received a telegram on June 1 from the State Department authorizing him to leave his post immediately.[71] It is clear that the State Department was seeking to get rid of Douglass, who was held completely responsible for the failure of the Môle negotiations. As the island was burning and bloodied with the government executing without trial its opponents, Douglass, terrified and disappointed, tied up loose ends and left the island on July 1, 1891.[72] Shortly afterward Douglass submitted his resignation in a short note sent from his home in Anacostia.[73] He later had to battle to receive the back pay that was due to him—a struggle that was further humiliating.[74] The Môle fiasco left many victims: first of all Haiti, since this affair stirred up tensions and reignited a bloody civil war; and also Frederick Douglass, whose only option was to resign given how unfavorably he was viewed by the government (Blaine and Tracy being the leading accusers) and in the press, which piled on in blaming Douglass for the failed negotiations.

Interestingly, Douglass, who up until then had always tried to defend his government against accusations of racism that were leveled against it, now responded to his detractors in the press by claiming that in the Môle affair he had been a victim of racial prejudice.[75] His overarching pride prevented him from accepting any responsibility for what happened, and he even said it was jealousy toward him that explained why certain Americans were hounding him from the moment of Haiti's refusal to hand over Môle to the Americans. Attacked and wounded by a barrage of criticism that he was probably not expecting, Douglass was forced to counter with his version of the facts. In two articles, both entitled "Haïti and the United States: Inside History of the Negotiations for the Môle St. Nicolas," published in the *North American Review* in the summer of 1891, Douglass unequivocally refused to accept responsibility for failure in the Môle Saint-Nicolas affair.

The first pages of part 1 settle some personal scores. Douglass positions himself as a righter of wrongs and apostle of truth as he attacks journalists who were part of "a premeditated attempt to make me a scapegoat to bear off the sins of others."[76] Douglass then evokes the anti-Black prejudice that he claimed he had endured. This Douglass-as-victim was different from the Douglass who had wanted to believe in the equality of the races and who had always done his utmost to convince others and himself that racism was a thing of the past and that people respected his personhood in all circumstances. He was now declaring that the criticism raining down on him over the preceding months was above all race-motivated. Whereas his critics had said that a Black man should not be sent to Haiti as a diplomat, Douglass claims, on the contrary, that sending a Black person was more likely to lead to successful negotiations with a Black government since the latter could hardly use skin color as an argument for refusal: "it would be shockingly inconsistent for Haiti to object to a black minister while she herself is black." Douglass also reminds Americans that Haiti was perfectly acquainted with the situation of Black people in the United States and in particular the prejudice they faced on a daily basis: "Haiti is no stranger to Americans or to American prejudice."[77]

Douglass next expresses his indignation that some believed it was necessary in this affair to exploit the relative weakness of Haiti and its fear of white nations to obtain the Môle territory. Douglass staunchly defends the right of this republic, or any republic in the world, to be respected by all, including the most powerful. Douglass the Black activist was reemerging out from behind Douglass the Republican and diplomat and even rising above Douglass the American citizen as he marked a certain distance between himself and his own country, which he accused of being mean and uncharitable.[78] Yet while denouncing the trickery of those who sought to seize on Haiti, Douglass confesses that it was a "weak" country, implying its inferiority to the United States. The ambiguity that troubled the Black activist reemerged: Haiti was a Black republic, which proved that Black people were capable of governing themselves; yet it was a weak and easily influenced country, which precipitated America's attempt to exploit it. Who was speaking? The expansionist or the representative of the Black diaspora defending the right to self-determination of all peoples?

To refute those who claimed he had not understood the strategic importance of acquiring the Môle territory, which was the second major accusation leveled by American newspapers, especially those in New York, Douglass replies that in fact he had been one of the first to evoke it, reminding his critics of the mission he had participated in under Grant. In almost the same words he had used to justify his pro-annexation position in 1871, Douglass repeats his uninhibited imperialist argument, still convinced of the reasonableness of an extension of American influence.[79] To be fair, he was calling for an extension of the benevolent force of an egalitarian America while opposing neocolonial imperialism. These contradictory arguments—on one hand a defense of oppressed peoples and of their right to independence, and on the other siding with imperialism—are representative of the divided feelings of the Sage of Anacostia. He was picked apart by his own paradoxes, and nothing reveals better the equivocation of his personality than the Môle Saint-Nicolas affair.

After carefully responding to all the accusations flung at him from various publications, Douglass turns to the facts as they occurred from his point of view. Along the way he notes Admiral Gherardi's impoliteness and transgressions of protocol toward himself and to the Haitians, thus implying that the failure of the negotiations was probably due to the admiral's arguments for acquiring Môle—arguments, Douglass claimed, that were close to blackmail and that he himself never subscribed to. He thus declines all responsibility for the failure of the negotiations and claims that Gherardi as the "principal speaker" and "also the principal negotiator" in the interviews with the Haitian government should be considered as singularly responsible.[80] The information related by Douglass in this first article is similar in every way to what was reported in his dispatches.

In the second article, Douglass gives an account of the negotiations themselves. Sticking to the same facts as in his dispatches, this retelling is filled with comments that all go toward insisting on how blameless he is, on the injustice of which he is a victim, and how the entire responsibility for this debacle belongs to Gherardi. Among the causes of the failure, beyond the alleged culpability of Gherardi, Douglass evokes Haiti's complex history and its fear of losing its independence, but also its distrust of a country (such as the United States) where racial prejudice still exists.[81] Douglass also attributes a large share of responsibility for failure to the New York press in comments that underline the (new) power of media at a moment in American history that experienced a rapid development of yellow journalism and sensationalism.[82] Finally, Douglass underlines the intimidation tactics, most obviously the insistent presence of American navy vessels off the coast of Haiti, and how they proved the American government's misunderstanding of the Haitian national character and were a sort of last straw that convinced the Haitians to refuse a lease arrangement of Môle Saint-Nicolas.[83]

Frederick Douglass's Black Atlantic

A decade before the start of this diplomatic crisis, Douglass made a speech in Elmira, New York, on the occasion of the emancipation of Black slaves in the British West Indies. That speech on August 1, 1880, would become famous. While he was supposed to speak about the abolition of slavery by Great Britain, Douglass gave his vision of what Paul Gilroy one hundred years later would call the "Black Atlantic." For Douglass, Black history was not national but transnational; and even what was, on the face of it, local, such as the emancipation in the British Caribbean islands, had an international resonance. Douglass claimed that the anniversary of Black emancipation in the West Indies was also the anniversary of the emancipation of the entire Black race, and therefore of Black people in the United States insofar as the two former slave populations were intimately linked. American slaves and British slaves were part of the Black diaspora for Douglass, and their local history was fully a part of their global history—in other words, a history of the Black race throughout the Americas and the world. The experience of one group ought to serve others; the victories of these people heralded the victories to come of those people; the history of some here or there would inspire and nourish the history of others there or here.[84] Besides affirming the importance of this universal connected history, Douglass seized the occasion to focus on what interested him the most: the situation of Black people in the United States. Even if in 1880 Black Americans were free on paper, so to speak, their true living conditions were visibly deteriorating; notably the citizenship rights granted by the Fourteenth and Fifteenth Amendments were not being respected.[85] Thus, beginning with an "exterior" event, the emancipation of Black people in the British West Indies, Douglass analyzed the specifics of a national situation: the condition of his Black compatriots in their own country.

Frederick Douglass's Haitian experience may be read alongside this famous speech in Elmira. Convinced that he and other Black Americans were part of a single transnational community, also called the Black diaspora, Douglass sees Haiti as much more than simply one of America's neighbors or a strategic location for expanding American civilization. By accepting the post of minister resident in Haiti, it is possible that Douglass, beyond having his ego stroked and being flattered by the president's confidence in him, wanted also to be on-site to analyze the situation of his Haitian brethren and see to what extent their experience could serve Black people in the United States. Unfortunately, the Haitian experience seems to have fallen below his expectations. After having tried to convince his government and himself that the Haitians had succeeded in establishing a stable and consistent political situation, he returned home in 1891 terribly disappointed. That frustration is particularly evident in the pair of articles published after his return.

Between the lines, one senses that Douglass believed the Black diaspora in Haiti needed the protection of more "civilized" Black people. Douglass makes direct use of imperialist language: Haiti is referred to as a "weak nation" whereas the United States is a "great nation."[86] More strikingly, Douglass comes off as a somewhat arrogant man using a rather paternalist discourse—a rather paradoxical position given that he was a former slave who had suffered deeply from the alleged superiority of white people. And yet he could describe Haiti as though it were a child who needed to be guided and to consider the Black American as superior to the Black Haitian, whom he must therefore guide. Douglass established a hierarchy within the Black community. This started to become clear in the last of his diplomatic writings sent off during the final weeks of his mission in Haiti. To a certain extent this idea of a hierarchy within the Black community recalls certain passages in his autobiographies in which he admits that more educated Black people constituted an elite group to which he belonged—suggesting that he considered himself superior to most Black people and even almost criticizing others as in part responsible for their lower station.[87] He now blamed Haiti and its people—scolding them for their fearful, timid character, for their outmoded traditions, and for the failure of the negotiations—in remarks that may be interpreted as rather contemptuous.[88]

The takeaway from a reading of the *North American Review* pieces is that Black Americans should protect Haiti from whites; Haiti is too weak to resist on its own; and Douglass was clearly divided between national and pan-African affinities: standing sometimes with his community in denying that his skin color could have been a factor in the failure of the negotiations, and yet sometimes detaching from that part of his identity when speaking as an American but as though he were colorless and not Black.[89] This is the case in those moments when he claims that Haiti was aware of American racial prejudice and writes, "Of course our peculiar and intense prejudice against the colored race was not forgotten."[90]

In the Môle affair, he was divided between his attachment to his country, as an American and patriotic expansionist, and his solidarity, as a Black person, with Haiti. It is clear from Douglass's writings—notably the diplomatic correspondence—that his experience as the minister resident and consul general in Haiti and his testimony concerning the diplomatic relations between the two countries at the time of the Môle Saint-Nicolas affair give much to think about within this crucial period of African American history. Nominally free while not yet equal, nor yet separated legally from whites, Black Americans were trying to find their proper place within the American nation, and while some were finally being promoted into important governmental positions—at the state, federal, or international level—that elevation could operate as an illusory success that hid the discrimination and segregation endured by a large majority. If the Môle affair seems particularly revealing of the personal paradoxes of one individual, Frederick Douglass, it speaks volumes about the equivocal behavior of his country of origin. One may rightly ask if America had perhaps extolled certain members of the Black American elite with the unspoken aim of winning over the new Black vote, and in certain cases, such as with Douglass, to recruit influential men to serve the imperialist cause or any other agenda of the Republican Party. In the present case we have been examining, it is worth asking if the nomination of Douglass was done to soften up the Haitians and get them to hand over Môle Saint-Nicolas. We are here at the intersection of emotion and realist politics with this instrumentalization of a race to serve the nation.

The Môle episode is revealing of the implicit fraternity between Black Americans and Haitians operating via the personal implication of Douglass in this affair, an involvement that demonstrates the intensity of the emotional bonds linking the two Black communities, which from a certain perspective are in fact but one—the singular Black diaspora.

It would seem that the Harrison administration posted Douglass to Haiti thinking perhaps that the Haitians would not be suspicious of a man of their own color who had combated slavery. Douglass, for his part, was very sensitive to the Haitian feeling of national unity, and his patriotism as a Republican and an American did not outstrip his wish to defend Black independence—American or otherwise. This is probably why some months later Douglass would be asked to serve as the first commissioner of the Haitian pavilion at the Chicago World's Fair of 1893. In any case, this permanent rift between Black race and American citizenship, poignantly incarnated by Douglass, corresponds point by point to the feeling of duality that will be described some years later by the Black historian W. E. B. Du Bois:

> The history of the American Negro is the history of this strife,—this longing to attain self-conscious manhood, to merge his double self into a better and truer self. In this merging he wishes neither of the older selves to be lost. He would not Africanize America, for America has too much to teach the world and Africa. He would not bleach his Negro soul in a flood of white Americanism, for he knows that Negro blood has a message for the world. He simply wishes to make it possible for a man to be both a Negro and an American, without being cursed and spit upon by his fellows, without having the doors of Opportunity closed roughly in his face.[91]

CHAPTER 7

Haiti and Frederick Douglass at the Chicago World's Fair

Never in modern times have men of widely different characteristics been brought together in a work that has resulted in such complete unity of action.[1]

—HALSEY C. IVES

The disgrace into which Frederick Douglass had fallen in the eyes of American public opinion—especially as conveyed by the press and his own government—in the aftermath of the failed Môle Saint-Nicolas negotiations destroyed any chance he might have had to be named to another position in government. It seemed as though the affair might even mark the end of public life for the Sage of Anacostia, who was no longer unanimously lionized within his own community. Already seventy-four years old, Douglass could have definitively withdrawn from public life and offered himself some well-deserved rest in retirement. And yet, less than two years after his resignation as minister resident, Douglass gave one of his most important speeches ever, "Lecture on Haiti," amid circumstances that the historical record has not fully elucidated.

Even though the speech has never been studied in relation to the particular place and the specific, immediate context in which it was given, it is commonly considered one of the major public statements made by Douglass, the former diplomat whose career had been abruptly interrupted by a diplomatic incident between Haiti and the United States. It turns out that this speech was much more than a thrilling homage to Haiti or fierce criticism of the imperialist foreign policy and domestic politics of the United States uttered by a fallen and disappointed ex-diplomat. But to understand this, it must be noted that the speech was not, on that day, spoken by Frederick Douglass the former minister resident and consul general of the United States in Haiti, but instead by Frederick Douglass the first commissioner of the Haitian Pavilion—nominated by the Haitian president himself, Florvil Hyppolite—at the World's Columbian Exposition in Chicago. In addition, on the day of the speech, January 2, 1893, Douglass had already contributed the introduction to a famous pamphlet co-edited with Ida B. Wells, *The Reason Why the Colored American Is Not in the World's Columbian Exposition.*

To understand why Douglass, Wells, and other Black activists felt the need to write and publish such a manifesto and how the Chicago World's Fair ignited so much activism, and to measure the impact of Douglass's lecture on Haiti, it is necessary to first place this Columbian Exposition, as it was called, within the context of domestic American history as well as within the wider context of universal exhibits of the nineteenth century more generally, before focusing on the Haitian Pavilion itself that served as Douglass's public forum and allowed his return into the political and media limelight.

The Chicago World's Fair and the Haitian Pavilion in the United States of the Late Nineteenth Century

When Frederick Douglass returned to the United States after spending two years in Haiti, he was unable to ignore the extent to which the situation of his fellow Black citizens had declined at a vertiginous pace. Segregation, which was already well established in southern mores in 1889, now regulated all relations between whites and Blacks in the public sphere, limiting Black access to public institutions and services. Beyond mere physical segregation, the South had constructed a more pernicious strategy for achieving added control over Black citizens and a lasting recapture of power from the hands of Republicans. The strategy consisted in simply depriving Black men of the right to vote, despite the guarantee enshrined in the Fifteenth Amendment to the Constitution. To do that, southern states made a series of local decisions during the 1890s that all aimed to circumvent the amendment by imposing voting eligibility rules on all their citizens. On paper these new conditions applied to both Blacks and whites. In practice, however, they essentially barred Black citizens, and on some occasions lower-class white people, from voting at all.

These measures varied from state to state, but most of the time these new laws imposed property-owning requirements or literacy tests. Some states adopted the so-called grandfather clause that only allowed descendants of those who had enjoyed the right to vote before 1867 to be exempt from the new education, property, or tax hurdles. One or more of these new laws setting preconditions for being placed on voting rolls were added to the constitutions of ex-Confederate states: in Mississippi in 1890, South Carolina in 1895, Louisiana in 1898, North Carolina in 1900, Alabama in 1901, Virginia in 1902, Georgia in 1908, and Oklahoma in 1910. In all these places, the eligibility hurdles were already in unofficial use before 1882, according to historian J. Martin Kousser.[2] All the above-named states, as well as Florida, Tennessee, Arkansas, and Texas, adopted the "poll tax" of one or two dollars to be paid by every person wishing to be added to voting rolls. That may seem today like a small fee, but of course it needs to be understood within the economic context of the time. The annual per capita income in ex-Confederate states averaged $86 in 1880 and $100 in 1900, and the vast majority of Black workers earned far less than that. For Black sharecroppers, one or two dollars represented a substantial portion of their income; therefore, the poll tax was in practice an effective tactic to prevent Black people from voting.[3] Some states also restricted the period during which one could register to vote, thus further discouraging certain categories of workers. For example, in Alabama after 1892, potential voters could only apply to be registered on voter rolls in the month of May each year, precisely the busiest month for all involved in farming.[4] In addition to these formal constraints, extremist groups such as the Ku Klux Klan led campaigns of intimidation and terror. It is thus no surprise that the number of Black registered voters plummeted during the 1890s and the first decade of the twentieth century. In 1896, for example, 130,334 Black men were registered to vote in Louisiana, but only 1,342—a roughly 99 percent drop—by 1904. The cause was clearly Louisiana's imposition of property and literacy clauses as well as a poll tax.[5]

While southern states were going about depriving Black citizens of the right to vote, they saw their system of racial segregation receive a boost of legitimation on the federal level thanks to the Plessy v. Ferguson decision handed down by the U.S. Supreme Court in 1896. The history of the Louisiana man Homer Plessy, a so-called octoroon—only one great-grandparent was Black, and he therefore had seven-eighths "white" blood—is notorious. We will simply recall that it was following his deliberately boarding a "whites-only" train car in Louisiana in 1892 that his case would rise to the Supreme Court in 1896. The decision handed down on May 18, 1896, was unquestionably a major victory for the South. It authorized states to impose laws of racial segregation so long as the public services proposed to the separate groups were of equal quality. This decision and the "separate but equal" doctrine that followed from it had a devastating effect on the entire Black population, and not just in the South but also in northern and western states, which now had the green light to pass segregationist legislation of their own—and they did.[6]

Thus, it should be noted that the Chicago World's Fair opened on May 1, 1893, amidst a particularly tense political situation of North–South reconciliation at the expense of Black exclusion. The small place allocated to Black

Americans at this universal exposition was a clear symptom of the larger social reality, as we shall see in the next chapter.

It is in the capital of the United Kingdom at the height of its power that the first such world's fair took place in 1851, the famous Crystal Palace Exhibition, whose official name was the Great Exhibition of the Works of Industry of All Nations.[7] At the time, "holding such a universal exposition was the fusion of diverse wishes and multiple objectives: instructing and entertaining the masses, a national statement in a time of peace and a sketch of the future [were] the principal goals pursued within the framework of these grandiose spectacles."[8] The nations organizing these universal exhibitions were pursuing more than mere entertainment. If one of the domestic objectives was to conglomerate the people around a grand public event, it is also the case that in the nineteenth century a universal exhibition was a major media campaign directed outward. It was the occasion for attracting millions of people from around the globe and amplifying to a great extent the attractiveness of the world of commerce and industry. As such it was a perfect propaganda tool because "nations [gave] the visitor the image they [had] constructed of themselves; and despite their cosmopolitan air, the universal exhibitions lent themselves to promoting their national values."[9] In 1851 England used the Great Exhibition to affirm its civilizing pretensions, positioning itself as the example to follow in the fight against slavery and the abolition of the international slave trade.[10] These universal exhibits were therefore not simply gigantic innocent parties. They were a means for the organizing nation to affirm its industrial, technological, and economic hegemony, its cultural and social dominance, and, one must remember in this second half of the nineteenth century, its military and imperial superiority. In this regard the British set the example that would be later imitated in the United States.[11]

The first official world's fair to be held on American soil took place in Philadelphia in 1876. The Centennial International Exhibition's official name was the International Exhibition of Arts, Manufactures, and Products of the Soil and Mine. This was the first in a long series of exhibits in America. The "world" and "universal" dimensions of these American exhibits were clearly designed to project America onto an international stage and reinforce its imperialist ambitions. It also offered the country, which was struggling to reunify at a national level, multiple occasions and levers to transform the political reconciliation process that had begun in 1877 into a durable reunification of North and South that would be respected by the powerful industrial nations of Europe.[12] Thus, one of the goals of the Chicago exhibition of 1893 was to present to the American people a general inventory and assessment of the scientific, intellectual, moral, and industrial prowess of the nation, while also advancing the claim of its superiority over all other nations. The fair's goal was to make American civilization more visible by exhibiting technological, industrial, and intellectual achievements via a series of "Congresses"; in other words, public lectures attended by millions of American and foreign visitors who traveled to Chicago in 1893.[13] Sixteen years after the end of Reconstruction, and four centuries after the iconic discovery of America by Columbus in 1492, one of the goals of the exhibition was clearly to reunify the country once and for all by gathering together northern and southern states in a celebration of the glory of the whole country, and thereby reignite the patriotic flame within every American. The 1893 exhibit would showcase the historian Frederick Jackson Turner, who presented his thesis about the importance of the frontier to the Congress of the American Historical Association three years after the American Census Bureau declared the end of the frontier, in other words the end of a line between unsettled and settled territories on the North American continent.[14]

The 1893 World's Fair, initially planned to coincide with the four hundredth anniversary of the discovery of America by Christopher Columbus, was intended to be the unforgettable celebration of the merits of American civilization, and therefore of the Caucasian race as a whole, in opposition to the supposed and demonstrated barbarism of Africa, which the rest of the civilized world had already begun to divvy up.[15] Chicago, the city chosen to host this gigantic exhibition, was faced with a colossal challenge. Moreover, it was given this mission barely twenty years after the great fire of 1871, and while memories of the labor dispute resulting in the Haymarket Massacre of 1886 were still fresh. Twenty-eight years after the abolition of slavery, sixteen years after the end of Reconstruction, during the height of the "Gilded Age," the organizers planned to showcase the grandeur of American civilization, display the unity of the nation, and highlight American inventiveness and technological know-how, all the while shunting aside the adjacent class war and racial tensions.[16]

The organizing committee put Daniel H. Burnham in charge of this difficult task, naming him director of works, with George R. Davis as director-general. The site chosen was Jackson Park, the third largest expanse in the city, situated at 57th Street along Lake Michigan south of the city center. The organizers also recruited the landscape architect Frederick Law Olmstead and the Harvard-educated naturalist and anthropologist Frederic Ward Putnam to design the exhibit in two distinct parts. One would be the "White City," an ensemble of grand buildings that would house the exhibits of nations and states (essentially the grand colonial powers of America and Europe and the individual American states). The other part would be a mile-long avenue named Midway Plaisance, simply called The Midway, which would consist of restaurants, attractions such as the Ferris wheel, belly dancers, and the reconstitutions of African villages and other displays. The Midway was a bustling space that Putnam envisioned as an open-air museum of entertainment and instruction where visitors would encounter peoples and creatures of lower, more "primitive" civilizations, which would likely nourish feelings of superiority when compared to the high grandeur of the civilizations represented in the other half of the exhibition. In addition, it was decided there would be a series of conferences associated with the exhibition. These public lectures, named "Congresses," were to assemble recognized world experts on large questions and important topics of the time such as religion, work, the condition of women, and Africa.[17]

Many Black Americans expressed their anger at what they considered to be the deliberate and racist marginalization by the exhibition's organizers of the Black community to the point of near total invisibility at the Chicago World's Fair. Close observation suggests that organizers sought to give Black people, whether American or foreign, the least importance possible. This would seem to be confirmed if one investigates the particulars surrounding the Haitian Pavilion.

This pavilion was not a miserable little hut.[18] On the contrary, the few photos that exist are proof that it was a majestic edifice; and even though it was "one of the three smallest pavilions," it was one of the most beautiful according to commentaries published at the time.[19] Moreover, it was ideally situated within Jackson Park, at the center of the White City, in the vicinity of the pavilions of powerful nations such as England, Spain, and Germany.[20] Photographs or drawings of it are very hard to come by, however. More surprisingly, various architectural plans and maps of the exhibition spaces make no mention of its existence. The large quantity of contemporary writings on the event make only passing reference to the Haitian Pavilion and often ignore its existence altogether. When it is mentioned in the literature, the Black republic appears indiscriminately in simple lists of other nations and structures.[21]

A handful of publications devote a few lines to the Haitian Pavilion, one of them describing it as "One of the prettiest structures in the foreign section. Pavilion shaped. Cost $20,000. It is filled with curiosities and beautiful things."[22] *The Book of the Fair* offers the most complete account of the Haitian Pavilion, describing its colonial architecture, façade decorated with the nation's flag, including the principal dates of Haitian history and an explanation

FIG. 9. "The Haitian Pavilion," *Pavillon de la République d'Haïti à l'Exposition Universelle de Chicago*, Chicago, Illinois, 1893. *Photograph. Library of Congress, Washington, D.C.*

of the nation's motto that appears on the flag (*l'Union fait la force*—Unity Is Strength). It also describes the pavilion's interior and the objects it contained. The book's author, Hubert Howe Bancroft, offers a list of the interesting items to be found inside the structure: vestiges of the Columbian era, works of art, portraits and busts of important figures such as Toussaint Louverture, Florvil Hyppolite, and even Frederick Douglass. Bancroft also includes praise for the national beverage, coffee, which was served to visitors in the pavilion, and for its leading prestigious crop, sugar, of which different varieties were presented to the public. The account also gives some information about when the building was inaugurated, its commissioners, and the celebration that took place at the pavilion to mark the anniversary of Haiti's independence.[23]

Unfortunately, very few publications exist that give a visual representation of the Haitian Pavilion. Two of them, *The World's Fair Souvenir Album* and *Official Views of the World's Columbian Exposition*, are souvenir albums, the first containing 268 photos of the Chicago exhibition and the second 115 reproductions of engravings.[24]

A third publication, *The Dream City*, is also a souvenir album of photographs accompanied by descriptions of various length of each building and point of interest for the visitor. A single paragraph of a few lines describes the

Haitian Pavilion. Besides the date of its opening and the objects it contains, one learns that the pavilion housed a restaurant:

> A restaurant was kept in the southern part of this building, at which colored people found it agreeable to refresh themselves, for notwithstanding the protestations of the colored people and in defiance of the laws, the race line is still sharply drawn in the great Northern cities.[25]

The near total absence of Haiti and its pavilion from the literature of the day is in one sense rather surprising. The small republic on the island of Hispaniola—"discovered" in 1492 by Christopher Columbus, the European explorer celebrated at this World's Fair and named in its very title, the World's Columbian Exposition—seems to have been set apart from the other nations represented at the 1893 exhibition and certainly did not enjoy the normal polite interest otherwise accorded by white Americans to the fair's various component parts. In another sense this lack of interest in the Black republic is not surprising at all, if one recalls the sociopolitical context within the United States in 1893. As we have already said, the great American nation was racially divided at that time. Two glaring facts, on one hand Haiti's very participation at the Chicago World's Fair as a Black republic, and on the other the widespread segregation throughout the territory of the host country, could hardly be held apart insofar as Black men and women who visited the fairgrounds were only allowed to get refreshments at the food stand of the Haitian Pavilion, the single nonsegregated locale. The prevalence of racist feelings among many of Douglass's fellow citizens at the end of the nineteenth century may explain the relative absence of publicity devoted to the Haitian Pavilion. White elites of the day, whether from the North or South, were probably made uneasy by the irritating and almost bothersome installation of this little Black nation among the great "civilized" nations.

Besides the near total absence of the Haitian Pavilion from the literature devoted to the exposition, most publications also disregard the presence and active participation of Frederick Douglass at the World's Fair of 1893. And yet Douglass was omnipresent. Not only was he named head commissioner of the Haitian Pavilion by President Hyppolite, Douglass also participated in the weeklong "Congress on Africa" that took place August 14–21. He was also among the Black Americans who applauded the creation of a "Colored People's Day," a cultural event on August 25, 1893, that he helped organize and spoke at, giving a stirring address denouncing segregation and pleading for equal civil rights for Black Americans throughout the United States.[26]

When he decided to accept the invitation of the United States to participate in the World Columbian Exposition of 1893, President Hyppolite immediately reached out to two individuals to represent Haiti in Chicago as its commissioners: the Haitian Charles A. Preston and the American Frederick Douglass.[27] In 1893 the Sage of Anacostia was still very much one of the most famous Black figures in America. Though his reputation was tarnished by the Môle Saint-Nicolas affair, he remained a respected and influential man internationally. And yet, like the Haitian Pavilion he oversaw, Douglass seems to have gone largely unnoticed. Douglass is even less present than the pavilion in the literature of the day. Most publications do not mention him at all. *Hill's Souvenir Guide,* which offers a list of participating countries and their commissioners, lists the name of Charles A. Preston, the second commissioner of the Haitian Pavilion, but leaves out Douglass, the first commissioner.[28] The few publications that do mention Douglass simply name him as commissioner of the Haitian Pavilion without further commentary. The *Photographic History of the World's Fair and Sketch of the City of Chicago* even misspells both Douglass and Frederick.[29] *The Dream City* also gets his name wrong ("Douglas") and leaves out his position as commissioner, stating only that he gave the inaugural speech at the Haitian Pavilion on January 2, 1893.[30] The *History of the World's Fair* is even more terse, including his name between two others with no explanation of his role at the exposition.[31] *The Book of the Fair* at least specifies the roles of Douglass and Preston and also mentions that a portrait of Douglass was displayed in the Haitian Pavilion.[32]

So, both Douglass and the nation he represented at the World's Fair of 1893 were snubbed by almost everyone charged with writing up the event. One wonders how such an "oversight" in the contemporary literature can be explained. The most likely answer is to be found in the domestic sociopolitical context as well as the international situation of the time.

The Origin of the Marginalization of the Haitian Pavilion: Frederick Douglass, President Hyppolite, and the Môle Saint-Nicolas Affair

Several elements must be taken into account in order to understand why the Haitian Pavilion and its first commissioner were left out of contemporary coverage of the event. They will also help explain the impact on Frederick Douglass of his role as commissioner. As we have seen in earlier chapters, the triangle Douglass–Haiti–United States was not simply a matter of diplomatic service but had important implications for the entire Black American community. It is an undeniable fact that in 1893 Douglass found himself in a delicate situation. Two years after the Môle Saint-Nicolas affair, Douglass was once again at the center of a diplomatic relationship between the United States and Haiti. This time, however, Douglass was not representing his country of origin, the country in which he was nominally an official citizen since the ratification of the Fourteenth Amendment in 1868, but was instead representing the country of his heart, the place he had always felt emotionally close to, the country that had served as a positive example first to abolitionists and later to militants seeking equal rights for Black Americans and more broadly for the entire Black diaspora. Moreover, this time the struggle he was leading was not taking place on a Caribbean island already sympathetic to his cause but in a major American city riven by segregation.

American public opinion, especially in the South, had always been wary of the Black republic, and that distrust went back to the first days of its war of independence more than a century before the Chicago World's Fair opened its doors. Twenty-eight years after the official abolition of slavery in the United States, as southern states were passing and implementing explicitly segregationist laws, Haiti the rebel nation continued to have a negative reputation among opinion makers and shapers. Even if the fear of "revolutionary contagion" had subsided since the end of the Civil War, white America's opinion of Haiti did not soften. After first recoiling in fear from its revolutionary spirit, it was now the island's bellicose character, its near-constant state of civil war, and the alleged incompetence and instability of its leading politicians who rotated in and out of office that alarmed Americans. This is clear from the many newspaper clippings from the time that Douglass compiled.

It must be remembered that the Chicago World's Fair was organized during a period of highly strained relations between the American government and Haiti. The United States had transmitted its invitation to Haiti to participate in this international cultural event through the diplomatic channel of its minister resident of the time, who was none other than Frederick Douglass himself; and this at the very moment when the Harrison administration was plotting to acquire Môle Saint-Nicolas. Douglass's diplomatic correspondence indicates that the American invitation reached Haiti in March 1891.[33] After this official invitation was received, the American government charged a certain Frederick A. Ober with the task of visiting various "West India Islands" to talk with their governments about their possible participation at the World's Fair.[34] Douglass reports in a dispatch that Firmin, Haiti's foreign affairs minister, was favorably disposed to the idea but could not give official confirmation of Haiti's participation without the approval of President Hyppolite, who was at the time conducting government business elsewhere on the island. Then, only a few weeks after having extended to Haiti the invitation to come to Chicago, the United States suffered the supreme humiliation of the failure of the Môle Saint-Nicolas negotiations. Finally, on June 24, 1891, insubmissive Haiti decided to confirm its participation at the Columbian World's Fair in a letter signed by Monsieur Lechaud, the former minister of public works who became the minister of foreign affairs following the resignation of Firmin on May 7, 1891.[35] From a purely diplomatic perspective, the situation was complicated, to say the least, and provoked high tension between two countries who were officially friends but unofficially felt hostile toward each other.

The diplomatic fiasco the United States experienced in the spring of 1891 around the Môle Saint-Nicolas affair could on its own explain the quasiboycott of the Haitian Pavilion and the near-total silence about its existence in write-ups of the time. But as if the refusal to hand over the Môle were not enough to anger its American neighbor, the Haitian president made a rather unexpected request to Douglass in early 1892 that no doubt further irritated the American government and public opinion. Although the American government and press had more or less made Douglass the scapegoat for the failed Môle negotiations, here was President Hyppolite asking the same Douglass to accept the title of first commissioner as Haiti's representative at the Chicago World's Fair and at the Haiti Pavilion in particular.

The Haitian authorities conferred on Monsieur C. Archin, then "secretary of state of exterior relations," the task of announcing to Douglass his nomination as first commissioner. In a letter dated February 11, 1892, Archin states that "his Excellency the President of Haiti has chosen Douglass to be First Commissioner of the Republic of Haiti at the World's Columbian Exposition in Chicago."[36] Some weeks earlier, on January 16, 1892, President Hyppolite had sent a personal letter to "Frédérick Douglass, former Minister of the United States in Haiti," in which he obsequiously thanks Douglass for the "lecture" that he had recently given "on Haiti":

> Dear Sir, I read the text of the lecture that you gave on Haiti before a large American audience. This lecture impressed me—not because of the praise you extended to my country, but because you judged it fairly and because you spoke of its faults and its merits with an impartiality that does you honor. . . .
>
> Bear with me, a citizen of Haiti, as I thank you for the justice you have rendered to my country.[37]

Archin's February letter to Douglass clearly states that choosing him as first commissioner was principally motived by the "Lecture on Haiti," which had been so complimentary toward the Black republic: "This choice . . . was inspired . . . by the feeling of patriotic sympathy and admiration present in our Nation for the remarkable man whose plain words defended it recently with eloquence and conviction to the Great America."[38] It is worth noting that the enthusiasm generated by this speech among the Haitian people was such that Hannibal Price, then Haitian consul in New York, asked Douglass's permission to have the speech, as well as the articles about the Môle Saint-Nicolas affair that had appeared some months earlier in the *North American Review,* translated into French and published in Haiti.[39] It was therefore in thanks to "the one whose name commands respect . . . and whose long career is a shining testimony to the power of a sentiment of right and of faith in God in the fight against injustices"—in short, for all his work on behalf of Haiti—that President Hyppolite named Frederick Douglass first commissioner of the Republic of Haiti at the World's Columbian Exposition in Chicago in early 1892.[40]

We have already commented in the preceding chapter on Douglass's two articles published in the highly respected *North American Review* soon after he resigned from his post as minister resident and consul general in the summer of 1891. Those documents, along with the no less famous speech of January 2, 1893, entitled "Lecture on Haiti" that was delivered to "Fifteen hundred of the best citizens of Chicago"[41] in Quinn Chapel, are usually the only texts cited by historians and biographers in their accounts of the Môle Saint-Nicolas affair and the special relation that linked Douglass and the Black republic. There is, however, another text signed by Douglass that also focuses on Haiti. It is a speech given on October 13, 1891, at the Metropolitan African Methodist Episcopal (AME) Church in Washington, D.C., with a newspaper giving it the somewhat misleading title "The Negotiations for the Mole Saint-Nicolas."[42] No other written record of this speech exists besides the document in the personal archives of Douglass, and its inadequate title may explain why it has gone unnoticed by historians and Douglass's biographers. Based on the title alone, one would expect it to be a condensed version of the articles published in the *North American Review.* However, that is not the case. In this October 1891 speech, Douglass offers a rather flattering portrait of the Haitian republic and praises President Hyppolite. There is no doubt that Hyppolite is referring to this long speech in his letter of January 16, 1892, and that it most likely contributed to Douglass being named first commissioner of the Haitian Pavilion at the World's Fair of 1893.

The transcription of this speech is conserved in the Frederick Douglass archives in the form of clippings from an unidentifiable newspaper published in

Washington and cut out and saved by Douglass himself. It is particularly interesting that Douglass seems to have crossed out certain passages of this transcription, passages that were later replaced by handwritten annotations made on the pieces of paper to which the columns of this newspaper piece were glued. One can make the strong deduction that this annotated scrapbook page was then used by Douglass as the initial draft for the speech he would give one year later, the famous "Lecture on Haiti" of January 2, 1893. It is clear that the first speech on Haiti from October 1891 served as the foundation for the second speech of the same name, since entire passages from the first are carried over word for word in the second. If one analyzes the first speech in relation to its historical context and immediate consequences—the Môle Saint-Nicolas affair, Douglass's resignation from his diplomatic functions, Haiti's positive response to the American invitation to participate in the 1893 World's Fair, and the nomination of Douglass as first commissioner—Douglass's intentions appear unequivocal: praise the Haitian people and the country's president, Louis Mondestin Florvil Hyppolite, while seizing the occasion to remind his audience of the precarious status of the civil rights of the Black American community in the United States. In short, Douglass, as so often when he spoke on a topic without any direct and obvious relation to the American nation, was using his ostensive subject, Haiti, as a springboard for making a proclamation about America's domestic politics and in particular the condition of Black people. Besides that, there was also an Atlanticist and diasporic dimension that may have escaped his audience, one perhaps not fully conscious to Douglass himself. However, to historians of the Atlantic space, this broader dimension speaks to the complexity of the process of identity construction within the Black American community of the second half of the nineteenth century and allows one to see in Douglass the emergence of Pan-African and diasporic ideas that are generally attributed to his successors, W. E. B. Du Bois and Marcus Garvey.[43]

Whereas in the *North American Review* pieces Douglass had insisted on Haiti's relative weakness, in this speech he underlines the country's grandeur and never once uses the adjective "weak." Even though he recognized that Haiti could still improve, that it was a young nation "still in her childhood," Douglass insisted on its capacity to progress more, to become even more civilized than it already was, and expressed no doubts about its future prospects. In his assessment based on twenty years of personal acquaintance with the island, Douglass assured his audience of its belonging in the near future to the family of "the most enlightened and highly civilized nations of the world," alongside Prussia, France, England, Italy, and Spain, while granting that it had not yet quite arrived at that level.[44]

If Frederick Douglass was, in this particular speech, so optimistic about the future of Haiti, it is because even while recognizing certain faults—a turbulent spirit, egoism, ignorance, superstition, and depravity among certain of its inhabitants—he also saw the characteristics of a solid and independent democracy.[45] According to Douglass, the best proof of this was its capacity to maintain a republican form of government similar to that of the United States since 1804.[46] These arguments were no doubt pleasing to President Hyppolite, all the more since Douglass not only praised the Haitian people, while also refuting the negative stereotype of laziness that Americans had always had about Haitians, but also praised the president. Douglass could not have been more lyrically exuberant in both his physical and moral description of Hyppolite and with his encouragement that the United States earnestly support this exemplary leader.[47]

But the principal interest of this forgotten speech of Douglass is certainly its transatlantic and diasporic dimension. For Douglass, Haiti is clearly the center of the Atlantic world. After succinctly recalling certain elements of Haitian history, he places the country at the heart of the Atlantic triangle, insisting on its location on Hispaniola, the first island on this side of the Atlantic where Christianity arrived with whites who had traveled from the other side of the Atlantic, because it was the Caribbean island where Christopher Columbus first set foot. Hispaniola was also, he said, the first island to which African slaves were first imported as well as the first island to abolish that institution.[48] It was this singular history marked by paradoxes that placed Haiti at the center of the Atlantic. It seems undeniable that in Douglass's retelling, Haiti's Atlantic dimension inspires the construction of a Black American identity that in turn recognizes itself as part of the existence of a Black diaspora. Obviously, Douglass does not use the term "diaspora," but he does affirm that Black Americans and Haitians are linked by a common destiny, a "common cause, and common ancestral identity." In this speech the destiny of Black Americans and Haitians is depicted as indissociable, and moreover linked to the destiny of all Black people around the world. This common destiny is the destiny of the whole Black diaspora:

> We talk of going to this place and that, to better our condition, but wherever we go, whether we go to Europe, Asia or Africa, or remain where we are, we are still identified with the colored people of Haiti and with colored people everywhere else, and whatever helps or hinders any, helps or hinders

> all. We are, therefore, deeply and practically interested in the experiment of self-government of the Republic of Haiti. Success there means success here and success everywhere.[49]

In refusing emigration, in other words colonization, of Black Americans to Africa or anywhere else, Douglass transforms his argument in favor of Haiti into an anticolonization diatribe that deftly touches on a sensitive domestic political topic.[50] In the margin at this particular moment in his speech, Douglass wrote by hand that Black people would never be respected anywhere in the world if they were not first respected in the United States, adding that therefore Black Americans would do better to resist the emigrationist temptation. He then went even further, claiming that Black Americans owe their liberty to Haiti and its courageous people.[51]

Relentlessly linking the destiny of Haitians to the destiny of the entire Black race, Douglass anchored his discourse in the imperialist spirit of the times by evoking the "manifest destiny" of the island. If every nation was given a divine mission, it is clear that for him Haiti's was to enlighten the world by proving that Black people were capable of governing themselves. Douglass thus claimed that the entire abolitionist movement was indebted to Haiti and that Haiti, in fact, was "the Great Emancipator" of the nineteenth century, in a clear allusion to the honorific that had been given to Abraham Lincoln after he freed the slaves in the United States.[52] The transfer of this nickname from Lincoln to Haiti may be interpreted as a way of revising and reducing Lincoln's role in the abolition of slavery. For Douglass it was the actions of Black Haitians that inspired antislavery and abolitionist whites. Therefore, he is in effect opening up a debate about the writing and reading of history via his alternative retelling. Finally, as an ultimate homage to Haiti the emancipator, Douglass concludes his speech by comparing the country to the North Star that will guide the Black diaspora toward the advent of a world where the entire Black race will enjoy liberty, justice, and equal rights, just as the literal North Star had guided fugitive slaves on the Underground Railroad toward Canada, a land of liberty within the slavery-stained North American continent in the first half of the nineteenth century:

> [I] believe that, like the steady star of the North, with its constellations sweeping around, [Haiti] will shine on till freedom, justice and equal liberty, shall be the possession of the whole colored race throughout the world.[53]

Therefore, the relative silence about the Haitian Pavilion may also be explained by Douglass's loud, public political stand in favor of the Haitian republic. Beyond the fresh wound of the Môle Saint-Nicolas humiliation, beyond the racial prejudice in America evidenced by the increasing power of Jim Crow laws throughout the South and in northern cities, and beyond white America's denigration of Haiti's history, Douglass himself was the major obstacle to any sanitizing of relations between Haiti and the United States. More than ever, Douglass was torn between his belonging to the Black diasporic community and his attachment to the American nation, the country of his birth that had granted him citizenship, but which on honest inspection turned out to be only second-class citizenship.

By accepting to represent a foreign country at a world's fair taking place in a major city within his own country, was Douglass launching a challenge to America? Or was he simply trying to be agreeable toward the republic whose esteem for him took on a near-cultlike status ever since he first set foot there some years earlier, a republic he also felt united to by racial ties? Douglass never stated the reasons that led him to accept the nomination as first commissioner of the Haitian Pavilion. Observing his long career, and in light of the identity paradoxes that beset him, one can imagine that his reasons intermixed both his activist and narcissistic sides. Douglass the activist was surely eager to seize the occasion to have a legitimate platform to publicly express himself on the subject of Haiti and on the condition of Black Americans; while Douglass the narcissist could hardly resist the heavy flattery coming from the Haitian president whom he respected, nor the chance to occupy one last time a position of prestige on the international stage.

First Commissioner of the Haitian Pavilion at the Chicago World's Fair: The American Experience of Douglass . . . the Haitian?

By falling into the good graces of President Hyppolite, Frederick Douglass seems to have taken his revenge on all those who believed his political career to be over. Contrary to all expectations, the World's Fair of 1893 was without doubt a key moment in Douglass's life. In naming him first commissioner of the Haitian Pavilion, Haiti and President Hyppolite offered Douglass one more chance to make his voice heard, to speak to the nation and to the world; and Douglass did not pass up the chance, disgruntled detractors notwithstanding. Once again Haiti served as a catalyzing pretext to take a stand on the domestic political problem that was undermining the United States: "the

FIG. 10. "Frederick Douglass, Commissioner from Hayti, March 1893." *Manuscript/Mixed Material. Frederick Douglass Papers, Library of Congress, Washington, D.C.*

Negro problem."[54] After explaining Douglass's official role regarding the Haitian Pavilion, we will see how that occasion acted as a spur for the renaissance of Douglass the activist.

Douglass is named first commissioner of the Haitian Pavilion at the start of 1892. It is very difficult, however, to measure the size and shape of Douglass's involvement in the preparations for the World's Fair and the Haitian Pavilion in particular. There is no proof of his directly taking part in the organization of festivities or the construction of the pavilion between the moment he accepted to serve as first commissioner and its official inauguration on January 2, 1893. All we know for sure concerning this period is that Douglass accepted to attend the "meeting of the Foreign Commissioners" that was to take place on October 11–13, 1892, in Chicago.[55] The official invitation that remains within the Douglass archives confirms that the purpose was to attend the dedication ceremonies of some of the exposition's buildings.[56]

There is nothing odd in supposing that Douglass may not have been very involved in the exposition's organization. When it comes to the overall organization, an explanation of his scant involvement is quite simple: as Douglass and Ida B. Wells would say themselves a few months later, Black Americans generally were excluded from the exposition's organization. We shall return to this point in our next chapter. But when it comes to his light participation in organizing the Haitian Pavilion, the explanation may be that Douglass did not speak French well and was after all an old man by that time. All the tasks related to the installation, whether purely administrative or material in nature, were supervised by the second commissioner, Charles A. Preston, who, as a Haitian and native French speaker, was no doubt better suited to the job. It may also be true that this purely logistical side of his role was simply uninteresting to Douglass.

In fact, Douglass spent very little time in Chicago in 1892. He traveled there in mid-October, as planned, to attend the inaugural ceremonies of the buildings in the White City, and he returned briefly in early January 1893 for the inauguration of the Haitian Pavilion. He then returned in April 1893, a few weeks before the official opening of the exposition on May 1, and was hosted by S. Laing Williams and his wife, Fannie Barrier Williams, the only Black woman accepted on the exposition's Women's Committee. She was admitted following pressure from the Black community but was given no responsibilities or remuneration.[57] Therefore, with Charles A. Preston seeing to very detail, the honorable first commissioner of the Haitian Pavilion did not really begin to get involved until the structure was in the spotlight shortly before the inauguration and the exposition's official opening day.[58]

The day of the pavilion's inauguration was doubly special since it directly followed the eighty-ninth anniversary of Haiti's independence on January 1, 1804. Douglass's inaugural speech took place on January 2, 1893. The speech, commonly referred to by historians as Douglass's "Lecture on Haiti," must not be confused with the actual inaugural speech at the Haitian Pavilion. Though delivered the same day, the two speeches occurred at different places and before two distinct audiences. It is impossible to know which of the two was given first. They were published the same year by a small press, the Violet Agents' Supply Company, in a work entitled *Frederick Douglass Speech in Chicago*. It happens that the more well-known speech, the "Lecture on Haiti," appears before the inaugural speech at the pavilion.[59]

Douglass delivered his "Lecture" to "Fifteen hundred of the best citizens of Chicago" in Quinn Chapel, a magnificent structure belonging to the AME Church that was erected at the corner of Wabash Avenue and Twenty-Fourth Street in Chicago in 1891.[60] As its title suggests, the lecture is a sort of teacherly sermon in favor of the Haitian republic. But from the very first sentences, Douglass uses his leading subject, Haiti, to address in barely disguised fashion the situation of Black Americans in the United States and the situation of Black people more generally around the world. At the start, Douglass seems to be returning to the theme of Haiti's inferiority as a "weak nation," which he had developed in the two articles from the summer of 1891 published in the *North American Review*. However, it is not so much its weakness that is central to Douglass's rhetorical performance that day but rather its status as a Black republic and exemplary nation, a shining example for the entire Black community around the world.

After briefly asserting that Haiti is in every way similar to the United States in its form of government *of the people and for the people*, and recalling that the country offers economic and commercial interests for the United States, Douglass focuses on the topic he cares most about: the color prejudice that was devouring America from within. For Douglass, this prejudice underlies the tense relations between Haiti and the United States, going back to America's delayed recognition of Haiti and extending to the poor treatment of Haitians in the United States compared to their reception in other countries—suggesting thereby that they were victims of the country's segregation policies just like Black Americans.[61] Douglass does not flinch at denouncing the endemic segregation that had spread like a poison across the entire American territory. Indeed, this portion of the lecture received much applause—as evidenced by the numerous "[applause]" markers inserted in the body of the text by the publisher—and marked Douglass's reemergence as an activist.

His grand panegyric is sprinkled with criticism of the racialized domestic politics and racism of the American government. Borrowing word for word from his speech of October 1891, Douglass returns to the Môle Saint-Nicolas negotiations, explaining that in any case the United States had no legitimate right to seize it, and that those who wanted to take it by force should be ashamed of their actions. Though he praises the beauty of the country and its inhabitants, the abundance of natural resources, favorable climate, and fertile soil, Douglass also lucidly examines what he considers to be the gravest fundamental flaw in Haiti, namely a bellicose character evidenced by its propensity to regularly fall back into civil war, a tendency he attributes to Haiti's ill-intentioned elites, not the Haitian people, and to Americans who are quick to do everything in their power to foment mutual antagonisms between Haitian factions if it might advance their own strategic and economic interests. He makes thinly veiled accusations that American shipbuilders and arms dealers have destabilized the country, thus settling some scores, notably with the New Yorker shipbuilder William Pancoast Clyde.[62] President Hyppolite, however, is spared Douglass's ire. On the contrary, his portrait of Hyppolite is flattering even though the Haitian president was a dictator and hardly different from many others in the nineteenth century; and yet Douglass asks America to do right by this statesman, whom he even compares to Abraham Lincoln.[63]

Although somewhat chaotically constructed, the lecture is clearly organized around a central theme that one could call diasporic, summarized as follows: Haiti is a Black republic and land of experimentation; as such it is the prism or lens through which the destiny of the entire Black race should be examined. Thus, the two central points developed in his speech via descriptions that alternate between flattery and criticism of Haiti are, first, that there is a Black diaspora that collectively defines all Black peoples around the world, who all have Haiti as a common denominator, and second, the question of Haiti's future. As a baseline, Douglass wants to defend Haiti's honor and that of its leaders in the name of diasporic solidarity. Yet the fact that the country regularly collapsed into civil war was a problem in itself and cast doubt and discredit on the Black race. In conclusion, Douglass considers that in the future the outlook whites would have toward Blacks anywhere in the world depended on the way they perceived Haiti. In this regard, Douglass anticipates the Third World and Pan-African movements that would develop in the early twentieth century.

Beyond the fact that Douglass insisted on the global consequences of local politics in Haiti, he revealed in this speech his diasporic consciousness while also reasserting his firm opposition to emigration or colonization abroad by Black Americans.[64] Drawing a parallel between the Black community and the Jewish community—another diasporic people—Douglass stated that the latter distinguished themselves from the rest of humanity by their faith while the former distinguished themselves from all others by the color of their skin. It was color that defined this community no matter where in the world they resided, be it in Haiti, Africa, or the United States; this Black community was composed of individuals with a common destiny, which is why their place of residence was of secondary importance. Consequently, Douglass flatly rejected all ideas of colonization or emigration, and explicitly rejected the Black nationalism that often accompanied such projects.[65]

So what lay in store for Haiti, this living laboratory of successes and failures of the Black race? Would it plunge into barbarism, as some predicted, or would it rise to the level of great civilized nations and thereby be of service to the entire Black race? This is the question that Douglass asks several times in very direct language, and each time his answer is equally clear.[66] Considering all the trials it had gone through and everything it had already accomplished, Haiti could only rise to the rank of great civilized nations. Douglass concludes his lecture with this affirmation, just as in his October 1891 speech he concluded by comparing Haiti to the North Star: "I will rather believe that whatever may happen of peace or war Haiti will remain in the firmament of nations, and, like the star of the north, will shine on and shine on forever."[67]

How did Douglass arrive at this conclusion? In recalling Haiti's glorious history, especially the way it obtained and then preserved its liberty and independence, Douglass claimed that Haiti had been and would continue to be a role model for the entire world by freeing itself from the yoke of slavery and demonstrating thereby the capacity of Black people to emancipate themselves and govern themselves effectively and lastingly. Here Douglass gave his own interpretation of the doctrine of "Manifest Destiny" by conferring on Haiti, "the original pioneer emancipator of the nineteenth century," the mission of enlightening the world about the horrors of slavery and the meaning of the word "liberty." In so doing, he was wresting from the United States its exclusive control over the principle of liberty—a concept leading Americans proudly disseminated via the notion of their country's Manifest Destiny and civilizing mission.[68]

This highly partisan speech marked the reemergence of Frederick Douglass's aggressive activism. It merits its place in history for the role it played in reviving Douglass the activist, orator, and defender of the Black race. After some years of vacillation and doubt, during which many considered him isolated and washed up, including some within his own community, Douglass regained a position of leadership as incisive as any he had ever known.

The January 2, 1893, lecture can be considered the last great public speech of Frederick Douglass. But in truth, Douglass gave two speeches at the start of 1893. The one we have just discussed took place somewhat apart from the Chicago World's Fair in a church before a sympathetic audience. However, on that same freezing January day, Douglass gave another, shorter speech in the center of Jackson Park as part of the official inauguration ceremony of the Haitian Pavilion.

Before a smaller audience than the one that heard him speak at Quinn Chapel, in a park covered in snow and under a menacing sky, Douglass inaugurated the freshly completed Haitian Pavilion "in the presence of a few of Chicago's best citizens."[69] After first noting the cost of the structure, Douglass quickly departed from the ostensible focus, the pavilion, and instead launched into praising President Hyppolite and Haiti. He noted the great intelligence of the president of the *Black* republic, underscoring that Haiti was above all Black and that "She has never been ashamed of her cause or of her color."[70]

Moreover, Douglass affirmed again, Haiti was a great nation with its proper place among the great civilized nations of the nineteenth century. After a brief physical description of the pavilion, Douglass remarked on its location within the layout of the World's Columbian Exposition. He even compared the Haitian Pavilion, and by extension the Republic of Haiti, to "a city set upon a hill"—a statement that received great applause from the audience. It is difficult not to admire the boldness of it all. As the United States was setting out in a decidedly imperialist direction, Douglass appropriated on behalf of Haiti the biblical symbol so often invoked to characterize American exceptionalism. That symbol had been anchored in the American collective consciousness since it was first pronounced by John Winthrop, one of the Pilgrim fathers and founder and first governor of the state of Massachusetts, in his sermon entitled "A Modell of Christian Charity." Winthrop gave the sermon onboard the *Arbella*, a ship taking hundreds of Puritans to the New World in 1630. Placing Haiti on top of that "hill" was to place it in the center of the world and claim it as a role model for all of humanity. This substitution within the parable was finely calculated. By choosing the image that went straight to the heart of every American, and especially white Americans who took pride in the notion that among their ancestors were prestigious Pilgrim fathers, Douglass was erecting the legitimacy of Haiti. Just as, 250 years earlier, America had served as a refuge and the Puritans as guides to Europeans fleeing the religious and political oppression of which they were victims in the Old World, so too Haiti would now take on the role of refuge for the Black race, that victim of race prejudice in the United States and elsewhere. Just as the United States had been a welcoming land for immigrants from all nations—or was at least thought as such in the American collective imagination—Haiti was opening its arms wide to Black men and women from all countries, and in particular to Black Americans who wished to build a better life.[71] Just as America proclaimed its democracy as exemplary and fervently spread the good word about its democratic ideal over the entire American continent and beyond, so too Haiti was claiming to be a role model, the example of a Black republic with a government of Black people, for Black people, and by Black people. In other words, Haiti was the incarnation of Black success, proof that they were capable of successfully governing themselves. It should be noted that Douglass was familiar with the continuation of Winthrop's sermon, one often considered the precursor of the American "Manifest Destiny" doctrine, that other American identity "myth" Douglass had already appropriated and repurposed for Haiti. In the following portion of the sermon, Winthrop's city on a hill evolves under God's gaze. And woe to that "city" should it prove unworthy of God's trust.

Not only will God withdraw his protection and the city's servants will curse it and its inhabitants, but in addition the rest of the world will mock them too, and God's enemies will exploit an opportunity to denigrate it.

Thus, one must understand it as Haiti's duty to be exemplary and succeed. Haiti must prove to the rest of the world that Black people are capable of progressing and that it truly is a civilized nation—because the future of the entire Black race depends on what becomes of Haiti. To borrow the words of Douglass, the success of Haiti means the success of the Black diaspora everywhere in the world. Haiti must not let itself fail, because failure would provoke the irremediable failure of the Black diaspora in every corner of the globe where it resides.

The second half of Douglass's speech in the park no longer concerned the Haitian Pavilion but the nation it represented. That cold day in 1893 was the day after Haiti's January 1 celebration of the eighty-ninth anniversary of its independence. Therefore Douglass gave a very flattering portrait of the Haitian Revolution, comparing it to the American War of Independence, claiming that the task of combatting for independence was more arduous for the Haitians than for Americans. Unlike many Americans, Haitians were neither the descendants of heroes nor were they men seasoned by long experience of warfare. Instead, they were simple, uneducated slaves, held in contempt by the rest of the world, and they owed their victory to their own courage and to their love of liberty.[72]

After a final allusion to the race prejudice of his time and the principle of equality of races that was so dear to him—an allusion particularly applauded by the audience—Douglass concluded his speech by reaffirming the legitimacy of Haiti within the universal community of nations:

> Her presence here to-day in the grounds of this World's Columbian Exposition at the end of the four hundredth anniversary of the discovery of the American Continent, it is a re-affirmation of her existence and independence as a nation, and of her place among the sisterhood of nations.[73]

On that raw January day in 1893, Frederick Douglass gave two important speeches. What could have passed as ordinary praise for the foreign nation that had given him its complete trust at the very moment when his own country was turning away from him, turned out to be a rousing plea for race equality throughout the American territory. By drawing on concepts and images deeply embedded in the collective American imagination, Douglass was seeking to give legitimacy, a reason for being, and a destiny to the little Black republic. Thus he mobilized the myths about the American nation that all

Americans at the end of the nineteenth century massively believed in, such as Manifest Destiny and American exceptionalism, as illustrated by the parable of Winthrop's "city on the hill"; he used the idea of America as a welcoming land of liberty by recalling memorable events in the history of the young republic; and he evoked the American Revolution or War of Independence and the recent emancipation of its Black population—all in the service of Haiti. Yes, Haiti deserved its place in Jackson Park among the great civilized nations of the world.[74] Yes, Haiti had a reason for being, a mission: to enlighten the world by proving that Black people deserved to be treated on an equal footing with whites. And yes, Haiti had a destiny: not to return into barbarism, but to succeed in elevating itself to the same level of civilization as the moralizing nations of Europe and North America.

CHAPTER 8

From Haiti to Chicago, Frederick Douglass and the Renewal of Black American Activism

> The Colored American received from a foreign power [the Republic of Hayti] the place denied to him at home.[1]
>
> —FERDINAND LEE BARNETT

After two orations to the glory of Haiti and President Hyppolite, Frederick Douglass did not turn down the chance to give a third public expression of his admiration for Haiti and its president at the foreign commissioners' banquet organized by the directors of the world's fair some months later on October 7, 1893. When his turn came to raise a glass and make a toast in honor of Haiti, Douglass paid homage once again to the nation and, without a hint of irony, to the despot who had propelled him back into the public spotlight. Douglass praised the island nation whose pavilion had been the gathering point for Black American discontent—the nation that incarnated the motherland of the Black diaspora, the enlightened country, constantly progressing, whose place among civilized nations seemed to him entirely legitimate:

> The participation of Haiti in this sublime exposition means . . . that she is in the trend of civilization and does not intend to be out of line with the progress and enlightenment of the age. In this spirit and purpose, no ruler is more sincere, enlightened, and resolved than is General Florvil Hyppolite, the President of the Republic of Haiti.[2]

Even if Hyppolite was not a model president, he had the merit of naming Douglass first commissioner and thereby giving him a platform and the opportunity to use the Haitian Pavilion as the headquarters of discontented Black American activists who otherwise had been given little other space by the exposition's organizers to freely assemble.

Between the two January speeches and the October toast, Douglass was not a passive participant at the Chicago World's Fair. He was now aware that the purpose of the Columbian World's Exposition was ultimately to serve as a gigantic signing ceremony, with the entire world as witness, of the recent reconciliation between North and South, a reconciliation that was being constructed by white America at the expense of Black exclusion. Douglass skillfully used the international platform offered by Haiti to denounce the Republicans' abandonment of their values and their ignoble submission to the South's preference for segregation, denying Black people the right to vote, and relegating them to second-class status as marginalized citizens. Douglass used the Chicago World's Fair to denounce, also with the world as witness, the American evil that W. E. B. Du Bois would call some years later "the problem of the color line."[3]

The Reason Why: On Segregation and Firmly Established Race Prejudice in Turn-of-the-Century America

Most historians are in agreement—even without the prodding of the Black American activists Ida B. Wells and Frederick Douglass in their famous pamphlet *The Reason Why the Colored American Is Not in the World's Columbian Exposition*—that Black Americans were underrepresented if not exactly entirely absent from the Chicago World's Fair of 1893.[4] Although criticized at the time by a portion of the Black American community, we shall see in this chapter how this pamphlet became an important document at the end of the nineteenth century and that early twentieth-century historiography about Black exclusion from American society is in large part based on it. It was only one hundred years later, in the 1990s, that a few publications would make the opposite claim and argue that Black Americans were not excluded from the 1893 exposition and that the famous pamphlet was "misleading." A few historians even advanced the idea that the exposition was the birthplace of new hope in the hearts of many Black Americans, thanks to the organization of a "Colored People's Day" and Congress on Africa.[5] One must therefore ask if Black Americans were really present or not, and at what level or levels they could really be involved at the Columbian World's Exposition of 1893.

Black Americans had placed a lot of hope in this world's fair. It offered them a chance to show the world the "progress" of their community thirty years after the abolition of slavery on American soil. Unfortunately, their hopes were dashed rather quickly when it became clear that the event was being organized without them, in fact without a single Black man or woman named to any committee responsible for organizing a part of the exposition.

For starters, President Harrison named no Black person to the national commission supervising the exposition, supposedly to avoid hurting the feelings of other (especially southern) members of the commission. When the Association of Black American Newspapers and the Convention of People of Color explicitly requested that the president nominate Black people, Harrison replied that there were no openings left on the commission.[6] However, yielding to pressure from the Black community, Harrison finally named Hale G. Parker, a Black principal of a school in St. Louis, to the national commission, but only as an "alternate" with no real power within the Missouri delegation.[7]

There was also at first no Black woman named to the "Board of Lady Managers." After Black Americans complained about this situation, a Black woman in Chicago, A. M. Curtis, was nominated in January 1893 to hold a post within the all-female committee as "Secretary of Colored Interests."[8] But in truth she had no decision-making power and resigned after a few months. Why Ms. Curtis resigned, however, is not exactly clear. The Black American periodical the *Cleveland Gazette* devoted an article to the matter and raised the possibility that she was perhaps fired.[9] She was replaced by Fannie Barrier Williams, who received no salary and had no real authority attached to the exercise of her function.[10]

Thus the number of Black Americans involved in the organization of the Chicago World's Fair can be counted on the fingers of one hand, and that includes Frederick Douglass, the first commissioner of the Haitian Pavilion. Not only were Black Americans underrepresented on organizational committees and commissions, they were also absent from the rolls of employees, no matter in what job category, from office workers to cleaners, with the sole exception of "porters."[11]

The historian Christopher Reed tried to overturn this idea of underrepresentation in his study *All the World Is Here! The Black Presence at White City* (2000). Reed offers a list of all the Black figures who either crossed paths or may have met one other at the Chicago World's Fair, including Frederick Douglass, Booker T. Washington, Ida B. Wells, the musician Wendell Phillips Dabney, and the feminist Anna Julia Cooper.[12] Reed also includes some photographs that claim to prove the presence of Black people. His presentation, however, is less than convincing. The list of prominent Black figures extends to only twenty people, and the Black people in the photographs are almost always indiscernible and surrounded by dozens of whites. In the end, Reed's evidence strengthens the thesis of Wells and Douglass more than his own. While it is true that Black visitors were not denied entry to the exposition, a fact noted in numerous articles in the white and Black press, it is no less true that Black men and women were excluded from the exposition's many jobs, whether in planning, organizing, or the daily running of such a large and complex event.

Because Black Americans were excluded from organizing committees, they also worried they would be unable to participate as exhibitors. The National Committee denied them the right to present their work and products separately in a dedicated pavilion, and instead encouraged them to join the existing exhibit venues—in other words, to present their work and products in the buildings assigned to their state of residence. To do so, Black candidates had to first request permission to exhibit from the committee in charge of the pavilion of their state. But since most Black people resided in southern states, they had little chance of being heard and granted permission to exhibit their work and products since the committees were always composed of white men. The impossibility of presenting the work, products, and other visible proof of progress of the Black community in the thirty years following abolition is richly documented in the white (Republican) and Black press. One example is an article first published in the *Chicago Inter-Ocean*, a white Republican periodical, and reprinted in the Black *Cleveland Gazette*. It is written by the white radical Republican judge Albion W. Tourgée.[13] In this article published on March 11, 1893, two months before the official opening of the Columbian World's Exposition, Tourgée argues in favor of Black Americans' "right to a separate exhibit," clearly distinct from the other expositions, and also defends their right to be represented on organizing committees. He insists that they be given the chance to show their "progress" and to be on an equal footing with other Americans. Tourgée, who was well known for his radical positions in favor of race equality, even calls for an exhibit that gives a "realistic representation" of bigoted whites' mistreatment of Black people in the South:

> [T]he colored people of the United States should petition the managers of the fair for leave to erect upon the grounds of the exposition a realistic representation of the way in which colored citizens are hanged and burned alive for the gratification of immense throngs of white Christians in the United States. Such things were common enough in Catholic Spain four hundred years ago, though we must admit that they were regulated by law and conducted in a lawful manner.[14]

In the end, some drawing and sewing projects done by Black American women were displayed in the Woman's Building, and in other areas of the exposition there were exhibition kiosks decorated in the colors of what are today known as historically Black colleges and universities (HBCUs): Wilberforce University, Tennessee Central College, Clark Atlanta University, and the Hampton Normal and Agricultural Institute (later Hampton University).[15] In addition, non-American Black people were also present and able to exhibit thanks to the Haitian Pavilion and a kiosk dedicated to Liberia within the agricultural building. That kiosk was designed to display accomplishments of the Black Americans who had emigrated there. It is worth noting that the Haiti installation was the only one allowed in the White City to offer an autonomous representation of and by people of African origin.

The most striking presence of (non-American) Black people at the exposition was along the Midway Plaisance alley. Placed under the supervision of the exposition's Department of Ethnology, the Midway Plaisance was the location of restaurants, attractions for the masses, and exhibits of an ethnological character.[16] There were representations of the least-advanced European peoples and of peoples classified as primitive. For example, the alley contained a "Dahomey Village" representing the inhabitants of western Africa as typical of the region's barbarous, wild, uncivilized peoples.[17] The presence of this "village" received much commentary from the Black American community, notably by Frederick Douglass, who considered it as yet one more racist insult flung at Black Americans, seeing as how it was the only representation, besides the Haitian Pavilion, of Black experience and one of the most visited by white attendees. The popularity of the primitive village led Douglass to make a sharp rebuke some months later in his last major speech entitled "The Lessons of the Hour":

> [A]s if to shame the educated negro of America, the Dahomeyans were there to exhibit their barbarism, and increase American contempt for the negro intellect. All classes and conditions were there [at the Fair] save the educated Negro.[18]

Burton Benedict has noted that the world's fairs of the nineteenth century were a location for acting out rivalries between the world's major powers. As part of the strategy of impressing foreign and domestic visitors, the imperial powers would accord a large place to displaying their colonial possessions and colonized peoples. The ethnological exhibitions were very well attended. Crowds gathered to gawk at "human zoos," pushed by their curiosity to know more about the physical appearance and customs of these foreign peoples.[19] Individuals were displayed as types in ways that usually underlined an alleged inferiority and barbarous customs. In the case of the Dahomeyans, their supposed cannibalism attracted the base and morbid curiosity of visitors.[20]

In the case of the Chicago World's Fair of 1893, the Dahomeyans were exhibited neither in a colonial pavilion nor in the French Pavilion—even though an agreement between Britain and France had reassigned Dahomey as a French protectorate. Instead, they were displayed in a festive zone that constituted a sort of supplementary counterexposition, distinct from the exhibits devoted to knowledge and technology. There one found all manner of attractions, games, and rides such as the Ferris wheel, as well as restaurants and restrooms, all thrown together as a giant bustling amusement park.[21] Placing the Dahomeyans in the center of the Midway Plaisance was deliberately suggesting that these people were a monstrous oddity of nature. Their presence in this amusement park area of the exposition classified them as inferior and implied the inferiority of Black Americans who obviously had African ancestors—an insulting amalgamation that did not escape Douglass's sensitive attention.

Thus, when it comes to the presence of Black people at the Chicago World's Fair, one can wonder if perhaps, between the harsh denunciation by Wells and Douglass of "our lack of representation at the Exposition" and the positive outlook of Christopher R. Reed, the truth is somewhere in the middle.[22] One cannot deny that in sheer numbers, the Black American community was very underrepresented at the exposition. However, a select number of elite members of this community did have a chance to participate and express themselves, notably at the day set aside for colored people. Some of them, such as Booker T. Washington, were invited to speak at the congresses that took place on the margin of the exposition. Others, such as the violinist Joseph Douglass, a grandson of Frederick, and the poet Paul Laurence Dunbar, were able to show their artistic talents before a mixed audience on Colored People's Day, as we shall see later in this chapter.

But it was without question the voice and ideas of Frederick Douglass that rang out above all others, notably thanks to the pamphlet he co-authored with Ida B. Wells, a message of protest that might not have been distributed at all without the help of the Haitian Pavilion, which opened its doors to Black Americans who were largely silenced in their own country. Indeed, one can ask if the polite indifference to the Haitian Pavilion among the media of the day covering the exposition was linked to the pamphlet. Did the white press deliberately forget about the Haitian Pavilion as a way to avoid talking about the pamphlet that was being distributed inside its walls? It is impossible to give a definitive answer, but it would be naïve to think that the white-controlled media of the day had not heard of the pamphlet and that their disregard for the Haitian Pavilion was a pure coincidence which had nothing to do with its famous first commissioner, who had "betrayed" America by not accomplishing the capture of the Môle from the weak Haitians, nor with the daily presence in the pavilion of Ida B. Wells, whose numerous speeches in opposition to lynching had already traveled across the Atlantic and stained the reputation of the great American nation, nor with the skin color of Haiti's citizens.

Starting off as they did by recalling that 7,470,040 Blacks out of a total American population of 62,622,250 were excluded from the organization of the exposition—and therefore excluded from this great national and international festival, which could have been an opportunity to prove to the whole world that they had nothing in common with the primitive peoples of Africa embarrassingly represented by the Dahomeyan Village—Wells and Douglass were determined to publish a pamphlet that would allow them to state the facts and raise the consciousness of millions of visitors from around the world.[23] The co-authors, Wells and Douglass alongside Irvine Garland Penn and Ferdinand Lee Barnett, wished to inform visitors about the deliberate sidelining of Black Americans at the exposition but also draw attention to their degrading condition in the United States and also to the progress of Black people since the time of emancipation.

Wells and Douglass had the ambition of publishing the pamphlet in four languages—English, French, German, and Spanish—and distributing it free of charge at the exposition. In order to raise the necessary funds, the authors published open letters in various Black newspapers to "Call for the Publication of a Pamphlet Protesting the Exclusion of Colored Citizens' Participation in the World's Columbian Exposition."[24] One such letter appeared in the *Topeka Call* dated March 26, 1893, under the title "To the Friends of Equal Rights." Another appeared in the *African-American Advocate* dated April 14, 1893—this one, "Our World's Fair Effort," tinged with irony.[25] In the open letters signed by Wells and Douglass and disseminated by these newspapers, the authors announced their pursuit of justice for the Black community by publishing a pamphlet in four languages and distributing it at no cost for the duration of the exposition. To do so, they asked members of the Black community to send their donations to Frederick Douglass at his residence in Anacostia before May 1, 1893, which was to be the official opening day of the exposition. As proof of their good-faith efforts in this cause, they concluded their letter by stating the sums already donated by Douglass and Wells themselves, and by the Black singer F. J. Loudin.[26] The Black American papers that agreed to publish the open letter added their commentaries, usually entreating their readers to participate in this community effort. This is clear in the *Topeka Call* piece that exhorts Black Americans in Kansas to send donations and spread the word throughout the community, while also repeating how much the Black American community had been humiliated by the organizers of the Columbian World's Exposition.[27] The *Afro-American Advocate* states solemnly that "Every Afro-American should contribute something."[28]

That said, it should be noted that there was no real consensus in the African American community about the advisability of publishing this pamphlet. Some, as we have noted, were explicitly favorable to the idea, but other newspapers, such as the *Freeman* in Indianapolis, were frankly opposed on the grounds that publishing such a pamphlet was a self-defeating labeling of oneself as a ridiculous minority to the rest of the world and risked only increasing the hostility of white Americans and foreigners toward Black people.[29] The piece called the pamphlet idea "foolish" and said the money that Wells and Douglass were trying to raise could be used in better ways, before adding that the $5,000 fundraising goal could be reached simply with donations from those eminent members of the community who favored the idea such as Senator Blanche K. Bruce, John Mercer Langston, or Douglass himself.[30] The *Freeman* claimed that the pamphlet did not express the views of the whole Black American *people*, only of its fortunate *elites*. The newspaper also pointed out that the *Statesman* in Denver and the *Crusader* in New Orleans were equally opposed to the pamphlet idea.[31] The *Washington Bee* also energetically opposed the pamphlet, noting that what Black people needed was "money, real-estate, education and good manners. The negro is more in need of the above than he is of pamphlets to be printed in English, French, German and Spanish. . . . The race have [*sic*] too much in pamphlets now and too little in their pockets."[32]

It should be noted that the spirited debates in the Black community and its print media, either for or against publishing such a pamphlet, took place in March and April 1893, in other words during the two months before the official opening, while simultaneously other debates were taking place around the organization of the special "Colored People's Day." In the end, it seems that the call for donations went largely unheard or unheeded since only a few hundred dollars were collected. Wells and Douglass thus decided to only publish the pamphlet in English but with a preface translated into French, Spanish, and German.[33]

THE REASON WHY the Colored American Is Not in the World's Columbian Exposition: The Afro-American's Contribution to Columbian Literature is eighty-one pages of text consisting of, first, Ida B. Wells's preface along with three translations of it, followed by six chapters written by Frederick Douglass, Ida B. Wells, Irvine Garland Penn, and Ferdinand Lee Barnett. Wells was the driving force behind the initiative to write and publish the pamphlet, but Douglass also played an important role, especially in its dissemination.

Besides his involvement in financing the pamphlet, Douglass wrote the first chapter, soberly entitled "Introduction." Although in 1889–90 Douglass took pleasure in affirming that twenty-five years after the abolition of slavery, America was a great nation no longer plagued with race prejudice, here he claimed just the opposite. Douglass's introduction makes strong accusations of racism and discrimination by whites against Blacks. For Douglass, "the spirit of slavery" still hung over the American nation. Douglass perceived the slavery system as the origin of every evil in American society, or at least the starting point of the race prejudice endured still by Black Americans thirty years after the abolition of slavery, and the explanation of why they were largely excluded from the Universal Exposition of 1893.[34] Focusing on living conditions for Black people in the South and the rough justice meted out there under the "lynch law" that Wells would denounce later in the pamphlet, Douglass asserted that southerners had not evolved and their behavior was as abject as before the Civil War. He claimed they even killed Black people more casually now than before the abolition of slavery since the latter were no longer their property and therefore there was no cost incurred by mistreating them.[35] According to Douglass, accusing Black men of harassment and rape only became common from the moment they became citizens and voters—the claim being that freedom had transformed the Black man into a criminal and "moral monster." These accusations were clearly designed to prove that the Black man, once free, was incapable of controlling himself and behaving in a civilized manner—an idea furthered by the paternalist theories that were also the rationalization for the segregationist practices spreading throughout the southern states and in large northern cities, and for the gradual suppression of Black voting rights.[36]

Conscious of the national and international context surrounding the Chicago World's Fair, Douglass granted that the moment for publishing such a pamphlet was perhaps poorly chosen. It was certainly ill-timed if one believes the purpose of the Universal Exposition was to praise the American nation on an international stage and that doing so required adhering patriotically to the high opinion that the United States had of itself. But whereas America was inviting nations from around the world to present their treasures and latest industrial and technological discoveries, the Black man—not just the American Black but the Black man in general as belonging to a diasporic community—had as its showcase only the humiliating Dahomeyan Village "here to exhibit the Negro as a repulsive savage." Douglass then went on to underscore how the constitutional amendments granting citizenship and civil rights to Black people, amendments passed after the Civil War in which Black people had played an active role, had since been circumvented by state and local legislation; and

Douglass concluded by affirming that rights for Black Americans had been rescinded as part of "the restoration of friendship between the north and the south."[37] Douglass aimed to denounce the significant rollback of Black American rights and make known to the world via this pamphlet their deplorable situation within the great American nation. Going beyond mere observation and denunciation of the abominable living conditions of his fellow Black citizens, Douglass exhorted his peers to fight for their rights in a rousing conclusion that asserted their struggle was "ennobling" and that their day would come because their cause was just.[38] The reader of this introduction is forewarned that the words that follow in each of the chapters are deliberately very political.

In the chapter entitled "Class Legislation," Ida B. Wells briefly recounts with a few examples the laws passed in southern states to prevent Black people from voting and to regulate their lives through segregation measures in public transportation or through the interdiction of interracial marriage. The slightly longer next chapter, entitled "The Convict Lease System," describes what Wells considered the unjust system that resulted from the laws enumerated in the previous chapter.[39] Wells states that nine out of ten detainees held under these news laws were Black, and she asserts that the "convict lease" system was in fact a thinly disguised return of slavery. The next chapter, "Lynch Law," describes with shocking photographs and statistics the endemic problem that arose in the southern United States starting in the 1880s but also in certain states of the West and North; namely, lynching, which affected an increasing number of Black people each year and in conditions, according to Wells, that were increasingly horrific and brutal.[40]

After the introduction and Wells's three chapters testifying to the extreme violence imposed on Black people in the United States at the end of the nineteenth century comes a fifth chapter, written by Irvine Garland Penn, devoted to "The Progress of the Afro-American Since Emancipation" in the areas of education, work, commerce, religion, literature, and other arts.[41] This chapter contains, in addition to numerous statistics to support his claims, iconographic documents representing buildings housing these educated or prosperous Black Americans, such as the Tuskegee Institute. Finally, in the sixth and last chapter of the pamphlet, Ferdinand Lee Barnett, who was not yet the husband of Ida B. Wells, states "The Reason Why" Black Americans had been kept against their will from participating in the organization of the Universal Exposition of 1893.[42]

According to Wells, ten thousand copies of the pamphlet were distributed over three months to those visiting the Haitian Pavilion at the Chicago World's Fair, underlining that this happened thanks to Frederick Douglass or, more precisely, thanks to the little republic of Haiti that named Douglass first commissioner of its pavilion, thus giving Douglass a platform to reignite his former activist fervor.[43] It was indeed the Haitian Pavilion that served as the epicenter of the protest. Wells recognized later, as did her husband, F. L. Barnett, that the Black republic gave Black Americans the opportunity to affirm their existence by giving them a dignified, centrally located showcase; whereas their own country had only offered a racist and contemptuous sideshow of Black experience on the midway.[44] Thus it was perfectly understandable that the Haitian Pavilion would become the headquarters for Black Americans and other visitors, Black or white, American or foreign, who supported their cause or who simply wanted to meet the great Frederick Douglass. And it was also logical that Douglass would offer Wells a location inside the pavilion from which to distribute their pamphlet to interested visitors.[45]

In a way, it can be said that the constant lobbying undertaken by Black activists starting in early January 1893 was successful if one accepts as evidence the "Congress on Africa" and the "Colored People's Day" that took place in August at the height of the Exposition's popularity.

The Congress on Africa

None of the many attempts by Black Americans to obtain a full and just representation at the Universal Exposition were all that successful. As we have seen, they obtained no prestigious post, no building, not even a stand specifically dedicated to the arts, crafts, and inventiveness of Black Americans; and very few of them were recruited over the duration of the exposition, even for lesser jobs or to do simple unskilled labor.

Yet it cannot be said that their requests and grievances went totally unheard and unanswered. The organizers of the Chicago World's Fair, who were probably eager to answer the charges of racism leveled notably by the Black press, ended up organizing a "Congress on Africa" devoted to African populations and their descendants, in other words to the African diaspora. This gathering was to last eight days, from August 14 to 21, and was intended to be distinct from another event related to the subject of this congress: namely, for people of color, which was referred to in the press either as "Colored People's Day," "Nigger Day," or "Jubilee Day." Lacking equal representation, Black Americans had to content themselves with a single celebratory day out of the 184 days that the exposition was open to the public. What exactly their just representation would have been can be debated, but it should be remembered that Black people represented roughly 12 percent of the total American population in 1893.[46]

The idea of organizing "The World's Congresses of 1893" as a series of conferences on various general topics, ranging from "the economic, industrial and financial problems of the day" to "the most efficient and advisable means of preventing or decreasing pauperism, insanity, and crime," had been mentioned in the press as early as 1889 as the idea of Charles Carroll Bonney, a Chicago jurist and judge, teacher, writer, and public orator. These congresses, which would bring together researchers, public intellectuals, figures from the world of business, astronomers, geologists, religious leaders, and philosophers, were expressly designed to be "conducive to the welfare of mankind" by bringing together around the same table "the enlightened people of the whole world."[47] They were conceived as a complementary exposition of the spiritual progress of humanity, alongside the physical buildings, pavilions, and other structures of the White City that gathered the concrete material proof of the industrial, military, artistic, and technological progress of the countries represented. The Art Institute of Chicago would be the gathering place of the intellectual and more abstract spiritual progress of these same nations.

The organizing committee for these congresses created twenty subcommittees charged with filling out the programs for two hundred such congresses.[48] Some would last a few days, others weeks, and together they would stretch out over the duration of the Universal Exposition from May 15 to October 28, 1893. In total, 1,245 workshops took place involving 5,974 public lectures. An estimated 700,000 people attended, which the organizers considered to be a solid success.[49]

The Congress on Africa was given various names by the press covering the event. The *Daily Inter Ocean* referred to it by four different names, depending on the article and sometimes within the same piece: "Ethnological Congress," "Congress on African Ethnology," "Congress on Africa," and "African Congress." The *Independent* refers to it as "The Negro Congress."[50] All these names touch on aspects of what this congress hoped to be: namely, a colloquium whose subject would be Africa, Africans, and Black people in general whether born in Africa or elsewhere. Indeed, the designation of this congress would pose an interpretive problem from the start.[51]

The long list of speakers scheduled for this congress is proof that a very wide array of topics would be discussed, from the basic geographical description of Africa to the study of African languages and folklore, the colonization of Black Americans in Africa, and the place of Black people in the U.S. Constitution. The Congress would also reserve an important place for the evocation of religion, including Black churches, Christian missions in Africa, and African religions. A draft of the "schedule of subjects and speakers" for the congress as presented by the organizational committee and written in February 1893 enumerates seven workshops as follows: "Geography" (15 lectures), "History" (5 lectures), "Arts" (10 lectures), "Language and literature" (7 lectures), "Religion" (37 lectures), "Natural Science" (6 lectures), and "Sociology and Political Science" (33 lectures).[52] The names of these workshops group together wide-ranging contents. Within the "Arts" workshop, for example, one finds plans for lectures on painting, sculpture, and music but also on African medical practices, Black American crafts and inventions, as well as Black American journalism, agriculture, and industry. "Arts" is thus the rubric that gathers the savoir-faire of both Africans and Afro-Americans.

It is worth noting the preponderance of religion, sociology, and political science within the congress and the comparatively lesser weight given to history, languages, and literature. Closer inspection of the program reveals that the two workshops which received most attention were those giving open expression to race prejudice via lectures that stirred up European and American civilizations and exhorted them to expand into Africa with missions and colonization. This is hardly surprising. The congress organizers reached out to several members of the Berlin Congress and the Brussels Congress for advice—a call that was answered by having sixteen of the former and eighteen members of the latter participate within the "Advisory Council of the Chicago Congress on Africa." The official report on the congress makes frequent reference to the Berlin Conference and the Brussels Geographic Conference in its twenty-eight pages.[53] Many of the figures on the advisory council participated in both events.

The Chicago Congress on Africa was of course not merely a replica of the Berlin Conference; however, the goal of the former was clearly to reassure European and American powers about their role as protectors of Africa and as leading examples of civilization whose mission was to enlighten the "Dark Continent," to borrow the expression used by the congress organizers and newspapers of the day to refer to "savage" Africa. The congress organizers were perfectly open about their racist prejudices regarding Africa. As good philanthropists, they proposed uniting the leading experts to reflect on the best way to get this "backward" continent to advance in all areas. Citing one of the members of the advisory council, H. H. Johnston, the high commissioner of Zambezia, a province of Mozambique, the report leaves no ambiguity about the racialized and racist theories and ambitions that motivated the organization of this African Congress. For Johnston, it would have been pure madness to leave the African continent entirely in the hands of Africans, seeing as how perfectly incapable they were when left to themselves. That said, and while still grounding its argument in the supposed superiority of the great European nations and the United States over Africa, the report does raise some specific and less automatic questions. For example, John Mercer Langston is quoted on the same page as H. H. Johnston concerning complications surrounding the "Negro Problem" in the South. Langston considered the congress as "the most fitting occasion and auspicious opportunity to discuss and, if possible, solve the questions covered by the 'Negro Problem.'"[54]

It is clear that this congress was not only or even mainly a disinterested academic gathering about Africa, but rather a congress about the Black diaspora and the African in the most general terms—Africans born and living in Africa as well as men, women, and children of African origin born and living elsewhere outside the African continent. This is confirmed by the thematic groupings of the lectures, with a quarter of them devoted to Black Americans.[55] Is it not strange, then, that this congress was mostly organized by white people? Though one finds among the speakers "well-educated blacks as well as elite and middle-class whites," the report released in February 1893 is proof that Black people were once again underrepresented at the congress ostensibly dedicated to them.[56] And yet the report affirms that the president of the congress's organizing committee, the white Reverend Joseph Edwin Roy, had carefully selected "the best man for the best theme." The report gives precise figures about the number and provenance of the speakers. Of the 138 guest lecturers, 67 were foreign and 71 American. Of the 94 speakers who had accepted the invitation at the time of publication of the report, 60 were American, and the others were European or resided in Africa, though not necessarily African themselves. Of the 94 speakers, 17 or roughly 18 percent were Black—which may appear rather small considering it was to be a Congress on Africa.[57] However, since there was no publication of the actual proceedings of the congress, it is impossible to say what the actual numbers were of white and Black participation and attendance at this August 1893 Congress on Africa.[58]

Lacking an official trace of what took place, one might consider piecing together what happened from newspaper accounts published between August 14 and 22. Although this is possible, very little is conveyed about the exact content of the lectures. Only a handful of lectures considered noteworthy by the news editors of the day received any attention. One example is the talk by a famous explorer of the African continent, Dr. Carl Peters, which was reprinted and the object of commentary in the press.[59] Another example is the lecture by Reverend Turner of the African Methodist Church, which also received favorable commentary. Turner presented his version of the theory of evolution according to which white men descended from a Black ancestor—a rather modern and controversial theory for the late nineteenth century. Turner's talk placed the origin of humanity in Africa, insisted on humanity's debt to Africans, and praised African genius. Inscribed within the broader conversation on evolution since Darwin but with his own twist, Turner's theory was understandably well received by the Black public that attended his lecture.[60] Indeed, Turner's success seems to be representative of the general success of the entire congress as measured by high attendance and the enthusiastic reception of the lectures that were given. The *Daily Inter Ocean* noted that a large audience took interest in the "dark Continent," with the auditorium chosen for the congress practically full—an observation confirmed by the *Sun*, which remarked that "The programme was full of interest for those who follow the progress of civilization in Africa."[61]

It is worth mentioning that Black Americans also participated in other congresses. For example, Booker Taliaferro Washington spoke on September 1, 1893, as part of the Labor Congress. His talk, entitled "Progress of Negroes and Free Laborers," was part of a panel moderated by none other than Frederick Douglass. Booker T. Washington recounted his experience as principal of the Tuskegee Normal and Industrial Institute for Colored Students, a school founded in 1881 whose mission was to offer professional training to Black students. At the time Washington was considered a local southern leader. He would become a Black American leader of national importance two years later at the Cotton States and International Exposition in Atlanta, Georgia, where he would give a famous speech on September 18, 1895, marked by accommodationist and separatist rhetoric far from the egalitarian ideals of Frederick Douglass.

Differences aside, the African Congress was clearly an event that contributed to the emergence and awareness of the notion of a Black diaspora. Africans, Black Americans, and Black people from other countries mingled, conversed, and debated the future of their community scattered around the world. The African Congress of 1893 was a unique moment that stood as a precursor to the Pan-Africanist theories developed by W. E. B. Du Bois and Marcus Garvey some years later.

Colored People's Day and the Forgotten Speech of Frederick Douglass

Initially scheduled for August 17, 1893, during the African Congress, Colored People's Day, also known as Colored Jubilee Day, was moved to August 25, a few days after the congress was over. One can well imagine that the organizers thought it best to keep the two events separate in order to offer the jubilee more visibility and probably to relieve the public of having to choose between attending one or the other of the two events. That said, the organization of a Jubilee Day for Colored People was not welcomed by all Black Americans.

Little is known about the deep and contagious disagreement between Frederick Douglass and Ida B. Wells concerning this special day. It was the subject of much commentary at the time in the Black press well before the summer of 1893. Numerous articles about it appear as early as February 1893, and more still in March and April, often in parallel with articles debating the pros and cons of the *Reason Why* pamphlet. The first article to criticize the idea of a so-called "Nigger Day" was published in the *Freeman* on February 25, 1893. The article rejects outright what it describes as a "Massachusetts idea"—implying that it was the brainchild of northern bourgeois Black people.[62] In the following issue dated March 4, the *Freeman* repeats its opposition and includes a letter signed by Ida B. Wells thanking the *Freeman* for taking a stand against the "Nigger Day."[63] In each of its March issues the *Freeman* published articles opposing the idea while also often criticizing the pamphlet that Wells and Douglass intended to publish.

In her autobiography, Wells comments briefly on this event, which she refers to as "Negro Day." Her account contains some inaccuracies, however. Wells suggests that the idea for this special day for Black people originated among the exposition's organizers following the success of the Haitian Pavilion and "everything colored"; in other words, because of the popular success of attractions featuring Black populations. But the idea for a Jubilee for Colored People was discussed months before the exposition opened to the public. The first articles evoking a "Negro Day" were published in late February and early March 1893, whereas the exposition did not open until May 1. Whatever the details of its origin, Wells is certainly direct about her opposition to the organization of such a day, but also conciliatory in recognizing she was mistaken:

> Many of us disapproved of Mr. Douglass's acceptance. We resented this sop to our pride in this belated way, and we thought Mr. Douglass ought not to have accepted. I was among those who differed with our grand old man. . . . He persevered with his plans without any aid whatever from us hotheads and produced a program which was reported from one end of this country to the other. The American nation had given him his opportunity for scoring its unfairness toward Negro citizens and he did not fail to take advantage of it in the most fitting way.[64]

Although many Black Americans were unsatisfied with the scant place they were given at the Universal Exposition and tended to follow Wells in see-

FIG. 11. Frederick Burr Opper, "Darkies' Day at the Fair," *Puck*, August 21, 1893, 186–87.
Color lithograph. Library of Congress, Washington, D.C.

ing this slight as a form of exclusionary paternalism, others, more in line with Frederick Douglass, considered it wrong to reject the offer made in answer to a request of some within the Black American community. On the contrary, they wanted to make the most of this opportunity to showcase the artistic and intellectual talents of Black people. For Douglass it was better to have one special day than none at all. Granting even one day to Black Americans, given the reality within white America near the turn of the century, was a step toward recognition of the existence and progress of the Black community. Therefore, the Sage of Anacostia agreed to serve, alongside John Mercer Langston, Robert Purvis, and other notable Black Americans, on the organizing committee for this special day. There were fifteen members on the committee, with Joseph Banneker Adger acting as president. The detailed program included in the document released by the jubilee organizing committee indicates that the morning was to be devoted to speeches and prayers performed by leading Black figures and accompanied by a five-hundred-member choir composed of schoolchildren. The afternoon was to be given over entirely to musical performances with a two-thousand-member choir, hundred-piece Black American orchestra, and another all-male choir of fifty voices. Clearly the jubilee was not intended as a celebration of the Black diaspora, but uniquely focused on Black Americans by Black Americans and for Black Americans. It was to be a historic day, a unique occasion to display the progress achieved by Black Americans since their emancipation.[65]

According to newspaper articles that appeared the next day, the jubilee was an overall success. Douglass's biographer William S. McFeely notes, however, that on the morning of August 25 watermelon salesmen rushed to the jubilee location, allegedly to mock the Black American community expected to attend that day.[66] Douglass, put off by their presence, supposedly quit the scene, thus leaving Paul Laurence Dunbar alone to manage the logistics of the celebration, and Douglass only returned in the early afternoon to give his speech on "The Negro Problem."[67] However, an article dated August 26, 1893, published in the *Cleveland Gazette* under the title "The Watermelons Absent" completely contradicts McFeely's account. This newspaper, which from the beginning had taken a stand against the jubilee, claims that the day was a failure and a farce, and that even the watermelons so feared by the organizers did not appear, nor did some of the most important members of the Black American community.[68]

It is true that newspapers gave varying accounts, sometimes with direct contradictions, of how the day unfolded. For example, it is impossible to know for certain if the famous Black soprano Matilda Sissieretta Joyner Jones, better known by the name "Black Patti," actually performed on Jubilee Day. *The Herald*, published in Los Angeles, claims "Sister Etta Jones (black Patti) sang delightfully." A similar account appears in the *New York Daily Tribune* and the *Daily Public Ledger* in Philadelphia. However, the *Freeman* states that the public was greatly disappointed by the absence of Black Patti; and the *Topeka Call* attributes her absence to a dirty trick played by those opposed to the jubilee who directed her to the other end of the city.[69] As for the rest of the program, all accounts concur in reporting a speech was given by Frederick Douglass, and one also learns from various articles published on August 26 that songs were performed by Sidney Woodward and Harry Burleigh from an operatic adaptation of *Uncle Tom's Cabin* by Will M. Cook; that "Miss Hallie G. Brown, an elocutionist of note among her people, read patriotic selections"; that other songs were performed throughout the day; and that Joseph Douglass, the grandson of Frederick Douglass, played the violin.[70] Ida B. Wells in her account notes that the young poet Paul Laurence Dunbar, Douglass's personal assistant and the efficient logistics coordinator throughout the day, had the opportunity to read some of his poems.[71]

Just as there is no knowing exactly what took place that day, it is also impossible to say how many people actually witnessed it all because there are no

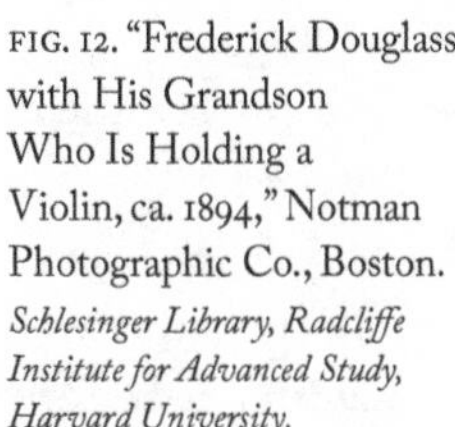

FIG. 12. "Frederick Douglass with His Grandson Who Is Holding a Violin, ca. 1894," Notman Photographic Co., Boston. *Schlesinger Library, Radcliffe Institute for Advanced Study, Harvard University.*

official attendance figures.[72] It is a pity that the only available numbers, also printed in the press, are the tallies of entrances registered each day at the ticket windows for the exposition. However, newspapers do provide some important information concerning the public gathered at the Festival Hall on August 25, 1893. First, the public was a mix of Black and white people. Among the white attendees, the *Saint Paul Daily Globe* insists on the noteworthy presence of the popular suffragette Isabella Beecher Hooker, the sister of Harriet Beecher Stowe, the famous author of *Uncle Tom's Cabin* (1852), as well as her two nieces.[73] It is impossible to know the exact number of white and Black people intermingled in the crowd that day, but it is probable that there were several thousand.[74] There were large numbers of Black Americans from the greater Chicago area as well as from other regions, including the Deep South. A journalist of the *Evening Herald* remarks jokingly that he had never seen so many Black people gathered in the same place—even in the South.[75] The large number of Black attendees, however, does not obscure the fact that "the audience . . . was largely composed of white people," as Booker T. Washington would attest some years later in his biography of Frederick Douglass.[76]

There is no doubt that the day was a big success, probably exceeding Douglass's expectations, and clearly beyond anything that Ida B. Wells could have imagined. Once again, it is likely that this success was due to Douglass's presence and personal involvement that took the form of one of his last great speeches, whose militant, activist ring was remarked on in the press.

No official written copy of the speech Douglass gave for the Jubilee Day at the Chicago World's Fair on August 25, 1893, has survived. In her autobiography, Wells laments that there is no written trace of his magisterial performance.[77] There are, however, transcriptions of parts of it in Black newspapers, including the *Topeka Call* of September 9, 1893, the *Freeman* of September 2 and 9, and the *Cleveland Gazette* of September 16.[78] We have assembled these transcriptions and propose a version of the speech for this commentary (see appendix).

The speech, which marks one of the last public appearances by the great orator, seems to have been relatively short, offering a brief reiteration of the ideas expressed in the *Reason Why* pamphlet. Douglass evokes the nonrepresentation of Black Americans at the world's fair, while yet thankfully acknowledging the organizers' better-late-than-never decision to allow a small place, however imperfect the conditions, for American colored citizens to gather on the side of the large national celebration glorifying, as he would say at the end of his speech, "the splendid civilization of the Caucasian." Between an introduction full of mock deference and a conclusion tinged with irony is a speech of Douglass the engaged activist who leaves aside the incidental conditions of the Universal Exposition in order to better focus on denouncing the atrocious overall situation of Black Americans, especially those condemned to live in the South. These individuals, he points out, who lack the resources to escape, are the victims of the most abominable conditions, from widespread lynching with impunity "in fourteen States of this Union [where] wild mobs have taken the place of law" to the systematic denial of "almost every reputable and decent employment." The state of relations between North and South was central to Douglass's speech, and he did not hesitate to use strong words to denounce the passive complicity of the North toward a contemptuous South that did not merit such goodwill: "You [northerners] fawn to the South and they despise you for it. They don't love you. You say you don't fawn to the South. Well, sometimes it seems to me that you do something very like it when you put us aside and under to please or to gratify the South."

His speech was short, to the point, and effective. It openly referred to the constitutional amendments trampled on by southern states. Douglass reminded his audience that he merely wanted (white) Americans to agree to respect their own Constitution, the document they held up as the supreme model of democracy and wished to spread around the world as the end of this imperial century was drawing near, a document that was supposed to guarantee equality for all its citizens regardless of the color of their skin: "Men talk of the Negro problem. There is no Negro problem. The problem is whether the American people have honesty enough, loyalty enough, honor enough, patriotism enough to live up to their own Constitution."

Douglass's conclusion is surprisingly abrupt. It comes after he has bitterly denounced the inadmissible behavior of the North, judged guilty of pardoning the traitorous South, which first massacred the young men of the North and then went on to disfigure the sacred text of the nation, the U.S. Constitution, with clear acts of contempt for the civil rights of a portion of its faithful and devoted citizens, "one tenth of its own people." It also follows a series of rhetorical questions that Douglass asks to underline the paradoxical attitude of the North toward Black Americans. Douglass then cuts short his speech and concludes with a few words about the North's rejection of Africa and a recommendation that America take an honest look at the "progress" accomplished by the Black community over the past thirty years. For Douglass, Black Americans are not comparable to the Dahomeyans whose presence at the Universal Exposition contributed to a harmful caricature of Black Americans. In one simple sentence Douglass asserted a rupture between America and Africa. For him, the Black American, whom he called the *Negro* and certainly not the *African-American,* had risen above the state of savagery incarnated by the Dahomeyans and was now civilized, and this gave him his legitimate place within the American nation: "But stop. Look at the progress the Negro has made in thirty years! We have come up out of Dahomey unto this. Measure the Negro. But not by the standard of the splendid civilization of the Caucasian. Bend down and measure him—measure him—from the depths out of which he has risen."

The speech was greatly appreciated by the Black community that had turned out in large numbers to hear the Sage of Anacostia. This is clear from the numerous newspaper reports published in the following days and weeks in both the white and Black press. Every article specifies that Douglass's speech was enthusiastically applauded. Although some Black newspapers claimed Colored People's Day was a failure and poorly attended, some white newspapers claimed it was a success and attendance very high.[79] In any case, the speech was positively received, functioning as the militant undertone of a day of Black American music and artistic performances. It was one of Douglass's best speeches according to Booker T. Washington, who claimed: "In voice, gesture, and spirit, he seemed like some great prophet, bearing a message to the civilized world."[80]

All newspaper accounts, Black and white, short or long, refer to the Douglass speech, often giving it the title "The Race Problem in America," and several publish their own synthesis and analysis of the words spoken by Frederick Douglass on August 25, 1893. From these accounts one learns that the magisterial and eloquent speaker politely got back at the exposition organizers: "Douglass mildly scorned the exposition management for having in a measure ignored the American negro"; that he criticized the North for yielding to southern prejudice; that he spoke "bitterly" about how Black Americans throughout the country were generally treated; and how he regretted that justice was not the same for all everywhere.[81]

It is worth noting that the *Cleveland Gazette* and *Afro-American Advocate*, which both strongly opposed holding a special celebration for Black people, did not publish a word, positive or negative, about Douglass's speech in the issues directly following the event; whereas Ida B. Wells, who had also expressed her opposition, eventually admitted she was wrong. She states in her autobiography, *Crusade for Justice*, that she read summaries of the day's events and of Douglass's speech in newspapers and that she immediately apologized to Douglass and asked him to forgive her poor behavior toward him on this matter and for not realizing earlier all the good that such a day could do for the Black community's cause.[82] It is interesting to notice that Wells links, perhaps unconsciously, Colored People's Day with other days commemorating a particular "nationality." In her recollections of this day and of how the organizers of the Universal Exposition suggested that Douglass be the one in charge, Wells writes, "Every other nationality had had its 'day,' and so in this way it was decided to give the Negroes a place on the program."[83] It would be no exaggeration to say this sentence fits perfectly within the rise of Pan-Africanism taking place at the end of the nineteenth century. Even if, as we have said, the organizers certainly considered the Jubilee Day for Colored People as uniquely focused on America and not about Black people around the world, it may have been obvious to the public, Black and white, attending the events on that day, and who may also have attended the Congress on Africa—a very ambiguous gathering where imperialists and Pan-Africanists both had opportunities to speak—that Black people everywhere did indeed constitute an entity defined by skin color, a community that transcended national borders, a nation with no country but one united by a "common cause."

There is no question that the Columbian World's Exposition in Chicago was the occasion for a renewal of Black American activism while also marking the final phase in the political career of Frederick Douglass that was made possible by the presence of Haiti, the Black republic. Thanks to the confidence and platform that Haiti extended to him, the Sage of Anacostia lived out in Chicago his last hours of glory as a spokesperson or at least a recognized and influential leader of the Black American community. The younger generation of Black American activists present in Chicago, from Ida B. Wells to Booker T. Washington, would quickly take up the torch after him. Unlike Wells, who would position herself in continuity with Douglass, Washington would go on to give a particularly conciliatory speech two years later that would be remembered as the "Atlanta Compromise." This speech would please the power elite in the South who welcomed Washington's accommodationist doctrine, which amounted to recommending that southern Black Americans go along with racial segregation and patiently accept their situation.[84] With this speech Washington temporarily occupied the place left vacant by Frederick Douglass, who had passed away some weeks before it was delivered; but his influence would soon be challenged by the arrival of a new militancy and passion via the theories of W. E. B. Du Bois starting in 1905.[85]

In sum, the Chicago World's Fair of 1893 both sealed the reconciliation between North and South at the expense of America's Black citizens and allowed that excluded minority to have a burst of activism on a national and international stage at the start of a somber period of institutionalized segregation that would be made official by the Supreme Court's *Plessy v. Ferguson* decision in 1896. That decision, handed down less than twenty years after the end of Reconstruction, would present Black activists with a dilemma. Whereas the federal government had been the defender and advocate of the Black community between 1865 and 1877, Black Americans then found they had to fend for themselves and that the choice of militant activism came with great risks since it would now be a combat they would have to pursue without any formal political support. This probably explains why Washington's accommodation speech was so successful. For Black southerners terrorized by lynch law and hemmed in by segregation, the choice of active resistance seemed nearly impossible and certainly reckless and dangerous.

EPILOGUE

The native land of the American negro is America.[1]

—FREDERICK DOUGLASS

Ninety years passed between the year of Haiti's independence and Frederick Douglass's famous last speech, "The Lessons of the Hour"—ninety years of a highly emotional relationship between Black Americans and the Black republic. One year after delivering his "Lecture on Haiti" at the Chicago AME Church in Quinn Chapel, the Sage of Anacostia returned to another AME church, this time in Washington, D.C., to speak again, this time more directly, about "the negro problem." On January 9, 1894, Douglass announced to his audience that he would give a frank assessment of the condition of Black Americans in their own country: "I propose to give you a colored man's view of the un-happy relations at present existing between the white and colored people of the Southern States of our union." He then says he must do this because, "the so-called, but mis-called, negro problem is one of the most important and urgent subjects that can now engage public attention."[2] Haiti was no longer a central preoccupation for Douglass or for any Black American activist in 1894. However, as we have seen, the country was never unimportant from the day it declared its independence on January 1, 1804.

The present study set out to cover a century of relations between Black Americans and Haiti. The nineteenth century was particularly unsettled and unsettling for Black Americans. It was a time of struggle and perpetual rethinking of the Black American situation and the protest movement led by individuals who were themselves subject to doubts and divisions between loyalty to their race and their nation. But throughout this century, Haiti was always present on the horizon. It is difficult to summarize in a few words the extent of the intensity and complexity of the dynamic relation between the Black republic and Black American activists. We will conclude this study by recalling its main features.

During the first half of the nineteenth century, from the time of Haiti's independence to the American Civil War, the Black republic was in the minds of Black Americans (at least those who were free and educated and whose writings have served as some of our source materials) as a place where full and genuine citizenship was accessible. Haiti was also an inspiration to slaves, but that story would require a separate study. Here we have seen how Haiti was viewed and concretely experienced as a refuge at critical times when free people of color despaired of obtaining rights on American territory. Thus, as the antislavery movement was starting to become a more radical and urgent abolitionist movement, Haiti was already an ideal and idealized place where diasporic, separatist, and nationalist ideals of certain Black activists converged. It was a place where Black nationality could be posited, and from there one could continue the combat for the emancipation and equality of all Black people around the world. This gave Haiti the status of a "promised land" for the Black diaspora. While firmly opposing the colonization projects of the American Colonization Society, supporters of a "chosen" emigration to Haiti saw the island destination as an acceptable alternative that would allow Black Americans to exercise rights which were denied to them in the United States, but that they would do without rather than emigrate to Africa. In two successive waves, thousands of Black men and women would experiment with emigrating to Haiti, but both attempts would be mostly unsuccessful. These emigrants, like so many others before and since, discovered that "the destination was sometimes only an alluring mirage and that the reality one had to face was very different from what the dream promised."[3] Nevertheless, these more and less successful experiments and the debates that surrounded them became fertile ground for meditations on Black American identity.

Starting in 1862, a new chapter in the history of Black American relations with Haiti was written. After the small Black republic received formal recognition from the American government under Abraham Lincoln and Black Americans obtained their legal emancipation at about the same time, relations between the two countries took on a new dimension. Even if around 1862–63 Lincoln was hatching his project for Black American colonization on Haiti's Île-à-Vache, interest in Haiti subsided among Black activists who were hopeful emancipation would lead to a better future in their own country. After obtaining the abolition of slavery, Black militants sought to redefine their combat, centering their efforts on gaining full citizenship and political representation at all levels of government. During Reconstruction, some Black men gained power as elected or appointed officials occupying posts of national or international importance. Unfortunately, the egalitarian dream that grew out of the initial success of a few was shattered by the termination of Reconstruction policies. Over that period Haiti maintained its privileged place in the hearts of Black Americans, notably because starting in 1869 and for the rest of the century, all American ambassadors posted to Haiti were Black. Also starting in the 1860s, Haiti quickly took on strategic importance for America's imperialist ambitions in the Caribbean that would continue for the next century. From the Santo Domingo mission launched by President Grant to the Môle Saint-Nicolas affair that was the flashpoint during Frederick Douglass's brief diplomatic career, Haiti remained a central concern for Americans, Black and white, during the decades following the American Civil War.

In 1893 Haiti called on Frederick Douglass to be its representative at the Universal Exposition in Chicago. It was an opportunity for the Sage of Anacostia to resume his pre-Emancipation activism. The Haitian Pavilion in Chicago became the headquarters for Black American discontent. The famous pamphlet *The Reason Why* was published during the exposition and distributed by its authors to visitors at the Haitian Pavilion. The present study concludes with this late nineteenth-century interaction between Haiti and Black American activists. As most of America, from large northern cities to urban and rural areas throughout the South, was sinking, body and soul, into systemic, institutionalized segregation; as state-sanctioned racism was infiltrating politics at the highest levels; and as Black Americans saw their living conditions deteriorate to levels not seen since slavery times and their constitutional protections thrown aside with each pseudolegal measure to prevent Black people from voting—against every expectation, key events from 1893 would be defining moments in the life of Frederick Douglass and for other activists at the end of the nineteenth century. By naming Douglass first commissioner of the Haitian Pavilion, Haiti's government was offering Douglass and his collaborators a golden opportunity to have their voices heard on an international stage. In this way, Haiti became an essential prism for facilitating, influencing, and understanding Black American consciousness of their identity throughout the nineteenth century.

Surprisingly, Douglass did not mention Haiti in his speech of January 9, 1894. However, he took the opportunity to refer to the Columbian World's Exposition, which had recently come to a close, denouncing yet again the general exclusion of Black Americans from the event's organization and daily operations:

> People from abroad noticed the fact that while we have eight millions of colored people in the United States, many of them gentlemen and schol-

> ars, not one of them was deemed worthy to be appointed a Commissioner, or a member of an important committee, or a guide, or a guard on the Exposition grounds. What a commentary is this upon our boasted American liberty and American equality! It is a silence to be sure, but it is a silence that speaks louder than words. It says to the world that the colored people of America are deemed by Americans not within the compass of American law and of American civilization. It says to the lynchers and mobocrats of the South, go on in your hellish work of negro persecution. What you do to their bodies, we do to their souls.[4]

With this parting tirade, Douglass settled scores with the exposition's organizers and northern politicians, who, he believed, had abandoned Black Americans and abandoned their principled defense of equality and liberty—in the name of a dubious North–South reconciliation—and thus opened the floodgates to daily violence, from intimidation to lynching, exercised with impunity by southern mobs against Black Americans. For Douglass, broad-based violence and terror was no longer only a local or regional problem but clearly a national one. If in the South certain white individuals and groups felt free to terrorize and flout procedures and precedent regarding court rules, juries, and other legal norms, it was partly the fault of northerners who lowered their guard and closed their eyes to the crimes committed by southerners. Moreover, Douglass considered the suppression of Black voting rights as an attack on American republicanism and a political surrender of the North to the South. Douglass also reaffirmed his attachment to the American territory, recalling that "the native land" of Black Americans was America, not Africa, that this had been so for well over two centuries, and therefore the Black American struggle ought to take place in the United States, while adding that it was a struggle for the good of "the whole race" in America and around the world:

> We have a fight on our hands right here, a fight for the whole race, and a blow struck for the negro in America is a blow struck for the negro in Africa. For until the negro is respected in America, he need not expect consideration elsewhere.[5]

Alongside his anti-imperialist and anticolonialist stance, Douglass's speech gave a damning summary of the Black economic situation. In certain places, he claimed, Black Americans in the 1890s were living in conditions that were in some respects less favorable than under slavery, because white southerners had succeeded in maintaining Black men and women in a state of economic dependence that prevented them from improving their situation. Therefore, he concluded, the evil plaguing the American nation had been misidentified. There was no "negro problem" but instead a problem of racial prejudice spread throughout the country.

Meanwhile, Haiti, the little Black republic whose destiny had seemed linked to that of the United States, the place where Black Americans imagined building a Black nationality with the aim of holding their own on the global political chessboard and proving to the rest of the world that Black people were as "civilized" and "enlightened" as whites, this plot of land that had been considered a sheltering asylum, a "promised land"—that Haiti now seemed far from the concerns of Black American activists.

The frank account Douglass gave of his home country was made more poignant by the disappointment and dashed hopes he felt about America. As Reconstruction was coming to an end in the 1870s, Douglass had gone along with the Pan-American project of his government by supporting the annexation of Santo Domingo.[6] However, while supporting this principle, Douglass also rejected the aggressivity of his country toward weaker nations; and as we have seen, he broke with the Pan-American project at the beginning of the 1890s after witnessing that the United States was prepared to use force against Haiti to satisfy its imperialist goals. It seemed nearly impossible to Douglass to remain loyal to both his nation and his race, which is why, according to the historian Millery Polyné, a project of "black pan-Americanism" took shape in Douglass's mind as a way to protect Black sovereignty in the Americas. By supporting the expansion of American values while both rejecting the racial domination of whites over Blacks and protecting Black national sovereignty, Douglass elaborated a project of Black Pan-Americanism. This project consisted in expanding only the American values of democracy and freedom to serve the Black cause in the Americas and allow for the progress of their race. Obviously, Douglass considered Black Americans to be the natural leaders of his Black Pan-Americanism that was to guide Black people throughout the Americas and particularly in the Caribbean toward further progress and the protection of their sovereignty.[7] It is likely that at the time, in 1891 and even more so in 1894, Douglass had set his sights even higher. After having witnessed during the Universal Exposition of 1893 the degree to which Black lives around the world were profoundly altered by the partitioning of Africa and the return to white domination in the southern states of America, it is not impossible that he was more in favor of Pan-Africanism and not just black Pan-Americanism, though he did not use that terminology.

Douglass had always refused to support the resettlement of Black Americans in Africa. He was uninterested in it because he judged a rapprochement between Black Americans and Africans to be degrading for the former, though later in 1894 he would declare his solidarity with the African continent. In short, Africa deserved solidarity, not colonization. For Douglass, Black Americans should feel solidarity toward peoples colonized by imperial powers because imperialism and racism were intertwined. And Black Americans were the leading victims of this racism, the supposed superiority of the white race over the Black race, in their own home in turn-of-the-century America. The consciousness of imperial exploitation of people of color characteristic of Pan-Africanism originated at the end of the nineteenth century in reaction to the imperialism and colonialism of America and the great European powers and took the form of expressions of solidarity between exploited peoples of color. Douglass's statements anticipated the Pan-Africanist theories later defended by Henry Sylvester-Williams of Trinidad and the Black American minister Alexander Walters. These two were the organizers of the fist Pan-African Congress that took place in London in 1900. Douglass's views also foreshadow the future activism of W. E. B. Du Bois and Marcus Garvey. Du Bois was one of the first theorizers of Pan-Africanism and a leader who pushed Black elites to link their cause to that of Africa to achieve a better defense of their interests inside America. He also participated in the founding of the National Association for the Advancement of Colored People, or NAACP, in 1909. Marcus Garvey would later emerge as another important voice for Pan-Africanism after World War I. Garvey considered Africa the motherland of Black people and directed his energy toward promoting Pan-Africanism and a "back-to-Africa" movement among working-class Black Americans. He founded the Universal Negro Improvement Association in 1916 and participated in the creation of the International League of Darker Peoples along with A. Philip Randolph in 1919.[8]

Unlike these Pan-Africanists, Douglass, while rejecting American domination over nonwhite nations, thought that financial and intellectual aid from the United States could help Black nations implement the structural changes necessary for social betterment and overall advancement of people of African origin, and that this would guarantee their sovereignty and reduce their dependence on other nations. At the end of the nineteenth century, Douglass passed the torch to the younger generation of Black American activists such as Du Bois, for whom the struggle would operate within a resolutely international framework.

At the memorial service for Douglass organized at Wilberforce University on March 9, 1895, Du Bois called on the audience to continue the combat led by Douglass for over fifty years, thus inscribing himself as the inheritor of that heritage:

> Douglass fought for us, but the main battle he has left for us. It is a stern strife where the trifler and idiot have no place but strong and fearless men, trained and experienced soldiers, will turn the tide of Battle![9]

One page of history was turning, but the combat would continue, extended now to another continent, Africa, which up until then had been looked on with condescension by Black Americans. The activists of the first generation, following Douglass's example, were inheritors of the ideology of natural rights as inscribed in the Declaration of Independence. They would now yield their place to a new generation of activists with new arguments and methods that would give the struggle for racial justice a more global dimension in the era of new social sciences.

The role of Black Americans in American foreign policy, and especially in the struggle against imperialism, became a subject of renewed interest by historians at the end of the 1990s. Brenda Gayle Plummer and Penny Von Eschen, for example, became interested in the links between Black Americans' national goals and their positions on foreign affairs during the twentieth century.[10] Plummer set out to prove that already in the nineteenth century and even starting in 1900 (after the first Pan-African Congress in London), many Black Americans, from both elite and working-class backgrounds, saw links between the racism they endured in the United States and the treatment of people of color in European colonies, and believed that one must fight on both fronts to advance their own condition in the United States. Von Eschen's study begins in the 1930s and demonstrates that starting at that time, Black American activists strongly criticized American imperialism throughout the world in order to improve their chances of obtaining radical reforms on a national scale in the areas of civil rights and worker rights. They too made the link between anticolonial struggles in the interest of the Black diaspora abroad and the struggle for racial equality within the United States.

Haiti was no longer a central concern of Black American activists. It had been displaced by Africa. At a time when an increasing number of activists were taking up a new form of anticolonial Black diaspora nationalism, the acquisition of full and effective citizenship was no longer the first aim of the struggle. The central focus of the new activism was now opposition to imperialism, to racism, and to prejudice on a global scale. Relations between Black Americans and Haitians were not terminated abruptly or totally, but their character and intensity did change. For example, it would be worth studying further the reactions of Black Americans to the American occupation of Haiti from 1915 to 1934 or examining how the question of Haiti is related to Black American struggles in the twentieth century and down to the present day. Those are different stories, which remain to be told.

APPENDIX

There exists no official version of the address that Frederick Douglass delivered on August 25, 1893, at Colored People's Day, not even in the Frederick Douglass Papers at the Library of Congress. Ida B. Wells herself lamented the absence of a written record of this masterly speech in her autobiography: "It is indeed a great pity that posterity has not been given a copy of that speech. . . . The newspapers gave what for them was large space to it, but no newspaper report did full justice to it."[1]

Christopher Reed published a tentative transcript of this speech as an appendix of his book *"All the World Is Here!"* in 2002, though he acknowledged that "the paragraphs may not be the exact order as when the speech was delivered. It has been reconstructed from two newspaper accounts, and the only paragraph definitely in its proper order is the final one."[2] Unfortunately, Reed does not source these two newspaper accounts, which makes it difficult to verify his text.

As I was searching for traces of Douglass's oration in the Black American newspapers published from late August to December 1893, I managed to find fragments of this masterpiece in four different articles published in the *Topeka Call*, the *Freeman*, and the *Cleveland Gazette* in September 1893.[3] I then assembled these documents into the following transcript. My transcript differs slightly from Reed's. Indeed, some words or phrases vary in the version I propose in this appendix, and the order of some of the central paragraphs is not the same. Moreover, I was not able to find one of the paragraphs that is published in Reed's book in the Black American newspapers I checked in 2012. Consequently, I chose not to include this unsourced passage in my version of Douglass's address. In any case, my analysis of Douglass's speech at Colored People's Day is based on the present transcript (see chapter 8).

Even though one might never be able to recover the full version of the address Douglass delivered on August 25, 1893, the *Topeka Call*, *Freeman*, and

Cleveland Gazette unanimously paid tribute to it and insisted on its being a success and the highlight of Colored People's Day. "Just before the last numbers on the program were given, Frederick Douglass came to the front of the stage, amid hearty cheers, and delivered the following address," wrote the *Topeka Call*, emphasizing that "Mr. Douglass was frequently applauded during his speech."[4] The *Freeman* concurred, asserting that "the feature of the occasion that most impressed the public was the masterly address of the Hon. Frederick Douglass. He was in a happy mood and when he had fairly set sail in his speech, applause again and again greeted him. . . . The applause was deafening."[5] "Frederick Douglass in his magnificent philippic delivered in Chicago 'Jubilee Day,' paid direct attention to the Northern whites in the following reflections, which we wish every mother son of them could read and ponder," the *Freeman* would point out a week later, hinting that Douglass was specifically addressing the white part of the crowd.[6] So did the *Cleveland Gazette* in its article entitled "Douglass' Truths," whose subtitle, "They Are Addressed to the Northern White People," eloquently set the tone of the speech.[7]

Frederick Douglass's Speech at Colored People's Day, August 25, 1893 (Festival Hall, Jackson Park, Chicago, Illinois)

Our presence here in such numbers is a vindication of our wisdom and of our good nature. I am glad that we have cheerfully embraced this occasion to show by our spirit, song, speech, and enthusiasm that we are neither ashamed of our cause nor of our company. It is known to many of you that there is a division of opinion among intelligent colored citizens as to the wisdom of accepting a "colored people's day" at the Fair.

This division of opinion has been caused, in part, by the slender recognition we have received from the management of the exposition. Without expressing any satisfaction with this phase of that management, I think we cannot wisely withhold our thanks to the World's Columbian Exposition for the opportunity now offered us to define our position and set ourselves right before the world. It might perhaps have done more and better for us at its inception, but we should not forget that it might also have done less and worse for us.

The question will be asked and is asked by our transatlantic visitors, why we do not more fully share in the glory of the great World's Exposition. To answer that question and to protect ourselves from the unfavorable inference and misrepresentation is, in part, the purpose for which we have assembled to-day.

Rejoicing in the liberty we have already secured and congratulating the nation upon the recognition given our rights in the fundamental law of the republic, we shall nevertheless fully expose and denounce the injustice, persecution, lawless violence and lynch law to which as a class we are still subjected. We wish especially to emphasize the fact that, owing to our two hundred years of slavery and the prejudices generated by that cruel system, all presumptions in law, government, and society in this republic are against us, so that it is only necessary to accuse one of our number of crime in order to secure his conviction and punishment. This state of affairs thus [i]ngenerated, will in a measure explain to our transatlantic friends why we have a share so slender in this World's Columbian Exposition. I deny with scorn and indignation the allegation, by whomsoever made, that our small participation in this World's Columbian Exposition is due either to our ignorance or to our want of public spirit.

That we are outside of the World's Fair is only consistent with the fact that we are excluded from every respectable calling, from workshops, manufactories and from the means of learning trades. It is consistent with the fact that we are outside of the church and largely outside of the state.

The people who held slaves are still the ruling class of the South. When you are told that the life of the Negro is held dog cheap in that section, the slave system tells you why it is so. Negro whipping, negro cheating, negro killing, is consistent with Southern ideas inherited from the system of slavery.

It has been affirmed on the one hand and denied on the other that the Negro since emancipation has made commendable progress. I affirm that no people emancipated under the same conditions could have made more commendable progress than has the negro in the same length of time. Under the whole heavens there never was an enslaved people emancipated under more unfavorable circumstances, or started from a lower condition in life.

Men talk of the Negro problem. There is no Negro problem. The problem is whether the American people have honesty enough, loyalty enough, honor enough, patriotism enough to live up to their own Constitution.

A statesman has recently discovered that the only solution of this Negro problem is the removal of the Negro to Africa. I say to this man that we Negroes have made up our minds to stay just where we are. We intend that the American people shall learn the great lesson of the brotherhood of man and the fatherhood of God from our presence among them.

During the war we were eyes to your blind, legs to your lame, shelter to the shelterless among your sons. Have you forgotten that now?

Today we number 8,000,000 people. Today a desperate effort is being made to blacken the character of the Negro and to brand him as a moral monster. In fourteen States of this Union wild mobs have taken the place of law. They hang, shoot, burn men of my race without justice and without right. Today the Negro is barred out of almost every reputable and decent employment.

We only ask to be treated as well as you treat the late enemies of your national life.

We love this country and we want that you should treat us as well as you do those who love only a part of it.

You fawn to the South and they despise you for it. They don't love you. You say you don't fawn to the South. Well, sometimes it seems to me that you do something very like it when you put us aside and under to please or to gratify the South.

The South hates you. It was the South that kept the colored race from a share in the glories of this great exposition. Fourteen States have abandoned their courts and judges and juries, and a wild mob invariably sit as a burlesque dispenser of justice to the colored man.

These same States were your enemies; they fought to trample in the dust the grandest republic the world can ever have. Why in the name of bare justice, are we not treated with as much consideration as were your foes?

We gave legs to your lame, shelter to your shelterless and tenderly bound the gushing wounds of your sons, riddled and torn with rebel bullets. Yet in your fawning upon these cruel slayers you slap us in the face, and with the same shallow prejudice which keeps us in the lowering rank in your estimation, this exposition denied mere recognition to eight million and one tenth of its own people. Kentucky and the rest object, and thus you see not a colored face in a single worthy place on these grounds.

Give us as much as you give your unforgiving enemies and we will cease to raise a voice in complaint. Treat us only as you do those who despise with unrelenting spleen your very selves and the colored man will begin to take a place he hopes by brains and education to acquire.

The sunny South does not love you; it never will. We do. Yet why in heaven's name do you take to your breast the serpent that once stung and crush down the race that grasped the saber that helped make the nation one and the exposition possible?

But stop. Look at the progress the Negro has made in thirty years! We have come up out of Dahomey unto this. Measure the Negro. But not by the standard of the splendid civilization of the Caucasian. Bend down and measure him—measure him—from the depths out of which he has risen.

NOTES

PREFACE

1. Douglass, *Life and Times* (1892); Douglass, *Lecture on Haiti.*

2. Blight, *Frederick Douglass.*

3. McFeely, *Douglass*, 247.

4. In this book, "the Black (American) community" must be understood as a generic term to refer to the Black Americans who actually interacted with Haiti in the nineteenth century. In the antebellum era, this meant mainly free or emancipated Black people—generally (self)-educated Black people—most of whom lived in the North of the United States. The use of the word "community" does not imply, however, that these people would speak with one voice on all important issues, as this book will demonstrate.

5. Bourhis-Mariotti, "'Go to our brethren, the Haytians.'"

6. Bourhis-Mariotti, *L'union fait la force.*

7. Johnson and Power-Greene, *In Search of Liberty.*

8. Fanning, *Caribbean Crossing.*

9. Byrd, *The Black Republic.*

10. See, for example, Dubois, *Avengers of the New World*; Fick, *The Making of Haiti*; Gómez, *Le spectre de la révolution noire*; Le Glaunec, *L'armée indigène.*

11. Dubois, "Esclavage, citoyenneté et République"; Fischer, *Modernity Disavowed.*

12. Johnson, *Diplomacy in Black and White*; Clavin, *Toussaint Louverture and the American Civil War.*

13. Ferrer, *Freedom's Mirror.*

14. Wells et al., *The Reason Why.*

INTRODUCTION

1. Douglass, *Lecture on Haiti*, 7.

2. Also spelled "L'Ouverture."

3. "A Trip to Hayti," *Douglass' Monthly*, May 1861, 449–50.

4. "In Paris, the failure of the expedition to Saint-Domingue, the death of General Leclerc . . . and encroaching hostilities with Great Britain gradually forced Bonaparte and Talleyrand to revise their plans for colonial expansion. . . . The First Consul decided to sell Louisiana rather than see it fall into the hands of the British." Marie-Jeanne Ros-

signol, *Le ferment nationaliste*, 252. François Barbé de Marbois clearly linked the sale of Louisiana to the United States to the Haitian Revolution and Napoleon's failure to win back Saint-Domingue: "The events of which Saint-Domingue was then the bloody theater are closely linked to the history of the Louisiana purchase treaty." François Barbé de Marbois, *Histoire de la Louisiane*, 201. On the consequences of the Haitian Revolution in the English-speaking world, see also Alejandro E. Gómez, *Le spectre de la révolution noire*; and Ashli White, *Encountering Revolution*.

5. In this book, "the first part of the nineteenth century" refers to the period starting in 1800 and ending in 1865 when slavery was abolished by the Thirteenth Amendment; "the second half of the century" refers to the postslavery period from 1865 to the end of the century.

6. The Caribbean island that is currently home to two countries—Haiti on the western third and the Dominican Republic on the eastern two-thirds—was referred to by several names in French and English since Christopher Columbus landed there in 1492. For the sake of simplicity, I will use "Hispaniola" when referring to the entire island, "Saint-Domingue" for the French colony, "Haiti" for the Black republic, and either "Dominican Republic" (its official name from 1844 on) or "Santo Domingo" for the part of the island under Spanish control.

7. Paul Gilroy, *The Black Atlantic*.

8. Patrick Manning, *The African Diaspora*.

9. Haiti is not part of the geographical, political, and cultural network Gilroy defines, but solely appears in his work in terms of its hypothetical arm's-length influence on Black American emancipatory and egalitarian thinking.

10. I am using "culture(s)" in the anthropological sense to refer to a "secondary" environment that is the result of human activity.

11. Brent Hayes Edwards, a diaspora theorist, identifies a relationship of cause and effect between the uptake of the term "diaspora" in Black studies and the institutionalization of the field in American universities in the 1970s, where Black studies departments were founded with the explicit aim of studying the history of African Americans (in the United States and the rest of the New World) in conjunction with the history of all the other Africans dispersed worldwide. As a result, from the outset, Black studies had an explicit leaning toward the diaspora with the Atlantic slave trade as its common origin. See Brent H. Edwards, "The Uses of Diaspora," 45–73, 56–57.

12. William J. Moses, *Classical Black Nationalism*.

13. Christine Chivallon, *The Black Diaspora of the Americas*, 132.

14. Douglass, *Life and Times* (1881), 244. This opinion is shared by historians with a recent interest in the history of Black American elites. The "movement" began with Julie Winch in the 1990s, then developed in the 2000s with Richard S. Newman. They studied the Black elites who used their free status to structure communication within the community, to enter into dialogue with white abolitionists, and so on. See Julie Winch, *Philadelphia's Black Elite*; and Richard S. Newman, *Freedom's Prophet*. See also Julie Winch, *A Gentleman of Color*, and *The Elite of Our People*.

15. Andrée-Anne Kekeh-Dika and Hélène Le Dantec-Lowry, eds., *Formes et écritures du départ*, 13.

16. Ibid.

17. Despite the closeness in space of the United States and Haiti and the closeness

in time of their respective revolutions, few American scholars have focused to date on the relationship between the two nations throughout the nineteenth century. By far the most exhaustive study is Rayford W. Logan's *Diplomatic Relations of the United States with Haiti, 1776–1891*. Logan lays the foundations for an Atlantic, postcolonial history of the revolutionary period, highlighting the interactions between the numerous powers (France and Britain, and to a lesser extent Spain) with a stake in Haiti (and the Dominican Republic). His book owes its strength and originality to the exhaustive reading of French diplomatic archives and other French-language sources, including secondary material and newspapers, as well as American diplomatic sources, Haitian government archives, and private documents located in Haiti.

18. See, for instance, Nell I. Painter, *Exodusters*; James R. Grossman, *Land of Hope*; and Nicholas Lemann, *Promised Land.*

19. See, for instance, Nathalie Dessens, *From Saint-Domingue to New Orleans.*

20. Sara Fanning, *Caribbean Crossing.*

21. Floyd J. Miller, *The Search for a Black Nationality.*

22. Chris Dixon, *African Americans and Haiti.*

23. Brandon R. Byrd, *The Black Republic.*

24. Ida B. Wells et al., *The Reason Why.*

CHAPTER 1. Haiti, the Promised Land?

1. Dewey, *Correspondence*, 7.

2. Fleming, *Deportation and Colonization*, 3.

3. Many terms, some of them shocking to us today, were used to name the concept of colonization in the American context. These included "expatriation," "deportation," and "emigration." They were all used interchangeably by colonizationists, by Black people themselves, and later by historians. In the present study, we consider as interchangeable synonyms the words *expatriation*, *expulsion*, and *deportation* to designate the idea of the movement of free and emancipated Black Americans to a location outside the United States. However, the word *colonization* will be used specifically in the way it was used in the United States at the beginning of the nineteenth century to speak of the creation of colonies composed of former slaves and free people of color and located outside American territory; in other words, a forced emigration of Black populations that was proposed principally by white abolitionists but also by a portion of elite (and often racist) southern whites. This term must be clearly distinguished from the parallel movement that we call the "emigration" of Black populations; in other words, a movement of voluntary departure undertaken on the initiative of Black people themselves, though it is true that certain Black emigrationist organizations were affiliated with analogous white organizations for essentially economic reasons.

4. On the creation of Liberia, see Clegg, *The Price of Liberty*; and Tyler-McGraw, *An African Republic.*

5. The American Colonization Society was a philanthropic organization founded in 1816. It was directed and financed by (racist) opponents of slavery and white politicians with the intention of helping American slaves, once freed, to return to their continent of origin. See Burin, *Slavery and the Peculiar Solution*. See also Power-Greene, *Against Wind and Tide.*

6. Jefferson, *Notes*, 154 (emphasis added).

7. See Melish, *Disowning Slavery*. See also Nash, *Race and Revolution*, 57–90.

8. See Berlin, *Many Thousands Gone*, 233–34.

9. This law was adopted in 1691 and suspended in 1782. See Burin, *Slavery and the Peculiar Solution*, 176.

10. Burin, *Slavery and the Peculiar Solution*, 7. See also Franklin, *From Slavery to Freedom*, 235.

11. See Burin, *Slavery and the Peculiar Solution*, 7–8.

12. For example, in 1786, Prince Hall, a free Black man from Boston, sent a petition to the town assembly in the name of the Black community of Boston recommending a plan to return to Africa. He declared that Black Americans would prefer "to return to Africa, our native country . . . where we shall live among our equals and be more comfortable and happy, than we can be in our present situation." Prince Hall, quoted by Nash, *Race and Revolution*, 66–67.

13. Needles, *An Historical Memoir*, 66. All ellipses are editorial here and in the rest of the manuscript.

14. See Berlin, *Many Thousands Gone*; Burin, *Slavery and the Peculiar Solution*.

15. See Staudenraus, *The African Colonization Movement*, 1–11.

16. In *William Thornton and Negro Colonization*, the historian Gaillard Hunt conducts a lengthy review of this "colonizationist" period in the life of William Thornton. He also briefly mentions the role of Samuel Adams, James Madison, and the Société des Amis des Noirs. The correspondence between Thornton and Etienne Clavières, then president of the Société des Amis des Noirs, reveals that Madison approved of the colonization plans, which he saw as the leading precondition for success of a possible emancipation of Black Americans. See Hunt, *William Thornton*, 12–13, 22–23.

17. Ferdinando Fairfax (1766–1820) was at the time the largest landowner in Virginia. He was also a slaveowner, justice of the peace in Jefferson County Virginia, and known to be in favor of the gradual emancipation (with compensation) of slaves.

18. Ferdinando Fairfax, "Plan for Liberating the Negroes within the United States," *American Museum* 8 (Dec. 1790): 285–87, qtd. in Nash, *Race and Revolution*, 146–50.

19. For more on the Virginia legal scholar and judge St. George Tucker (1752–1827), see Coleman, *St. George Tucker*.

20. See Jordan, *White over Black*, 559. The proposal for gradual emancipation put forward by St. George Tucker in 1796 is partially reproduced in Nash, *Race and Revolution*, 151–58.

21. The slave rebellion of Gabriel (Gabriel Prosser, sometimes spelled Proser) was repressed in Richmond, Virginia, on August 30, 1800.

22. See Jordan, *White over Black*, 561.

23. See Jefferson, *The Writings*, 457–58.

24. Thomas Jefferson to James Monroe, November 24, 1801, manuscript/mixed material. Retrieved from the Library of Congress, www.loc.gov/item/mtjbib010767 (last accessed July 6, 2021).

25. See Hunt, *Haiti's Influence on Antebellum America*.

26. On this topic, especially in the southern states, see Aje, "Entre désir d'intégration et séparatisme socio-racial."

27. In February 1806 the U.S. Senate ratified an act to suspend commercial exchange

between the United States and certain parts of the island of St. Domingo. See Rossignol, *Le ferment nationaliste*, 207.

28. A letter written in 1793 by Thomas Jefferson and quoted in Jordan, *White over Black*, 434.

29. Jordan, *White over Black*, 380–82.

30. Hunt, *Haiti's Influence on Antebellum America*, 107–46.

31. Aje, "Entre désir d'intégration et séparatisme socio-racial," 51–58.

32. Alderson, *This Bright Era*, 14–15.

33. Alderson, *This Bright Era*, 104–5, 107.

34. For more on Denmark Vesey's life and failed slave conspiracy (1822), see Egerton, *He Shall Go Out Free*.

35. Achates, *Reflections*, 6, 7.

36. Thomas Jefferson to Jared Sparks, February 4, 1824, manuscript/mixed material. Retrieved from the Library of Congress, www.loc.gov/item/mtjbib024921 (last accessed July 6, 2021).

37. Sometimes spelled "Sanders."

38. Christophe began corresponding with Wilberforce in 1814, then with Clarkson in 1815, hoping that with their help he could obtain the British government's recognition of Haiti. Without the support of the Royal Navy, Christophe doubted that his people could remain free for long. See Cole, *Christophe*, 223–24.

39. Saunders, *Haytian Papers*.

40. Madiou, *Histoire d'Haïti*, 5:424.

41. Cole, *Christophe*, 229.

42. Miller, *The Search for a Black Nationality*, 75.

43. In 1823 "Boyer, thinking of further populating the Samana peninsula, resolved to establish there families of Blacks and colored men whom he proposed to bring from the United States." Madiou, *Histoire d'Haïti*, 6:392–93.

44. See Montague, *Haiti and the United States*, 50–52.

45. This theory is elaborated by the historian Rayford Logan, who, after having asserted that between 1821 and 1823 no southern newspaper proposed recognizing Haiti whereas the northern press raised the matter while remaining divided about it, underlines that, overall, the press was unanimous in interpreting Boyer's generous offer as a thinly disguised stratagem to obtain recognition from the United States. See Logan, *Diplomatic Relations*, 217.

46. Dewey, *Correspondence*, 2.

47. Dewey, *Correspondence*, 7.

48. Dewey, *Correspondence*, 11.

49. Dewey, *Correspondence*, 14.

50. Dewey, *Correspondence*, 27.

51. Gannett, *Statistics*, 6–11.

52. Dewey, *Correspondence*, 22, 24.

53. *First Report of the New York Colonization Society*, 18.

54. See Newman, *Freedom's Prophet*; Winch, *A Gentleman of Color*; and Bethel, "Images of Hayti," 834.

55. *Address of the Board of Managers of the Haytian Emigration Society of Coloured People*, 3.

56. The *Niles' Weekly Register* (a Baltimore magazine) reprinted articles from other

sources, as well as its own pieces of a similar nature, particularly between 1818 and 1825. They all praised the stability of the Black republic, raved about the rare opportunity of emigrating or investing there, and so forth.

57. *Genius of Universal Emancipation* 4, no. 2, November 1824, 17, 19.

58. *Genius of Universal Emancipation* 4, no. 6, March 1825, 82: "The subscriber intends to despatch a ship to Hayti, on or about the 15th of April, with such free persons of colour as may wish to emigrate thither, who are requested to enter their names as early as possible, in order that the necessary preparations may be made."

59. Dillon, *Benjamin Lundy*, 87–90.

60. Dillon, *Benjamin Lundy*, 79–80.

61. *Genius of Universal Emancipation* 4, no. 1, October 1824, 2–4.

62. Lundy, *A Plan for the Gradual Abolition of Slavery in the United States*. Lundy went to Haiti for the first time in the spring of 1826 with the goal of negotiating more financial aid from the Haitian government for the transportation and resettlement of free Black Americans wishing to emigrate to Haiti. He made a second trip in June 1829 to accompany a group of twelve Black people who had been recently emancipated by their Maryland owner Joseph Leonard Smith, who had accepted to free them on condition that Lundy escort them to Haiti and help with their resettlement. See Dillon, *Benjamin Lundy*, 99–100, 142–43. See also Lundy, *Life, Travels and Opinions*, 23–24, 29.

63. "Emigrants to Hayti," 62–63.

64. See Waterman, *Frances Wright*. See also Eckhardt, *Fanny Wright*. According to Eckhardt, in 1825 Frances Fanny Wright was the first woman in the United States to take a public stand against slavery. In her letter number 28 to "a friend in England," reprinted in her *Views of Society and Manners in America; in a Series of Letters from That Country to a Friend in England, During the years 1818, 1819 and 1820*, Wright already spoke out at length against this institution, which she considered particularly degrading and revolting.

65. On February 5, 1783, Lafayette wrote to George Washington inviting him to join in an experimental plan for gradual emancipation. Having quickly understood that Washington, though sympathetic and kindly disposed toward him, would not get involved in the project, Lafayette acquired a clove and cinnamon plantation, "La Belle Gabrielle," along the Oyapok River in present-day French Guiana. His goal was to demonstrate the benefit of the gradual emancipation of approximately seventy African slaves between the ages of one and fifty-nine. They were paid for their labor, enrolled in school, and punished with the same rigor as white employees. Lafayette thought he would be able to demonstrate that this method of "soft" exploitation gave better results of productivity and natality than traditional slavery. See Gillard, "Lafayette, Friend of the Negro."

66. On the utopian theories of Robert Owen and his idea of "Villages of Unity and Mutual Cooperation," see Kumar, "Utopian Thought and Communal Practice."

67. She would return to this plan in detail some years later in the *New Harmony Gazette*. See Wright, "Explanatory Notes."

68. Albion was founded in 1817–18 by a colony of English citizens led by George Flower and his friend Morris Birkbeck. After crossing Ohio, Indiana, and Illinois, they decided to buy land in Edwards County, brought over two hundred of their English compatriots, and began their experiment. Americans called their colony "The En-

glish Settlement." However, relations with neighboring Americans quickly deteriorated around the question of slavery. The English, who were all opposed to the practice, soon found themselves in conflict with the local slaveowners. George Flower relates this experience very precisely in his *History of the English Settlement in Edward County Illinois, Founded in 1817 and 1818 by Morris Birkbeck and George Flower*, especially chapter 10.

69. Waterman, *Frances Wright*, 99.

70. Madison, "Letter to Lafayette."

71. See Connors, "Frances Wright."

72. Waterman, *Frances Wright*, 131.

73. Russwurm, "The Condition and Prospects of Hayti."

74. See Hunt, *Haiti's Influence on Antebellum America*; Baur, "Mulatto Machiavelli." See also Fanning, *Caribbean Crossing*, chap. 6.

75. Baur, "Mulatto Machiavelli," 326–27.

76. The ordinance of Charles X, signed by the king on April 17, 1825, recognized "the full and whole independence" of the Haitian government on condition of payment of "the sum of one hundred and fifty million francs to be used to indemnify former colonists." This measure was approved by the senate on July 11, 1825, once Boyer had accepted the terms in an official letter to Baron de MacKau dated July 8, 1825. See Blancpain, *Un siècle de relations financières*, 49–60. See also Logan, *Diplomatic Relations*, 219–20.

77. On the nonrecognition of Haiti by the Monroe administration, see Henry, "Vers une Amérique?" According to Monica Henry, it was first the Jefferson administration that decided not to recognize Haiti, and Monroe simply followed the policy of his predecessor.

78. See *American State Papers: Foreign Relations* 5:240. See also Logan, *Diplomatic Relations*, 204–5.

79. Logan, *Diplomatic Relations*, 221, 216.

80. We will discuss in greater detail the emigration plan encouraged by Holly in the 1850s in chapter 3.

81. Holly, *A Vindication of the Capacity of the Negro Race*, 38.

82. Manigat, *Eventail d'histoire vivante d'Haïti*, 110: "It is known that Dessalines nurtured the project to bring 500,000 Blacks from Africa to make them Haitian citizens, producers, and consumers. Boyer drew in 13,000 Black Americans."

83. Corvington, *Port-au-Prince au cours des ans*, 54–55.

84. *Genius of Universal Emancipation* 4, no. 7, May 1825, 100.

85. "Report from Hayti," 61–62: "From my short acquaintance with the Haytiens, and my observing their dispositions towards our American blacks amongst them, I am not disposed to encourage any free people of colour to go from the United States to settle in Hayti; but as a friend, I would suggest to them the propriety of emigrating to Liberia, where I believe they would live under good government and laws, enjoy equal privileges, and be among their own country people. . . . Added to which, they would be in the land of their forefathers' nativity; where, by proper application on their part, they might be instrumental in civilizing and christianizing benighted Africa."

86. "American Colonization," *Colored American*, August 11, 1838.

87. "The Chief of Sinners," *Colored American*, January 20, 1838.

88. "Colonization Convention," *Colored American*, June 2, 1838.

89. "A Mistake Corrected," *Colored American*, July 27, 1839.

90. "Republic of Hayti," *Colored American*, March 15, 1838.

CHAPTER 2. Haiti and the "Black Nationality" Project

1. Walker, *Walker's Appeal*, 62–63

2. For more on William Lloyd Garrison (1805–1879), see Mayer, *All on Fire*.

3. Harrold, *The Rise of Aggressive Abolitionism*, 7.

4. Walters, *The Antislavery Appeal*, xi.

5. Newman, *The Transformation of American Abolitionism*.

6. Walters, *The Antislavery Appeal*, 18.

7. For more on Nat Turner's rebellion, see Breen, *The Land Shall Be Deluged in Blood*.

8. U.S. Bureau of the Census, *Historical Statistics of the United States* (1975), 14.

9. For more on Henry Highland Garnet (1815–1882), see Schor, *Henry Highland Garnet*.

10. Garnet, "Address to the Slaves of the United States." Italics as in the original. This pamphlet, published in 1848, was in fact written in 1843, but many Black activists, Frederick Douglass first among them, objected to its publication. They considered it too virulent because it exhorted slaves to demand their freedom from their masters and to take it, whether by consent or by force.

11. Pease and Pease, "The Negro Convention Movement," 191.

12. Newman et al., *Pamphlets of Protest*, 166.

13. Pease and Pease, "The Negro Convention Movement."

14. *Proceedings* (1847), 32. Italics and caps as in the original.

15. Purvis, "Appeal of Forty Thousand Citizens."

16. Bell and Ennals, "An Address to the Citizens of New York."

17. Many first-rate studies have been written about the Black press in America. See especially Hutton, *The Early Black Press in America*; Pride and Wilson, *A History of The Black Press*; and Tripp, *Origins of the Black Press*.

18. See Bacon, "The History of Freedom's Journal."

19. "To Our Patrons," *Freedom's Journal*, March 16, 1827.

20. Kinshasa, *Emigration vs. Assimilation*, 75.

21. Wesley, *The Quest for Equality*.

22. Kinshasa, *Emigration vs. Assimilation*, xiii–xiv.

23. Kinshasa, *Emigration vs. Assimilation*, 1–2, 161.

24. Blackett, *Building an Antislavery Wall*, 209. The historian Richard Blackett claims to have identified one hundred Black American visitors by name, suggesting that still more left for Great Britain before the outbreak of the Civil War. In the 1830s, Blackett identifies Moses Roper, Robert Purvis, James McCune Smith, and Nathaniel Paul as all having taken part in the transatlantic abolitionist movement. In the 1840s the movement was led by a new generation including Frederick Douglass, Henry Highland Garnet, William Wells Brown, Alexander Crummell, J. W. C. Pennington, and Charles Lenox Remond, among others. Others would join in throughout the 1850s.

25. Blackett, *Building an Antislavery Wall*, 3.

26. Paul Cuffe was born in 1759 in the colony of Massachusetts to an Amerindian mother and a father who was a former slave who had purchased his freedom. In 1808

Cuffe became a Quaker and joined the Anglo-American abolitionist movement. He soon became interested in Sierra Leone, already the home of former British slaves, as a possible land of asylum for Black Americans. In short, Cuffe, who was also a merchant and sailor, was one of the first Black American emigrationists of the nineteenth century. On the invitation of British abolitionists, Cuffe made a first voyage to Sierra Leone in 1811 with the idea of organizing annual transports to Africa of skilled Black American workers. The War of 1812 prevented him from carrying out his project. He embarked for Sierra Leone a second time in December 1815, accompanying nine families, a total of thirty-eight free people of color, with the support of the Black abolitionists James Forten, Absalom Jones, and Richard Allen. After returning to the United States, Cuffe, who was convinced of the necessity of massive emigration of Black Americans to Africa, joined forces with the American Colonization Society. He died in 1817 before he was able to set up his own emigration project, which he hoped would contribute to African prosperity and improve the living conditions of Black Americans. See Thomas, *Rise to Be a People*.

27. "American Colonization," *Colored American*, August 11, 1838.

28. "New Jersey," *Colored American*, September 1, 1838. Italics as in the original.

29. Walker, *Walker's Appeal*, 62–63.

30. Janvier, *Les Constitutions d'Haïti*, 32, Art. 12: "Aucun blanc, quelle que soit sa nation, ne mettra le pied sur ce territoire, à titre de maître ou de propriétaire et ne pourra à l'avenir y acquérir aucune propriété."

31. Janvier, *Les Constitutions d'Haïti*, 117, Art. 44:—"Tout Africain, Indien et ceux issus de leur sang, nés dans les colonies ou en pays étrangers, qui viendraient résider dans la République sont reconnus Haïtiens, mais ne jouiront des droits de citoyen qu'après une année de résidence."

32. The first colored convention that took place in 1830 discussed the question of emigration toward Upper Canada, coming out in favor of this idea on the grounds that it was a humanitarian measure in response to the persecution experienced by Black people in many northern states. The convention decided to create auxiliary chapters whose mission would be to raise funds for the purchase of land in Canada to establish a colony for Black Americans. See *Constitution of the American Society of Free Persons of Colour*.

33. Francis and Cork, "A Voice from Trenton!"

34. Whitfield, *Blacks on the Border*, 9–24.

35. Gallant, "Perspectives," 392–93.

36. See Whitfield, *Blacks on the Border*, 30–31; Gallant, "Perspectives," 394.

37. Whitfield, *Blacks on the Border*, 59–60.

38. Dodson and Diouf, *In Motion*, 71. On emigration to Trinidad at the end of the 1830s, see also Power-Greene, "Look Well Before You Leap."

39. The Abolition Act of 1833, implemented on August 1, 1834, officially abolished slavery in British colonies in the Americas. It is estimated that between 20,000 and 30,000 Black Americans took refuge in Canada following the enactment of the Fugitive Slave Act of 1850. See Landon, "The Negro Migration to Canada"; Gallant, "Perspectives," 399.

40. For more on the Underground Railroad, see Foner, *Gateway to Freedom*.

41. See Gallant, "Perspectives," 395.

42. The colonies welcoming the highest number of Black Americans at the time were Wilberforce, Chatham, Amherstburg, and Toronto. See Gallant, "Perspectives," 391, 395.

However, it is estimated that approximately 30,000 Black Americans who had fled to Canada returned to the United States to fight in the Union army during the Civil War and to reunite with their families. See Dodson and Diouf, *In Motion*, 71–72.

43. Williams, *Discourse Delivered in St. Philip's Church*.

44. "Emigration vs. Colonization," *Colored American*, November 16, 1839.

45. Editor, "Our Prospects," *Colored American*, September 14, 1839.

46. "Philip A. Bell to Charles B. Ray," *Colored American*, September 28, 1839.

47. Editor, "Emigration," *Colored American*, September 28, 1839.

48. See Pamphile, *Haitians and African Americans*.

49. Dunbar, *Masterpieces of Negro Eloquence*, 14.

50. Russwurm, "The Condition and Prospects of Hayti," 396.

51. Smith, *A Lecture on the Haytien Revolutions;* Brown, *St. Domingo*.

52. Black Americans were not the only ones to take an interest in Haiti. Despite the reservations or outright fear of southerners toward Haiti, a large number of white historians and/or abolitionists spoke and published on Haiti, its revolution, and on Toussaint Louverture at that time. It is more than likely that Black elites had access to these publications. Of particular note are the works of Beard, *The Life of Toussaint L'Ouverture*; Franklin, *The Present State of Hayti*; and Hunt, *Remarks on Hayti*.

53. Editor, "Haiti," *Colored American*, November 3, 1838.

54. Editor, "Hayti," *Colored American*, February 2, 1839.

55. Smith, *A Lecture on the Haytien Revolutions*, 6.

56. See Bell, "Negro Nationalism in the 1850s"; Miller, *The Search for a Black Nationality*; Dixon, *African Americans and Haiti*; and Moses, *The Golden Age of Black Nationalism*. A few historians, such as J. Herman Blake and August Meier, imagine the possibility that a certain early form of Black nationalism may have emerged from the start of the nineteenth century, but they remain prudent about using this controversial term. See Blake, "Black Nationalism"; and Meier, "The Emergence of Negro Nationalism."

57. Dixon, *African Americans and Haiti*, 11.

58. Watkins, *The Pine and Palm*, November 23, 1861, Black Abolitionist Archives, doc. no. 24731, University of Detroit Mercy Special Collections, Black Abolitionist Digital Archives, http://research.udmercy.edu/find/special_collections/digital/baa/index.php (my emphasis).

59. Holly, "Thoughts on Hayti, Number VI," 364. Caps as in the original.

60. "Wanted! A Nation!" *Weekly Anglo-African*, May 11, 1861. My emphasis and caps as in the original.

61. *Proceedings* (1847), 25.

62. Garland, Henry H. "The West—the West!" *North Star*, January 26, 1849, 3.

63. Henry Walton Bibb (1815–1854) was born a slave, the son of Kentucky senator James Bibb and a female slave. He managed to flee in 1837 and emigrated to Canada in 1851. He founded the abolitionist newspaper *The Voice of the Fugitive* the same year. Mary Ann Shadd Cary (1823–1893) was born free in the state of Delaware. She was a teacher, journalist, abolitionist, and the first Black editor in chief in North America. After passage of the Fugitive Slave Act, she moved to Windsor, Ontario, where she published *The Provincial Freemen*. A large portion of chapter 3 is devoted to James Theodore Holly (1829–1911).

64. Miller, *The Search for a Black Nationality*, 110–14.

65. *Minutes and Proceedings*, 15–16. Caps as in the original.

66. See Miller, *The Search for a Black Nationality*, 94–97. See also the issues of *Colored American* dated December 2 and 9, 1837.

67. See Delany, *The Condition*.

68. Stowe, *Uncle Tom's Cabin*.

69. More than 300,000 copies of *Uncle Tom's Cabin* were sold in the first months following its publication. See Parfait, *The Publishing History of Uncle Tom's Cabin*.

70. Stowe, *Uncle Tom's Cabin*, 608–9.

71. Levine, *Martin Delany*, 58–60.

72. James Monroe Whitfield (1822–1871) was a Black American abolitionist and poet born free in the state of New Hampshire.

73. *Proceedings* (1853), 10.

74. Reverend William J. Watkins Sr. was a Black American abolitionist and educator born free in Baltimore, Maryland. He ran his own school for Black Americans, Watkins' Academy for Negro Youth, from the 1820s to the 1850s. He was the uncle of Frances Ellen Watkins Harper (1825–1911), the famous Black American feminist. The correspondence between Whitfield and Watkins in 1853–54 was soon published as a pamphlet that analyzed emigration, possible destinations for expatriation, and so forth. See Newsom, *Arguments*.

75. Newsom, *Arguments*, 26.

76. *Proceedings* (1854).

77. *Proceedings* (1854), 37. Caps as in the original.

78. Martin R. Delany, whose children are all named after famous Black figures, would give two of his sons Haitian names. He named his oldest son Toussaint L'Ouverture and the fifth Faustin Soulouque. See Sterling, *The Making of an Afro-American*, 86.

79. *Proceedings* (1854), 42.

80. For more on James William Charles Pennington, see Webber, *American to the Backbone*.

81. *Proceedings* (1856), 37. See also Dixon, *African Americans and Haiti*, 95.

CHAPTER 3. The Second Wave of Emigration to Haiti

1. Holly, "Thoughts on Hayti, Number V," 329.

2. There are only two books on Reverend Holly: Dean, *Defender of the Race*; and Wipfler, *James Theodore Holly in Haiti*. The papers of Reverend Holly and those relating to his Haitian Mission (the Haiti Mission Records) are preserved in the archives of the Episcopal Church of Austin, Texas. The archives contain just under 4,600 documents. Of note are Holly's papers from 1855 to 1911, which number 1,100 items. All the documents from the collection were made available thanks to the cooperation of the archives of the Episcopal Church, which has kindly granted me permission to quote from them in this study.

3. "The Protestant Episcopal Mission in Haïti," from Holly to the Bishop of the Protestant Episcopal Church in the U.S., May 29, 1862, in Overseas Department, Haiti Records 1855–1967, Record Group 68, Series 1: Missionary Personnel Files, 1855–1967, Box 3, Folder 20, Holly, James Theodore, Bishop, 1855–1865.

4. Holly wrote the introduction to Newsom's *Arguments* as well as the pages of the

appendix that examine the advantages and drawbacks of Haiti as a possible emigration destination: "Emigration there [Haiti] in large numbers on the part of the colored Americans would do much to strengthen the hands of that government, and forward in an uncalculable [*sic*] degree the cause of our elevation in America."

5. This argument is perfectly consistent with the thesis of Brenda Gayle Plummer, who suggests that the lobbying by ethnic minorities on matters of foreign policy is inseparable from the goals of these groups in the area of domestic politics inside their country. This thesis, though applied to the twentieth century by the author, seems to us to be also applicable to the nineteenth century. See Plummer, *Rising Wind*, 9–15.

6. Hutchison, *Errand to the World*, 5–8, 43–45.

7. See Park, *White Americans in Black Africa*.

8. Williams, *Black Americans and the Evangelization of Africa*, 174–76.

9. See Holly, *Facts about the Church's Mission in Haiti*.

10. One can find many details about this crossing in a letter he wrote while his ship was entering the harbor of Port-au-Prince. See, From Holly to "Rev. and Dear Sir," August 1, 1855, in Overseas Department, Haiti Records 1855–1967, Record Group 68, Series 1: Missionary Personnel Files, 1855–1967, Box 3, Folder 20, Holly, James Theodore, Bishop, 1855–1865.

11. Essentially Black Americans who had arrived in Haiti in the 1820s in the wake of Boyer's incentivizing campaign. See, From Holly to "Rev. and Dear Sir," Document A—Remarks, September 10, 1855, in Overseas Department, Haiti Records 1855–1967, Record Group 68, Series 1: Missionary Personnel Files, 1855–1967, Box 3, Folder 20, Holly, James Theodore, Bishop, 1855–1865.

12. Contrary to what has been written in the few commentaries that exist, Holly did not meet Haitian emperor Faustin-Elie Soulouque, which is not surprising because at the time Soulouque was directly involved in an attempt to invade the Spanish portion of the island in order to (re)unite Santo Domingo. See Logan, *Diplomatic Relations*, 281–89.

13. See, From Holly to "Rev. and Dear Sir," Document A, September 10, 1855, in Overseas Department, Haiti Records 1855–1967, Record Group 68, Series 1: Missionary Personnel Files, 1855–1967, Box 3, Folder 20, Holly, James Theodore, Bishop, 1855–1865.

14. *Minutes of Stated Meeting of Foreign Committee*, October 23, 1855. Record Group 41, the Domestic and Foreign Missionary Society, Records of the Board of Missions, 1822–1919, Volume 38, October 1855 to June 1857 (Manuscript). "Mr. Holly has prepared a course of lectures in reference to the condition and wants of St. Domingo and desires opportunity to deliver them in various parts of the Country."

15. Rev. G. J. Bedell to Rev. Denison, Nov. 13, 1855, in Overseas Department, Haiti Records 1855–1967, Record Group 68, Box 8, Folder 1, Series 2: General Records, 1855–1955, General Correspondence, 1855–1916.

16. Holly indicates that this association had links with the publication committee created by the Emigration Convention that was convened in 1854 and 1856 (Holly, *Vindication*, 3). The last two pages of his document in fact promote other works that the association intended to publish in the future. He also reasserts the link between the association and the convention (Holly, *Vindication*, 47). This information is confirmed by Howard H. Bell in his *A Survey of the Negro Convention Movement*, 207.

17. Holly, *Vindication*, 44–45.

18. It should be noted that Holly specifies neither the sources nor his method for making this estimation. The population of Haiti was difficult to determine with any precision, the first official census only taking place in 1950.

19. Holly, *Vindication*, 45–46.

20. The Blair family (notably Frank P. Blair Sr. and his sons Frank Jr. and Montgomery) included a number of Republican politicians who, though part of the establishment in a proslavery state, were among the most active promoters of colonization.

21. Blair, *The Destiny of the Races of This Continent*, 22–23.

22. Blair, *Destiny of the Races*, 26–29.

23. See, for example, the remarks of Robert Purvis and Charles L. Remond at a meeting at the Israel Church in Philadelphia on April 3, 1857, published in *The Liberator*, April 10, 1857, in Aptheker, *A Documentary History*, 392–94.

24. Blair, *Destiny of the Races*, 37: "An intelligent and able commissioner ought to be dispatched in behalf of this association, to enter into stipulations with the Central American Government in regard to these contemplated emigrants. And this commissioner might be accompanied by some intelligent colored man, to be named by their Board or Central Committee, in whom they might repose the utmost confidence, when he brought back a report of the condition, prospects, and advantages, of that country."

25. Garnet, *The African Civilization Society*.

26. "The African Civilization Society; Response to Its Opponents; No Connection with the Colonization Society," *New York Times*, May 16, 1860.

27. Dixon, *African Americans and Haiti*, 118–19.

28. Blackett, "Martin R. Delany and Robert Campbell," 5–6.

29. Holly, "Thoughts on Hayti, Number V."

30. Holly, "Thoughts on Hayti, Number IV."

31. Holly, "Thoughts on Hayti, Number III," 243.

32. Holly, "Thoughts on Hayti, Number VI," 366.

33. Holly, "Thoughts on Hayti, Number III," 241.

34. "The Late Haytian Revolution," *Frederick Douglass' Paper*, March 11, 1859, vol. 12, issue 13, 2.

35. "Hayti Invites the People of Color," *Frederick Douglass' Paper*, April 22, 1859, vol. 12, issue 19, 1.

36. "Emigration to Hayti," *Frederick Douglass' Paper*, April 29, 1859, vol. 12, issue 20, 3.

37. "Black Emigration to Hayti," *Frederick Douglass' Paper*, May 6, 1859, vol. 12, issue 21, 2.

38. "The Haytian Emigration Movement," *Frederick Douglass' Paper*, May 6, 1859, vol. 12, issue 21, 2.

39. "Emigration of Free Blacks to Hayti," *Frederick Douglass' Paper*, July 8, 1859, vol. 12, issue 30, 3.

40. In the *Guide to Hayti* written by James Redpath and published in 1861, it is said that the decision to name "agents" across the United States was made by presidential decree on August 14, 1860. See Redpath, *A Guide to Hayti*, 120; Miller, *The Search for a Black Nationality*, 236; and Boyd, "James Redpath," 172–76.

41. For more on James Redpath (1833–1891), see McKivigan, *Forgotten Firebrand*.

42. Redpath, *A Guide to Hayti*, 9–10.

43. "Weekly Report of James Redpath, General Agent of Emigration to Hayti, in

Boston, to the Honorable M. Plésance, Secretary of State of Exterior Relations of the Republic of Hayti, Report No. 1, from September 27, 1860, to November 3, 1860," in Haytian Bureau of Emigration, *Reports and Correspondence*, 13.

44. Redpath, *A Guide to Hayti*, 94–96, 100–103.

45. Redpath, *A Guide to Hayti*, 120.

46. Redpath, *A Guide to Hayti*, 124. The Haitian "carreau" is equivalent to 1.29 hectares or roughly three acres.

47. Dorsainvil, *Manuel d'histoire d'Haïti*, 278.

48. Price-Mars, *La République d'Haïti*, 249–69. See also Dorsainvil, *Manuel d'histoire d'Haïti*, 275–76.

49. Logan, *Diplomatic Relations*, 293–96.

50. Haytian Bureau of Emigration, *Reports and Correspondence*, 18. As we shall see in the next chapter, Senator Charles Sumner is today considered to be the initiator of the recognition of Haiti that occurred in 1862.

51. Haytian Bureau of Emigration, *Reports and Correspondence*, 13–19.

52. See the letter of instructions sent by Redpath to Holly on November 9, 1860 (Haytian Bureau of Emigration, *Reports and Correspondence*, 24).

53. Haytian Bureau of Emigration, *Reports and Correspondence*, 14–15.

54. See "About *New York Daily Tribune*. (New York [N.Y.]) 1842–1866," in *Chronicling America*, Library of Congress, Washington D.C., 2012.

55. Haytian Bureau of Emigration, *Reports and Correspondence*, 15–16.

56. Haytian Bureau of Emigration, *Reports and Correspondence*, 17–18. Caps as in the original.

57. "Emigration to Hayti," *Douglass' Monthly*, January 1861.

58. See "Hayti," *North Star*, April 21, 1848, vol. 1, issue 17, 2: "The people of this country in general, and the colored people in particular, are quite ignorant in regard to the character and condition of this most interesting Republic. It is strange that this should be so, considering the importance of her example. . . . Hayti should be an object of constant curiosity, especially to the oppressed of this country."

59. Harold, "Haytian Correspondence—No. I.," *North Star*, April 21, 1848, vol. 1, issue 17, 3.

60. Douglass, "The Haytian Emigration Movement," *Douglass' Monthly*, July 1861. "I hold up both hands for Hayti, grateful for her humanity, rejoice in her prosperity, point to her example with pride and hope, and would smite down any band that would fling a shadow upon the pathway of her glory."

61. Douglass is speaking in eloquent, laudatory terms of his (future) trip to Haiti, which he does not yet know will be cancelled: "A dream, fondly indulged, a desire, long cherished, and a purpose, long meditated, are now quite likely to be realized." See Frederick Douglass, "A Trip to Hayti," *Douglass' Monthly*, May 1861.

62. "Haïti," *L'Union*, October 1, 1862, 1.

63. For example, the manuscript of the reports and correspondence of the bureau confirm the correspondence between Redpath and Montgomery Blair. The latter promised, among other things, to work on behalf of Haitian recognition. See Haytian Bureau of Emigration, *Reports and Correspondence*, 56.

64. Redpath, "Editorial," *Pine and Palm*, May 18, 1861. Caps and italics as in the original.

65. Brown, *Pine and Palm*, August 17, 1861.

66. Brown, *Pine and Palm*, August 31, 1861.

67. Mason, *Life of Isaac Mason as a Slave*, chap. 5.

68. It is interesting to note that in a letter to Reverend Denison, Holly states that the emigration began in 1859, but he confirms that these émigrés had no connection with the Haytian Bureau of Emigration. See, From Theodore Holly to Rev. S. D. Denison, March 19, 1860, in Overseas Department, Haiti Records 1855–1967, Record Group 68, Series 1: Missionary Personnel Files, 1855–1967, Box 3, Folder 20, Holly, James Theodore, Bishop, 1855–1865.

69. Seraille, "Afro-American Emigration," 200, 195.

70. Boyd, "James Redpath," 176.

71. "Emigration to Hayti," *The Sun*, April 28, 1859, 1.

72. "Free Negroes Leaving New-Orleans for Hayti," *New York Daily Tribune*, May 19, 1859, 6.

73. "Colored Emigrants to Hayti," *The Sun*, June 8, 1859, 4.

74. "Emigration to Hayti," *Daily Confederation*, June 29, 1859, 2.

75. "Emigration of Free Blacks to Hayti," *New York Daily Tribune*, June 29, 1859, 5; "Emigration of Free Blacks to Hayti," *Frederick Douglass' Paper*, July 8, 1859, vol. 12, issue 30, 3.

76. In a letter addressed to Reverend Denison from March 1860, Holly speaks of a large number of Black Americans from Florida and also from Washington, D.C., who planned to go to Haiti. See, From Theodore Holly to Rev. S. D. Denison, March 19, 1860, in Overseas Department, Haiti Records 1855–1967, Record Group 68, Series 1: Missionary Personnel Files, 1855–1967, Box 3, Folder 20, Holly, James Theodore, Bishop, 1855–1865.

77. *Commercial Advertiser*, October 26, 1860, 5.

78. "Emigration to Hayti," *The Liberator*, November 30, 1860, vol. 30, issue 48, 191.

79. "Haytien Emigration," *Weekly Anglo-African*, January 12, 1861.

80. "Pour Port-au-Prince (Haïti.)," *L'Union*, January 28, 1864, 1. "Un navire partira pour le port ci-dessus [Port-au-Prince] vers le 20 mars prochain, si d'ici à cette date il se présente un nombre suffisant de passagers."

81. See Haytian Bureau of Emigration, *Reports and Correspondence*, 138, 151–52, 165.

82. Holly to the Bishop of the Protestant Episcopal Church in the U.S., "The Protestant Episcopal Mission in Haïti," May 29, 1862, in Overseas Department, Haiti Records 1855–1967, Record Group 68, Series 1: Missionary Personnel Files, 1855–1967, Box 3, Folder 20, Holly, James Theodore, Bishop, 1855–1865: "Thousands of American emigrants are now here. . . . Thousands more will doubtlessly follow, under the auspices and inducements of the Haïtien government, among whom a large number of contrabands now on the hands of the government of the U.S. will probably be included."

83. "Story of Another Returned Emigrant from Hayti," *Weekly Anglo-African*, April 5, 1862.

84. Holly, "A General View of Hayti," *The Liberator*, June 19, 1863.

85. See Holly, to the Bishop of the Protestant Episcopal Church in the U.S., "The Protestant Episcopal Mission in Haïti," May 29, 1862, in Overseas Department, Haiti Records 1855–1967, Record Group 68, Series 1: Missionary Personnel Files, 1855–1967, Box 3, Folder 20, Holly, James Theodore, Bishop, 1855–1865.

86. Seraille, "Afro-American Emigration to Haiti," 200; Dixon, *African Americans and Haiti*, 206–7.

87. See Holly, *Facts*; *Fourth Anniversary of the American Church Missionary Society*; and From Holly to Rev. Arthur Cleveland Coxe, D.D. (Bishop of the Diocese of Western New York, Buffalo, Erie County), September 22, 1864, in Overseas Department, Haiti Records 1855–1967, Record Group 68, Series 1: Missionary Personnel Files, 1855–1967, Box 3, Folder 20, Holly, James Theodore, Bishop, 1855–1865.

88. Holly to the Bishop of the Protestant Episcopal Church in the U.S., "The Protestant Episcopal Mission in Haïti," May 29, 1862, in Overseas Department, Haiti Records 1855–1967, Record Group 68, Series 1: Missionary Personnel Files, 1855–1967, Box 3, Folder 20, Holly, James Theodore, Bishop, 1855–1865.

89. See *Minutes of the Executive Council of the American Church Missionary Society*, in Overseas Department, Haiti Records 1855–1967, Record Group 68, Box 8, Folder 11.

90. "Trinity Church, Port-au-Prince, Haïti," 69.

91. From Holly to Rev. Arthur Cleveland Coxe, D.D. (Bishop of the Diocese of Western New York, Buffalo, Erie County), September 22, 1864, in Overseas Department, Haiti Records 1855–1967, Record Group 68, Series 1: Missionary Personnel Files, 1855–1967, Box 3, Folder 20, Holly, James Theodore, Bishop, 1855–1865.

92. Archives of the Episcopal Church, *Inventory to the Records*, 1–2.

CHAPTER 4. Abraham Lincoln's Project for Haiti

1. Lincoln, "Address on Colonization," 237

2. See Brooks, *Washington in Lincoln's Time*, 220–22; Sandburg, *Abraham Lincoln*, 2:423–24.

3. Brooks, *Washington in Lincoln's Time*, 221.

4. See Paludan, "Lincoln and Colonization."

5. See, for example, Randall, *Lincoln the President;* Bennett, "Was Abe Lincoln a White Supremacist?"; Neely, *The Abraham Lincoln Encyclopedia.*

6. Bennett, *Forced into Glory*, 151.

7. Lind, *What Lincoln Believed.*

8. Foner, "Lincoln and Colonization," 137.

9. Smith, *No Party Now*, 56.

10. Lincoln, "Reply to Loyal Colored People."

11. Lincoln was born in Kentucky, but his family later lived in Indiana before finally moving to Illinois. See McPherson, *Abraham Lincoln*, 1–4.

12. See McPherson, *Abraham Lincoln*, 21–24.

13. Quarles, *Lincoln and the Negro*, 108.

14. At the start of 1862, Liberia had sent two emissaries to the United States with the mission of recruiting volunteers from among the free Black population to emigrate to Liberia. One of the two, Alexander Crummell, was a Black American minister who had voluntarily emigrated to Liberia in 1853. He spent the first months of 1862 meeting with Black Americans and trying to win the support of the American government. Lincoln did not meet with the two delegates, but he did receive Joseph Jenkins Roberts at the White House on August 10, 1862. Roberts was the first president of Liberia (1848–56) and afterward president of Liberia College, a position he still held in August 1862. Roberts made a positive impression on Lincoln but did not convince him to choose Liberia as a colonization destination. Lincoln considered Liberia to be too far away and that

transportation alone would be too costly. He also thought the climate was unhealthy and that Black emigrationists would prefer to remain on the American side of the Atlantic. See Quarles, *Lincoln and the Negro*, 110–12.

15. Léger, *Haïti*, 175.

16. We may add that in 1804, recognizing a Black republic whose independence had been won by open revolt was completely impossible—not just for the United States, but also for the great slavery-practicing nations of Europe: France, Spain, and Great Britain. See Logan, *Diplomatic Relations*, 152.

17. For Logan, the request for recognition fell exactly along the sectional divide of the country. Pennsylvania, a free state, was the most southerly location in favor of recognition. Further south were slave states. While the North spread prorecognition propaganda in its newspapers, the South let it be known in its newspapers that it was resolutely opposed to recognition for Haiti. See Logan, *Diplomatic Relations*, 191–97, 200–201.

18. Wesley, "The Struggle for the Recognition of Haiti," 376, 378.

19. Nicolay and Hay, *Abraham Lincoln*, 6:99.

20. Redpath, "Special Report of James Redpath . . . On the Question of Independence, December 12, 1860," in Haytian Bureau of Emigration, *Reports and Correspondence*, 92–93.

21. Redpath, "Letter to the President Elect, Mr. Lincoln, via Judge Army, December 18, 1860," in Haytian Bureau of Emigration, *Reports and Correspondence*, 98–101.

22. Redpath, "Special Report of James Redpath," 249.

23. Redpath, "Special Report of James Redpath," 254.

24. These commercial agents were representatives in Haiti of American merchants who did business in the Black republic. It is difficult to say exactly when these agents were sent to Haiti, however the historian Tim Matthewson claims that already during the revolution in Saint-Domingue, American commercial agents were present in the French colony. See Matthewson, "Jefferson and Haiti."

25. Logan, *Diplomatic Relations*, 297. Seth Webb sent a second letter dated December 12, 1861, with the same message. It was read aloud in the Senate just before the bill for the recognition of Haiti and Liberia was approved on April 24, 1862. See Sumner, *Independence of Hayti and Liberia*, 13–14.

26. Lincoln, "Annual Message to Congress, December 3, 1861," 5:39.

27. Lincoln's proposal for the recognition of Liberia was welcomed and a great relief for the American Colonization Society. This sense of relief was expressed by its president, John H. Latrobe, the successor of Henry Clay, who wrote two days later in a letter to William Seward that he hoped Congress would rapidly carry out this recognition. He also took the opportunity to plead in favor of colonization to Liberia, which he considered a necessity. See John H. B. Latrobe to William Seward, Thursday, December 5, 1861, in the Abraham Lincoln Papers at the Library of Congress, Series 1, General Correspondence (1833–1916).

28. Wilson, *History of the Antislavery Measures*, 175. See also Sumner, *Charles Sumner*, 8:309–10.

29. Sumner, *Independence of Hayti and Liberia*, 8.

30. Sumner, *Independence of Hayti and Liberia*, 7.

31. Sumner, *Independence of Hayti and Liberia*, 14.

32. Wilson, *History of the Antislavery Measures*, 179.

33. Cox, *Eight Years in Congress*, 154, 156, 161.

34. For the details of these debates, see Cox, *Eight Years in Congress*, 157–61; and Kelley, *The Recognition of Hayti and Liberia*, 3–4.

35. *The Statutes at Large*, 421.

36. *Journal of the Executive Proceedings*, 329, 404.

37. Foner, *The Fiery Trial*, 184.

38. During a conversation with Charles Sumner, Lincoln is said to have spoken of colonization as being his hobby." See Lester, *Life and Public Services*, 386.

39. Foner, *The Fiery Trial*, 184.

40. Page, "Lincoln and Chiriquí," 295.

41. "An act to confiscate property used for insurrectionary purposes," August 6, 1861, in *Statutes at Large*, 319.

42. Lincoln, "Annual Message to Congress, December 3, 1861," 5:48.

43. See Select Committee on Emancipation and Colonization, *Report*, 1.

44. *Statutes at Large*, 376–78.

45. *Statutes at Large*, 582–83.

46. *Statutes at Large*, 592.

47. Ambrose Thompson to Abraham Lincoln, Friday, April 25, 1862, Abraham Lincoln Papers at the Library of Congress, Series 1, General Correspondence (1833–1916).

48. In other words, a colony independent from the local government. See Page, "Lincoln and Chiriquí," 297.

49. Page, "Lincoln and Chiriquí," 297–98.

50. Vorenberg, "Abraham Lincoln," 33.

51. Foner, *The Fiery Trial*, 127. See also Foner, "Lincoln and Colonization," 154.

52. See the Abraham Lincoln Papers at the Library of Congress, Series 1, General Correspondence (1833–1916).

53. On this subject, see Quarles, *The Negro in the Civil War*, 147. See also Quarles, *Lincoln and the Negro*, 115–16; Lockett, "Abraham Lincoln and Colonization"; Masur, "The African American Delegation."

54. See Masur, "The African American Delegation," 129–30.

55. Foner, *The Fiery Trial*, 224–25.

56. Lincoln, "Address on Colonization," 236–37, 237.

57. Lincoln, "Address on Colonization," 238.

58. Lincoln, "Address on Colonization," 239.

59. One regrets Lincoln's use of the expression "native land" to describe Africa, since nearly all slaves present in the United States in 1862 were, following the end of the transatlantic slave trade in 1808, born on American soil.

60. Lincoln, "Address on Colonization," 239–41.

61. Edward M. Thomas to Abraham Lincoln, Saturday, August 16, 1862, Abraham Lincoln Papers at the Library of Congress, Series 1, General Correspondence (1833–1916).

62. Masur, "The African American Delegation," 136, 148. Unlike Masur, Lockett claims that the five men left their interview with Lincoln largely won over to the idea and had promised to spread the idea within the Black community. See Lockett, "Abraham Lincoln and Colonization," 435.

63. Henry McNeal Turner even signed a petition in favor of colonization to Chiriquí

that was drafted by Joseph E. Williams, an agent of Ambrose Thompson, and presented in the House of Representatives on April 7, 1862, by Francis P. Blair Jr. See *Journal of the House of Representatives of the United States*, 578.

64. See Page, "Lincoln and Chiriquí," 300–303; and Vorenberg, "Abraham Lincoln," 34–35.

65. The abolitionist newspaper *The Liberator*, for example, published Lincoln's speech on the front page of its August 22, 1862, issue. Alongside it was an article sharply criticizing the president's proposal. See "The President on African Colonization," *The Liberator*, August 22, 1862, vol. 32, no. 34, 134.

66. See Page, "Lincoln and Chiriquí," 314. Lincoln approved this contract on September 11, 1862, via a note containing but one sentence: "The within contract is approved, and the Secretary of the Interior is directed to execute the same. A. Lincoln." See Abraham Lincoln, "Approval of Contract with Ambrose W. Thompson, September 11, 1862," in *Collected Works of Abraham Lincoln*, 5:414, Abraham Lincoln Association, http://quod.lib.umich.edu/l/lincoln.

67. Lincoln, "Preliminary Emancipation Proclamation, September 22, 1862," in *Collected Works of Abraham Lincoln*, 5:433–36, Abraham Lincoln Association, http://quod.lib.umich.edu/l/lincoln.

68. According to Lockett, Lincoln and Smith ignored for too long the advice of Navy Secretary Gideon Welles, who, suspicious of Thompson, whom he suspected was trying to get rich by bilking the government, had tried with no success to discourage them from entering into any agreement with them. See Lockett, "Abraham Lincoln and Colonization," 432. On Welles's mistrust of Thompson and Pomeroy, see also Fleming, *Deportation and Colonization*, 19.

69. See Nicolay and Hay, *Abraham Lincoln*, 357.

70. Page, "Lincoln and Chiriquí," 308.

71. Page, "Lincoln and Chiriquí," 315–16.

72. L'Île-à-Vache(s), is a small island of 45.96 square kilometers located approximately ten kilometers southeast of the Haitian city of Les Cayes.

73. See Fleming, *Deportation and Colonization*, 20–21; Carroll, *Henri Mercier*, 246; Magness and Page, *Colonization after Emancipation*, 18.

74. Nicolay and Hay, *Abraham Lincoln*, 357; Fleming, *Deportation and Colonization*, 17.

75. See Boyd, "The Île à Vache," 47–48.

76. See Bernard Kock, "To His Excellency, Abraham Lincoln, President of the United States," Washington, D.C., 1862, www.loc.gov/item/rbpe.20406700, Library of Congress, Rare Book and Special Collections Division (last accessed July 8, 2021).

77. Bernard Kock to Abraham Lincoln, October 4, 1862, Abraham Lincoln Papers at the Library of Congress, Series 1, General Correspondence (1833–1916).

78. Jacob R. S. Van Vleet to Abraham Lincoln, October 4, 1862, Abraham Lincoln Papers at the Library of Congress, Series 1, General Correspondence (1833–1916). Van Vleet sends a second letter to Lincoln on December 11, 1862, in which one learns that on Mitchell's advice Lincoln accepted to receive him. It is impossible to say with certainty if this meeting took place. See Jacob R. S. Van Vleet to Abraham Lincoln, December 11, 1862, Abraham Lincoln Papers at the Library of Congress, Series 1, General Correspondence (1833–1916).

79. Lockett, "Abraham Lincoln and Colonization," 437.

80. William E. Robinson to Abraham Lincoln, December 13, 1862, Abraham Lincoln Papers at the Library of Congress, Series 1, General Correspondence (1833–1916). On the contrary, Boyd asserts that Lincoln became very suspicious of Kock starting in the fall of 1862. See Boyd, "The Île à Vache," 47–48.

81. Lincoln, "Annual Message to Congress, December 1, 1862," 5:535.

82. Lincoln, "Annual Message to Congress, December 1, 1862," 5:520–21.

83. The content of the so-called final Emancipation Proclamation is quite different from what the "draft" of September 1862 might lead one to expect. In the final document there is no mention of any financial compensation to slaveowners, emancipation is to be immediate not gradual, and there is no mention of colonization. See Lincoln, "Emancipation Proclamation. January 1, 1863," in *Collected Works of Abraham Lincoln*, 6:28–30, Abraham Lincoln Association, http://quod.lib.umich.edu/l/lincoln.

84. See William H. Seward to Abraham Lincoln, January 3, 1863, Abraham Lincoln Papers at the Library of Congress, Series 1, General Correspondence (1833–1916).

85. Boyd, "The Île à Vache," 50; Lockett, "Abraham Lincoln and Colonization," 438.

86. See Charles K. Tuckerman to Abraham Lincoln, March 31, 1863, Abraham Lincoln Papers at the Library of Congress, Series 1, General Correspondence (1833–1916).

87. Lockett, "Abraham Lincoln and Colonization," 438–39.

88. The exact number of passengers onboard the *Ocean Ranger* as well as the exact date of its departure are still unable to be determined with certainty. Lockett writes that 453 Black people left for Haiti on April 14, 1863, but newspaper reports speak of 500 émigrés and state that the ship was still not ready to depart as of April 21, 1863. See "The New Colonization Scheme," *Milwaukee Daily Sentinel*, April 21, 1863, vol. 20, no. 109, 1. Fleming states that 500 Black people had left Fort Monroe, where hundreds of contrabands were being held in deplorable conditions, but he gives no date. See Fleming, *Deportation and Colonization*, 22.

89. Some of this currency was intercepted by De Long and later sent by Whidden to Seward on July 30, 1863. See Benjamin F. Whidden to William H. Seward, July 30, 1863, Abraham Lincoln Papers at the Library of Congress, Series 1, General Correspondence (1833–1916).

90. James De Long to Henry Conard, June 25, 1863, Abraham Lincoln Papers at the Library of Congress, Series 1, General Correspondence (1833–1916).

91. Lockett, "Abraham Lincoln and Colonization," 439–40.

92. See Boyd, "The Île à Vache," 55; Quarles, *Lincoln and the Negro*, 194; Fleming, *Deportation and Colonization*, 25.

93. Foner, *The Fiery Trial*, 259–60.

94. Vorenberg, "Abraham Lincoln," 41.

95. See Vorenberg, "Abraham Lincoln," 41; Quarles, *Lincoln and the Negro*, 194; Lockett, "Abraham Lincoln and Colonization," 442.

96. See Foner, *The Fiery Trial*, 260.

97. Magness and Page, *Colonization after Emancipation*, 32.

98. Magness and Page, *Colonization after Emancipation*, 36. See also Foner, "Lincoln and Colonization," 162.

99. Gold, "Negro Colonization Schemes in Ecuador."

100. Guyatt, "A Vast Negro Reservation."

CHAPTER 5. Haiti's Growing Strategic Importance

1. Douglass, *Life and Times* (1881), 485

2. See Foner, *Reconstruction*, 281–91.

3. Foner, *Reconstruction*, 198–201.

4. See Litwack, *Been in the Storm so Long*, 366.

5. For a study of living conditions for free people of color in the South prior to the Civil War, see Berlin, *Slaves without Masters*. On voting during this same period, see Keyssar, *The Right to Vote*, 54–59.

6. Foner, *Reconstruction*, 78.

7. The Civil Rights Act of 1866, which was approved on April 9 of that year, established equal protection for all citizens regardless of race or skin color. Its purpose was to prevent states from passing laws that would restrict the rights of (Black) citizens. Three Enforcement Acts also became law in 1870, 1871, and 1875. Their intent was to require states, particularly in the South, to respect the amendments passed by Congress in 1870 and 1871, and to prevent discrimination in public places (1875). All these laws marked a turning point in so far as they gave the federal government the power to intervene in the internal affairs of individual states. This federal interventionism contributed to the collapse of the Republican Party in the South and to the resurgence of the Democratic Party starting in the mid-1870s.

8. See Woodward, *The Strange Career of Jim Crow*, 22–29, 34.

9. See Foner, *Freedom's Lawmakers*. This study offers the first lists and biographical notices of roughly three-quarters of elected Black officials during Reconstruction. Foner considers that Reconstruction came to an end in each state the year when Democrats retook power—defined as Democratic control of the governorship and Democratic majorities in both houses of the state legislature. This occurred as early as 1870 for Tennessee and by 1876 for the two Carolinas, Louisiana, and Florida.

10. Ebenezer Don Carlos Bassett was the son of a fugitive slave father and an Amerindian mother. He was born in Connecticut in 1833. During the Civil War he helped recruit Black soldiers into the Union army. It was then that he became friends with Frederick Douglass. For more information on Bassett, see Dockett-Mcleod, *Ebenezer Don Carlos Bassett.*

11. *Leavenworth Bulletin*, March 18, 1869, vol. 13, no. 156, 1.

12. "The Mission to Hayti," *Farmers' Cabinet*, April 8, 1869, vol. 67, no. 38, 2.

13. "The Senate," *Manufacturers' and Farmers' Journal*, April 19, 1869, vol. 48, no. 31, 1.

14. "Too Much of the Nigger," *New York Herald*, April 19, 1869, vol. 34, no. 109, 6.

15. "The Kind of Distinction Demanded," *Georgia Weekly Telegraph*, April 30, 1869, vol. 43, no. 24, 3.

16. "Colored Ministers Appointed for the Haytien and Liberian Missions," *New York Herald*, April 13, 1869, vol. 34, no. 103, 5.

17. *New York Daily Tribune*, April 13, 1869, vol. 29, no. 8740, 4.

18. McFeely, *Douglass*, 270.

19. Douglass, *Life and Times* (1881), 425.

20. "Mr. Frederick Douglass," *National Republican*, April 23, 1869, vol. 9, no. 125, 3.

21. "The Negro in a New Attitude," *Elevator*, July 16, 1869, vol. 5, no. 15, 2.

22. See *Journal of the Executive Proceedings of the Senate*, 199.

23. See Brantley, "Black Diplomacy," 197–98.

24. See Dockett-Mcleod, *Ebenezer Don Carlos Bassett.*

25. See Teal, *Hero of Hispaniola.*

26. Teal, *Hero of Hispaniola*, 52.

27. Teal, *Hero of Hispaniola*, 53–54.

28. The title ambassador was only used to designate the chief American diplomat in Haiti starting in 1943.

29. Padgett, "Diplomats to Haiti," 277.

30. Padgett, "Diplomats to Haiti," 279–80.

31. Léger, *Haïti*, 210–15. See also Teal, *Hero of Hispaniola*, 63.

32. Léger, *Haïti*, 222–24. See also Teal, *Hero of Hispaniola*, 103–16.

33. See Padgett, "Diplomats to Haiti," 276.

34. Bassett to Douglass, July 3, 1869, in the Frederick Douglass Papers at the Library of Congress, Manuscript Division, Series: General Correspondence. Underlining as in the original.

35. Langston, *From the Virginia Plantation to the National Capitol.*

36. We borrow this expression from a piece by journalist Kevin Merida in the *Washington Post*. See Merida, "He Was the Obama before Obama."

37. See Padgett, *Diplomats to Haiti*, 281.

38. The circumstances that allowed the three men to meet remain somewhat mysterious. Langston does not speak of his first meeting with Douglass in his autobiography, but his biographers claim they met during circumstances surrounding the Underground Railroad. They could also have met during the Civil War since both were working actively to recruit Black soldiers into the Union army. In his third autobiography, Douglass makes passing reference to meeting the two men in their younger years but without giving details about it or the date.

39. Padgett, *Diplomats to Haiti*, 281–86.

40. Langston, *From the Virginia Plantation*, 350–74.

41. See Langston, *From the Virginia Plantation*, 350–54.

42. Despite the long-standing recommendations of Senator Sumner, Langston did not think it necessary that he learn French or school himself in international law—convinced as he was that he would be named to a prestigious governmental post within the United States.

43. Langston, *From the Virginia Plantation*, 355–56. Caps as in the original.

44. Langston, *From the Virginia Plantation*, 360. Langston wrote in the third-person singular.

45. Langston, *From the Virginia Plantation*, 360.

46. Langston, *From the Virginia Plantation*, 361.

47. Langston, *From the Virginia Plantation*, 372.

48. Léger, *Haïti*, 220.

49. Rogers, *Our Representatives Abroad.*

50. These figures come from a table published by the Institute of Education Sciences National Center for Education Statistics on its website. The table was constructed from statistics gathered by the census bureau. See Bureau of the Census, *Historical Statistics of the United States* (1979). See National Assessment of Adult Literacy, "120 Years of Literacy."

51. Langston, *From the Virginia Plantation*, 409–12.
52. See Franklin, *George Washington Williams*, 149–53.
53. Padgett, "Diplomats to Haiti," 289.
54. Léger, *Haïti*, 234, 240–42.
55. Gaillard, *La République exterminatrice*, 161, 165–66, 173.
56. Gaillard, *La République exterminatrice*, 171.
57. LaFeber, *The American Age*, 157–61.
58. See Logan, *Diplomatic Relations*, 315–33. On the different American attempts to annex Santo Domingo, see also Tansill, *The United States and Santo Domingo*.
59. Logan, *Diplomatic Relations*, 331.
60. The project to annex Santo Domingo has been studied by historian Nicholas Guyatt. He argues that the debate over the possible annexation was a central episode in the history of Reconstruction as it reveals profound differences that divided Republicans from the general American population at the time on the question of the integration of Black people into American society. Santo Domingo raised important questions about Black citizenship in the United States, since annexing that territory and making it into the thirty-eighth state of the Union would inevitably raise questions about the situation of Black people in the United States. See Guyatt, "America's Conservatory."
61. Logan, *Diplomatic Relations*, 333.
62. Price-Mars, *La République d'Haïti*, 294.
63. Logan, *Diplomatic Relations*, 335–37.
64. Léger, *Haïti*, 216.
65. In 1821, faced with the general liberation movements of Spanish colonies in the Americas, the population of the Spanish portion of the island of Hispaniola rebelled and proclaimed its independence on December 1. Some weeks later, in answer to some insurgents, Haitian president Jean-Pierre Boyer invaded the country and reunited the entire island at the start of 1822. Haitian occupation of the eastern portion of the island lasted until Boyer's fall in 1843. At that moment Dominican separatists led by General Pedro Santana managed to regain control of the little republic, declaring its independence on February 27, 1844. The name Dominican Republic was inscribed in the constitution of 1844. In 1854 U.S. president Franklin Pierce attempted to win concessions from the Dominican Republic. In June 1854 William L. Cazneau was sent to the island to negotiate formal recognition of Santo Domingo in exchange for its willingness to give up a portion of the Bay of Samaná, where the Americans planned to establish a coal depot and naval base. European leaders panicked at the idea of the United States establishing a permanent presence on the island of Hispaniola, and to prevent it they disrupted the negotiations by sending consuls and consular agents to the island. Later, when the Civil War erupted in the United States and with Haiti threatening to again invade its territory, Dominican president Pedro Santana sought a rapprochement with Spain. On March 18, 1861, he publicly announced the annexation of his country by Spain, but this new Spanish occupation caused many popular uprisings against the authoritarian Spanish administration. Consequently, on March 3, 1865, the queen of Spain published a decree declaring the abandonment of Santo Domingo by the Spanish throne. The following year, as the United States was looking for new markets to sell its agricultural and industrial products, Seward, convinced of the strategic importance of the Caribbean, traveled to the Dominican Republic to search for places suitable for constructing coal fu-

eling stations and naval bases. He entered into negotiations with Dominican president Buenaventura Báez, however they did not last long because the U.S. Congress came out against any territorial expansion. Nevertheless, the United States accepted to recognize the Dominican Republic in 1866.

66. Logan, *Diplomatic Relations*, 343. See also Brantley, "Black Diplomacy," 202.

67. See Brantley, "Black Diplomacy," 202; Logan, *Diplomatic Relations*, 345–46; and Léger, *Haïti*, 219.

68. See Douglass, *Life and Times* (1881), 418.

69. Pitre, "Frederick Douglass," 391–92.

70. Pitre, "Frederick Douglass," 392.

71. "The St. Domingo Question in Congress—a Decisive Victory for General Grant," *New York Herald*, January 11, 1871, vol. 36, no. 11, 6.

72. See "Santo Domingo," *New York Daily Tribune*, February 21, 1871, vol. 30, no. 9322, 1. See also "The Good News from Santo Domingo," *New York Herald*, February 21, 1871, 6.

73. See "Fred Douglass and the Santo Domingo Commission," *New York Tribune*, August 10, 1872, vol. 32, no. 9782, 1; "San Domingo," *Cincinnati Daily Gazette*, March 17, 1871, 1.

74. "The Good News from Santo Domingo," *New York Herald*, February 21, 1871, 6; "Santo Domingo," *New York Daily Tribune*, February 21, 1871, vol. 30, no. 9322, 8.

75. "Santo Domingo," *New York Daily Tribune*, February 21, 1871, vol. 30, no. 9322, 8.

76. "The Santo Domingo Commission—Address of Frederick Douglass to the Negro Colonizers from the United States." In *Frank Leslie's Illustrated Newspaper*, March 11, 1871, 1. These Black attendees were probably the descendants of a few thousand who emigrated voluntarily to Haiti in the mid-1820s on the incentives of President Boyer and the American Loring D. Dewey (see chapter 1). At the time the island of Hispaniola had been "reunified" by President Jean-Pierre Boyer in 1822; in other words, the Dominican Republic and Haiti were one and the same nation.

77. "The Good News from Santo Domingo," *New York Herald*, February 21, 1871, 6.

78. "Hayti," *New York Daily Tribune*, March 17, 1871, vol. 30, no. 9343, 2.

79. In April 1846 Douglass wrote a letter to Horace Greeley from Glasgow, Scotland. It was later published in the *New York Tribune* where Greeley, a moderate antislavery advocate, was editor. In the letter Douglass denounced the expansionist (and therefore annexationist) plans of the American government toward Haiti. He believed the Polk administration wanted to "exterminate" the Black republic in order to better preserve, propagate, and perpetuate slavery. Frederick Douglass to Horace Greeley, April 15, 1846, Frederick Douglass Papers at the Library of Congress, Series: General Correspondence. It is worth noting that the historian Rayford Logan asserts that Douglass, along with other abolitionists, was deeply mistaken in believing the United States wanted to swallow up Haiti at that time. According to Logan, the U.S. had no interest in annexing Haiti in 1846 and had not the least intention of doing so. See Logan, *Diplomatic Relations*, 242–43.

80. Douglass, *Life and Times* (1881), 417.

81. See Guyatt, "America's Conservatory," 982–83, 990–91, 994; "African Giants at War," *Weekly Louisianian*, May 28, 1871, 2.

82. "Colored Sentiment against San Domingo Annexation," *Richmond Whig*, April 4, 1871, vol. 50, no. 27, 4. It is highly probable that "Wyland Garnett" was no other than

Henry *Highland* Garnet. The journalist of the *Richmond Whig* may have misspelled his name.

83. "Coming to the Point," *Richmond Whig*, April 7, 1871, vol. 50, no. 28, 4.

84. "Negro Barbarism and Suffrage," *Georgia Weekly Telegraph*, April 11, 1871, vol. 44, no. 41, 4.

85. Douglass was one of the financial partners of the *New Era*, which was founded in early 1870, and had taken a 50 percent stake in the paper by the summer of 1870. In September the paper was renamed the *New National Era*, with Douglass as "Mr. Editor"; in other words, editor in chief. See McFeely, *Douglass*, 270–73.

86. "Frederick Douglass on the Haytiens," *New York Daily Tribune*, April 3, 1871, vol. 30, no. 9357, 5.

87. See *Weekly Louisianian*, May 28, 1871, 3.

88. Douglass, *Life and Times* (1881), 417. See also Pitre, "Frederick Douglass," 393.

CHAPTER 6. Frederick Douglass's Diplomatic Career in Haiti

1. Du Bois, *The Souls of Black Folk*, 3.

2. Douglass was not entirely certain of his birthday, as he says in his third autobiography: "I suppose myself to have been born in February, 1817." Douglass, *Life and Times* (1881), 14.

3. Douglass was the first Black recorder of deeds in Washington, D.C. President James A. Garfield named him to that post in 1881, and he held that job until 1886.

4. Douglass, *Life and Times* (1892), 639.

5. *New-York Daily Tribune*, June 29, 1889, 6.

6. *Washington Bee*, July 6, 1889, 1. This is also the view of the *Washington Critic*, a white newspaper, which also states that Haitians considered Douglass to be "a model of their race." *Washington Critic*, June 29, 1889: "A representative Afro-American citizen is nominated as Minister to Hayti, and the people of that island will find a model of their race in Mr. Frederick Douglass."

7. *Omaha Daily Bee*, June 30, 1889, 4.

8. "With Mixed Feelings," *Pittsburgh Despatch*, June 29, 1889, 5.

9. "Hopeful Preston," *Pittsburgh Despatch*, June 30, 1889, 7.

10. See Bassett to Frederick Douglass, July 3, 1869, in the Frederick Douglass Papers at the Library of Congress, Series: General Correspondence, 1869. See also Langston, *From the Virginia Plantation*, 370.

11. Douglass, *Life and Times* (1892), 723.

12. Harlan to Frederick Douglass, July 1, 1889, in the Frederick Douglass Papers at the Library of Congress, Series: General Correspondence, 1889, July.

13. Mitchell to Frederick Douglass, July 1, 1889, in the Frederick Douglass Papers at the Library of Congress, Series: General Correspondence, 1889, July.

14. National Archives, Records of the Department of State, Diplomatic Despatches, Haiti, vol. 24, unnumbered letter of Frederick Douglass to James G. Blaine, Secretary of State, June 25, 1889.

15. See Léger, *Haïti*, 242.

16. See Logan, *Diplomatic Relations*, 405–9, 415–20.

17. Gaillard, *La République exterminatrice*, 168–69.

18. Logan, *Diplomatic Relations*, 426.

19. Gaillard, *La République exterminatrice*, 172–73.

20. Logan, *Diplomatic Relations*, 415.

21. The construction of a canal in Nicaragua to compete with the Panama Canal had been authorized by the American government through a federal law creating the Maritime Canal Company of Nicaragua on February 20, 1889.

22. Himelhoch, "Frederick Douglass," 162. See also Logan, *Diplomatic Relations*, 447–48.

23. See LaFeber, *The New Empire*, 104, 111.

24. See, for example, National Archives, Records of the Department of State, Diplomatic Despatches, Haiti, vol. 24, despatch 13, November 18, 1889. Frederick Douglass would insist on this position further in two pieces published in 1891 in the *North American Review*. We discuss these articles in more detail at the end of this chapter.

25. Bassett to Frederick Douglass, July 11, 1889, in the Frederick Douglass Papers at the Library of Congress, Series: General Correspondence, 1889, July.

26. Bassett to Frederick Douglass, July 11, 1889, in the Frederick Douglass Papers at the Library of Congress, Series: General Correspondence, 1889, July.

27. Bassett to Frederick Douglass, July 11, 1889, in the Frederick Douglass Papers at the Library of Congress, Series: General Correspondence, 1889, July. Underlining as in the original. In a letter dated September 30, 1889, Clyde suggested that Douglass try to profit from the recent military victory of Hyppolite, with U.S. aid, to obtain concessions from the Haitian government. See William P. Clyde & Co. to Frederick Douglass, September 30, 1889, in the Frederick Douglass Papers at the Library of Congress, Series: General Correspondence, 1889, August–September.

28. Douglass to James G. Blaine, June 25, 1889, in the Frederick Douglass Papers at the Library of Congress, Series: General Correspondence, 1889, June.

29. Harrison's administration recognized Hyppolite tacitly by finally sending Douglass to the island. The Haitian historian Roger Gaillard states that Douglass took up his functions on October 8, 1889. See Gaillard, *La République exterminatrice*, 180.

30. National Archives, Records of the Department of State, Diplomatic Despatches, Haiti, vol. 24, despatch 1, October 15, 1889. As minister resident, Douglass was under the authority of the secretary of state.

31. National Archives, Records of the Department of State, Diplomatic Despatches, Haiti, vol. 24, despatch 5, October 26, 1889.

32. Numerous dispatches from Douglass to Blaine evoke a large number of cases of Americans in opposition to the Haitian government. One example is the case of Charles Adrian Van Bokkelen; another involved the indemnity paid to the shipbuilder Clyde for the loss of his ship the *Ozama*. See National Archives, Records of the Department of State, Diplomatic Despatches, Haiti, vols. 24 and 25.

33. Roger Gaillard confirms that Douglass was sent to Haiti without having been assigned "any task of negotiating for the acquisition of any portion whatsoever of Haiti's territory." Gaillard, *La République exterminatrice*, 180.

34. National Archives, Records of the Department of State, Diplomatic Despatches, Haiti, vol. 24, Mr. Douglass's remarks on presenting his letter of credence, November 14, 1889, enclosure no. 4 in despatch 13, November 18, 1889.

35. National Archives, Records of the Department of State, Diplomatic Despatches,

Haiti, vol. 24, President Hyppolite's response to Frederick Douglass, November 14, 1889, enclosure no. 6 in despatch 13, November 18, 1889.

36. It is an argument against him that will return many times throughout his term. As an example, see the *Dallas Morning News*, December 8, 1889, vol. 5, no. 69, 6.

37. Gaillard, *La République exterminatrice*, 180.

38. In any event, it is what Douglass will claim later on many occasions. Responding to attacks in American newspapers, he will write that at no time during his first year in Haiti did his government inform him of its interest in Môle, nor did it ask him to negotiate a lease.

39. National Archives, Records of the Department of State, Diplomatic Despatches, Haiti, vol. 24, despatch 17, December 9, 1889.

40. National Archives, Records of the Department of State, Diplomatic Despatches, Haiti, vol. 24, despatch 18, December 14, 1889.

41. Ibid., enclosure no. 5.

42. National Archives, Records of the Department of State, Diplomatic Despatches, Haiti, vol. 24, despatch 31, January 17, 1890.

43. National Archives, Records of the Department of State, Diplomatic Despatches, Haiti, vol. 24, despatch 64, May 14, 1890.

44. Volwiler, "Harrison, Blaine," 637–38.

45. National Archives, Records of the Department of State, Diplomatic Despatches, Haiti, vol. 24, despatch 79, June 27, 1890.

46. National Archives, Records of the Department of State, Diplomatic Despatches, Haiti, vol. 24, despatch 80, June 27, 1890.

47. National Archives, Records of the Department of State, Diplomatic Despatches, Haiti, vol. 24, despatch 72, May 30, 1890; National Archives, Records of the Department of State, Diplomatic Despatches, Haiti, vol. 24, Douglass to Blaine, May 31, 1890; National Archives, Records of the Department of State, Diplomatic Despatches, Haiti, vol. 24, despatch 75, June 6, 1890.

48. This triple recognition was officially reported in the *Moniteur* on July 12 with a copy included in despatch no. 89 of July 16, 1890. See National Archives, Records of the Department of State, Diplomatic Despatches, Haiti, vol. 24, despatch 89, July 16, 1890.

49. The first despatch written by Douglass after his return to Haiti notes that he was welcomed as a hero, with the same honors as a head of state, before even setting foot on the island. Hyppolite sent his personal guards to Douglass's ship to escort him to shore. See National Archives, Records of the Department of State, Diplomatic Despatches, Haiti, vol. 24, despatch 95, December 18, 1890.

50. See Logan, *Diplomatic Relations*, 436.

51. This reciprocal treaty gave Blaine the power to suspend by decree the importation of sugar, coffee, and tea from a country he judged to be applying excessively high border tariffs against American products. See LaFeber, *The New Empire*, 119.

52. See Himelhoch, "Frederick Douglass," 173; Logan, *Diplomatic Relations*, 438.

53. National Archives, Records of the Department of State, Diplomatic Despatches, Haiti, vol. 25, unnumbered "private and confidential" letter of Frederick Douglass to James G. Blaine, Secretary of State, January 6, 1891.

54. National Archives, Records of the Department of State, Diplomatic Despatches, Haiti, vol. 25, despatch 120, January 26, 1891.

55. See Sears, "Frederick Douglass," 232.

56. National Archives, Records of the Department of State, Diplomatic Despatches, Haiti, vol. 25, letter no. 1 of Bancroft Gherardi to Secretary of State, January 31, 1891.

57. National Archives, Records of the Department of State, Diplomatic Despatches, Haiti, vol. 25, "confidential" despatch 123, January 29, 1891.

58. National Archives, Records of the Department of State, Diplomatic Despatches, Haiti, vol. 25, letter no. 2 of Bancroft Gherardi to Secretary of State, February 7, 1891.

59. National Archives, Records of the Department of State, Diplomatic Despatches, Haiti, vol. 25, unnumbered telegram of Frederick Douglass to Secretary of State, April 23, 1891.

60. National Archives, Records of the Department of State, Diplomatic Despatches, Haiti, vol. 25, despatch 156, April 23, 1891, enclosure 1, Firmin to Douglass and Gherardi, Plénipotentiaires etc. Port-au-Prince, April 22, 1891.

61. Ibid.

62. Ibid.

63. Logan, *Diplomatic Relations*, 451.

64. As part of its mission as the official journal of the Republic of Haiti, *Le Moniteur*, founded in 1845 under the direction of the Presses Nationales d'Haïti, publishes the proceedings of the executive branch and thereby acts as the reference for all judicial matters of the country.

65. National Archives, Records of the Department of State, Diplomatic Despatches, Haiti, vol. 25, despatch 159, May 2, 1891, enclosure 1. Italics as in the original.

66. National Archives, Records of the Department of State, Diplomatic Despatches, Haiti, vol. 25, despatch 161, May 2, 1891.

67. National Archives, Records of the Department of State, Diplomatic Despatches, Haiti, vol. 25, despatch 162, May 7, 1891.

68. National Archives, Records of the Department of State, Diplomatic Despatches, Haiti, vol. 25, despatch 163, May 7, 1891.

69. National Archives, Records of the Department of State, Diplomatic Despatches, Haiti, vol. 25, despatch 164, May 7, 1891.

70. National Archives, Records of the Department of State, Diplomatic Despatches, Haiti, vol. 25, despatch 165, May 9, 1891.

71. National Archives, Records of the Department of State, Diplomatic Despatches, Haiti, vol. 25, despatch 171, June 3, 1891.

72. National Archives, Records of the Department of State, Diplomatic Despatches, Haiti, vol. 25, despatch 174, June 19, 1891.

73. National Archives, Records of the Department of State, Diplomatic Despatches, Haiti, vol. 25, despatch 180bis, July 30, 1891. As a handwritten note on this despatch attests, his resignation was officially accepted on August 11, 1891.

74. See National Archives, Records of the Department of State, Diplomatic Despatches, Haiti, vol. 25, Frederick Douglass to Wharton, September 4, 1891.

75. Douglass received word that his resignation was accepted on August 11, 1891, which was also the day he began letting loose in the press. It is interesting to notice that the white press rushed to publish articles affirming that Douglass was let go by his government because of the failed negotiations, among other arguments. See, for example, "Fred Douglass Resigns," *Washington Post*, August 11, 1891, 1. Even the historian LaFeber, prob-

ably based on his reading of such articles, notes that Douglass "was fired by President Benjamin Harrison for not showing sufficient enthusiasm for U.S. imperialistic ventures in the black Caribbean nation." LaFeber, *The Cambridge History*, 49.

76. Douglass, "Haïti and the United States. I," 338.

77. Douglass, "Haïti and the United States. I," 338, 339.

78. Douglass, "Haïti and the United States. I," 339–40.

79. Douglass, "Haïti and the United States. I," 340.

80. Douglass, "Haïti and the United States. I," 345, 343.

81. Douglass, "Haïti and the United States. II," 453–54.

82. The number of newspapers in America more than doubled between 1880 and 1900, going from 850 to almost 2,000.

83. Douglass, "Haïti and the United States. II," 454–55.

84. Douglass, *Life and Times* (1881), 505–6.

85. Douglass, *Life and Times* (1881), 511–12.

86. Douglass, "Haïti and the United States. I," 339–40.

87. Douglass, *Life and Times* (1881), 291, 488.

88. Douglass, "Haïti and the United States. II," 453.

89. According to historian James Oakes, this ambivalence in Douglass's statements was observable as early as the 1850s: "By 1855 Douglass sometimes sounded like the proud Yankee boasting the superiority of the northern way of life." Oakes, *The Radical and the Republican*, 36.

90. Douglass, "Haïti and the United States. II," 454.

91. Du Bois, *The Souls of Black Folk*, 3–4.

CHAPTER 7. Haiti and Frederick Douglass

1. *The Dream City*, introduction.

2. See Woodward, *The Strange Career of Jim Crow*, 83–86; Kousser, *The Shaping of Southern Politics*, 17.

3. Kousser, *The Shaping of Southern Politics*, 65.

4. Kousser, *The Shaping of Southern Politics*, 48.

5. Woodward, *The Strange Career of Jim Crow*, 85.

6. For more information on this affair, see Fireside, *Separate and Unequal*.

7. For a history of universal expositions in the nineteenth century, see Aimone and Olmo, *Les Expositions universelles*.

8. Pinot de Villechenon, *Fêtes géantes*, 6.

9. Pinot de Villechenon, *Fêtes géantes*, 6–7.

10. See Plum, *Les Expositions universelles*, 133.

11. Rydell et al., *Fair America*, 8.

12. Rydell et al., *Fair America*, 10.

13. The official number of entrances from March 1 to October 31, 1893, the span of time that the Chicago World's Fair was open to the public, is recorded as 27,539,521. It is impossible to say what percentage of these were foreign visitors. See *Report of the President to the Board of Directors*, 408.

14. For more on Frederick Jackson Turner's frontier thesis, see Turner and Faragher, *Rereading Frederick Jackson Turner*.

15. Notably during the Berlin Conference of 1884–1885. See *infra*.

16. Rydell et al., *Fair America*, 30.

17. Rydell, *All the World's a Fair*, 40–41.

18. "The term 'pavilion,' associating the notion of free-standing autonomy to specific architectural form, was the regular term used to name any construction outside the palace and halls of the exposition." Schroeder-Gudehus and Rasmussen, *Les fastes du progrès*, 17. These pavilions were the first attempt to articulate a national spirit through a specific architectural project in the nineteenth century.

19. Reed, *"All the World Is Here,"* 173.

20. *Cosmopolitan Magazine*, 543.

21. Truman, *History of the World's Fair*, 211–12.

22. Flinn, *The Best Things to Be Seen*, 143.

23. Bancroft, *The Book of the Fair*, 918–20.

24. *The World's Fair Souvenir Album*; Arnold and Higinbotham, *Official Views*.

25. *The Dream City*, chap. 5.

26. In the newspapers of the time, the "Congress on Africa" was sometimes referred to as the "Congress on African Ethnology" or the "Congress on the Negro."

27. Little is known about Charles A. Preston other than that he was the son of Stephen Preston, who had been the Haitian ambassador to the United States at the time of Douglass's nomination as minister resident to Haiti. See McFeely, *Douglass*, 338, 366.

28. Hill, *Hill's Souvenir*, 230.

29. Pierce, *Photographic History*, 309.

30. *The Dream City*, chap. 5.

31. Truman, *History of the World's Fair*, 84.

32. Bancroft, *The Book of the Fair*, 918.

33. National Archives, Records of the Department of State, Diplomatic Despatches, Haiti, vol. 25, despatch 138, March 3, 1891. The archives of the diplomatic dispatches do not contain a copy of the letter sent by the American government to Douglass inviting Haiti to participate in the exposition.

34. See National Archives, Records of the Department of State, Diplomatic Despatches, Haiti, vol. 25, despatch 144, "Mr Frederick A. Ober's visit to Port-au-Prince," March 19, 1891. Douglass gives no list of the Caribbean islands that Ober was to visit. The Dominican Republic was the only other Caribbean nation to participate in the 1893 Exposition.

35. See National Archives, Records of the Department of State, Diplomatic Despatches, Haiti, vol. 25, despatch 178, "Haïti and the Chicago Exposition of 1893," June 24, 1891.

36. Archin to Frederick Douglass, February 11, 1892, Frederick Douglass Papers at the Library of Congress, Series: General Correspondence.

37. Hyppolite to Frederick Douglass, January 16, 1892, Frederick Douglass Papers at the Library of Congress, Series: General Correspondence.

38. Archin to Frederick Douglass, February 11, 1892, Frederick Douglass Papers at the Library of Congress, Series: General Correspondence.

39. Price to Frederick Douglass, February 10, 1892, Frederick Douglass Papers at the Library of Congress, Series: General Correspondence.

40. Hyppolite to Frederick Douglass, January 16, 1892, Frederick Douglass Papers at the Library of Congress, Series: General Correspondence.

41. Douglass, *Lecture on Haiti*, 7.

42. Douglass, "The Negotiations for the Mole St. Nicolas. Haiti Becomes More and More Interesting on Account of the Columbian Exposition," unknown newspaper, Washington D.C., Saturday, October 17, 1891, Frederick Douglass Papers at the Library of Congress, Series: Speech, Article, and Book File, 1846–1894 and Undated. Douglass crosses out the title of this article and replaces it with "A Lecture by Frederick Douglass on Hayti."

43. James Sidbury is one of the few historians to have recently studied the presence of a diaspora consciousness among some Black Americans from the colonial period onward, but his investigation does not go further than the 1830s. See Sidbury, *Becoming African in America.*

44. Douglass, "The Negotiations for the Mole St. Nicolas," 18–19.

45. Douglass, "The Negotiations for the Mole St. Nicolas," 11.

46. Douglass, "The Negotiations for the Mole St. Nicolas," 18.

47. Douglass, "The Negotiations for the Mole St. Nicolas," 7, 9, 12.

48. Douglass, "The Negotiations for the Mole St. Nicolas," 4.

49. Douglass, "The Negotiations for the Mole St. Nicolas," 5.

50. In fact, he posits the existence of a Black diaspora as an incontrovertible reality, and his prophetic tone indicates a global struggle.

51. Douglass, "The Negotiations for the Mole St. Nicolas," 15.

52. Douglass, "The Negotiations for the Mole St. Nicolas," 15–16.

53. Douglass, "The Negotiations for the Mole St. Nicolas," 19.

54. Douglass employs and discusses this term on August 25, 1893, in his speech during the Jubilee Day for Black Americans. See chapter 8.

55. "The Meeting of the Foreign Commissioners in the City of Chicago," Frederick Douglass to Haiti Foreign Affairs Secretary, March 21, 1892, Frederick Douglass Papers at the Library of Congress, Series: General Correspondence.

56. See the Frederick Douglass Papers at the Library of Congress, "World's Columbian Exposition, Chicago, Ill.," Series: Subject File, 1845–1939. This ceremony was to mark the end of the major portions of the exposition's construction. The ceremonies to inaugurate the pavilions took place as the building of each was completed along with the installations within each one.

57. See McFeely, *Douglass*, 366. See also Reed, *"All the World Is Here,"* 30.

58. McFeely, *Douglass*, 366.

59. Douglass, *Lecture on Haiti.*

60. Douglass, *Lecture on Haiti*, 7.

61. Douglass, *Lecture on Haiti*, 9–10.

62. Douglass, *Lecture on Haiti*, 16–17.

63. It is difficult to interpret this tendency of Douglass to not recognize that Hyppolite maintained order in his country through bloody repression. Perhaps one must see it as part of Douglass's deep wish to support Black regimes in a spirit of diasporic solidarity at a time when Black Americans were victims of segregation and violence in the South. Perhaps it was a sort of pre–Third World attitude of a man who was conscious of

the flaws of the Black republic but who only wanted to see its positive side, namely its capacity to remain independent. See Douglass, *Lecture on Haiti*, 20–21.

64. Douglass, *Lecture on Haiti*, 18.

65. Douglass, *Lecture on Haiti*, 26–27.

66. Douglass, *Lecture on Haiti*, 27–28.

67. Douglass, *Lecture on Haiti*, 44.

68. Douglass, *Lecture on Haiti*, 35.

69. Douglass, *Lecture on Haiti*, 45.

70. Douglass, *Lecture on Haiti*, 47.

71. Douglass, *Lecture on Haiti*, 49.

72. Douglass, *Lecture on Haiti*, 51–52.

73. Douglass, *Lecture on Haiti*, 56.

74. The Haitian pavilion was placed next to the German and Spanish pavilions and not far from the British pavilion.

CHAPTER 8. From Haiti to Chicago

1. Wells et al., *The Reason Why*, 81

2. Douglass, untitled document, October 1893, Frederick Douglass Papers at the Library of Congress, Series: Speech, Article, and Book File C: Frederick Douglass, Undated and Untitled.

3. Du Bois, *The Souls of Black Folk*, vii.

4. Among the many books and articles supporting this thesis, one can cite Lorini, *Rituals of Race*; Meier and Rudwick, "Black Man in the 'White City'"; Rydell, *All the World's a Fair*.

5. Reed, *"All the World Is Here,"* xi. See also Muccigrosso, *Celebrating the New World*.

6. Meier and Rudwick, "Black Man in the 'White City,'" 354. See also Reed, *"All the World Is Here,"* 23.

7. Rydell, *All the World's a Fair*, 52.

8. Meier and Rudwick, "Black Man in the 'White City,'" 355–56.

9. "Did Mrs Curtis Resign?" *Cleveland Gazette*, April 15, 1893, 1.

10. See McFeely, *Douglass*, 366–67.

11. Meier and Rudwick, "Black Man in the 'White City,'" 357.

12. Reed, *"All the World Is Here,"* 101–4.

13. Born in Ohio, Albion Winegar Tourgée (1838–1905) was a Republican known for his radical positions in favor of equality between the races and his fervent defense of civil rights and the vote for Black people. From 1888 to 1898 he wrote a weekly editorial column entitled "A Bystander's Note" for the *Chicago Inter Ocean*. His column was the perfect example of the sort of continuous crusade he led in favor of social reforms and racial equality. As a result, Tourgée was much appreciated within the Black American community, and the Black press regularly reprinted his editorials.

14. "That Day at the World's Fair for Afro-Americans—What Judge Tourgee Has to Say Relative to the Separate Day Movement," *Cleveland Gazette*, March 11, 1893, 1.

15. Meier and Rudwick, "Black Man in the 'White City,'" 359.

16. See Rydell, *All the World's a Fair*, 40.

17. See Ballard, "A People Without a Nation." Dahomey is an ancient African kingdom located in present-day Benin.

18. Douglass, *The Lessons of the Hour*, 20.

19. On mass cultures and the interests of colonial powers, and especially the exhibits of sometimes deformed humans (coming from colonial Africa, the Americas, Oceania, or Asia) placed on the margins of learned gatherings and discourses, from the European display of Sarah Baartman, known as the Hottentot Venus, in the early nineteenth century to the 1930s, see Bancel, Blanchard, et al., *Zoos humains*.

20. Burton, "Rituals of Representation," 29.

21. Burton, "Rituals of Representation," 39.

22. Wells et al., *The Reason Why*, preface.

23. These are the official numbers of the 1890 census. See Census Office, *Report on Population of the United States*, xciii–xciv.

24. Frederick Douglass, "Call for the Publication of a Pamphlet Protesting the Exclusion of Colored Citizens' Participation in the World's Columbian Exposition," Frederick Douglass Papers at the Library of Congress, Series: Speech, Article, and Book File A: Frederick Douglass, Dated.

25. "To the Friends of Equal Rights," *Topeka Call*, March 26, 1893; "Our World's Fair Effort," *Afro-American Advocate*, April 14, 1893.

26. It is surprising to see that the sums supposedly given by Douglass, Wells, and Loudin vary from one newspaper to another. The *Topeka Call* reports Douglass contributed $50, Wells $25, and Loudin $100, while the *Afro-American Advocate* reports they gave $50, $10, and $50, respectively.

27. "To the Friends of Equal Rights," *Topeka Call*, March 26, 1893.

28. "Our World's Fair Effort," *Afro-American Advocate*, April 14, 1893.

29. Among the newspapers supporting this view, one can cite the *Topeka Call*, the *Afro-American Advocate*, the *Baltimore Afro-American*, the *Cleveland Gazette*, the *Philadelphia Tribune*, and the *Richmond Planet*. The *Freeman* published many articles that were hostile to the initiative such as "No 'Nigger Day' No 'Nigger Pamphlet'" that appeared in the March 25, 1893, issue, and "Douglass's Wasted Zeal" in the issue for August 5, 1893.

30. "Statesman: Against the Pamphlet Idea," *Freeman*, April 1, 1893; "No 'Nigger Day' No 'Nigger Pamphlet,'" *Freeman*, March 25, 1893.

31. "Statesman: Against the Pamphlet Idea," *Freeman*, April 1, 1893.

32. "World's Fair Appeal," *Washington Bee*, April 15, 1893, 2.

33. Wells, *Crusade for Justice*, 117.

34. Wells et al., *The Reason Why*, 4, 6.

35. Wells et al., *The Reason Why*, 6–7.

36. Wells et al., *The Reason Why*, 7–8.

37. Wells et al., *The Reason Why*, 7–8.

38. Wells et al., *The Reason Why*, 11–12.

39. Wells et al., *The Reason Why*, 19.

40. Wells et al., *The Reason Why*, 26.

41. Wells et al., *The Reason Why*, 40.

42. Wells et al., *The Reason Why*, 65.

43. Wells, *Crusade for Justice*, 117.

44. Wells et al., *The Reason Why*, 81; Wells, *Crusade for Justice*, 115–16.

45. Wells, *Crusade for Justice*, 116–17.

46. Most of the information about the organization of the Congress on Africa and the Jubilee Day for Black Americans comes from a February 1893 document entitled *Report in Behalf of the General Committee, by Its Chairman, Joseph E. Roy, D.D.* This twenty-eight-page report on the genesis of the Congress on Africa and its organization, program, and the progress of its preparation at the moment of its publication exists intact in the digital archives of Frederick Douglass. See World's Columbian Exposition, Chicago, Illinois, 1897, in the Frederick Douglass Papers at the Library of Congress, Series: Subject File.

47. *Report of the President to the Board of Directors*, 326.

48. The subcommittees were composed exclusively of men; however, "on all subjects suitable for the coöperation of women in the congresses," parallel subcommittees composed exclusively of women were organized. These women's groups were together called the Women's Branch of the World's Congress Auxiliary, with Mrs. Bertha Potter Palmer (1849–1918) serving as president. Palmer was a musician and writer but also a philanthropic businesswoman, a member of the Chicago Woman's Club, and married to a Chicago millionaire. See *Report of the President to the Board of Directors*, 334.

49. See *Report of the President to the Board of Directors*, 333, 336.

50. "The Negro Congress at Chicago," *The Independent*, August 24, 1893, 10.

51. *Report in Behalf of the General Committee*, 17.

52. *Report in Behalf of the General Committee*, 8–16.

53. On the Berlin Conference (1884–1885) and the Brussels Geographic Conference (1876), see Comte, *L'empire triomphant*, 41–44, 333–35; Wesseling, *Le partage de l'Afrique*, 159–64; and Hochschild, *Les fantômes du roi Léopold*.

54. *Report on Behalf of the General Committee*, 7.

55. *Report on Behalf of the General Committee*, 17.

56. See Reed, *"All the World Is Here,"* 180.

57. *Report on Behalf of the General Committee*, 17.

58. Despite efforts by the organizing committee, the proceedings of the congress were never published. This lack is regrettable and probably contributed to the limited impact of the congress at the time and certainly hinders research and reflection about this event today. One must make do with a few summaries of certain lectures that appeared in some newspapers.

59. See "From the Wilds of Africa—Dr. Carl Peters, the Noted Explorer of the Dark Continent Is Here," *New York Herald-Tribune*, August 19, 1893. See also "A Talk with Dr. Peters," *The Sun*, August 19, 1893.

60. "African Evolution," *Daily Times-Picayune*, August 21, 1893, 4.

61. "Congress on Africa," *Daily Inter Ocean*, August 16, 1893; "Conventions in Chicago," *The Sun*, August 15, 1893, 6.

62. "No 'Nigger Day' Wanted," *Freeman*, February 25, 1893, 4.

63. "Miss Well's [*sic*] Congratulations," *Freeman*, March 4, 1893, 5.

64. Wells, *Crusade for Justice*, 118–19.

65. "Afro-American Jubilee Day Committee," World's Columbian Exposition, Chicago, Illinois, 1893, 1, in the Frederick Douglass Papers at the Library of Congress, Series: Subject File.

66. Watermelon was present in many nineteenth-century caricatures as the favorite food of Black people, depicted with pudgy faces and exaggeratedly swollen lips. The fruit was frequently used symbolically as part of the general derision of Black Americans by slaveowners and by southerners in general after the Civil War and Emancipation. The drawing by Frederick Opper, "Darkies' Day at the Fair," a particularly flagrant example, appeared in a special issue of *Puck* devoted to the Universal Exposition of 1893. The illustration was published in August of that year only days before the jubilee event. The caricature repeats the stereotype of the Black-American-eater-of-watermelon associated with the Black-African-barbarian. One is shown Black Americans strolling with Black Africans with no difference between them but their clothing. See Opper, "Darkies' Day at the Fair" (lithograph, color), in *Puck*, August 21, 1893, 186–87.

67. See McFeely, *Douglass*, 371.

68. "The Watermelons Absent," *Cleveland Gazette*, August 26, 1893, 2.

69. "World's Fair Notes," *Los Angeles Herald*, August 26, 1893, 1; "Wiping Out the Fair's Debt," *New-York Daily Tribune*, August 26, 1893, 6; "Black Friday," *Daily Public Ledger*, August 26, 1893, 3; "Honor to Their Race," *Topeka Call*, September 9, 1893, 1.

70. "Negro Day at the Fair," *New-York Herald*, August 26, 1893, 5. See also "Colored People's Day," *The Sun*, August 26, 1893, 8; "Colored People's Day," *The Sun*, August 26, 1893, 8; "Wiping Out the Fair's Debt," *New-York Daily Tribune*, August 26, 1893, 6; "At the Fair," *Daily Picayune*, August 26, 1893.

71. See Wells, *Crusade for Justice*, 119; McFeely, *Douglass*, 370–71.

72. See "Wiping Out the Fair's Debt," *New-York Daily Tribune*, August 26, 1893, 6; "At the Fair," *Saint Paul Daily Globe*, August 26, 1893, 8; "At the Fair," *Evening Herald*, August 29, 1893.

73. "At the Fair," *Saint Paul Daily Globe*, August 26, 1893, 8.

74. See Wells, *Crusade for Justice*, 119; "At the Fair," *Evening Herald*, August 29, 1893; "At the Fair," *Saint Paul Daily Globe*, August 26, 1893, 8.

75. See "World's Fair Notes," *Los Angeles Herald*, August 26, 1893, 1; "At the Fair," *Saint Paul Daily Globe*, August 26, 1893, 8; "Wiping Out the Fair's Debt," *New-York Daily Tribune*, August 26, 1893, 6; "At the Fair," *Evening Herald*, August 29, 1893.

76. See "Black Friday," *Daily Public Ledger*, August 26, 1893, 3. See also "Wiping Out the Fair's Debt," *New-York Daily Tribune*, August 26, 1893, 6; Washington, *Douglass*, 336.

77. Wells, *Crusade for Justice*, 119.

78. "Honor to Their Race—Fred Douglass' Address," *Topeka Call*, September 9, 1893, 1; "Douglass' Brilliant Metaphor," *Freeman*, September 2, 1893, 1; "Northern Whites Attention!" *Freeman*, September 9, 1893, 4; "Douglass' Truths," *Cleveland Gazette*, September 16, 1893, 1.

79. See "Honor to Their race," *Topeka Call*, September 9, 1893, 1; "The World in Miniature. By Chicago's Changing Lights," "Colored Americans' Day, Minus the Negro," *Freeman*, September 2, 1893, 1.

The *New-York Daily Tribune* also reported that the crowd was predominantly white. See "Wiping out the Fair's Debt," *New-York Daily Tribune*, August 26, 1893, 6.

80. Washington, *Douglass*, 336.

81. See "At the World's Fair," *Wheeling Register*, August 26, 1893, 1. See also "At the Fair," *Daily Times-Picayune*, August 26, 1893; "Black Friday," *Daily Public Ledger*, August 26, 1893, 3; "The World's Fair," *Idaho Daily Statesman*, August 26, 1893, 1.

82. Wells, *Crusade for Justice*, 119.

83. Wells, *Crusade for Justice*, 118. A special day was devoted to each of the nationalities represented at the exposition. For example, "German Day" took place on June 15, 1893. See *Report of the President to the Board of Directors*, 222.

84. See Washington, "The Atlanta Exposition Address."

85. In 1895 W. E. B. Du Bois, still quite young, was not as influential as Booker T. Washington. Moreover, he built his fame thanks to his strong opposition to the accommodationist theories of Washington in 1895, then thanks to his virulent criticism toward Washington's autobiography, *Up from Slavery*, published in 1901.

EPILOGUE

1. Douglass, *The Lessons of the Hour*, 26.

2. Douglass, *The Lessons of the Hour*, 3.

3. Kekeh and Le Dantec-Lowry, *Formes et écritures du départ*, 15.

4. Douglass, *The Lessons of the Hour*, 19–20.

5. Douglass, *The Lessons of the Hour*, 25–26.

6. For the United States, Pan-Americanism consisted in elaborating a foreign policy prioritizing North America; in other words, serving America's financial, military, and political interests for the nineteenth and twentieth centuries. Officially, Pan-Americanism was a policy of nonintervention, commercial equality, and political cooperation between the United States and Caribbean and Latin American countries. It claimed inspiration from the Monroe Doctrine of 1823. Stated plainly, the goal was to protect American interests from possible European interference. See Polyné, *From Douglass to Duvalier*, 27–30.

7. Polyné, *From Douglass to Duvalier*, 27–28, 42–43, 48.

8. See Plummer, *Rising Wind*, 14–16.

9. See Aptheker, "DuBois on Douglass," 268.

10. See Plummer, *Rising Wind;* and Von Eschen, *Race against Empire*.

APPENDIX

1. Wells, *Crusade for Justice*, 119.

2. Reed, *"All the World Is Here,"* 194.

3. The following 1893 African American newspaper titles were part of the Readex collection of America's Historical Newspapers called "African American Newspapers" when I did my research in 2012: *Afro-American*, *Broad Axe*, *Atchison Blade*, *Cleveland Gazette*, *Elevator*, *Freeman*, *Huntsville Gazette*, *Parsons Weekly Blade*, *Richmond Planet*, *Savannah Tribune*, *State Ledger*, *Topeka Call*, and *Washington Bee*.

4. "Frederick Douglass' Address," *Weekly Call* (aka *Topeka Call*), September 9, 1893, vol. 3, no. 39, 1.

5. "Jubilee Day," *Freeman*, September 2, 1893, vol. 5, no. 15, 1.

6. "Northern Whites, Attention!" *Freeman*, September 9, 1893, vol. 5, no. 16, 4. N.B. A philippic is a verbal denunciation.

7. "Douglass' Truths," *Cleveland Gazette*, September 16, 1893, 1.

BIBLIOGRAPHY

PRIMARY SOURCES

Archives

The Abraham Lincoln Papers, Manuscript Division, Library of Congress, Washington, D.C.

The Booker T. Washington Papers, University of Illinois, Urbana-Champaign, Illinois.

A Century of Lawmaking for a New Nation: U.S. Congressional Documents and Debates, 1774–1875, 2003, American Memory collections, Library of Congress. http://memory.loc.gov/ammem/amlaw/lawhome.html.

The Collected Works of Abraham Lincoln, 2006, Abraham Lincoln Association. http://quod.lib.umich.edu/l/lincoln.

Diplomatic Despatches, Despatches from U.S. Ministers to Haiti, Vol. 24: Oct. 15, 1889–Dec. 31, 1890. Washington, D.C.: National Archives, Records of the Department of State.

Diplomatic Despatches, Despatches from U.S. Ministers to Haiti, Vol. 25: Jan. 8, 1891–Oct. 23, 1891. Washington, D.C.: National Archives, Records of the Department of State.

The Frederick Douglass Papers, Manuscript Division, Library of Congress, Washington, D.C.

The Haiti Mission Records, Archives of the Episcopal Church, Austin, Texas.

The Right Reverend James Theodore Holly Papers, Archives of the Episcopal Church, Austin, Texas.

The Thomas Jefferson Papers, Manuscript Division, Library of Congress, Washington, D.C.

Historical newspapers and periodicals

The African Repository and Colonial Journal
Afro-American Advocate
Baltimore Afro-American
Chicago Inter Ocean
Cincinnati Daily Gazette
Cleveland Gazette
Colored American
Commercial Advertiser
The Daily Confederation
Daily Public Ledger
The Daily Times-Picayune
The Dallas Morning News
Douglass' Monthly
Elevator

The Evening Herald
The Farmers' Cabinet
Frank Leslie's Illustrated Newspaper
Frederick Douglass' Paper
Freedom's Journal
Freeman
Genius of Universal Emancipation
Georgia Weekly Telegraph
The Idaho Daily Statesman
The Independent
Liberator
The Los Angeles Herald
Manufacturers' and Farmers' Journal
The Milwaukee Daily Sentinel
Le Moniteur
National Republican
New-York Daily Tribune
New York Herald
The New York Herald-Tribune
The New York Times
The North Star
The Omaha Daily Bee
Philadelphia Tribune
The Pine and Palm
The Pittsburgh Dispatch
Puck
Richmond Planet
Richmond Whig
The Saint Paul Daily Globe
The Sun
Topeka Call
L'Union
Washington Bee
The Washington Critic
Washington Post
Weekly Anglo-African
Weekly Louisianian
The Wheeling Register

Governmental and congressional journals, reports, and statistics

Journal of the Executive Proceedings of the Senate of the United States of America, from December 2, 1861, to July 17, 1862, Inclusive. Vol. 12. Washington, D.C.: Government Printing Office, 1887.

Journal of the Executive Proceedings of the Senate of the United States of America, 1869–1871, Friday, April 16, 1869, 199. In *A Century of Lawmaking for a New Nation: U.S. Congressional Documents and Debates, 1774–1875.* American Memory collections, Library of Congress, 2003.

Journal of the House of Representatives of the United States, 1861–1862, Monday, April 21, 1862, 578. In *A Century of Lawmaking for a New Nation: U.S. Congressional Documents and Debates, 1774–1875.* American Memory collections, Library of Congress, 2003.

The Statutes at Large, Treaties, and Proclamations of the United States of America. Vol. 12. Boston: Little, Brown, 1863.

U.S. Department of Commerce, U.S. Bureau of the Census. *Historical Statistics of the United States, Colonial Times to 1970.* Part 1. Washington, D.C.: Government Printing Office, 1975.

———. *Historical Statistics of the United States, Colonial Times to 1970; and Current Population Reports.* Series P-23, Ancestry and Language in the United States: November 1979. Washington, D.C.: Government Printing Office, 1979.

U.S. Department of Education, National Assessment of Adult Literacy. "120 years of Literacy." In Institute of Education Sciences National Center for Education Statistics, 2012. http://nces.ed.gov/NAAL/lit_history.asp (last accessed July 9, 2021).

U.S. Department of the Interior, Census Office. *Report on Population of the United States at the Eleventh Census: 1890.* Part 1. Washington, D.C.: Government Printing Office, 1895.

United States 37th Congress, 2nd session. House of Representatives. Select Committee on Emancipation and Colonization. *Report of the Select Committee on Emancipation and Colonization: With an Appendix.* Washington: Government Printing Office, 1862.

Books, pamphlets, reports, speeches, articles, and manuscripts

Achates (Thomas Pinckney). *Reflections, Occasioned by the Late Disturbances in Charleston.* Charleston: A. E. Miller, 1822.

Address of the Board of Managers of the Haytian Emigration Society of Coloured People, to the Emigrants Intending to Sail to the Island of Hayti in the Brig De Witt Clinton. New York: Mahlon Day, 1824.

Arnold, Charles D., and H. D. Higinbotham. *Official Views of the World's Columbian Exposition.* [Chicago]: Press Chicago Photo-Gravure Co., 1893.

Bancroft, Hubert H. *The Book of the Fair.* Chicago; San Francisco: Bancroft Company, 1893.

Beard, John R. *The Life of Toussaint L'Ouverture: The Negro Patriot of Hayti: Comprising an Account of the Struggle for Liberty in the Island, and a Sketch of Its History to the Present Period.* London: Ingram, Cooke, 1853.

Bell, Phillip A., and Samuel Ennals. "An Address to the Citizens of New York, January 26, 1831." In *The Black Abolitionist Papers*, 1830–1865, Document no. 407. Sanford, N.C.: Microfilming Corporation of America, 17 reels, 35mm microfilm.

Blair, Frank P., Jr. *The Destiny of the Races of This Continent: An Address Delivered before the Mercantile Library Association of Boston, Massachusetts, on the 26th of February, 1859.* Washington, D.C.: Buell & Blanchard, 1859.

Brown, William W. *St. Domingo: Its Revolutions and Its Patriots.* Boston: Bela Marsh, 1855.

Constitution of the American Society of Free Persons of Colour, for Improving Their Condition in the United States; for Purchasing Lands; and for the Establishment of a Settlement in Upper Canada, Also the Proceedings of the Convention, with Their Address to the Free Persons of Colour in the United States. Philadelphia: Printed by J. W. Allen, 1831.

The Cosmopolitan Magazine: A World's Fair Number 15, no. 5. New York: Walker, September 1893.

Cox, Samuel S. *Eight Years in Congress, from 1857–1865: Memoir and Speeches.* New York: D. Appleton, 1865.

Delany, Martin R. *The Condition, Elevation, Emigration, and Destiny of the Colored People of the United States, Politically Considered.* Philadelphia: Privately published, 1852. Reprint, New York: Arno, 1968.

The Dream City: A Portfolio of Photographic Views of the World's Columbian Exposition, with an Introduction by Halsey C. Ives. St. Louis: Thompson, 1893–94.

Dewey, Loring D. *Correspondence Relative to the Emigration to Hayti, of the Free People of Colour, in the United States. Together with the Instructions to the Agent Sent Out by President Boyer.* New York: Mahlon Day, 1824.

Douglass, Frederick. *Address by Hon. Frederick Douglass, Delivered in the Metropolitan A.M.E. Church, Washington, D.C., Tuesday, January 9th, 1894, on the Lessons of the Hour: In Which He Discusses the Various Aspects of the So-Called, but Mis-Called, Negro Problem.* Baltimore: Press of Thomas & Evans, 1894.

———. "Haïti and the United States. Inside History of the Negotiations for the Môle St. Nicolas. I." *North American Review* 153, no. 418 (Sept. 1891): 337–45.

———. "Haïti and the United States. Inside History of the Negotiations for the Môle St. Nicolas. II." *North American Review* 153, no. 419 (Oct. 1891): 450–59.

———. *Lecture on Haiti.* Washington, D.C.: Violet Agents Supply, 1893.

———. *Life and Times of Frederick Douglass, His Early Life as a Slave, His Escape from Bondage, and His Complete History to the Present Time.* Hartford: Park, 1881.

———. *Life and Times of Frederick Douglass, Written by Himself.* New rev. ed. Boston: De Wolfe & Fiske, 1892.

Du Bois, W. E. B. *The Souls of Black Folk; Essays and Sketches.* 2nd ed. Chicago: A. C. McClurg, 1903.

First Report of the New York Colonization Society. New York: J. Seymour, 1823.

Flinn, John J. *The Best Things to Be Seen at the World's Fair.* Chicago: Columbian Guide, 1893.

Flower, George. *History of the English Settlement in Edward County Illinois, Founded in 1817 and 1818 by Morris Birkbeck and George Flower.* Chicago: Fergus, 1882.

Fourth Anniversary of the American Church Missionary Society, Held in the Church of the Epiphany, Philadelphia, Thursday, October 15th, 1863. New York: John A. Gray & Green, 1863.

Franklin, James. *The Present State of Hayti (Saint Domingo) with Remarks on Its Agriculture, Commerce, Laws, Religion, Finances, and Population, Etc.* London: J. Murray, 1828.

Gannett, Henry. *Statistics of the Negroes in the United States.* Baltimore: Trustees of the John F. Slater Fund, 1894.

Garnet, Henry H. "Address to the Slaves of the United States." In *Pamphlets of Protest: An Anthology of Early African-American Protest Literature, 1790–1860*, edited by Richard Newman, Patrick Rael, and Philip Lapsansky, 162–64. New York: Routledge, 2001.

Garnet, Henry H., et al. *The African Civilization Society.* New York: Office of the Civilization Society, 1859.

Haytian Bureau of Emigration. *Reports and Correspondence.* Manuscript, Boston Public Library, 1860–61.

Hill, Thomas E. *Hill's Souvenir Guide to Chicago and the World's Fair.* Chicago: Laird & Lee, 1892.

Holly, James T. *Facts about the Church's Mission in Haiti: A Concise Statement by Bishop Holly.* New York: Thomas Whittaker, 1897.

———. "Thoughts on Hayti, Number III." *Anglo-African Magazine* 1, no. 8 (August 1859): 241–43.

———. "Thoughts on Hayti, Number IV." *Anglo-African Magazine* 1, no. 9 (September 1859): 298–300.

———. "Thoughts on Hayti, Number V." *Anglo-African Magazine* 1, no. 10 (October 1859): 327–29.

———. "Thoughts on Hayti, Number VI." *Anglo-African Magazine* 1, no. 11 (November 1859): 363–67.

———. *A Vindication of the Capacity of the Negro Race for Self-Government, and Civilized Progress, as Demonstrated by Historical Events of the Haytian Revolution: And the*

Subsequent Acts of That People Since Their National Independence. New Haven: William H. Stanley, 1857.

Hunt, Benjamin S. *Remarks on Hayti as a Place of Settlement for Afric-Americans; and on the Mulatto as a Race for the Tropics*. Philadelphia: T. B. Pugh, 1860.

Janvier, Louis J. *Les Constitutions d'Haïti (1801–1885)*. Paris: Marpon & Flammarion, 1886.

Jefferson, Thomas. *Notes on the State of Virginia*. Philadelphia: Prichard & Hall, 1788.

———. *The Writings of Thomas Jefferson*. Edited by Paul Leicester Ford, vol. 7, 1795–1801. n.p.: Putnam, Knickerbocker, 1896.

Journal of the Eightieth Annual Convention of the Protestant Episcopal Church in the Diocese of Connecticut, Held in Norwich, June 14th and 15th, 1864. Hartford: Press of Case, Lockwood, 1864.

Kelley, William D. *The Recognition of Hayti and Liberia. Speech of Hon. William D. Kelley, of Pennsylvania, Delivered in the House of Representatives, June 3, 1862*. Washington, D.C.: Scammel, 1862.

Langston, John M. *From the Virginia Plantation to the National Capitol, or the First and Only Negro Representative in Congress from the Old Dominion, John Mercer Langston. Self-Reliance the Secret of Success.* Hartford: American, 1894.

Lincoln, Abraham. "Address on Colonization to a Deputation of Negroes." In *Lincoln on Race and Slavery*, edited by H. Louis Gates Jr., 235–41. Princeton: Princeton University Press, 2009.

———. "Annual Message to Congress, December 3, 1861." In *Collected Works of Abraham Lincoln*, vol. 5 (2006): 35–53. Abraham Lincoln Association. http://quod.lib.umich.edu/l/lincoln.

———. "Annual Message to Congress, December 1, 1862." In *Collected Works of Abraham Lincoln*, vol. 5 (2006): 518–37. Abraham Lincoln Association. http://quod.lib.umich.edu/l/lincoln.

———. "Reply to Loyal Colored People of Baltimore upon Presentation of a Bible, September 7, 1864." In TeachingAmericanHistory.org, 2006–2021, Ashbrook Center at Ashland University, https://teachingamericanhistory.org/library/document/reply-to-loyal-colored-people-of-baltimore-upon-presentation-of-a-bible (last accessed June 28, 2021).

Lundy, Benjamin. *The Life, Travels and Opinions of Benjamin Lundy, Including His Journeys to Texas and Mexico; with a Sketch of Contemporary Events, and a Notice of the Revolution in Hayti. Compiled under the Direction and on Behalf of His Children.* Philadelphia: Parrish, 1847.

———. *A Plan for the Gradual Abolition of Slavery in the United States, Without Danger or Loss to the Citizens of the South*. Baltimore: Printed by Benjamin Lundy, 1825.

Mason, Isaac. *Life of Isaac Mason as a Slave*. Worcester, Mass.: n.p., 1893.

Merida, Kevin. "He Was the Obama before Obama: John Mercer Langston." *Journal of Blacks in Higher Education*, no. 60 (Summer 2008): 70–73.

Minutes and Proceedings of the General Convention for the Improvement of the Colored Inhabitants of Canada, Held by Adjournments in Amhrstburgh [sic], *C. W., June 16th and 17th, 1853*. Windsor, C.W.: Bibb & Holly, 1853.

Needles, Edward. *An Historical Memoir of the Pennsylvania Society for Promoting the Abolition of Slavery*. Philadelphia: Merrihew & Thompson, 1848.

Newsom, M. T. *Arguments, Pro and Con, on the Call for a National Migration Convention, to Be Held in Cleveland, Ohio, August, 1854, by Frederick Douglass, W. J. Watkins, and James Whitfield. With a Short Appendix of the Statistics of Canada West, West Indies, Central and South America.* Detroit: George Pomeroy, 1854.

Pierce, James W. *Photographic History of the World's Fair and Sketch of the City of Chicago: Also a Guide to the World's Fair and Chicago.* n.p.: Lennox, 1893.

Proceedings of the Colored National Convention, Held in Franklin Hall, Sixth Street, Below Arch, Philadelphia, October 16th, 17th and 18th, 1855. Printed by Order of the Convention. Salem, N.J.: National Standard Office, 1856.

Proceedings of the Colored National Convention, Held in Rochester, July 6th, 7th, and 8th, 1853. Rochester, N.Y.: Office of Frederick Douglass' Paper, 1853.

Proceedings of the National Convention of Colored People and Their Friends; Held in Troy, NY; on the 6th, 7th, 8th, and 9th of October, 1847. Troy: Steam Press of J. C. Kneeland, 1847.

Proceedings of the National Emigration Convention of Colored People: Held at Cleveland, Ohio, Thursday, Friday and Saturday, the 24th, 25th and 26th of August 1854; with a Reference Page of Contents. Pittsburgh: Anderson, 1854.

Purvis, Robert. "Appeal of Forty Thousand Citizens, Threatened with Disfranchisement, to the People of Pennsylvania (1837)." In *Pamphlets of Protest: An Anthology of Early African-American Protest Literature, 1790–1860*, edited by Richard Newman, Patrick Rael, and Philip Lapsansky, 140. New York: Routledge, 2001.

Redpath, James. *A Guide to Hayti.* Boston: Haytian Bureau of Emigration, 1861.

Report of the President to the Board of Directors of the World's Columbian Exposition. Chicago, 1892–1893. Chicago: McNally, 1898.

Rogers, Augustus C. *Our Representatives Abroad: Biographical Sketches of Embassadors* [sic], *Ministers, Consuls-General, and Consuls of the United States in Foreign Countries; Including Also a Few Representative Americans Residing Abroad in Unofficial Capacities.* 2nd ed. New York: Atlantic, 1876.

Russwurm, John B. "The Condition and Prospects of Hayti." *Journal of Negro History* 54, no. 4 (Oct. 1969): 395–97.

Saunders, Prince. *Haytian Papers, a Collection of the Very Interesting Proclamations and Other Official Documents . . . of the Kingdom of Hayti.* London: Reed, 1816.

Smith, James McC. *A Lecture on the Haytien Revolutions; with a Sketch of the Character of Toussaint L'Ouverture. Delivered at the Stuyvesant Institute . . . February 26, 1841.* New York: Fanshaw, 1841.

Stowe, Harriet B. *Uncle Tom's Cabin; or, Life among the Lowly.* 1852. Reprint, New York: Penguin, 1986.

Sumner, Charles. *Charles Sumner, His Complete Works, with Introduction by Hon. George Frisbie Hoar.* 20 vols. Boston: Lee & Shepard, 1900.

———. *Independence of Hayti and Liberia. Speech of Hon. Charles Sumner, of Massachusetts, on the Bill to Authorize the Appointment of Diplomatic Representatives to the Republics of Hayti and Liberia, with the Debate Thereon; in the Senate of the United States, April 23 and 24, 1862.* Washington: Printed at the Congressional Globe Office, 1862.

"Trinity Church, Port-au-Prince, Haïti. The Rev. J. Theodore Holly, Rector." In *Jour-*

nal of the Eightieth Annual Convention of the Protestant Episcopal Church in the Diocese of Connecticut, Held in Norwich, June 14th and 15th, 1864, 69. Hartford: Press of Case, Lockwood, 1864.

Truman, Benjamin C. *History of the World's Fair: Being a Complete Description of the Columbian Exposition from Its Inception*. Philadelphia: Mammoth, 1893.

Tuckerman, Charles, to Abraham Lincoln, March 31, 1863. The Abraham Lincoln Papers, Series 1, General Correspondence (1833–1916), Library of Congress.

Walker, David. *Walker's Appeal, in Four Articles; Together with a Preamble, to the Coloured Citizens of the World, but in Particular, and Very Expressly, to Those of the United States of America, Written in Boston, State of Massachusetts, September 28, 1829*. Boston: David Walker, 1830.

Washington, Booker T. "The Standard Printed Version of the Atlanta Exposition Address." In *The Booker T. Washington Papers*, edited by Louis L. Harlan, 3:583–87. Urbana: University of Illinois Press, 1974.

———. *Up from Slavery: An Autobiography*. 1901. Reprint, New York: Doubleday, Page, 1907.

Wells, Ida B. *Crusade for Justice: The Autobiography of Ida B. Wells*. Edited by Alfreda M. Duster. Chicago: University of Chicago Press, 1970.

Wells, Ida B., et al. *The Reason Why the Colored American Is Not in the World's Columbian Exposition*. Chicago: Ida B. Wells, 1893.

Williams, Peter (Reverend). *Discourse Delivered in St. Philip's Church, for the Benefit of the Coloured Community of Wilberforce, in Upper Canada, on the Fourth of July, 1830*. New York: Bunce, 1830.

Wilson, Henry. *History of the Antislavery Measures of the Thirty-seventh and Thirty-eighth United States Congresses, 1861–1864*. Boston: Walker, Wise, 1864.

The World's Fair Souvenir Album, Containing General Views of the Columbian Exposition, Grounds, Main Buildings, Foreign and State Buildings, Peristyles, Lagoons, Statuary, Fountains, Architectural Details, Midway Plaisance, etc., Covering the Whole Scope of the White City. Chicago: Ropp, 1894.

Wright, Frances. "Explanatory Notes, Respecting the Nature and Objects of the Institution of Nashoba, and of the Principles upon Which It Is Founded. Addressed to the Friends of Human Improvement, in All Countries and of All Nations." *New Harmony Gazette* 3, no. 16 (January 30, 1828): 124–25; 3, no. 17 (February 6, 1828): 132–33; 3, no. 18 (February 13, 1828): 140–41.

———. *Views of Society and Manners in America; in a Series of Letters from That Country to a Friend in England, During the Years 1818, 1819, and 1820*. London: Longman, Hurst, Rees, Orme & Brown, 1821.

SECONDARY SOURCES

Journal articles and unpublished conference papers

Aptheker, Herbert. "DuBois on Douglass: 1895." *Journal of Negro History* 49, no. 4 (October 1964): 264–68.

Bacon, Jacqueline. "The History of Freedom's Journal: A Study in Empowerment and Community." *Journal of African American History* 88, no. 1 (Winter 2003): 1–20.

Ballard, Barbara. J. "A People Without a Nation: African Americans at the 1893 World's Columbian Exposition." *Chicago History* (Summer 1999): 27–43.

Baur, John E. "Mulatto Machiavelli, Jean Pierre Boyer, and the Haiti of His Day." *Journal of Negro History* 32, no. 3 (July 1947): 307–53.

Bell, Howard H. "Negro Nationalism in the 1850s." *Journal of Negro Education* 35, no. 1 (Winter 1966): 100–104.

Bennett, Lerone, Jr. "Was Abe Lincoln a White Supremacist?" *Ebony* 23, no. 4 (Feb. 1968): 35–43.

Bethel, Elizabeth R. "Images of Hayti: The Construction of an Afro-American Lieu de Mémoire." *Callaloo* 15, no. 3 (Summer 1992): 827–41.

Blackett, Richard J. M. "Martin R. Delany and Robert Campbell: Black Americans in Search of an African Colony." *Journal of Negro History* 62, no. 1 (January 1977): 1–25.

Blake, J. Herman. "Black Nationalism." *Annals of the American Academy of Political Science* 382 (Mar. 1969): 15–25.

Bourhis-Mariotti, Claire. "'Go to our brethren, the Haytians': Haiti as the African Americans' Promised Land in the Antebellum Era." *Revue française d'études américaines* 2015/1, no. 142 (2015): 6–23.

Boyd, Willis D. "The Île à Vache Colonization Venture, 1862–1864." *The Americas* 16, no. 1 (July 1959): 45–62.

———. "James Redpath and American Negro Colonization in Haiti, 1860–1862." *The Americas* 12, no. 2 (October 1955): 169–82.

Brantley, Daniel. "Black Diplomacy and Frederick Douglass' Caribbean Experiences, 1871 and 1889–1891: The Untold History." *Phylon* 45, no. 3 (3rd Qtr., 1984): 197–209.

Connors, Robert J. "Frances Wright: First Female Civic Rhetor in America." *College English* 62, no. 1 (Sept. 1999): 30–57.

Dubois, Laurent. "Esclavage, citoyenneté et République dans les Antilles françaises à l'époque révolutionnaire." *Annales Histoire Sciences Sociales*, no. 2 (2003): 281–303.

Edwards, Brent H. "The Uses of Diaspora." *Social Text* 19, no. 1 (Spring 2001): 45–73.

Gallant, Sigrid N. "Perspectives on the Motives for the Migration of African-Americans to and from Ontario, Canada: From the Abolition of Slavery in Canada to the Abolition of Slavery in the United States." *Journal of Negro History* 86, no. 3 (Summer 2001): 391–408.

Gillard, John T. "Lafayette, Friend of the Negro." *Journal of Negro History* 19, no. 4 (Oct. 1934): 355–71.

Gold, Robert L. "Negro Colonization Schemes in Ecuador, 1861–1864." *Phylon* 30, no. 3 (3rd Qtr. 1969): 306–16.

Guyatt, Nicholas. "'A vast negro reservation': Black Colonization in the Postbellum United States, 1863–1871." International Conference of the Association pour l'Etude de la Colonisation Européenne (June 16–18, 2011), "Réorientations des empires et nouvelle colonisation: Couleurs, esclavage, libérations aux Amériques—1804–1860," Université Paris Diderot, France, June 17, 2011.

———. "America's Conservatory: Race, Reconstruction, and the Santo Domingo Debate." *Journal of American History* 97, no. 4 (March 2011): 974–1000.

Himelhoch, Myra. "Frederick Douglass and Haiti's Mole St. Nicolas." *Journal of Negro History* 56, no. 3 (July 1971): 161–80.

Kumar, Krishan. "Utopian Thought and Communal Practice: Robert Owen and the Owenite Communities." *Theory and Society* 19, no. (Feb. 1990): 1–35.

Landon, Fred. "The Negro Migration to Canada after the Passing of the Fugitive Slave Act. *Journal of Negro History*, no. 5 (1920): 22–27.

Lockett, James D. "Abraham Lincoln and Colonization: An Episode That Ends in Tragedy at l'Ile à Vache, Haiti, 1863–1864." *Journal of Black Studies* 21, no. 4 (June 1991): 428–44.

Masur, Kate. "The African American Delegation to Abraham Lincoln: A Reappraisal." *Civil War History* 56, no. 2 (June 2010): 117–44.

Matthewson, Tim. "Jefferson and Haiti." *Journal of Southern History* 61, no. 2 (May 1995): 209–48.

Meier, August. "The Emergence of Negro Nationalism." *Midwest Journal* 4 (Winter 1951): 96–104.

Meier, August, and Elliott M. Rudwick. "Black Man in the 'White City': Negroes and the Columbian Exposition, 1893." *Phylon* 26 (Winter 1965): 354–61.

Padgett, James A. "Diplomats to Haiti and Their Diplomacy." *Journal of Negro History* 25, no. 3 (July 1940): 265–330.

Page, Sebastian N. "Lincoln and Chiriquí Colonization Revisited." *American Nineteenth Century History* 12, no. 3 (September 2011): 289–325.

Paludan, Phillip S. "Lincoln and Colonization: Policy or Propaganda?" *Journal of the Abraham Lincoln Association* 25, no. 1 (Winter 2004): 23–37.

Pitre, Merline. "Frederick Douglass and the Annexation of Santo Domingo." *Journal of Negro History* 62, no. 4 (Oct. 1977): 390–400.

Power-Greene, Ousmane. "'Look Well Before You Leap': African Americans and the Debate over Emigration to Trinidad in the Urban North, 1839–1841." *Revue française d'études américaines* 2020/3, no. 164 (March 2020): 71–84.

Sears, Louis M. "Frederick Douglass and the Mission to Haiti, 1889–1891." *Hispanic American Historical Review* 21, no. 2 (May 1941): 222–38.

Seraille, William. "Afro-American Emigration to Haiti During the American Civil War." *The Americas* 35, no. 2 (October 1978): 185–200.

Volwiler, A. T. "Harrison, Blaine, and American Foreign Policy, 1889–1893." *Proceedings of the American Philosophical Society* 79, no. 4 (Nov. 15, 1938): 637–48.

Vorenberg, Michael. "Abraham Lincoln and the Politics of Black Colonization." *Journal of the Abraham Lincoln Association* 14, no. 2 (Summer 1993): 22–45.

Wesley, Charles H. "The Struggle for the Recognition of Haiti and Liberia as Independent Republics." *Journal of Negro History* 2, no. 4 (Oct. 1917): 369–83.

Monographs, books, book chapters, and unpublished PhD dissertations

Aimone, Linda, and Carlo Olmo. *Les Expositions universelles, 1851–1900*. Paris: Belin, 1993.

Aje, Lawrence. "Entre désir d'intégration et séparatisme socio-racial: naissance et autonomisation des libres de couleur de Charleston, Caroline du Sud, 1790–1865." PhD diss., Université de Versailles-Saint-Quentin-en-Yvelines, 2012.

Alderson, Robert J., Jr. *This Bright Era of Happy Revolutions*. Columbia: University of South Carolina Press, 2008.

Aptheker, Herbert. *A Documentary History of the Negro People in the United States*. New York: Citadel Press, 1951.

Bancel, Nicolas, et al., eds. *Zoos humains et exhibitions coloniales: 150 ans d'inventions de l'autre*. Paris: Découverte, 2011.

Barbé de Marbois, François. *Histoire de la Louisiane et de la cession de cette colonie par la France aux États-Unis de l'Amérique septentrionale; précédée d'un Discours sur la constitution et le gouvernement des États-Unis*. Paris: Firmin Didot, 1829.

Bell, Howard H. *A Survey of the Negro Convention Movement, 1830–1861*. New York: Arno, 1953.

Bennett, Lerone, Jr. *Forced into Glory: Abraham Lincoln's White Dream*. 2nd ed. Chicago: Johnson, 2007.

Berlin, Ira. *Many Thousands Gone: The First Two Centuries of Slavery in North America*. Cambridge: Belknap, 2003.

———. *Slaves Without Masters: The Free Negro in the Antebellum South*. New York: Oxford University Press, 1981.

Blackett, Richard J. M. *Building an Antislavery Wall: Black Americans in the Atlantic Abolitionist Movement, 1830–1860*. Baton Rouge: Louisiana State University Press, 1983.

Blancpain, François. *Un siècle de relations financières entre Haïti et la France, 1825–1922*. Paris: L'Harmattan, 2001.

Blight, David W. *Frederick Douglass: Prophet of Freedom*. New York: Simon & Schuster, 2018.

Bourhis-Mariotti, Claire. *L'union fait la force: Les Noirs américains et Haïti, 1804–1893*. Rennes: Presses Universitaires de Rennes, 2016.

Breen, Patrick H. *The Land Shall Be Deluged in Blood: A New History of the Nat Turner Revolt*. Oxford: Oxford University Press, 2015.

Brooks, Noah. *Washington in Lincoln's Time*. New York: Century, 1895.

Burin, Eric. *Slavery and the Peculiar Solution: A History of the American Colonization Society*. Gainesville: University Press of Florida, 2005.

Burton, Benedict. "Rituals of Representation: Ethnic Stereotypes and Colonized People at World's Fairs." In *Fair Representations: World's Fairs and the Modern World*, edited by Robert W. Rydell and Nancy Gwinn, 28–61. Amsterdam: VU University Press, 199.

Byrd, Brandon R. *The Black Republic: African Americans and the Fate of Haiti*. Philadelphia: University of Pennsylvania Press, 2019.

Carroll, Daniel B. *Henri Mercier and the American Civil War*. Princeton: Princeton University Press, 1971.

Chivallon, Christine. *The Black Diaspora of the Americas: Experiences and Theories out of the Caribbean*. Translated by Antoinette Titus-Tidjani Alou. Kingston, Jamaica: Ian Randle, 2011.

Clavin, Matthew J. *Toussaint Louverture and the American Civil War: The Promise and Peril of a Second Haitian Revolution*. Philadelphia: University of Pennsylvania Press, 2010.

Clegg, Claude A., III. *The Price of Liberty: African Americans and the Making of Liberia*. Chapel Hill: University of North Carolina Press, 2004.

Cole, Hubert. *Christophe: King of Haiti*. London: Eyre & Spottiswoode, 1967.

Coleman, Mary H. *St. George Tucker: Citizen of No Mean City*. Richmond: Dietz, 1938.

Comte, Gilbert. *L'empire triomphant*. Paris: Denoël, 1988.

Corvington, Georges. *Port-au-Prince au cours des ans. La Métropole haïtienne du XIXe siècle: 1804–1888*. Port-au-Prince: Deschamps, 1975.

Dean, David M. *Defender of the Race: James Theodore Holly, Black Nationalist Bishop*. Boston: Lambeth, 1978.

Dessens, Nathalie. *From Saint-Domingue to New Orleans: Migration and Influences*. Gainesville: University Press of Florida, 2007.

Dillon, Merton L. *Benjamin Lundy and the Struggle for Negro Freedom*. Urbana: University of Illinois Press, 1966.

Dixon, Chris. *African Americans and Haiti: Emigration and Black Nationalism in the Nineteenth Century*. Westport: Greenwood, 2000.

Dockett-McLeod, Wilma. *Ebenezer Don Carlos Bassett: A Biographical Sketch of America's First American of African Descent Diplomat*. Bloomington: AuthorHouse, 2005.

Dodson, Howard, and Sylviane A. Diouf, eds. *In Motion: The African-American Migration Experience*. Washington, D.C.: National Geographic, 2004.

Dorsainvil, J.-C. *Manuel d'histoire d'Haïti*. Port-au-Prince: Procure des Frères de l'Instruction Chrétienne, 1934.

Dubois, Laurent. *Avengers of the New World: The Story of the Haitian Revolution*. Cambridge: Belknap, 2004.

Dunbar, Alice M., ed. *Masterpieces of Negro Eloquence: The Best Speeches Delivered by the Negro from the Days of Slavery to the Present Time*. New York: Bookery, 1914.

Eckhardt, Celia M. *Fanny Wright, Rebel in America*. Cambridge: Harvard University Press, 1984.

Egerton, Douglas R. *He Shall Go Out Free: The Lives of Denmark Vesey*. Rev. ed. Lanham: Rowman & Littlefield, 2004.

Fanning, Sara. *Caribbean Crossing: African Americans and the Haitian Emigration Movement*. New York: New York University Press, 2015.

Ferrer, Ada. *Freedom's Mirror: Cuba and Haiti in the Age of Revolution*. New York: Cambridge University Press, 2014.

Fick, Carolyn. *The Making of Haiti: The Saint Domingue Revolution from Below*. Knoxville: University of Tennessee Press, 1990.

Fireside, Harvey. *Separate and Unequal: Homer Plessy and the Supreme Court Decision That Legalized Racism*. New York: Carroll & Graf, 2004.

Fischer, Sybille. *Modernity Disavowed: Haiti and the Cultures of Slavery in the Age of Revolution*. Durham: Duke University Press, 2004.

Fleming, Walter L. *Deportation and Colonization, an Attempted Solution of the Race Problem*. New York: n.p., 1914.

Foner, Eric. *The Fiery Trial: Abraham Lincoln and American Slavery*. New York: Norton, 2010.

———. *Freedom's Lawmakers: A Directory of Black Officeholders During Reconstruction*. New York: Oxford University Press, 1993.

———. *Gateway to Freedom: The Hidden History of the Underground Railroad*. New York: Norton, 2016.

———. "Lincoln and Colonization." In *Our Lincoln: New Perspectives on Lincoln and His World*, edited by Eric Foner, 135–66. New York: Norton, 2008.

———. *Reconstruction: America's Unfinished Revolution, 1863–1877*. New American Nation Series. New York: Harper & Row, 1988.

Foner, Eric, ed. *Our Lincoln: New Perspectives on Lincoln and His World.* New York: Norton, 2008.

Franklin, John H. *From Slavery to Freedom*. New York: Alfred A. Knopf, 1947.

———. *George Washington Williams: A Biography*. Durham: Duke University Press, 1998.

Gaillard, Roger. *La République exterminatrice. Première partie: une modernisation manquée (1880–1896)*. 2nd ed. Port-au-Prince: Imprimerie Le Natal, 1995.

Gilroy, Paul. *The Black Atlantic: Modernity and Double Consciousness*. Cambridge: Harvard University Press, 1993.

Gómez, Alejandro E. *Le spectre de la révolution noire*. Rennes: Presses Universitaires de Rennes, 2013.

Grossman, James R. *Land of Hope: Chicago, Black Southerners, and the Great Migration.* Chicago: University of Chicago Press, 1989.

Harrold, Stanley. *The Rise of Aggressive Abolitionism: Addresses to the Slaves*. Lexington: University Press of Kentucky, 2004.

Henry, Monica A. "Vers une Amérique? Les relations entre les États-Unis et les nouvelles républiques hispano-américaines, 1810–1826." PhD diss., Université Paris-Diderot, 2004.

Hochschild, Adam. *Les fantômes du roi Léopold*. Paris: Belfond, 1998.

Hunt, Alfred N. *Haiti's Influence on Antebellum America: Slumbering Volcano in the Caribbean*. Baton Rouge: Louisiana State University Press, 2006.

Hunt, Gaillard. *William Thornton and Negro Colonization*. Worcester, Mass.: American Antiquarian Society, 1921.

Hutchison, William R. *Errand to the World: American Protestant Thought and Foreign Missions*. Chicago: University of Chicago Press, 1987.

Hutton, Frankie. *The Early Black Press in America, 1827–1860*. Westport: Greenwood, 1993.

Johnson, Ronald A. *Diplomacy in Black and White: John Adams, Toussaint Louverture, and Their Atlantic World Alliance*. Athens: University of Georgia Press, 2014.

Johnson, Ronald A., and Ousmane K. Power-Greene, eds. *In Search of Liberty: African American Internationalism in the Nineteenth-Century Atlantic World*. Athens: University of Georgia Press, 2021.

Jordan, Winthrop D. *White over Black: American Attitudes toward the Negro, 1550–1812*. Chapel Hill: University of North Carolina Press, 1968.

Kekeh-Dika, Andrée-Anne, and Hélène Le Dantec-Lowry, eds. *Formes et écritures du départ : incursions dans les Amériques noires.* Paris: L'Harmattan, 2000.

Keyssar, Alexander. *The Right to Vote: The Contested History of Democracy in the United States*. Rev. ed. New York: Basic Books, 2009.

Kinshasa, Kwando M. *Emigration vs. Assimilation: The Debate in the African American Press, 1827–1861*. Jefferson: McFarland, 1988.

Kousser, J. Morgan. *The Shaping of Southern Politics: Suffrage Restriction and the Establishment of the One-Party South, 1880–1910*. New Haven: Yale University Press, 1974.

LaFeber, Walter. *The American Age: United States Foreign Policy at Home and Abroad Since 1750*. New York: Norton, 1989.

———. *The Cambridge History of American Foreign Relations*. Vol. 2. New York: Cambridge University Press, 1993.

———. *The New Empire: An Interpretation of American Expansion, 1860–1898*. 35th anniversary ed. Ithaca: Cornell University Press, 1998.

Le Glaunec, Jean-Pierre. *L'armée indigène: La défaite de Napoléon en Haïti*. Montréal: Lux éditeur, 2014.

Léger, Jacques N. *Haïti, son histoire et ses détracteurs*. New York and Washington: Neale, 1907.

Lemann, Nicolas. *Promised Land: The Great Black Migration and How It Changed America*. London: Macmillan, 1991.

Lester, Charles E. *Life and Public Services of Charles Sumner*. New York: United States Publishing, 1874.

Levine, Robert S. *Martin Delany, Frederick Douglass and the Politics of Representative Identity*. Chapel Hill: University of North Carolina Press, 1997.

Lind, Michael. *What Lincoln Believed: The Values and Convictions of America's Greatest President*. New York: Doubleday, 2005.

Litwack, Leon F. *Been in the Storm so Long: The Aftermath of Slavery*. New York: Knopf, 1979.

Logan, Rayford W. *The Diplomatic Relations of the United States with Haiti, 1776–1891*. 1941. Reprint, New York: Kraus Reprint, 1969.

Lorini, Alessandra. *Rituals of Race: American Public Culture and the Search for Racial Democracy*. Charlottesville: University Press of Virginia, 1999.

Madiou, Thomas. *Histoire d'Haïti*. 3 vols. Port-au-Prince: J. Courtois, 1847–48. Reprint, *Histoire d'Haïti*. 8 vols. Port-au-Prince: H. Deschamps, 1987–91.

Magness, Phillip W., and Sebastian N. Page. *Colonization after Emancipation: Lincoln and the Movement for Black Resettlement*. Columbia: University of Missouri Press, 2011.

Manigat, Leslie. *Éventail d'histoire vivante d'Haïti*. Vol. 4: "Définition, fondements, conditions et constantes de l'histoire des relations internationales d'Haïti." Port-au-Prince: Collection du CHUDAC, 2006.

Manning, Patrick. *The African Diaspora: A History through Culture*. New York: Columbia University Press, 2010.

Mayer, Henry. *All on Fire: William Lloyd Garrison and the Abolition of Slavery*. New York: St. Martin's Press, 1998.

McFeely, William S. *Frederick Douglass*. New York: Norton, 1995.

McKivigan, John R. *Forgotten Firebrand: James Redpath and the Making of Nineteenth-Century America*. Ithaca: Cornell University Press, 2008.

McPherson, James M. *Abraham Lincoln*. New York: Oxford University Press, 2009.

Melish, Joanne P. *Disowning Slavery: Gradual Emancipation and Race in New England, 1780–1860*. Ithaca: Cornell University Press, 2000.

Miller, Floyd J. *The Search for a Black Nationality: Black Emigration and Colonization, 1787–1863*. Urbana: University of Illinois Press, 1975.

Montague, Ludwell L. *Haiti and the United States, 1714–1938*. Durham: Duke University Press, 1940.

Moses, William J. *Classical Black Nationalism: From the American Revolution to Marcus Garvey*. New York: New York Press, 1996.

———. *The Golden Age of Black Nationalism, 1850–1925*. Hamden: Archon, 1978.

Muccigrosso, Robert. *Celebrating the New World: Chicago's Columbian Exhibition of 1893*. Chicago: Ivan R. Dee, 1993.

Nash, Gary B. *Race and Revolution*. Madison: Madison House, 1990.

Neely, Mark E. *The Abraham Lincoln Encyclopedia*. New York: DaCapo, 1982.

Newman, Richard S. *Freedom's Prophet: Bishop Richard Allen, the AME Church, and the Black Founding Fathers*. New York: New York University Press, 2008.

———. *The Transformation of American Abolitionism: Fighting Slavery in the Early Republic*. Chapel Hill: University of North Carolina Press, 2002.

Nicolay, John G., and John Hay. *Abraham Lincoln: A History*. 10 vols. New York: Century, 1890.

Oakes, James. *The Radical and the Republican: Frederick Douglass, Abraham Lincoln, and the Triumph of Antislavery Politics*. New York: Norton, 2007.

Painter, Nell I. *Exodusters: Black Migration to Kansas after Reconstruction*. New York: Knopf, 1977.

Pamphile, Leon D. *Haitians and African Americans: A Heritage of Tragedy and Hope*. Gainesville: University Press of Florida, 2001.

Parfait, Claire. *The Publishing History of* Uncle Tom's Cabin, *1852–2002*. Aldershot: Ashgate, 2007.

Park, Eunjin. *White Americans in Black Africa: Black and White American Methodist Missionaries in Liberia, 1820–1875*. New York: Routledge, 2001.

Pease, Jane H., and William H. Pease. "The Negro Convention Movement." In *Key Issues in the Afro-American Experience*, Volume 1 to 1877, edited by Nathan I. Huggins, Martin Kilson, and Daniel M. Fox, 191–205. New York: Harcourt Brace Jovanovich, 1971.

Pinot de Villechenon, Florence. *Fêtes géantes: les expositions universelles, pour quoi faire?* Paris: Éd. Autrement, 2000.

Plum, Werner. *Les Expositions universelles au 19ème siècle, spectacles du changement socio-culturel: aspects sociaux et culturels de l'industrialisation*. Bonn-Bad Godesberg: Friedrich-Ebert-Stiftung, 1977.

Plummer, Brenda G. *Rising Wind: Black Americans and U.S. Foreign Affairs, 1935–1960*. Chapel Hill: University of North Carolina Press, 1996.

Polyné, Millery. *From Douglass to Duvalier: U.S. African Americans, Haiti, and Pan Americanism, 1870–1964*. Gainesville: University Press of Florida, 2011.

Power-Greene, Ousmane. *Against Wind and Tide: The African American Struggle against the Colonization Movement*. New York: New York University Press, 2014.

Price-Mars, Jean. *La République d'Haïti et la République dominicaine: Les aspects divers d'un problème d'histoire, de géographie et d'ethnologie*. Vol. 2. Port-au-Prince: Collection du Tricinquantenaire de l'Indépendance d'Haïti, 1953.

Pride, Armistead, and Clint C. Wilson II. *A History of the Black Press*. Washington, D.C.: Howard University Press, 1997.

Quarles, Benjamin. *Lincoln and the Negro*. New York: Oxford University Press, 1962.

———. *The Negro in the Civil War*. 1953. Reprint, New York: Da Capo, 1989.

Randall, James G. *Lincoln the President: Springfield to Gettysburg*. 2 vols. New York: Dodd, Mead, 1945.

Reed, Christopher R. *"All the World Is Here!": The Black Presence at White City.* Bloomington: Indiana University Press, 2000.

Rossignol, Marie-Jeanne. *Le ferment nationaliste.* Paris: Belin, 1994.

Rydell, Robert W. *All the World's a Fair: Visions of Empire at American International Expositions, 1876–1916.* Chicago: University of Chicago Press, 1984.

Rydell, Robert W., John E. Findling, and Kimberly Pelle. *Fair America: World's Fairs in the United States.* Washington, D.C.: Smithsonian, 2000.

Sandburg, Carl. *Abraham Lincoln: The Prairie Years.* 2 vols. New York: Harcourt, Brace, 1926.

Schor, Joel. *Henry Highland Garnet: A Voice of Black Radicalism in the Nineteenth Century.* Westport, Conn.: Greenwood, 1977.

Schroeder-Gudehus, Brigitte, and Anne Rasmussen. *Les fastes du progrès: le guide des expositions universelles, 1851–1992.* Paris: Flammarion, 1992.

Sidbury, James. *Becoming African in America: Race and Nation in the Early Black Atlantic.* New York: Oxford University Press, 2007.

Smith, Adam. *No Party Now: Politics in the Civil War North.* New York: Oxford University Press, 2006.

Staudenraus, P. J. *The African Colonization Movement, 1816–1865.* New York: Columbia University Press, 1961.

Sterling, Dorothy. *The Making of an Afro-American: Martin Robinson Delany, 1815–1882.* Garden City: Doubleday, 1971.

Tansill, Charles C. *The United States and Santo Domingo, 1798–1873.* Baltimore: Johns Hopkins Press, 1938.

Teal, Christopher. *Hero of Hispaniola: America's First Black Diplomat, Ebenezer D. Bassett.* Westport: Praeger, 2008.

Thomas, Lamont D. *Rise to Be a People: A Biography of Paul Cuffe.* Urbana: University of Illinois Press, 1986.

Tripp, Bernell. *Origins of the Black Press: New York, 1827–1847.* Northport: Vision, 1992.

Turner, Frederick J., and John M. Faragher. *Rereading Frederick Jackson Turner: "The Significance of the Frontier in American History" and Other Essays.* New Haven: Yale University Press, 1999.

Tyler-McGraw, Marie. *An African Republic: Black and White Virginians in the Making of Liberia.* Chapel Hill: University of North Carolina Press, 2007.

Von Eschen, Penny. *Race against Empire: Black Americans and Anticolonialism, 1937–1957.* Ithaca: Cornell University Press, 1997.

Walters, Ronald G. *The Antislavery Appeal: American Abolitionism after 1830.* Baltimore: Johns Hopkins University Press, 1976.

Washington, Booker T. *Frederick Douglass.* Philadelphia: Jacobs, 1907.

Waterman, William R. *Frances Wright.* New York: n.p., 1924.

Webber, Christopher L. *American to the Backbone: The Life of James W. C. Pennington, the Fugitive Slave Who Became One of the First Black Abolitionists.* New York: Pegasus, 2011.

Wesley, Charles H. *The Quest for Equality: From Civil War to Civil Rights.* New York: Publishers Co., 1968.

Wesseling, Henri. *Le partage de l'Afrique, 1880–1914.* Paris: Denoël, 1996.

White, Ashli. *Encountering Revolution: Haiti and the Making of the Early Republic.* Baltimore: Johns Hopkins University Press, 2010.

Whitfield, Harvey A. *Blacks on the Border: The Black Refugees in British North America, 1815–1860.* Burlington: University of Vermont Press, 2006.

Williams, Walter L. *Black Americans and the Evangelization of Africa, 1877–1900.* Madison: University of Wisconsin Press, 1982.

Winch, Julie. *The Elite of Our People: Joseph Willson's Sketches of Black Upper-Class Life in Antebellum Philadelphia.* University Park: Pennsylvania State University Press, 2000.

———. *A Gentleman of Color: The Life of James Forten.* Oxford: Oxford University Press, 2002.

———. *Philadelphia's Black Elite: Activism, Accommodation, and the Struggle for Autonomy, 1787–1848.* Philadelphia: Temple University Press, 1993.

Wipfler, William L., and National Council of the Episcopal Church. *James Theodore Holly in Haiti.* New York: National Council, 1956.

Woodward, Comer V. *The Strange Career of Jim Crow.* 3rd rev. ed. New York: Oxford University Press, 1974.

INDEX

Locators in italics indicate a figure.

Race in the Atlantic World, 1700–1900

The Hanging of Angélique: The Untold Story of Canadian Slavery and the Burning of Old Montréal
BY AFUA COOPER

Christian Ritual and the Creation of British Slave Societies, 1650–1780
BY NICHOLAS M. BEASLEY

African American Life in the Georgia Lowcountry: The Atlantic World and the Gullah Geechee
EDITED BY PHILIP MORGAN

The Horrible Gift of Freedom: Atlantic Slavery and the Representation of Emancipation
BY MARCUS WOOD

The Life and Letters of Philip Quaque, the First African Anglican Missionary
EDITED BY VINCENT CARRETTA AND TY M. REESE

In Search of Brightest Africa: Reimagining the Dark Continent in American Culture, 1884–1936
BY JEANNETTE EILEEN JONES

Contentious Liberties: American Abolitionists in Post-Emancipation Jamaica, 1834–1866
BY GALE L. KENNY

We Are the Revolutionists: German-Speaking Immigrants and American Abolitionists after 1848
BY MISCHA HONECK

The American Dreams of John B. Prentis, Slave Trader
BY KARI J. WINTER

Missing Links: The African and American Worlds of R. L. Garner, Primate Collector
BY JEREMY RICH

Almost Free: A Story about Family and Race in Antebellum Virginia
BY EVA SHEPPARD WOLF

To Live an Antislavery Life: Personal Politics and the Antebellum Black Middle Class
BY ERICA L. BALL

Flush Times and Fever Dreams: A Story of Capitalism and Slavery in the Age of Jackson
BY JOSHUA D. ROTHMAN

Diplomacy in Black and White: John Adams, Toussaint Louverture, and Their Atlantic World Alliance
BY RONALD ANGELO JOHNSON

Enterprising Women: Gender, Race, and Power in the Revolutionary Atlantic
BY KIT CANDLIN AND CASSANDRA PYBUS

Eighty-Eight Years: The Long Death of Slavery in the United States, 1777–1865
BY PATRICK RAEL

Finding Charity's Folk: Enslaved and Free Black Women in Maryland
BY JESSICA MILLWARD

The Mulatta Concubine: Terror, Intimacy, Freedom, and Desire in the Black Transatlantic
BY LISA ZE WINTERS

The Politics of Black Citizenship: Free African Americans in the Mid-Atlantic Borderland, 1817–1863
BY ANDREW K. DIEMER

Punishing the Black Body: Marking Social and Racial Structures in Barbados and Jamaica
BY DAWN P. HARRIS

Race and Nation in the Age of Emancipations
EDITED BY WHITNEY NELL STEWART AND JOHN GARRISON MARKS

Vénus Noire: Black Women and Colonial Fantasies in Nineteenth-Century France
BY ROBIN MITCHELL

City of Refuge: Slavery and Petit Marronage in the Great Dismal Swamp, 1763–1856
BY MARCUS P. NEVIUS

An American Color: Race and Identity in New Orleans and the Atlantic World
BY ANDREW N. WEGMANN

Maroons in Guyane: Past, Present, Future
BY RICHARD PRICE AND SALLY PRICE

Almost Dead: Slavery and Social Rebirth in the Black Urban Atlantic, 1680–1807
BY MICHAEL LAWRENCE DICKINSON

Race and Reproduction in Cuba
BY BONNIE A. LUCERO

Escapes from Cayenne: A Story of Socialism and Slavery in the Age of Revolution and Reaction
BY LÉON CHAUTARD, EDITED AND WITH AN INTRODUCTION BY MICHAËL ROY

Wanted! A Nation!: Black Americans in Haiti, 1804–1893
BY CLAIRE BOURHIS-MARIOTTI, TRANSLATED BY C. JON DELOGU AND WITH A FOREWORD BY RONALD ANGELO JOHNSON

Printed in the USA
CPSIA information can be obtained
at www.ICGtesting.com
LVHW091032031123
762979LV00005B/141

9 780820 362700